Something's Wrong With Us

NATSUMI ANDO

STORY

When Nao hides her identity and marries Tsubaki to get access to Kogetsuan, she gradually finds herself falling in love with him. However, once Nao discovers the secret behind their parentage, she decides she has to leave. Tsubaki also finds out that Nao is actually "Sakura," the girl from his childhood.

Then a fire breaks out in Kogetsuan, during which Nao passes out, and Tsubaki is left unconscious in a critical state, separating the two against their will.

The years go by, and Nao opens her own shop called Hanagasumi. With Takigawa's help, she's determined to take over Kogetsuan to avenge her late mother. Meanwhile, Tsubaki resolves to forget his feelings for Nao and finally gets back on his feet, giving everything he has into winning the *wagashi* selection against Hanagasumi.

What exactly happened to Nao in the three years since she left Kogetsuan?

CONTENTS

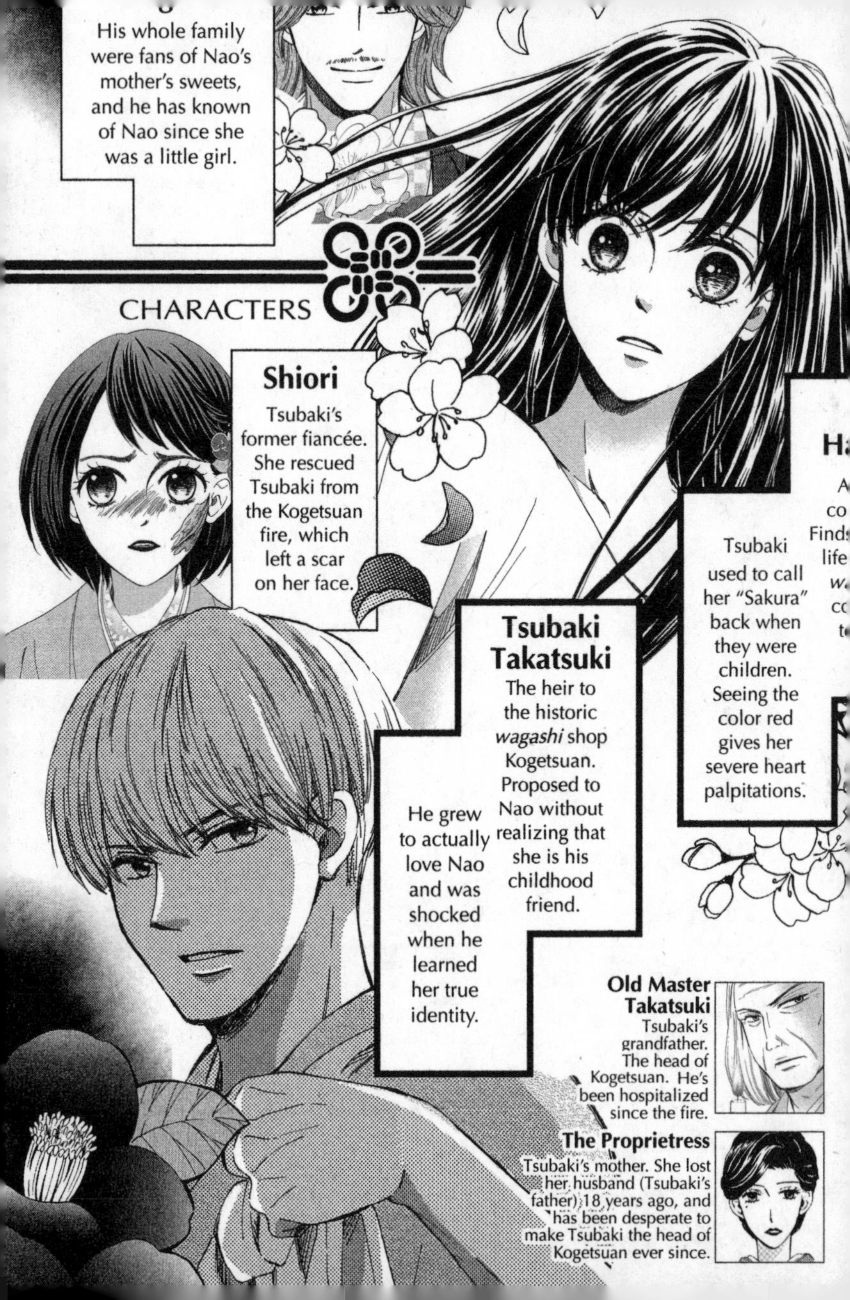
His whole family were fans of Nao's mother's sweets, and he has known of Nao since she was a little girl.
CHARACTERS
Tsubaki used to call her "Sakura" back when they were children. Seeing the color red gives her severe heart palpitations.
Tsubaki Takatsuki
The heir to the historic *wagashi* shop Kogetsuan. Proposed to Nao without realizing that she is his childhood friend.
He grew to actually love Nao and was shocked when he learned her true identity.
Shiori
Tsubaki's former fiancée. She rescued Tsubaki from the Kogetsuan fire, which left a scar on her face.
Old Master Takatsuki
Tsubaki's grandfather. The head of Kogetsuan. He's been hospitalized since the fire.
The Proprietress
Tsubaki's mother. She lost her husband (Tsubaki's father) 18 years ago, and has been desperate to make Tsubaki the head of Kogetsuan ever since.

Chapter 42 *The Three-Year Blank*

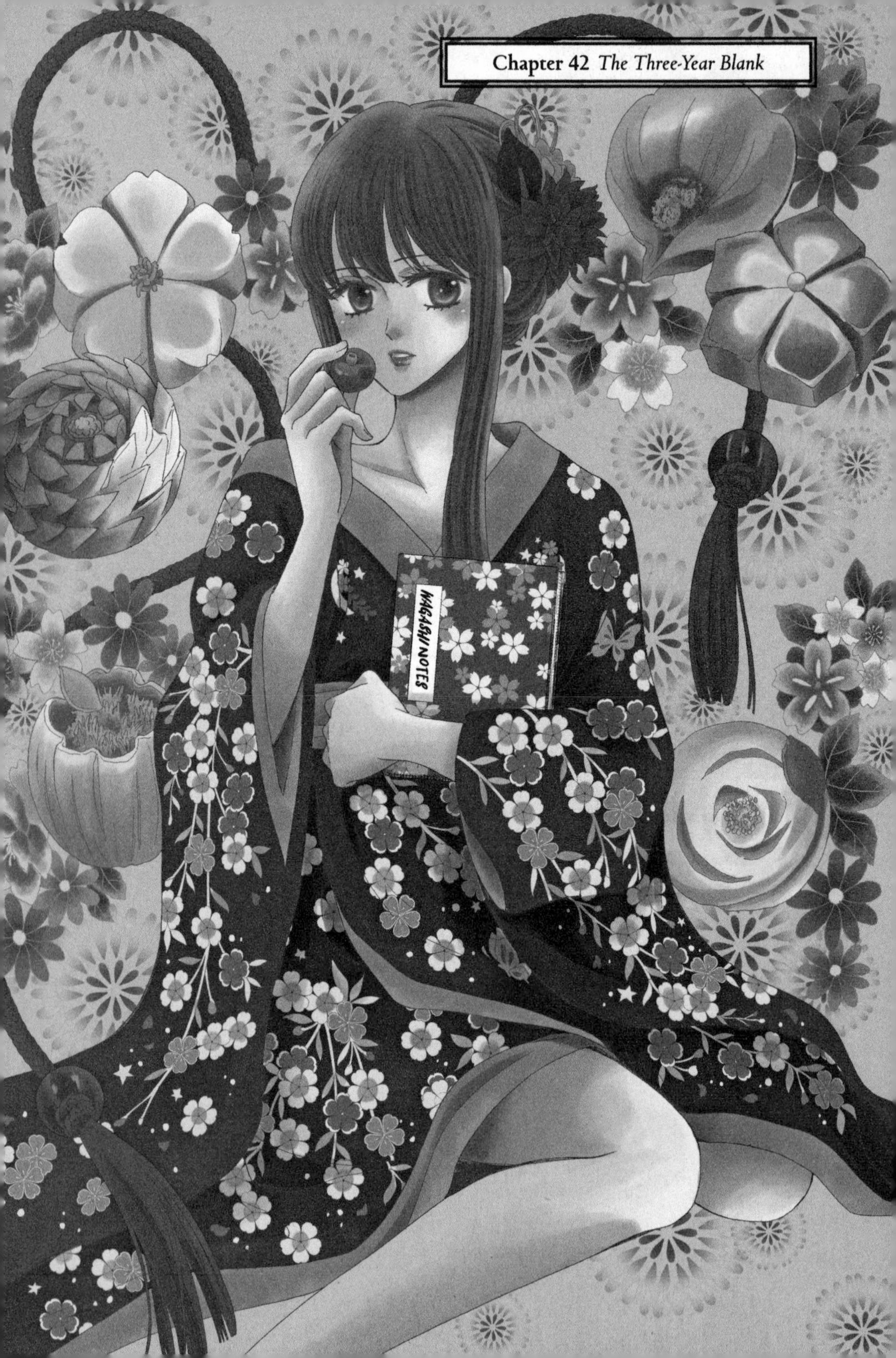
WAGASHI NOTES

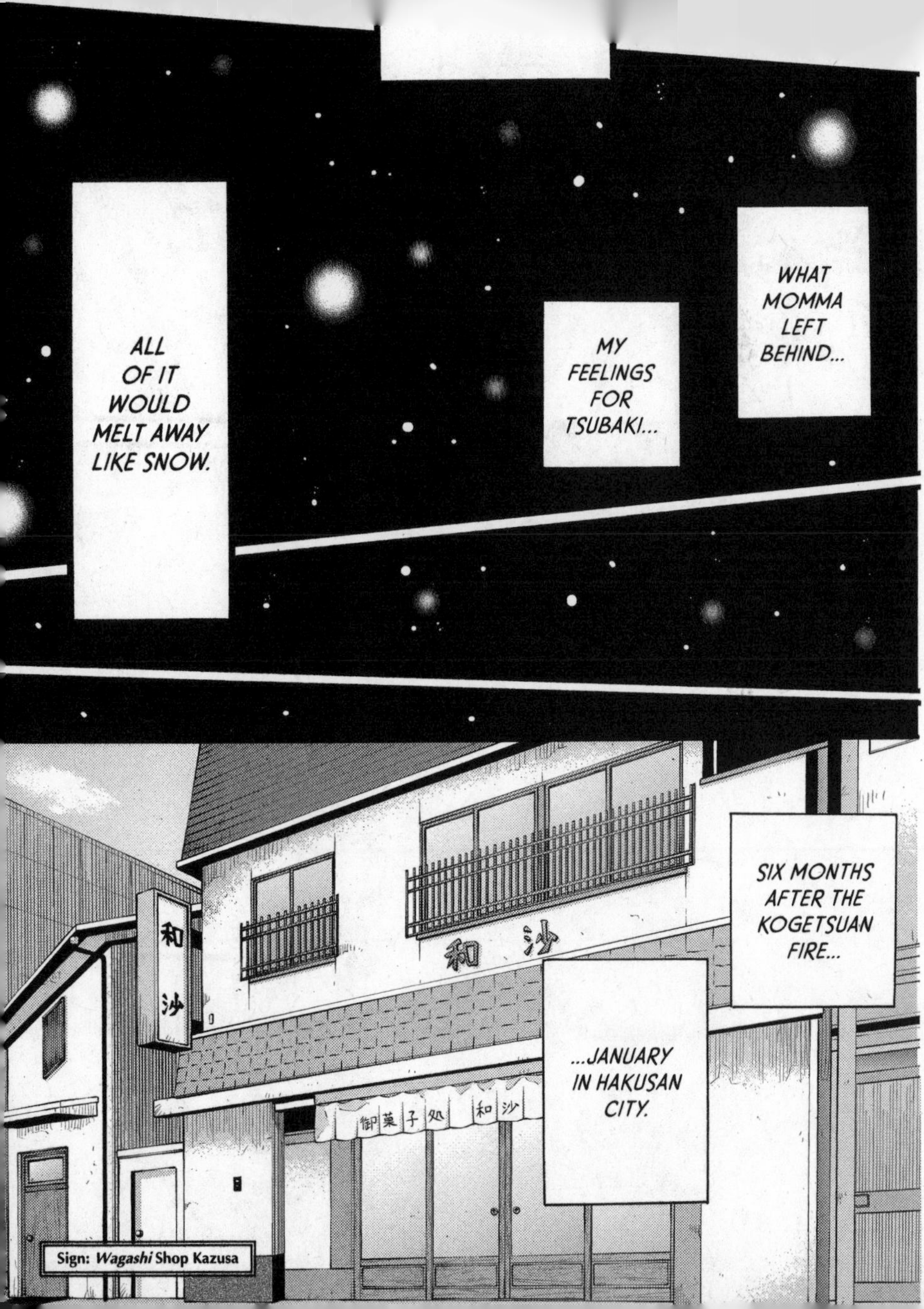
WHAT MOMMA LEFT BEHIND...
MY FEELINGS FOR TSUBAKI...
ALL OF IT WOULD MELT AWAY LIKE SNOW.
SIX MONTHS AFTER THE KOGETSUAN FIRE...
...JANUARY IN HAKUSAN CITY.
和沙
和沙
御菓子処 和沙
Sign: *Wagashi* Shop Kazusa

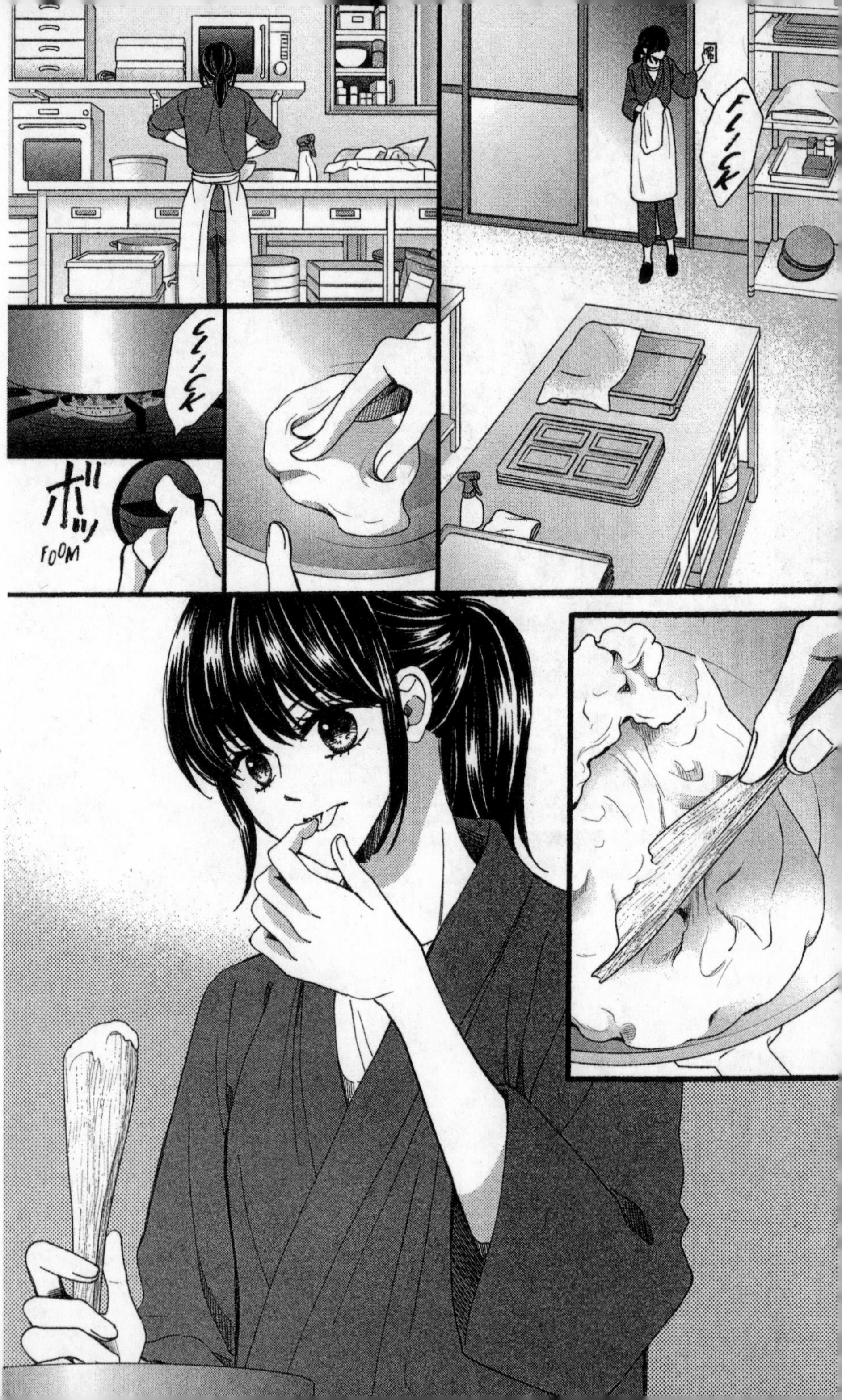
FLICK
CLICK
ボッ
FOOM

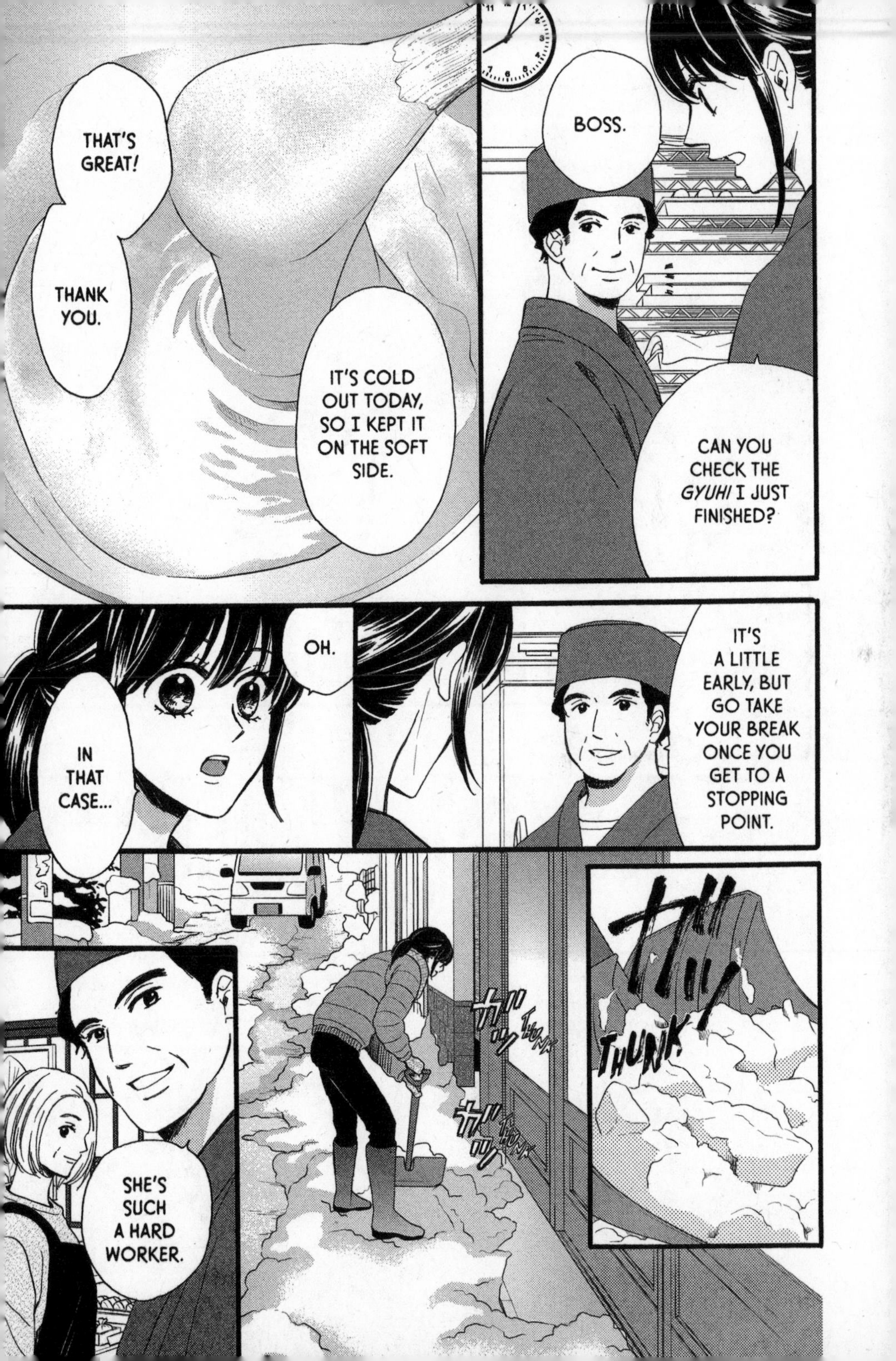

BOSS.
CAN YOU CHECK THE *GYUHI* I JUST FINISHED?
IT'S COLD OUT TODAY, SO I KEPT IT ON THE SOFT SIDE.
THAT'S GREAT!
THANK YOU.
IT'S A LITTLE EARLY, BUT GO TAKE YOUR BREAK ONCE YOU GET TO A STOPPING POINT.
OH.
IN THAT CASE...
THUNK
THUNK
THUNK
SHE'S SUCH A HARD WORKER.

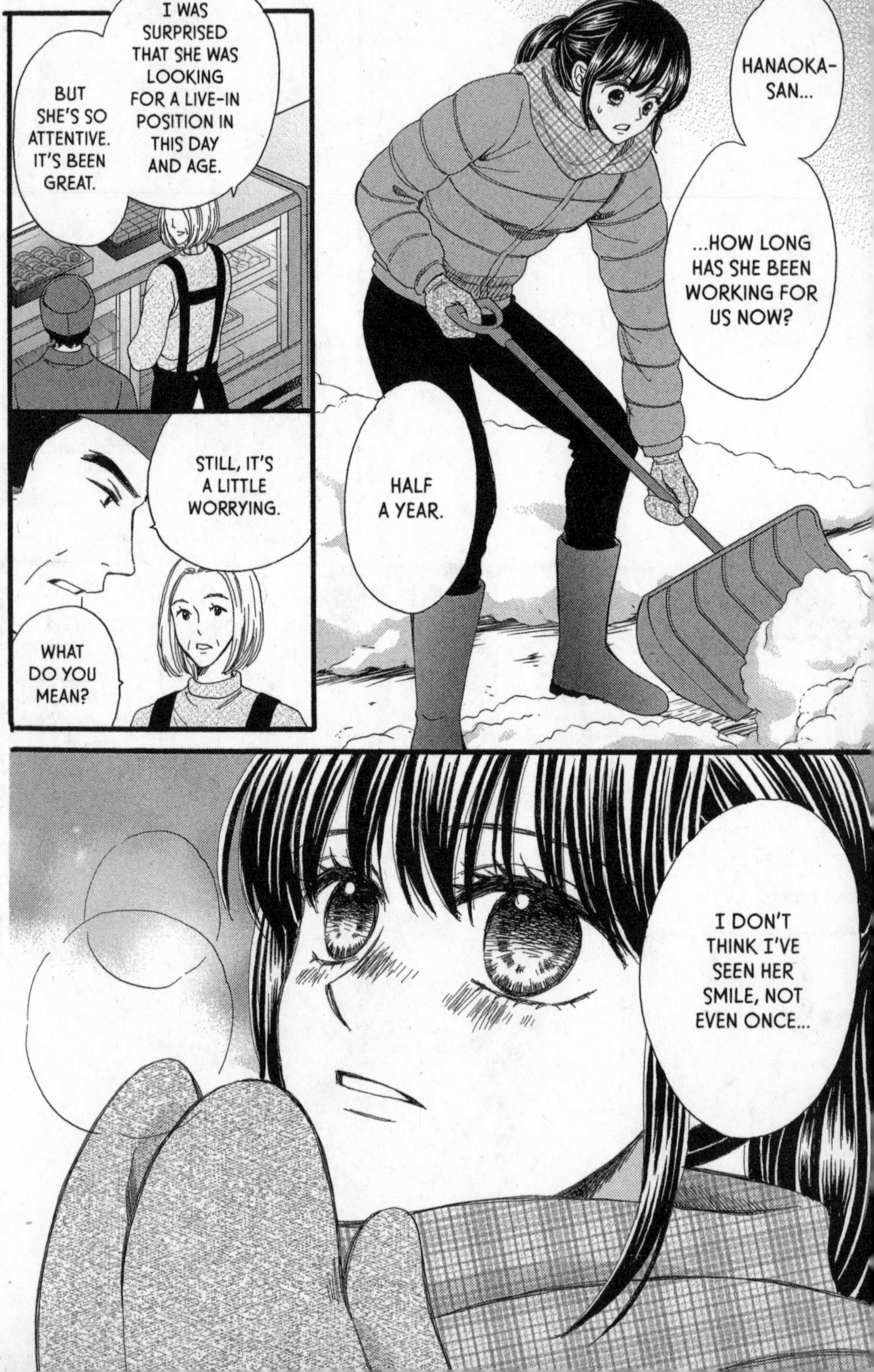
HANAOKA-SAN...
...HOW LONG HAS SHE BEEN WORKING FOR US NOW?
HALF A YEAR.
I WAS SURPRISED THAT SHE WAS LOOKING FOR A LIVE-IN POSITION IN THIS DAY AND AGE.
BUT SHE'S SO ATTENTIVE. IT'S BEEN GREAT.
STILL, IT'S A LITTLE WORRYING.
WHAT DO YOU MEAN?
I DON'T THINK I'VE SEEN HER SMILE, NOT EVEN ONCE...

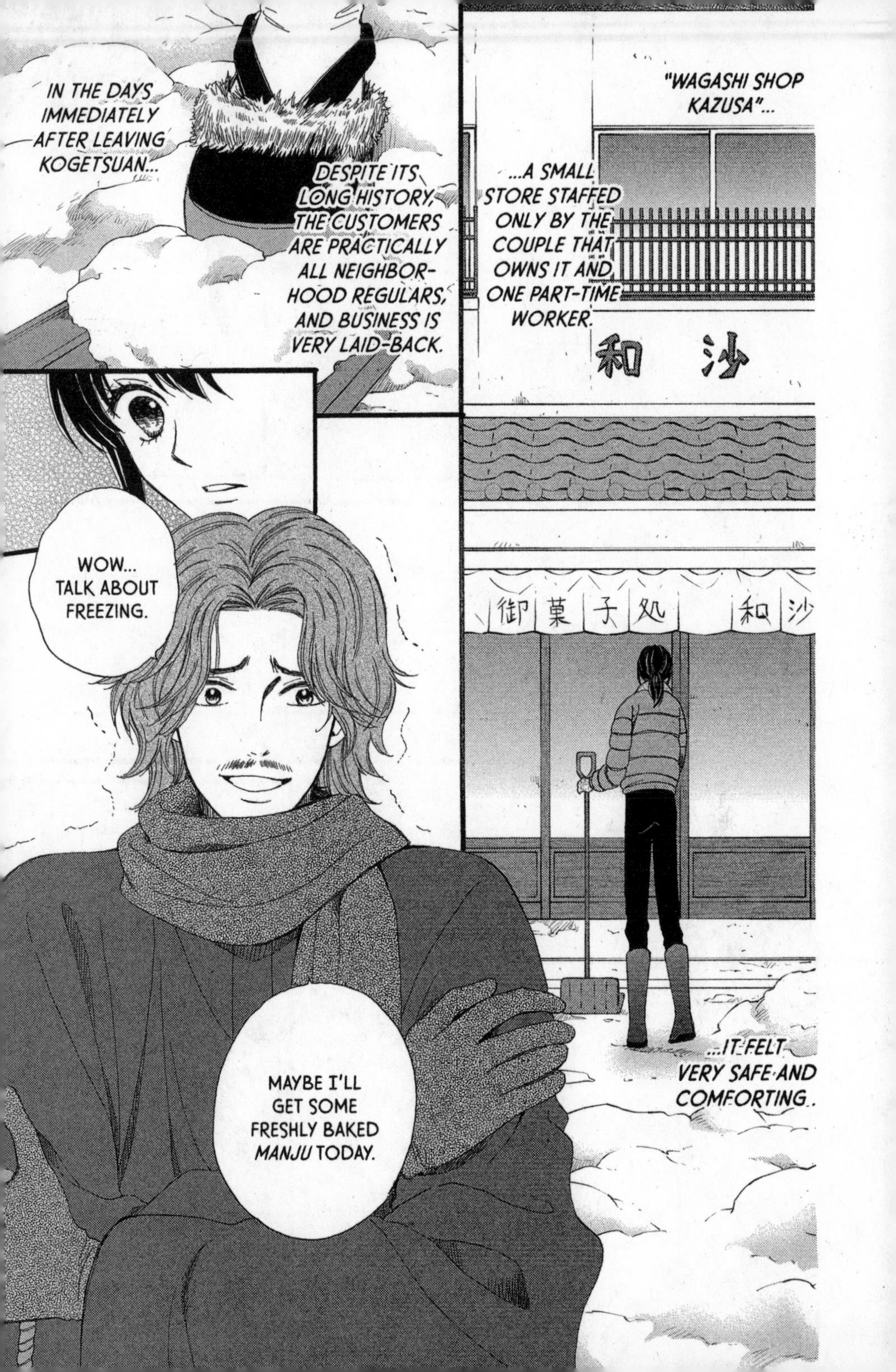
"WAGASHI SHOP KAZUSA"...
...A SMALL STORE STAFFED ONLY BY THE COUPLE THAT OWNS IT AND ONE PART-TIME WORKER.
和 沙
IN THE DAYS IMMEDIATELY AFTER LEAVING KOGETSUAN...
DESPITE ITS LONG HISTORY, THE CUSTOMERS ARE PRACTICALLY ALL NEIGHBOR-HOOD REGULARS, AND BUSINESS IS VERY LAID-BACK.
御菓子処 和沙
...IT FELT VERY SAFE AND COMFORTING.
WOW... TALK ABOUT FREEZING.
MAYBE I'LL GET SOME FRESHLY BAKED *MANJU* TODAY.

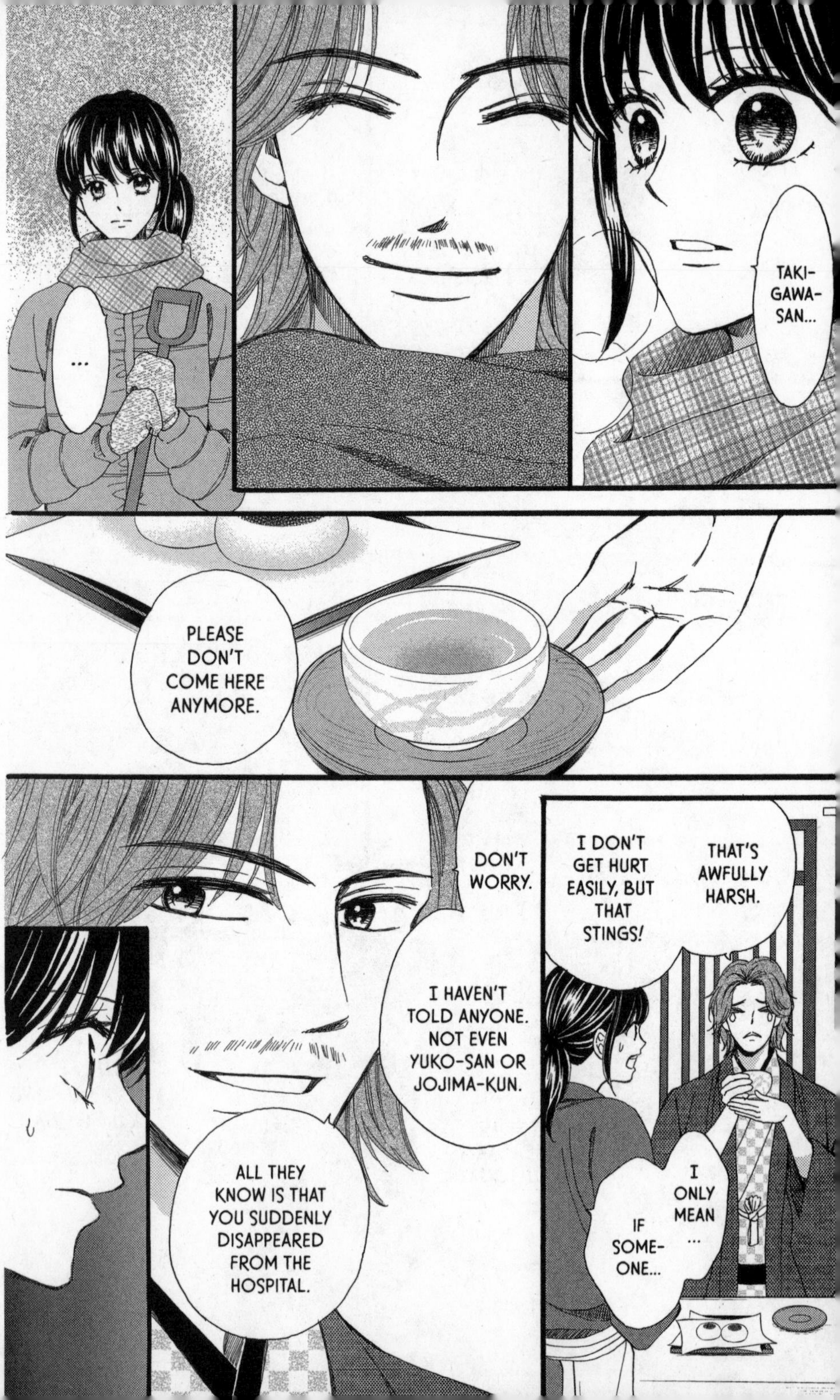
TAKI-GAWA-SAN...
...
PLEASE DON'T COME HERE ANYMORE.
THAT'S AWFULLY HARSH.
I DON'T GET HURT EASILY, BUT THAT STINGS!
I ONLY MEAN ...
IF SOME-ONE...
DON'T WORRY.
I HAVEN'T TOLD ANYONE. NOT EVEN YUKO-SAN OR JOJIMA-KUN.
ALL THEY KNOW IS THAT YOU SUDDENLY DISAPPEARED FROM THE HOSPITAL.

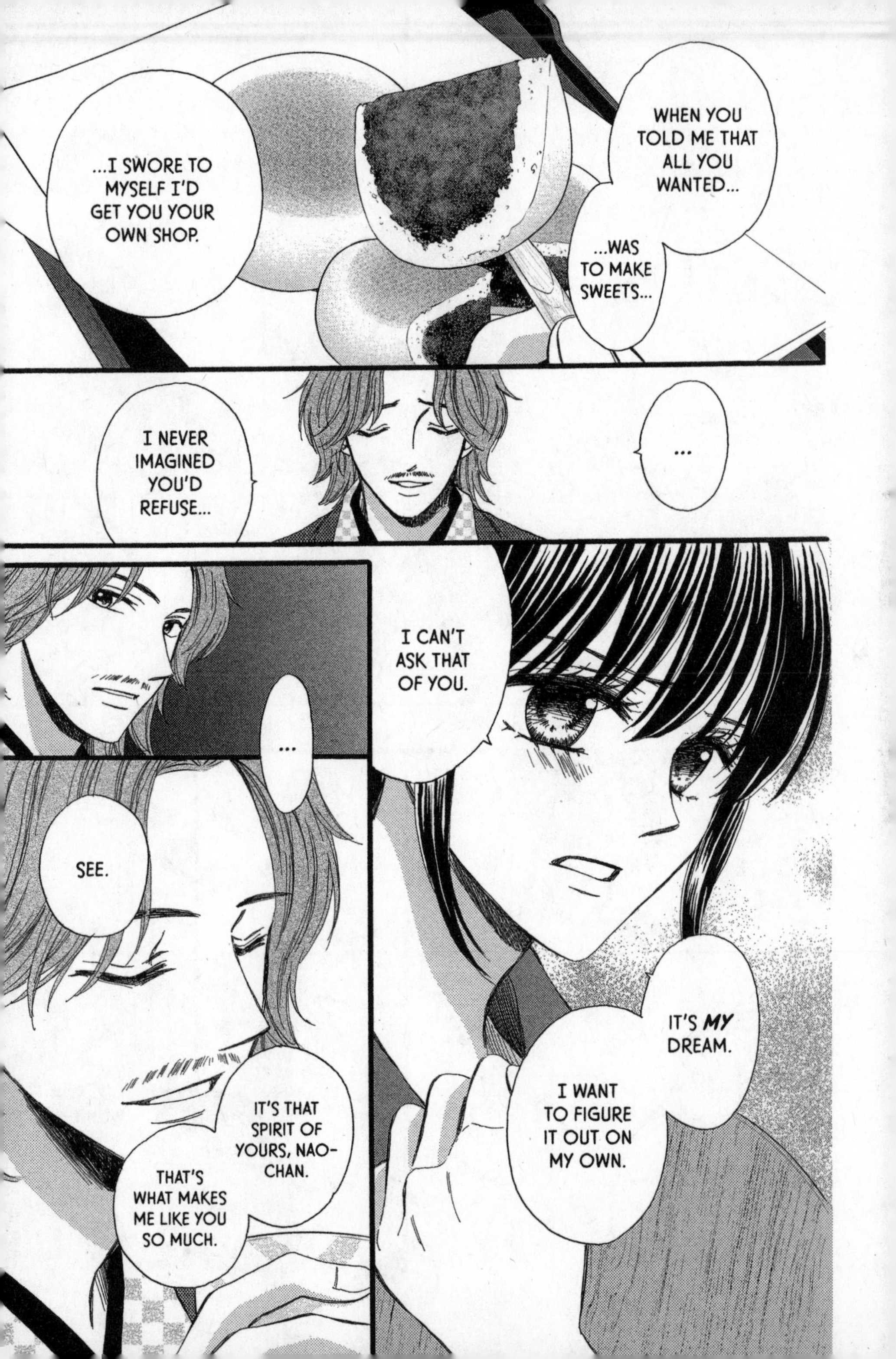
WHEN YOU TOLD ME THAT ALL YOU WANTED...
...WAS TO MAKE SWEETS...
...I SWORE TO MYSELF I'D GET YOU YOUR OWN SHOP.
...
I NEVER IMAGINED YOU'D REFUSE...
I CAN'T ASK THAT OF YOU.
IT'S *MY* DREAM.
I WANT TO FIGURE IT OUT ON MY OWN.
...
SEE.
IT'S THAT SPIRIT OF YOURS, NAO-CHAN.
THAT'S WHAT MAKES ME LIKE YOU SO MUCH.

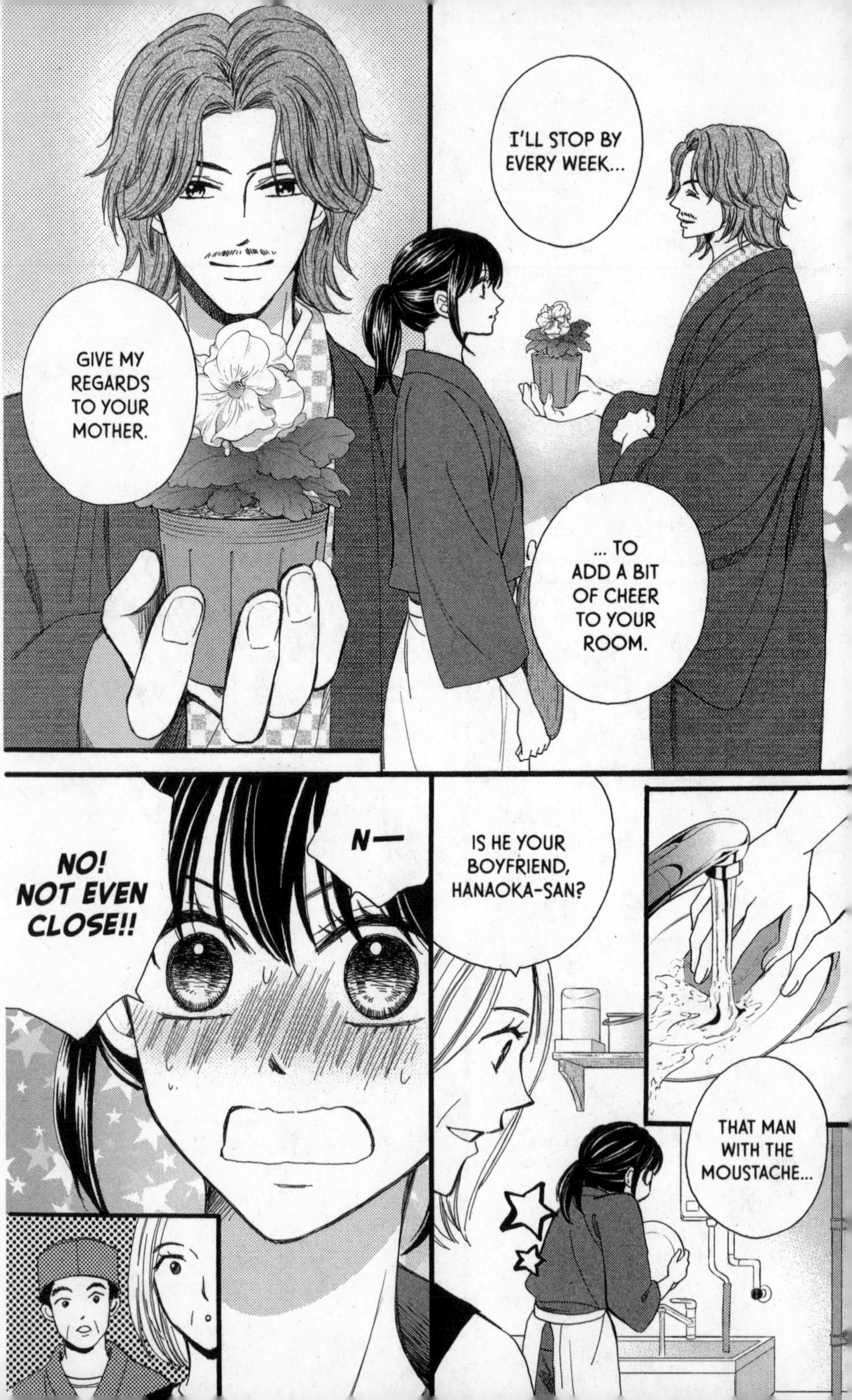

I'LL STOP BY EVERY WEEK...
... TO ADD A BIT OF CHEER TO YOUR ROOM.
GIVE MY REGARDS TO YOUR MOTHER.
IS HE YOUR BOYFRIEND, HANAOKA-SAN?
THAT MAN WITH THE MOUSTACHE...
N—
NO! NOT EVEN CLOSE!!

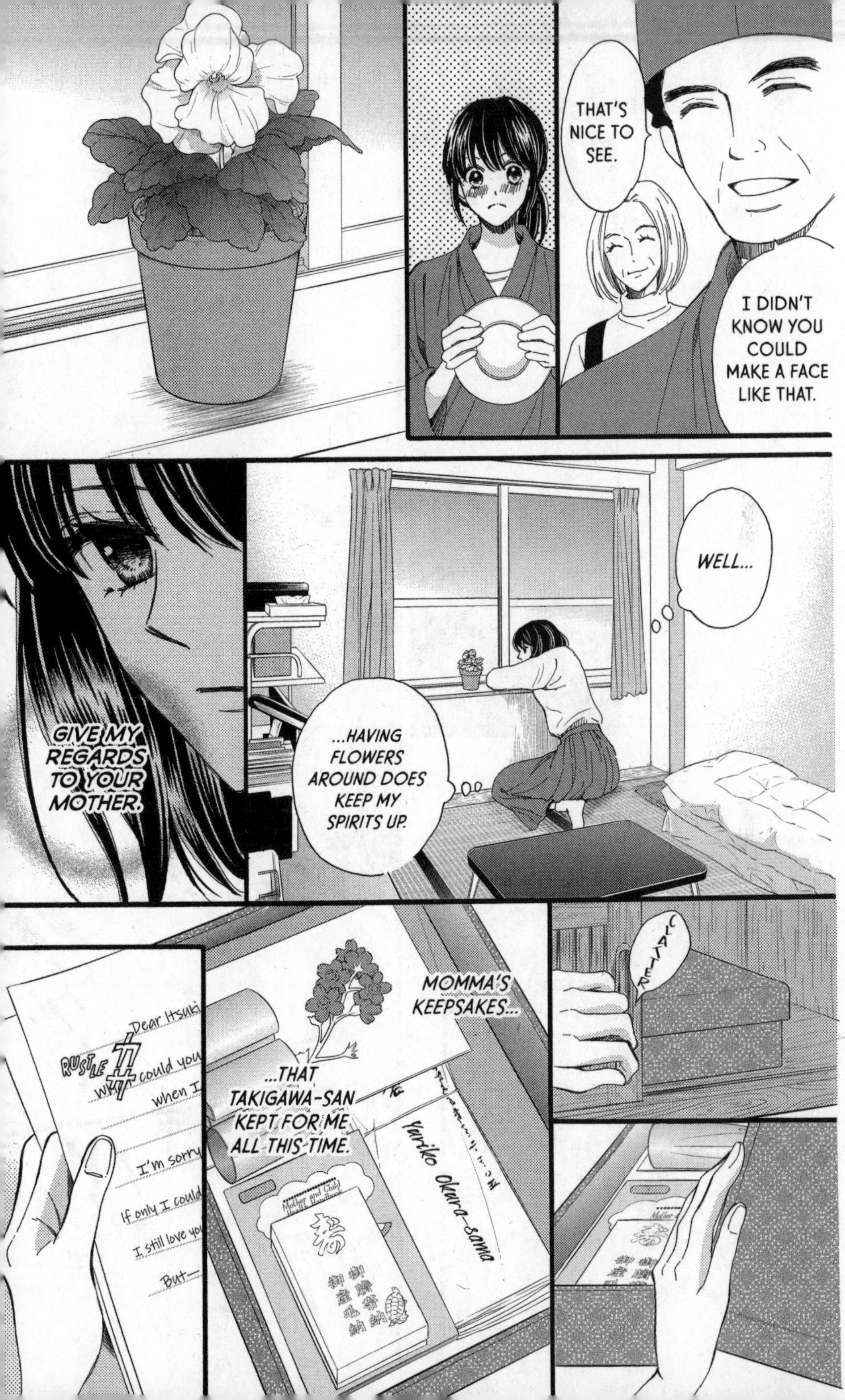
THAT'S NICE TO SEE.
I DIDN'T KNOW YOU COULD MAKE A FACE LIKE THAT.
WELL...
...HAVING FLOWERS AROUND DOES KEEP MY SPIRITS UP.
GIVE MY REGARDS TO YOUR MOTHER.
CLATTER
MOMMA'S KEEPSAKES...
...THAT TAKIGAWA-SAN KEPT FOR ME ALL THIS TIME.
Yuriko Okura-sama
Mother and Child Health Handbook
Dear Itsuki
RUSTLE
could you
when I
I'm sorry
If only I could
I still love you
But—

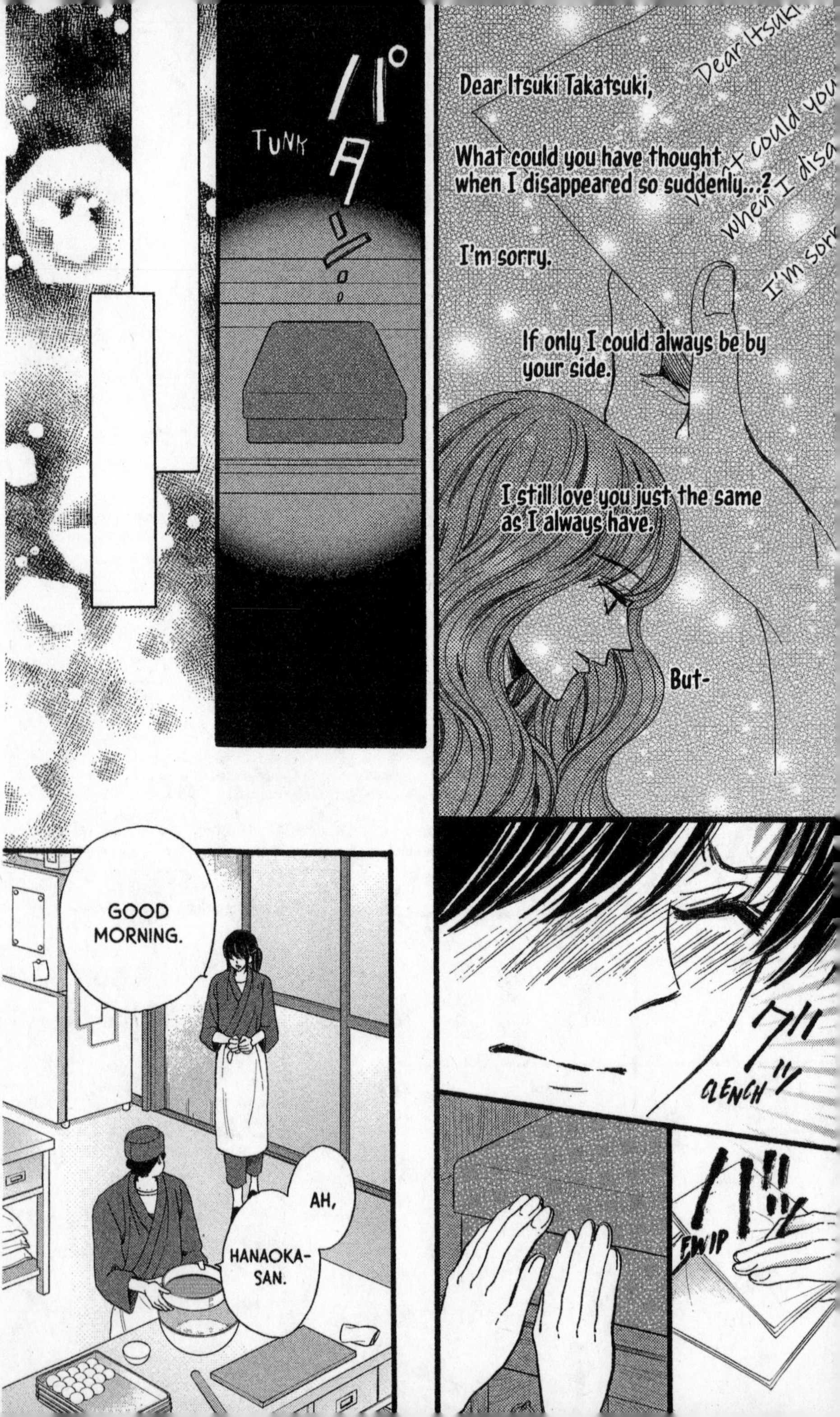
Dear Itsuki Takatsuki,
What could you have thought when I disappeared so suddenly...?
I'm sorry.
If only I could always be by your side.
I still love you just the same as I always have.
But-
TUNK
CLENCH
FWIP
GOOD MORNING.
AH, HANAOKA-SAN.

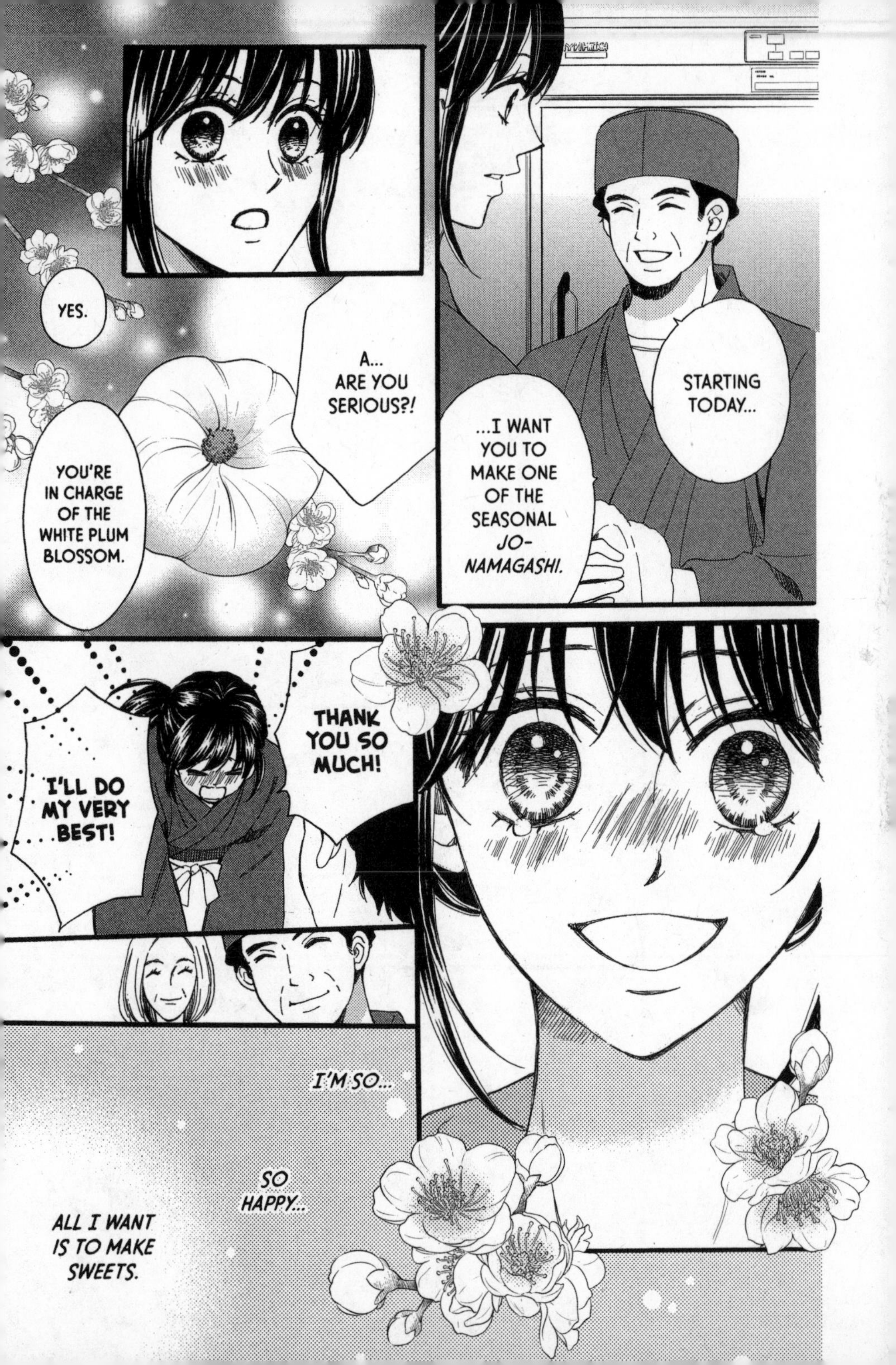
STARTING TODAY...
...I WANT YOU TO MAKE ONE OF THE SEASONAL *JO-NAMAGASHI.*
A... ARE YOU SERIOUS?!
YES.
YOU'RE IN CHARGE OF THE WHITE PLUM BLOSSOM.
THANK YOU SO MUCH!
I'LL DO MY VERY BEST!
I'M SO...
SO HAPPY...
ALL I WANT IS TO MAKE SWEETS.

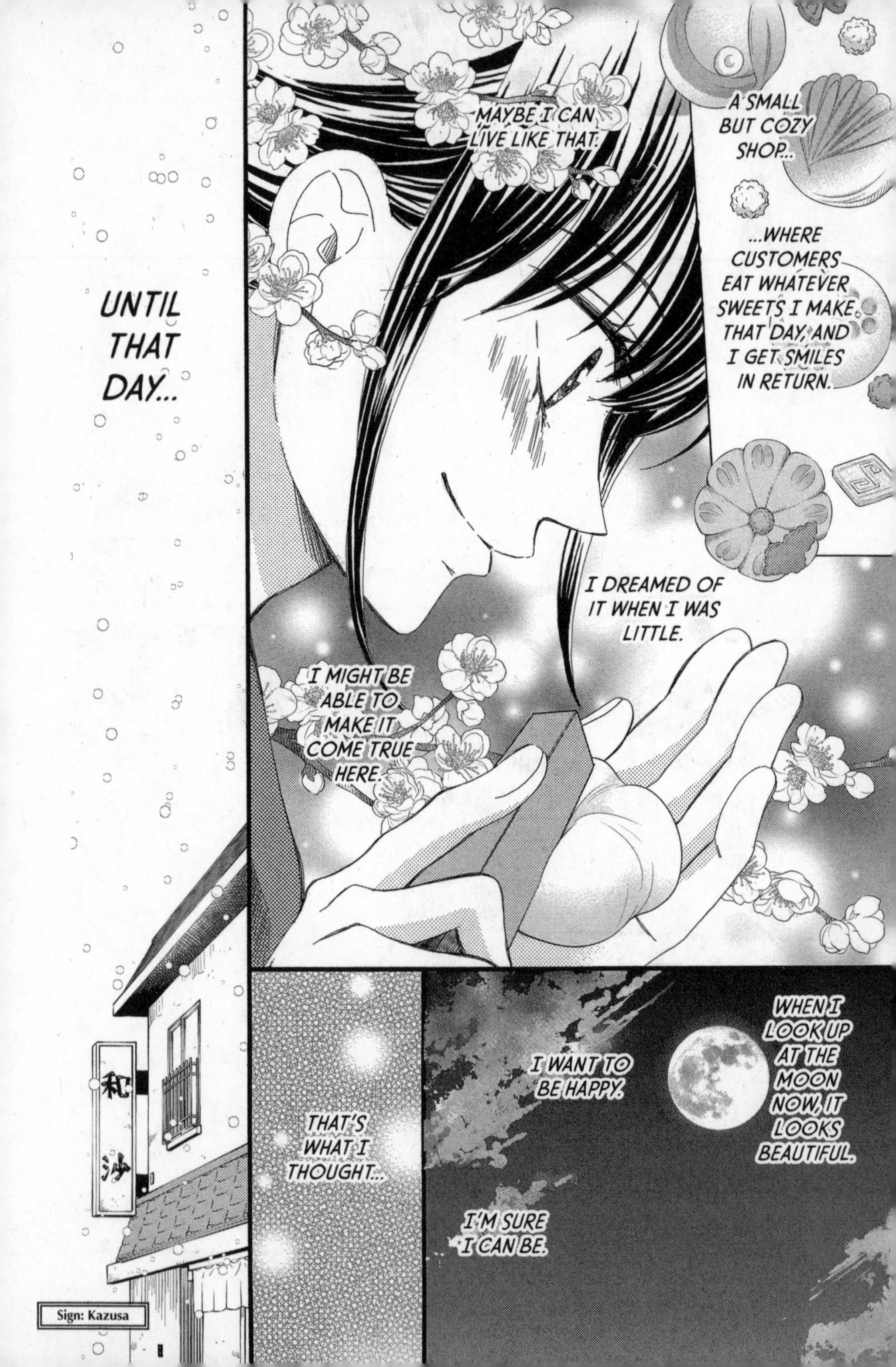
A SMALL BUT COZY SHOP...
...WHERE CUSTOMERS EAT WHATEVER SWEETS I MAKE THAT DAY, AND I GET SMILES IN RETURN.
MAYBE I CAN LIVE LIKE THAT.
I DREAMED OF IT WHEN I WAS LITTLE.
I MIGHT BE ABLE TO MAKE IT COME TRUE HERE.
WHEN I LOOK UP AT THE MOON NOW, IT LOOKS BEAUTIFUL.
I WANT TO BE HAPPY.
I'M SURE I CAN BE.
THAT'S WHAT I THOUGHT...
UNTIL THAT DAY...
和
沙
Sign: Kazusa

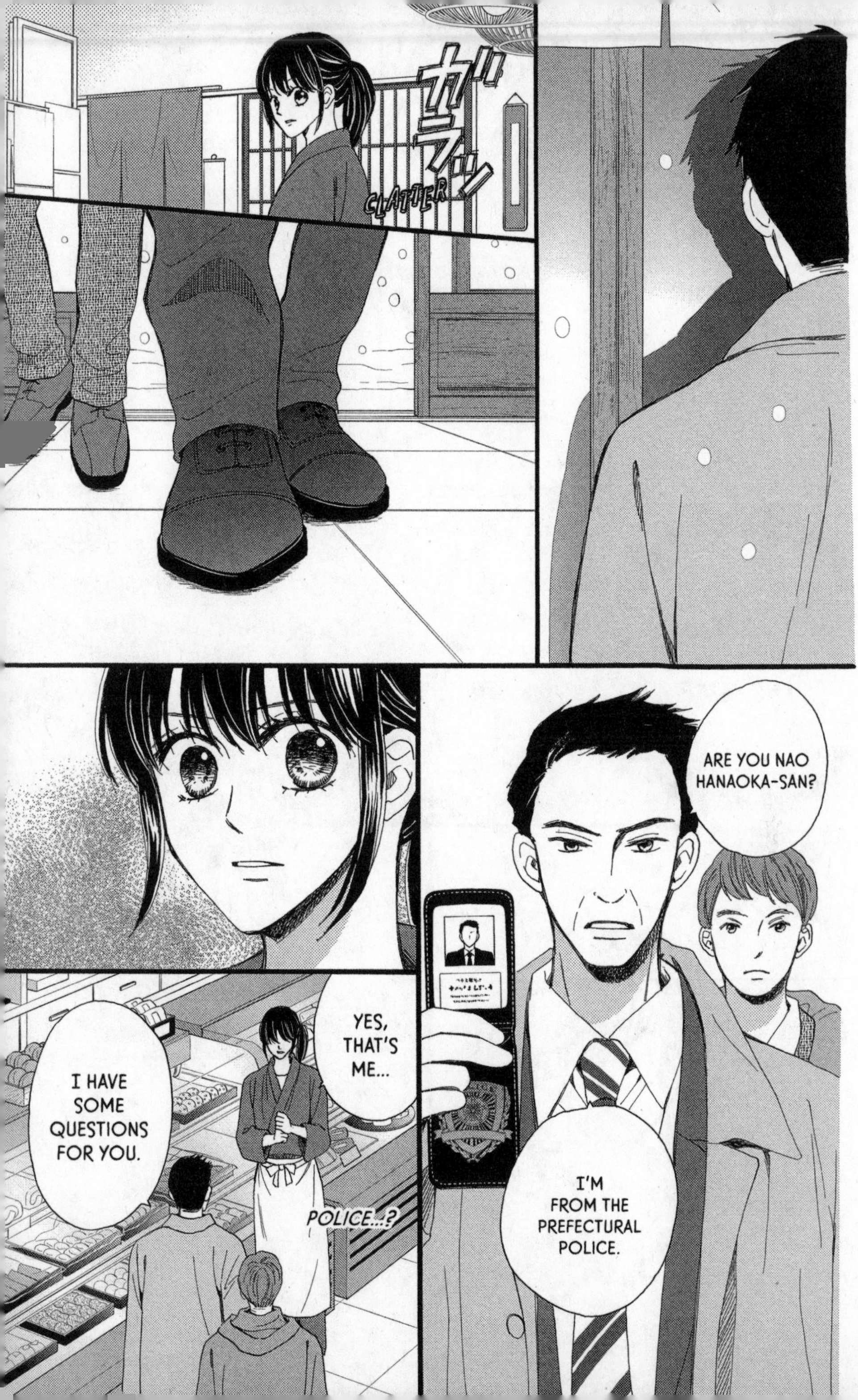
ガラッ
CLATTER
ARE YOU NAO HANAOKA-SAN?
I'M FROM THE PREFECTURAL POLICE.
YES, THAT'S ME...
I HAVE SOME QUESTIONS FOR YOU.
POLICE...?

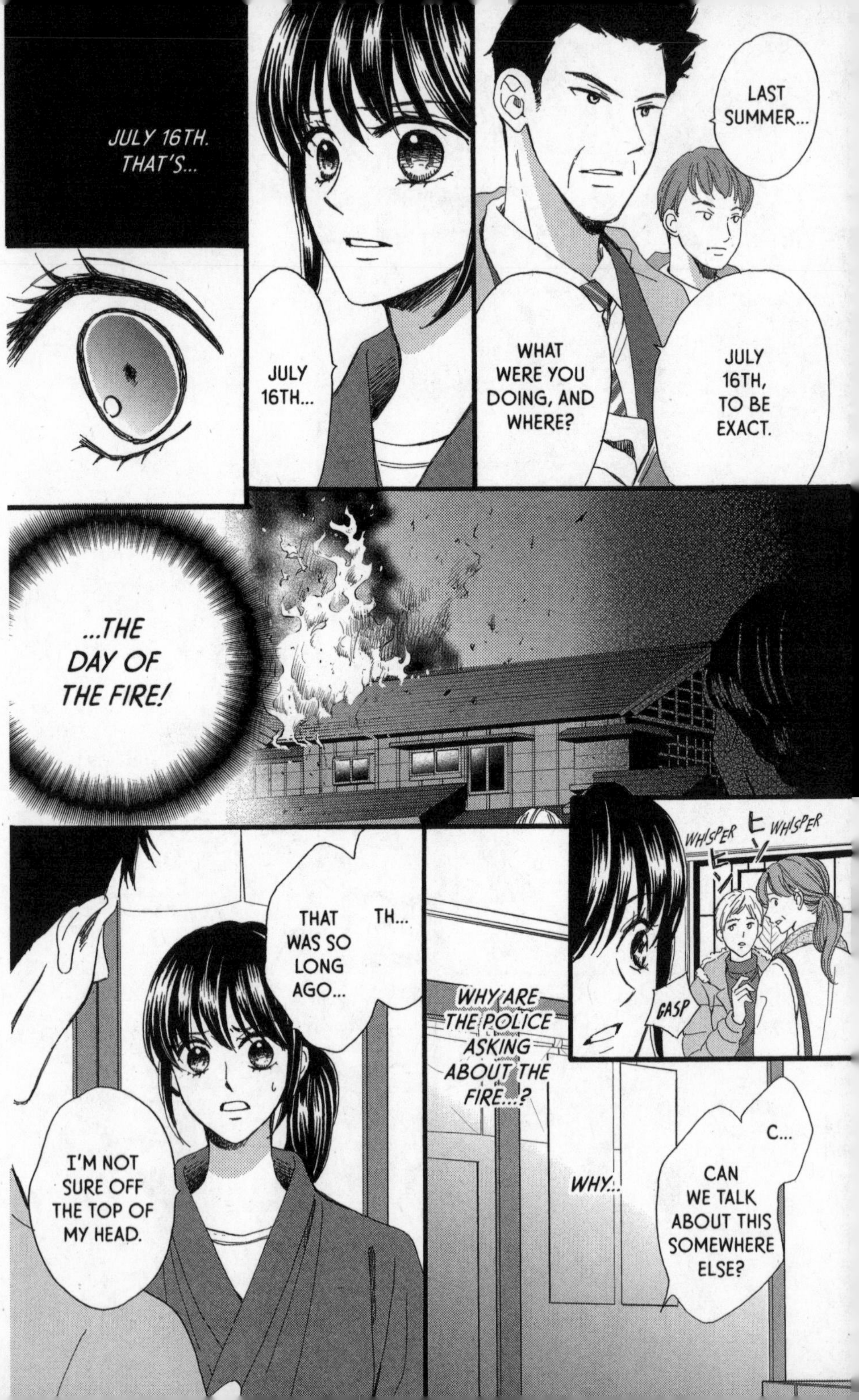
LAST SUMMER...
JULY 16TH, TO BE EXACT.
WHAT WERE YOU DOING, AND WHERE?
JULY 16TH...
JULY 16TH. THAT'S...
...THE DAY OF THE FIRE!
WHISPER
WHISPER
GASP
WHY ARE THE POLICE ASKING ABOUT THE FIRE...?
WHY...
C...
CAN WE TALK ABOUT THIS SOMEWHERE ELSE?
TH...
THAT WAS SO LONG AGO...
I'M NOT SURE OFF THE TOP OF MY HEAD.

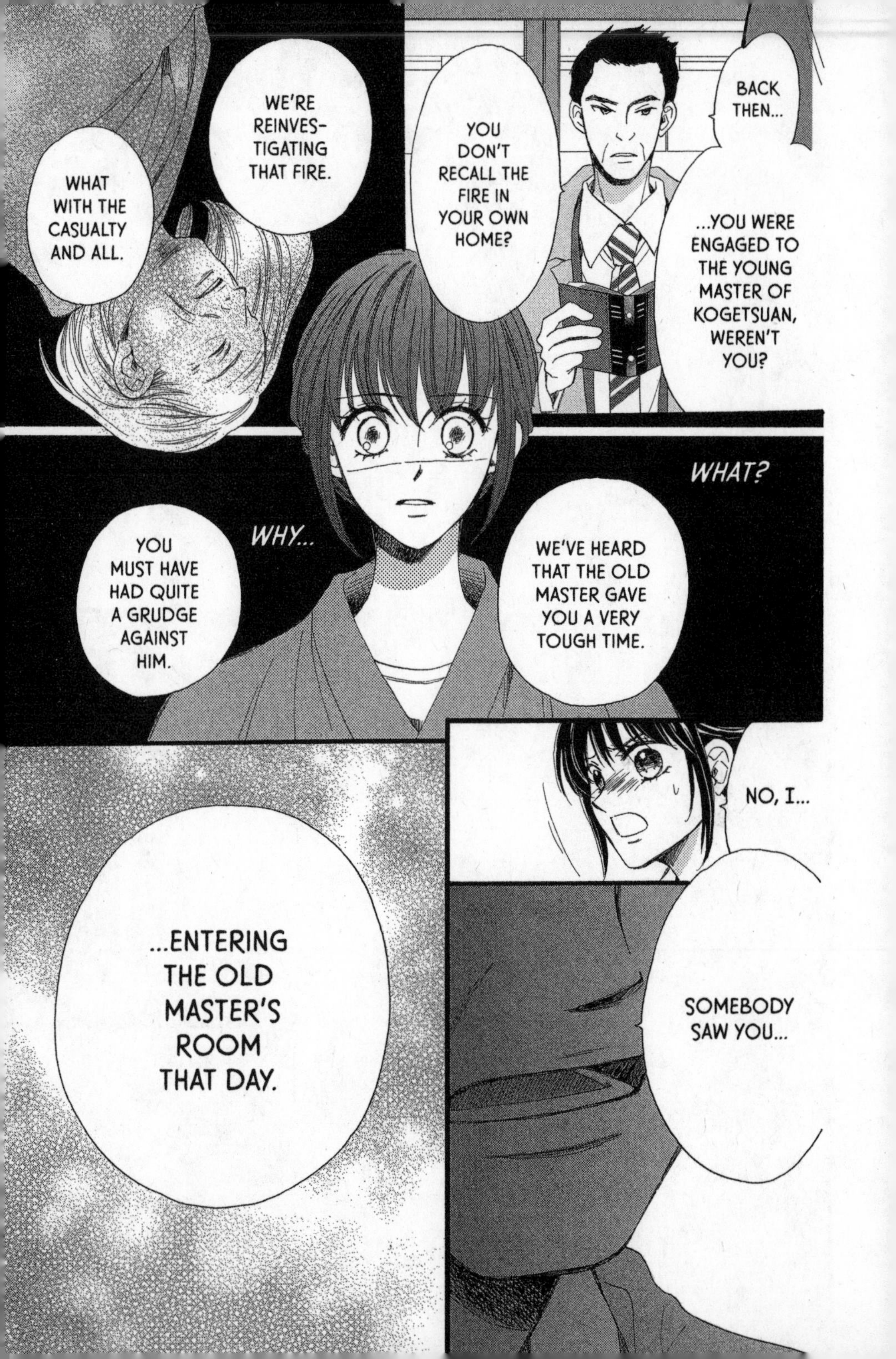
BACK THEN...
...YOU WERE ENGAGED TO THE YOUNG MASTER OF KOGETSUAN, WEREN'T YOU?
YOU DON'T RECALL THE FIRE IN YOUR OWN HOME?
WE'RE REINVES-TIGATING THAT FIRE.
WHAT WITH THE CASUALTY AND ALL.
WHAT?
WE'VE HEARD THAT THE OLD MASTER GAVE YOU A VERY TOUGH TIME.
WHY...
YOU MUST HAVE HAD QUITE A GRUDGE AGAINST HIM.
NO, I...
SOMEBODY SAW YOU...
...ENTERING THE OLD MASTER'S ROOM THAT DAY.

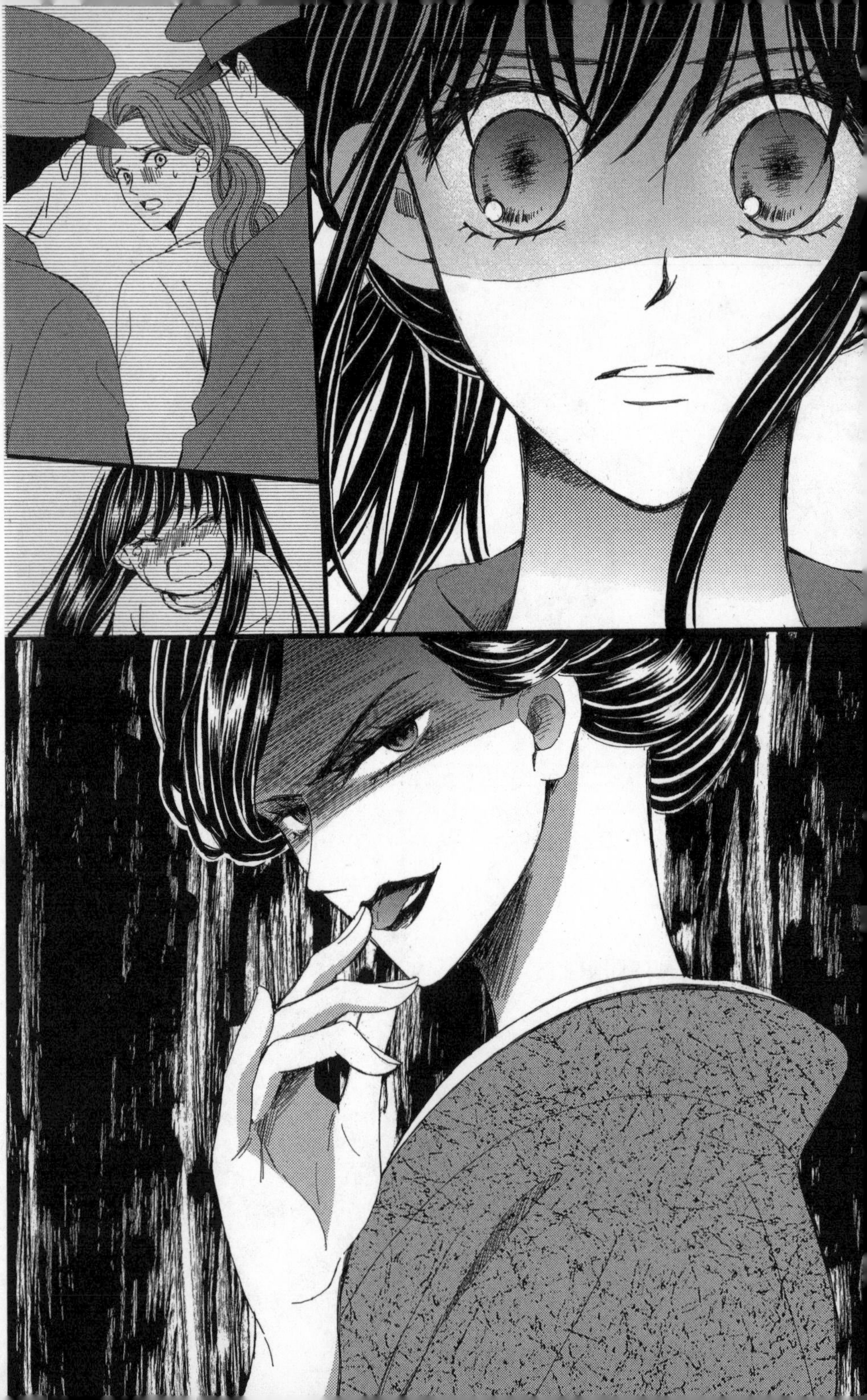

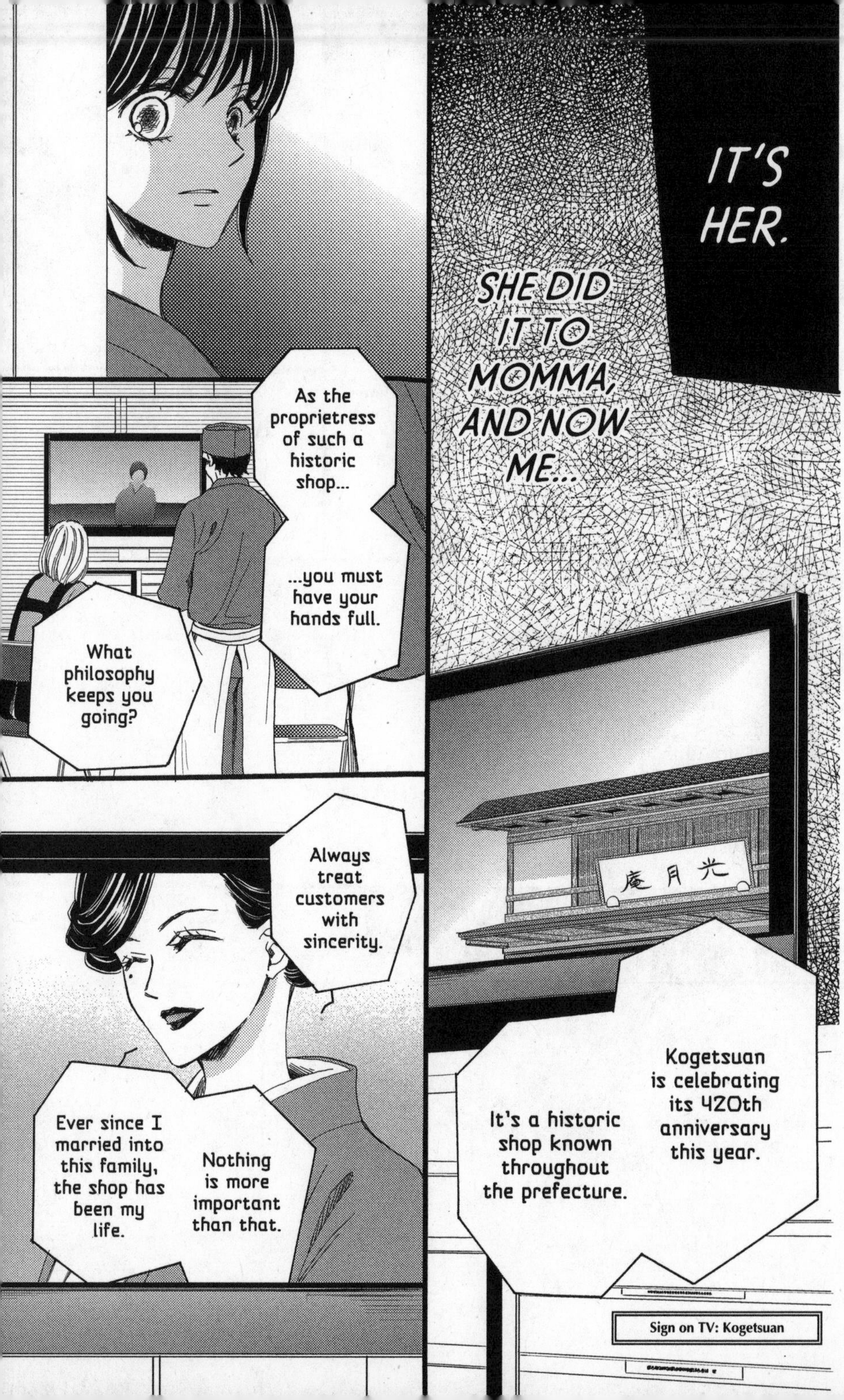
IT'S HER.
SHE DID IT TO MOMMA, AND NOW ME...
Kogetsuan is celebrating its 420th anniversary this year.
It's a historic shop known throughout the prefecture.
Sign on TV: Kogetsuan
As the proprietress of such a historic shop...
...you must have your hands full.
What philosophy keeps you going?
Always treat customers with sincerity.
Ever since I married into this family, the shop has been my life.
Nothing is more important than that.

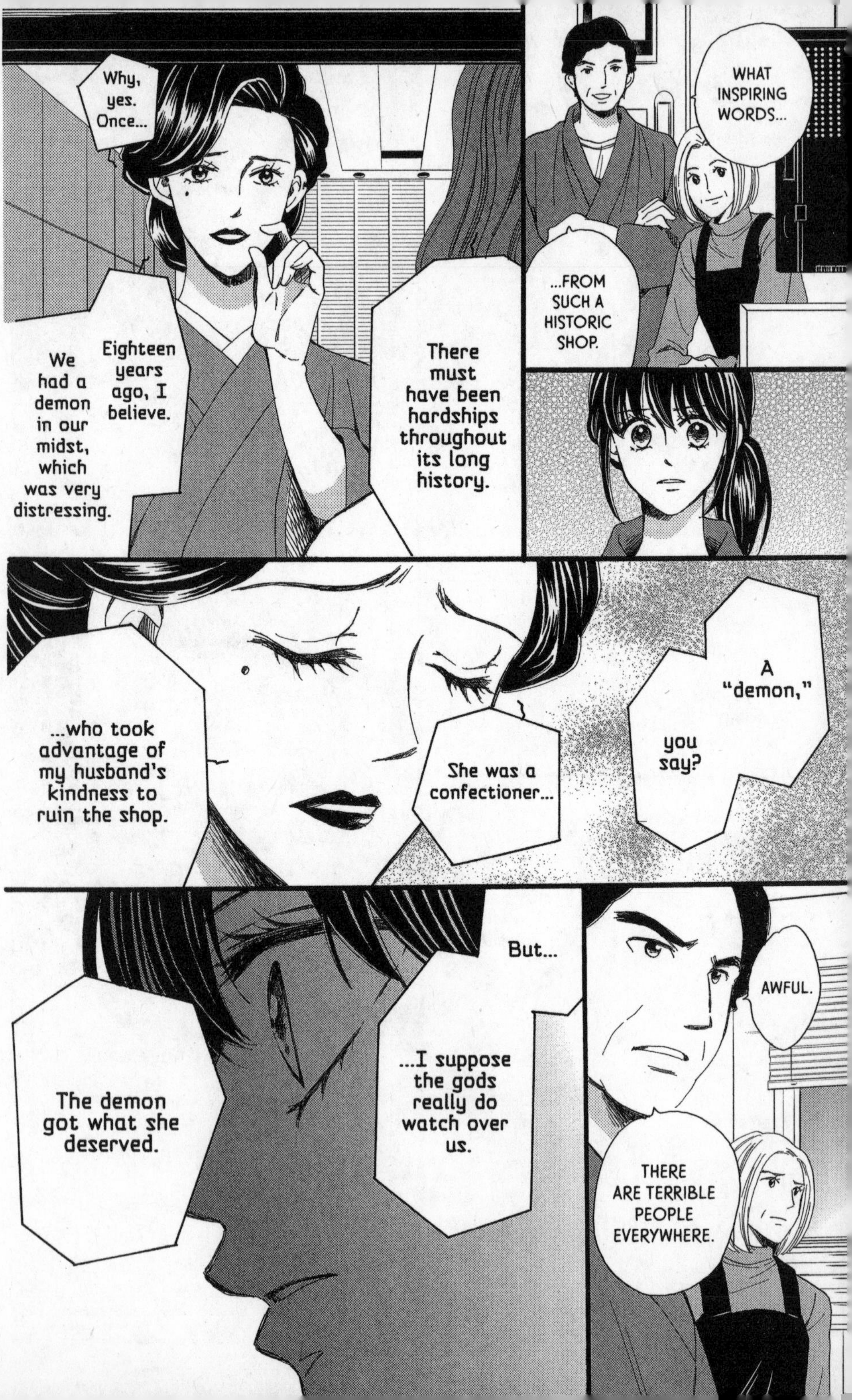
WHAT INSPIRING WORDS...
...FROM SUCH A HISTORIC SHOP.
There must have been hardships throughout its long history.
Why, yes. Once...
Eighteen years ago, I believe.
We had a demon in our midst, which was very distressing.
A "demon," you say?
She was a confectioner...
...who took advantage of my husband's kindness to ruin the shop.
AWFUL.
THERE ARE TERRIBLE PEOPLE EVERYWHERE.
But...
...I suppose the gods really do watch over us.
The demon got what she deserved.

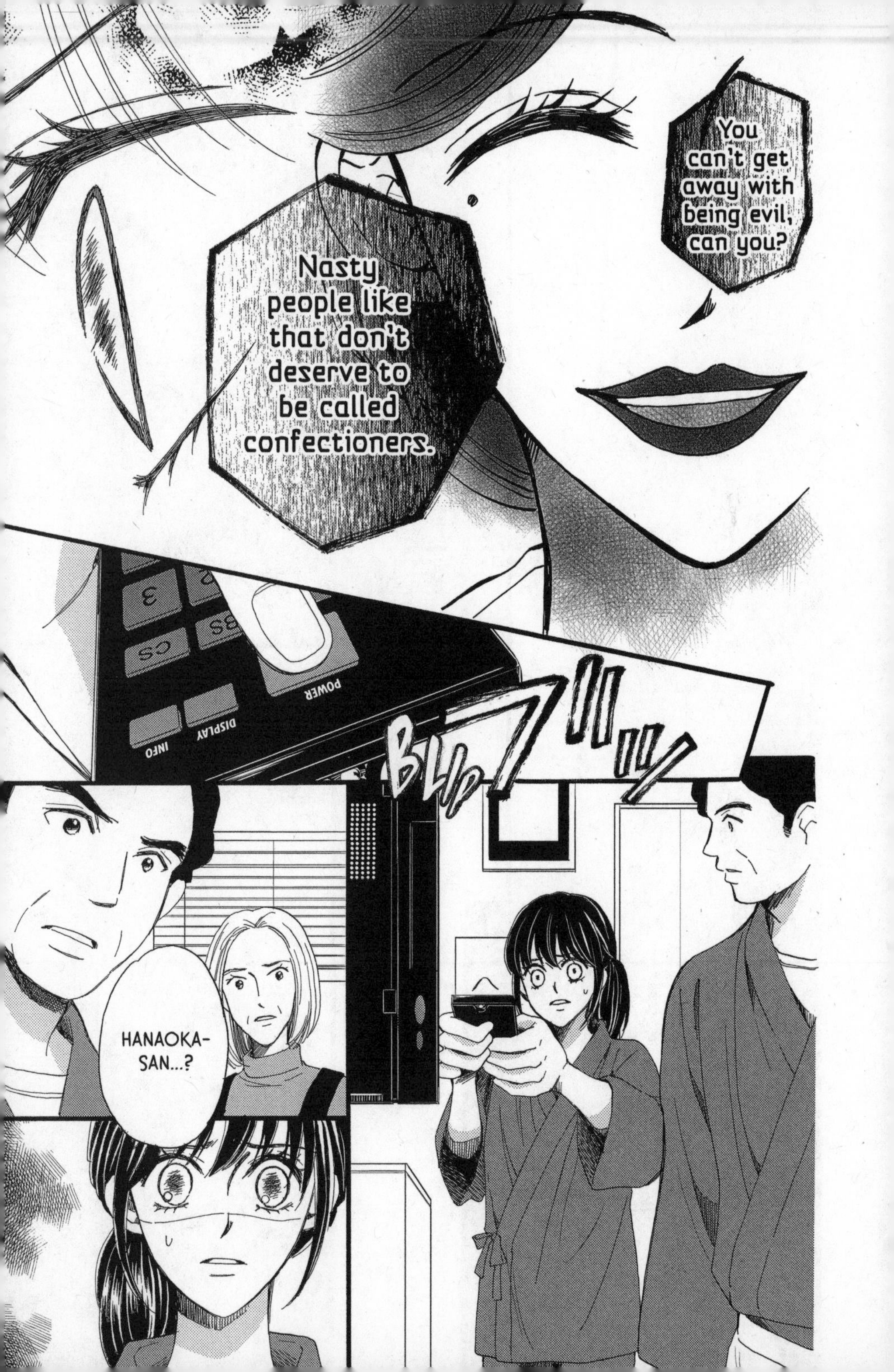
You can't get away with being evil, can you?
Nasty people like that don't deserve to be called confectioners.
HANAOKA-SAN...?

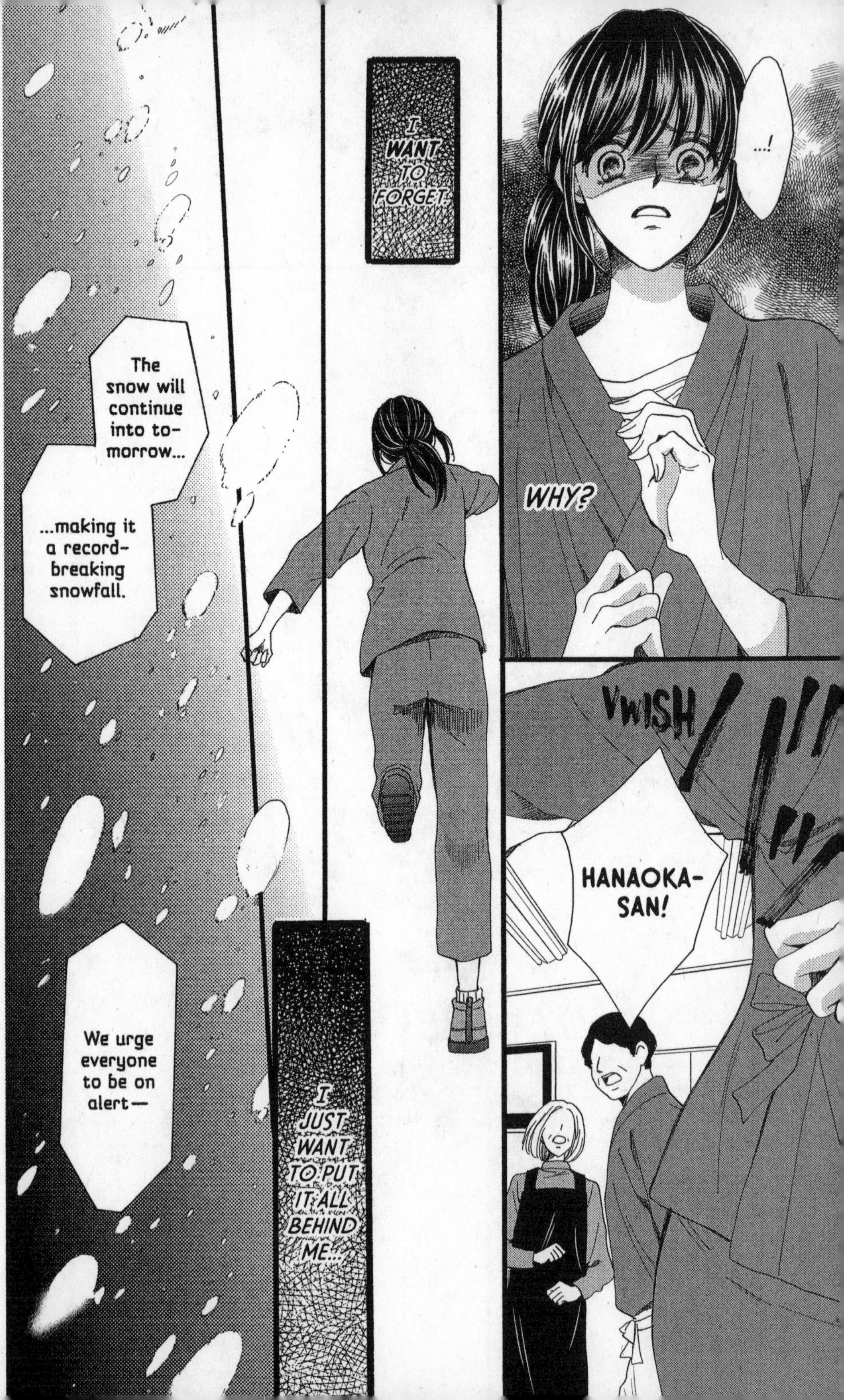
...!
WHY?
VWISH
HANAOKA-SAN!
I WANT TO FORGET.
I JUST WANT TO PUT IT ALL BEHIND ME...
The snow will continue into tomorrow...
...making it a record-breaking snowfall.
We urge everyone to be on alert—

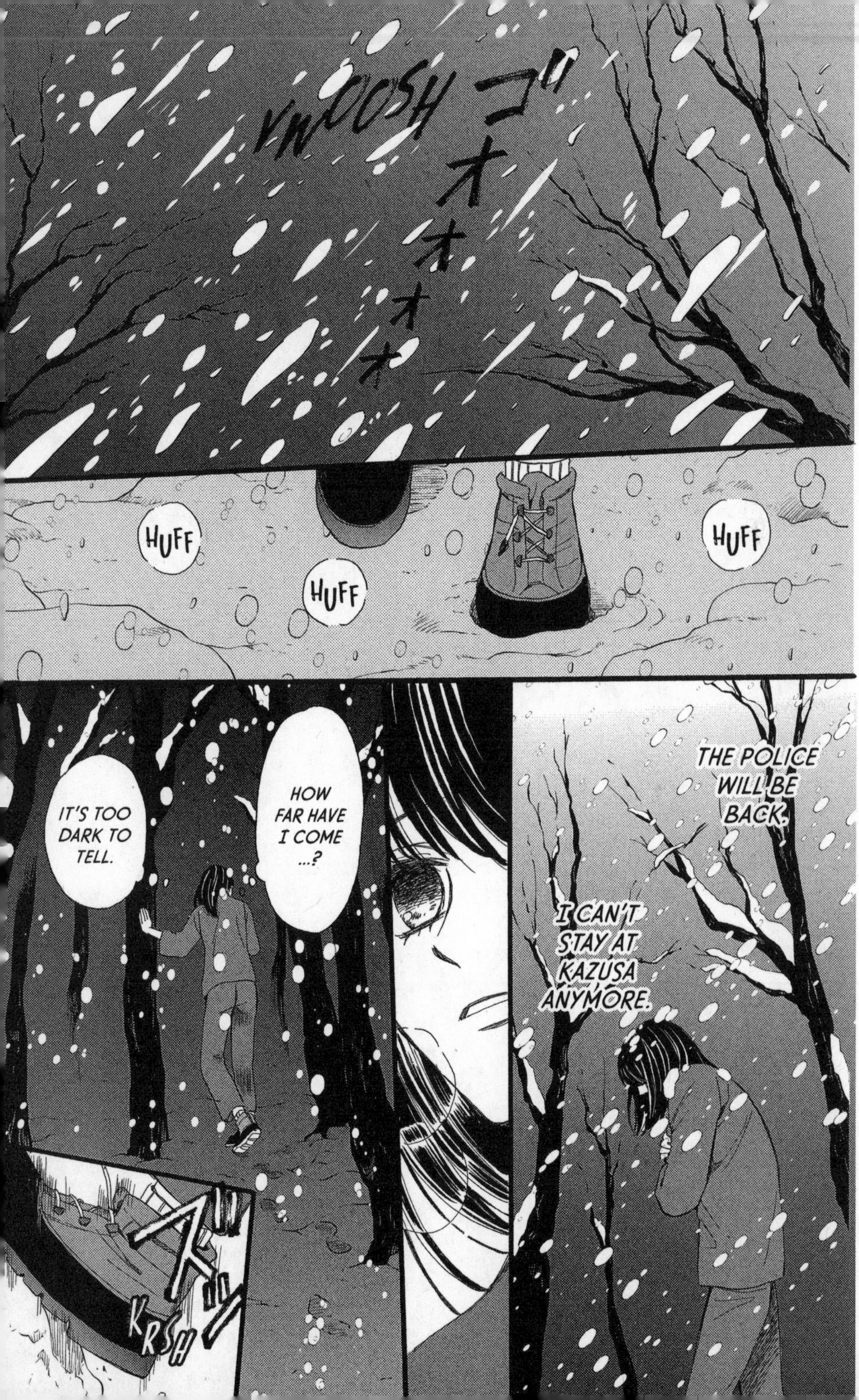
VWOOSH
ゴオオオオ
HUFF
HUFF
HUFF
THE POLICE WILL BE BACK.
I CAN'T STAY AT KAZUSA ANYMORE.
HOW FAR HAVE I COME ...?
IT'S TOO DARK TO TELL.
KRSH

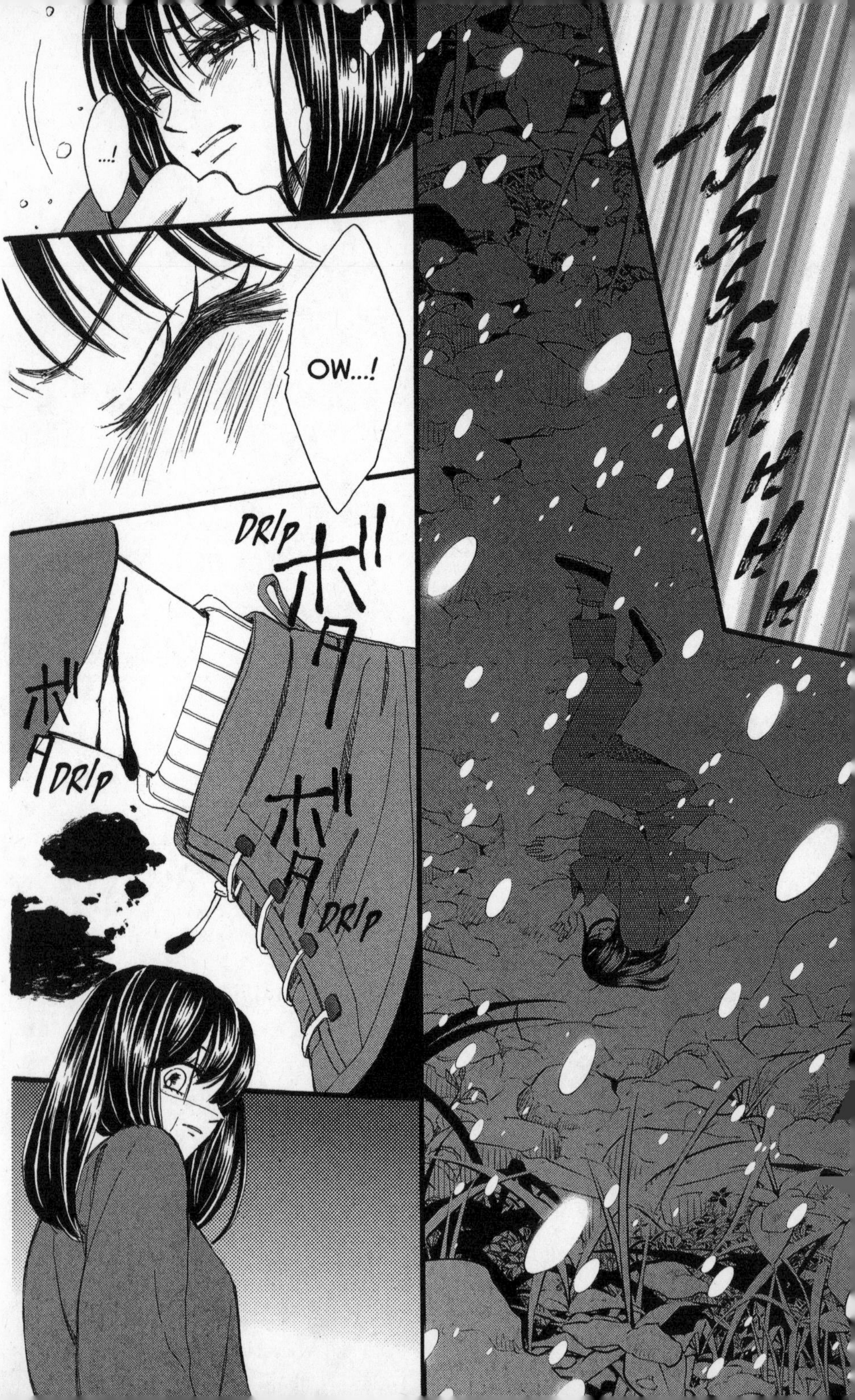
FSSSHHHH
...!
OW...!
DRIP
ボタ
ボタ
DRIP
ボタ
DRIP

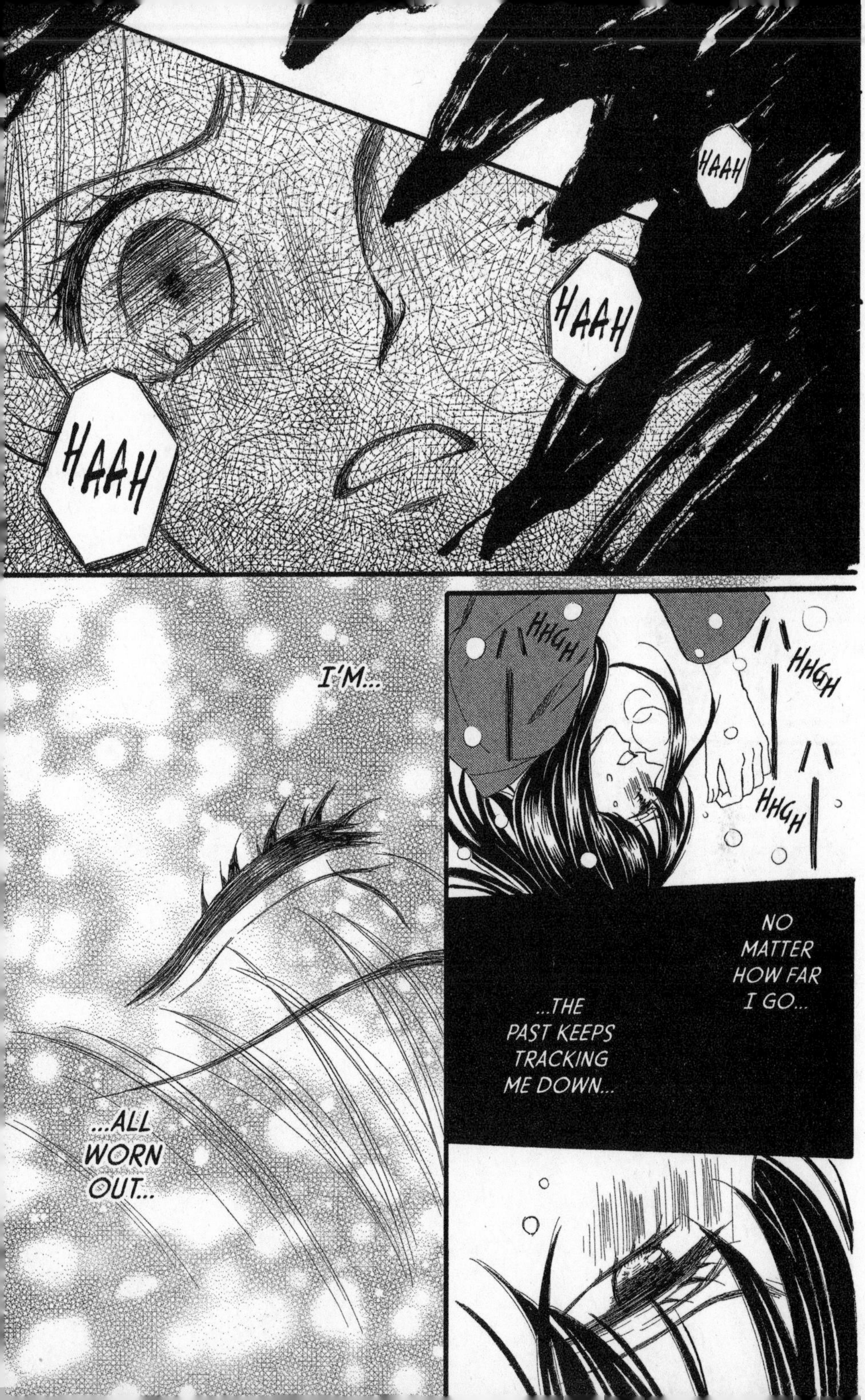
HAAH
HAAH
HAAH
HHGH
HHGH
HHGH
NO MATTER HOW FAR I GO...
...THE PAST KEEPS TRACKING ME DOWN...
I'M...
...ALL WORN OUT...

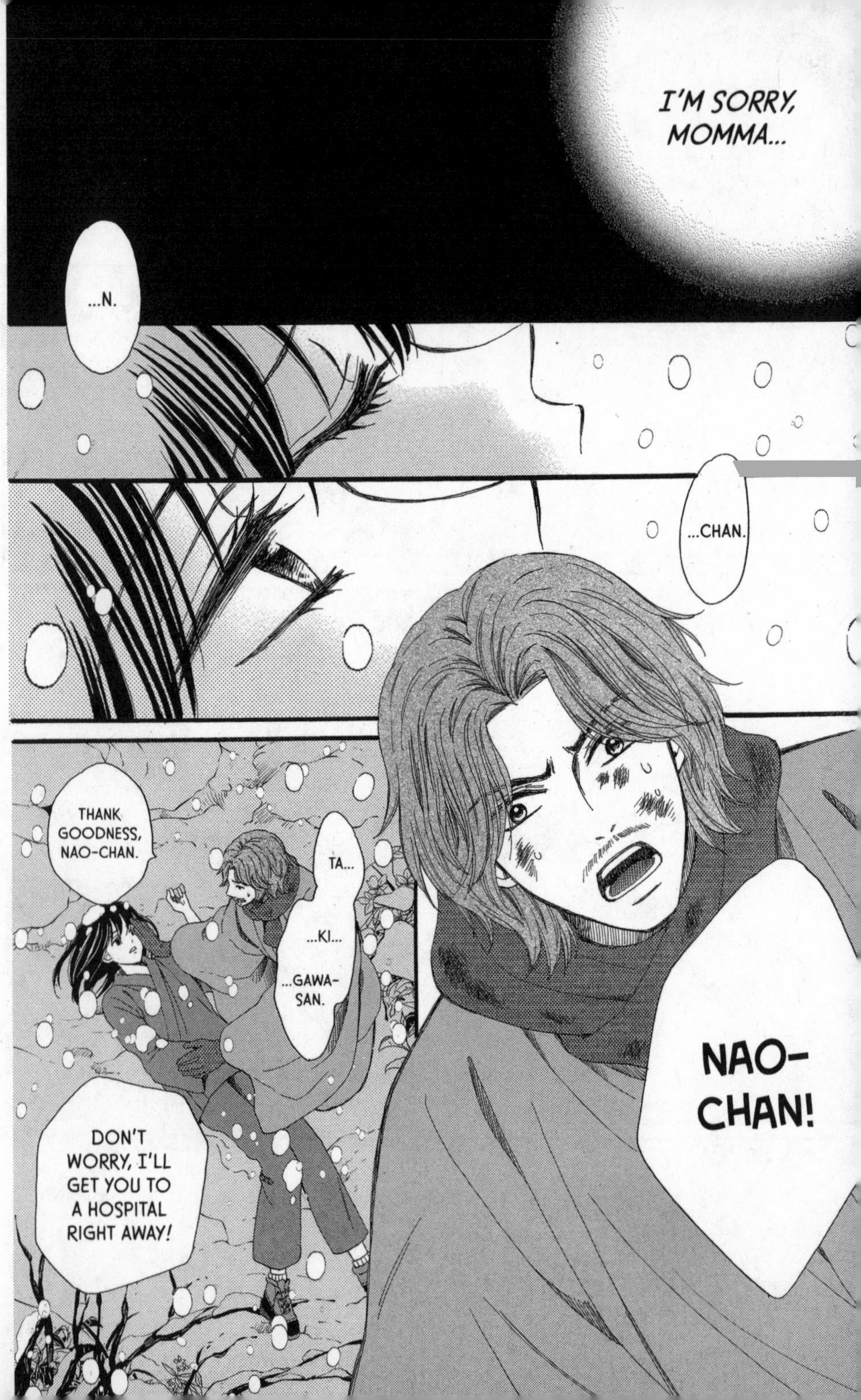
I'M SORRY, MOMMA...
...N.
...CHAN.
NAO-CHAN!
TA...
...KI...
...GAWA-SAN.
THANK GOODNESS, NAO-CHAN.
DON'T WORRY, I'LL GET YOU TO A HOSPITAL RIGHT AWAY!

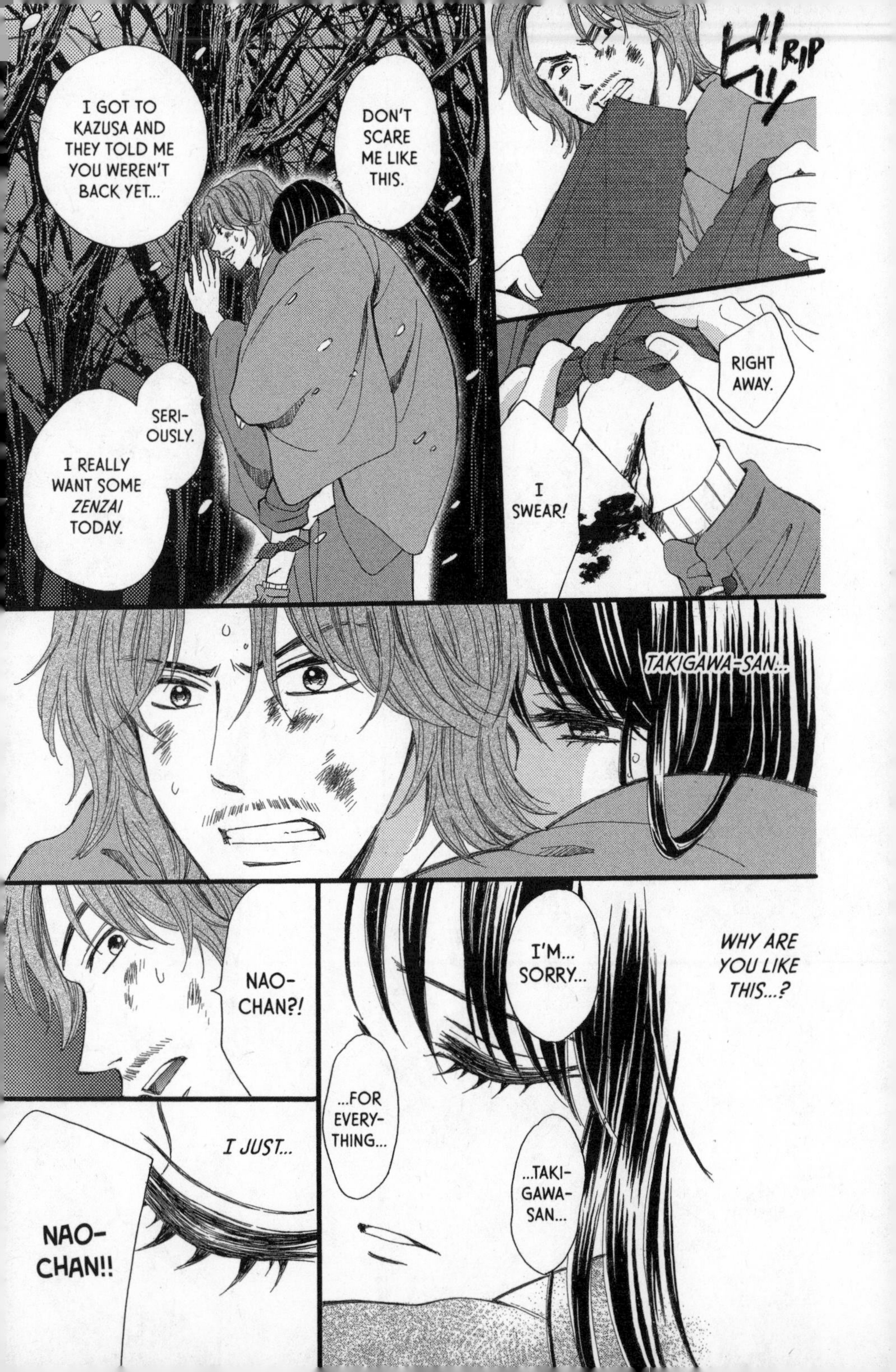
RIP
RIGHT AWAY.
I SWEAR!
DON'T SCARE ME LIKE THIS.
I GOT TO KAZUSA AND THEY TOLD ME YOU WEREN'T BACK YET...
SERIOUSLY.
I REALLY WANT SOME *ZENZAI* TODAY.
TAKIGAWA-SAN...
WHY ARE YOU LIKE THIS...?
I'M... SORRY...
...FOR EVERYTHING...
...TAKIGAWA-SAN...
NAO-CHAN?!
I JUST...
NAO-CHAN!!

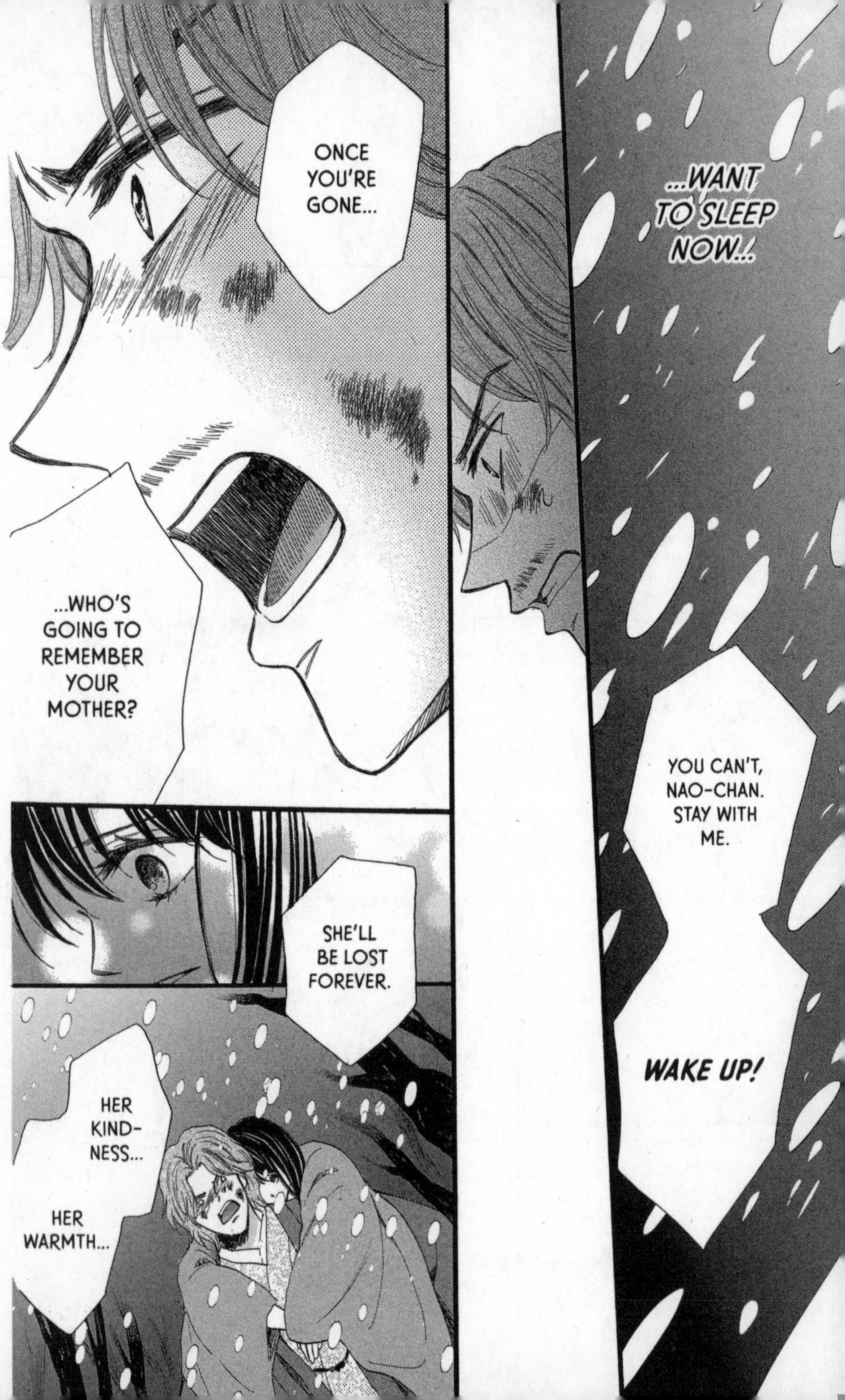
...WANT TO SLEEP NOW..
YOU CAN'T, NAO-CHAN. STAY WITH ME.
WAKE UP!
ONCE YOU'RE GONE...
...WHO'S GOING TO REMEMBER YOUR MOTHER?
SHE'LL BE LOST FOREVER.
HER KIND-NESS...
HER WARMTH...

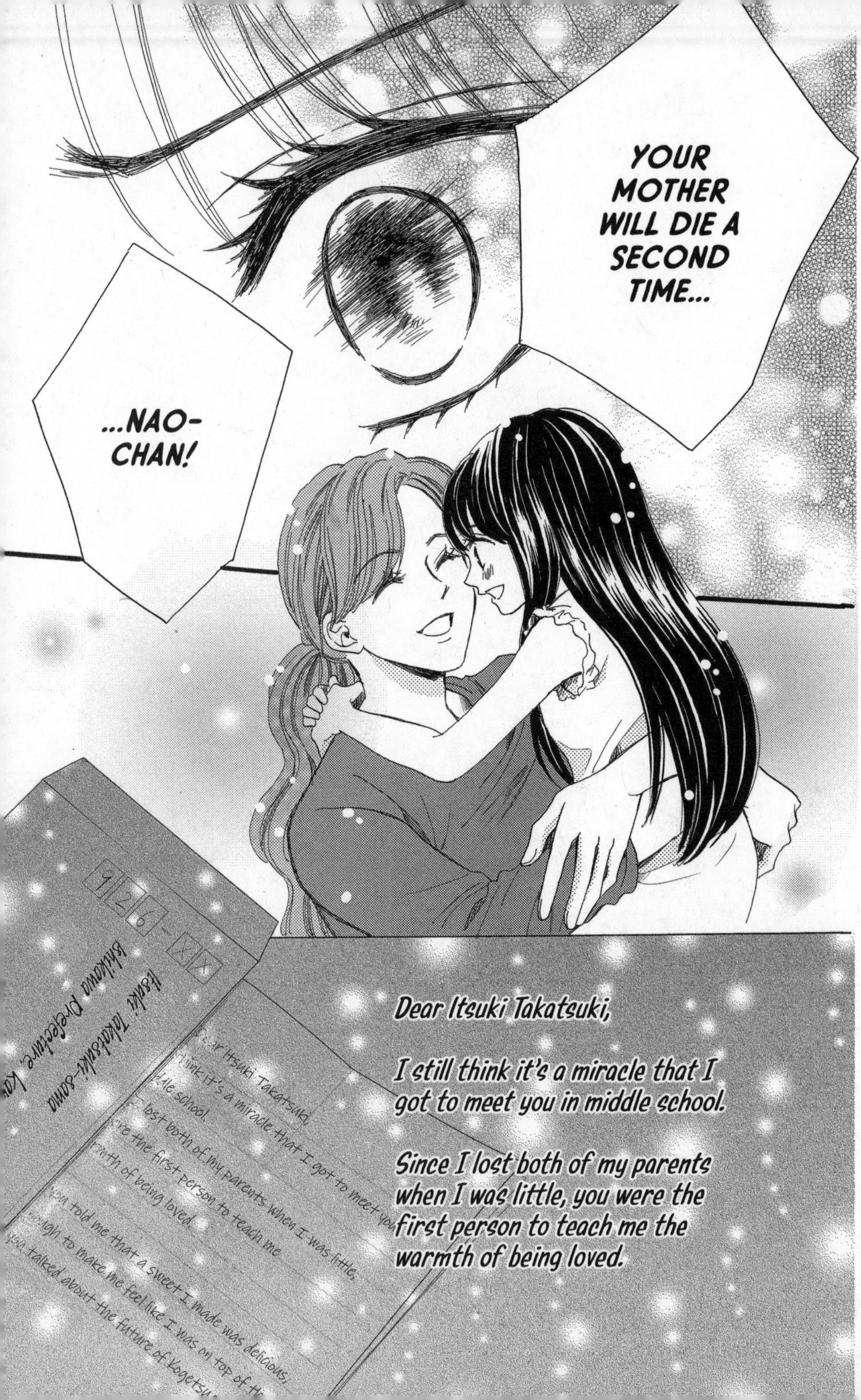
YOUR MOTHER WILL DIE A SECOND TIME...
...NAO-CHAN!
Dear Itsuki Takatsuki,
I still think it's a miracle that I got to meet you in middle school.
Since I lost both of my parents when I was little, you were the first person to teach me the warmth of being loved.

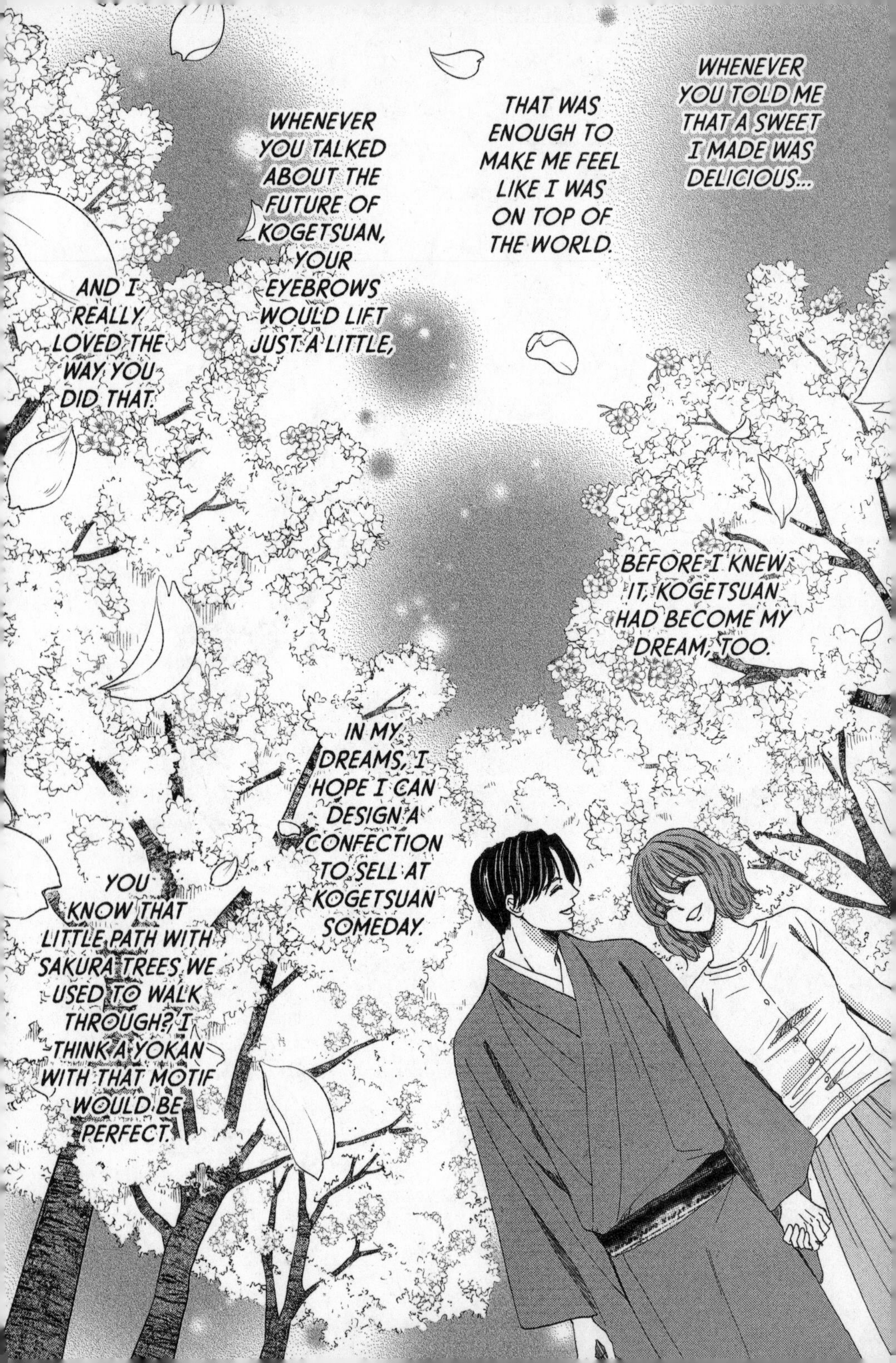
WHENEVER YOU TOLD ME THAT A SWEET I MADE WAS DELICIOUS...
THAT WAS ENOUGH TO MAKE ME FEEL LIKE I WAS ON TOP OF THE WORLD.
WHENEVER YOU TALKED ABOUT THE FUTURE OF KOGETSUAN, YOUR EYEBROWS WOULD LIFT JUST A LITTLE,
AND I REALLY LOVED THE WAY YOU DID THAT.
BEFORE I KNEW IT, KOGETSUAN HAD BECOME MY DREAM, TOO.
IN MY DREAMS, I HOPE I CAN DESIGN A CONFECTION TO SELL AT KOGETSUAN SOMEDAY.
YOU KNOW THAT LITTLE PATH WITH SAKURA TREES WE USED TO WALK THROUGH? I THINK A YOKAN WITH THAT MOTIF WOULD BE PERFECT.

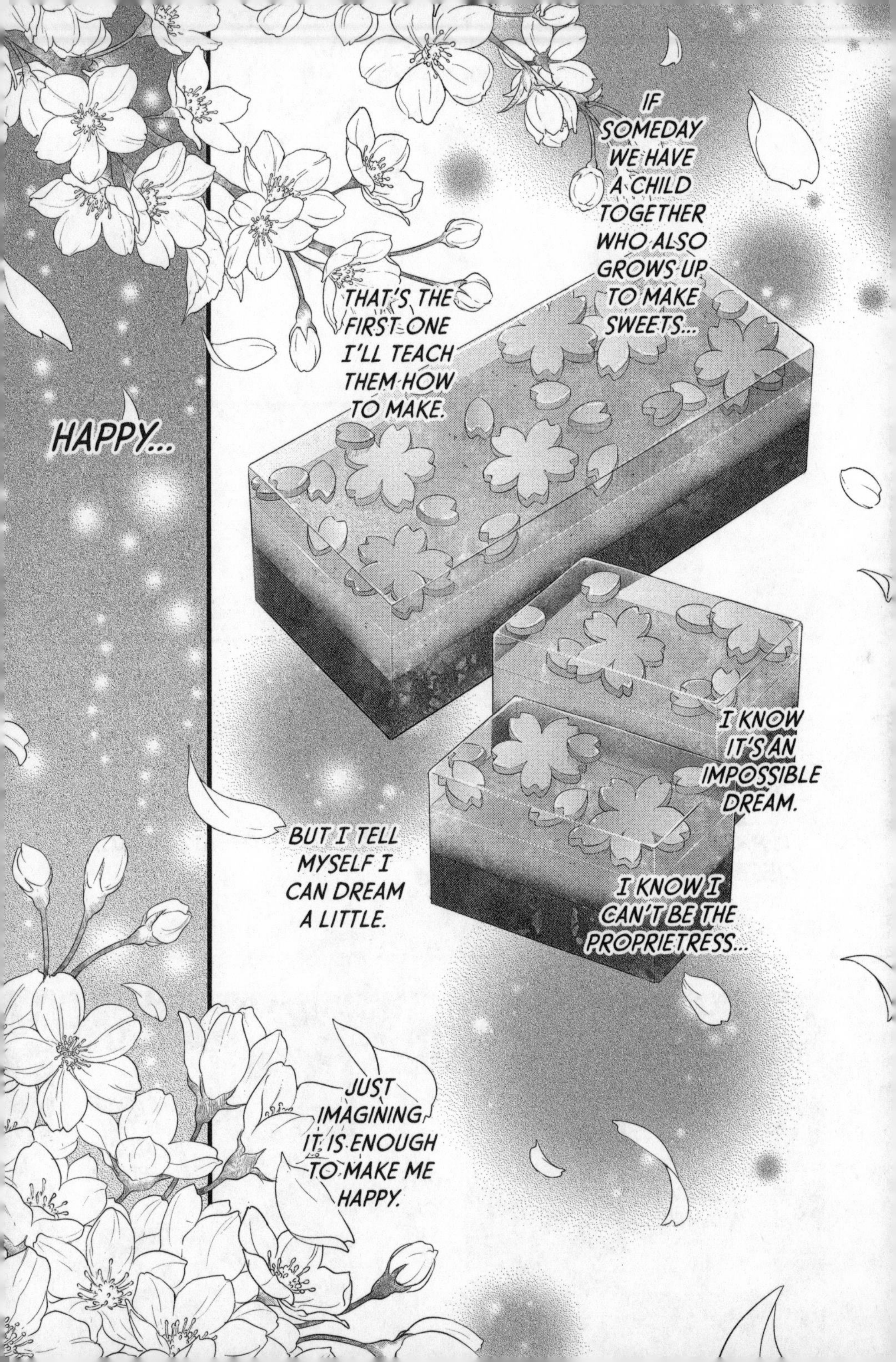
IF SOMEDAY WE HAVE A CHILD TOGETHER WHO ALSO GROWS UP TO MAKE SWEETS...
THAT'S THE FIRST ONE I'LL TEACH THEM HOW TO MAKE.
I KNOW IT'S AN IMPOSSIBLE DREAM.
I KNOW I CAN'T BE THE PROPRIETRESS...
BUT I TELL MYSELF I CAN DREAM A LITTLE.
JUST IMAGINING IT IS ENOUGH TO MAKE ME HAPPY.
HAPPY...

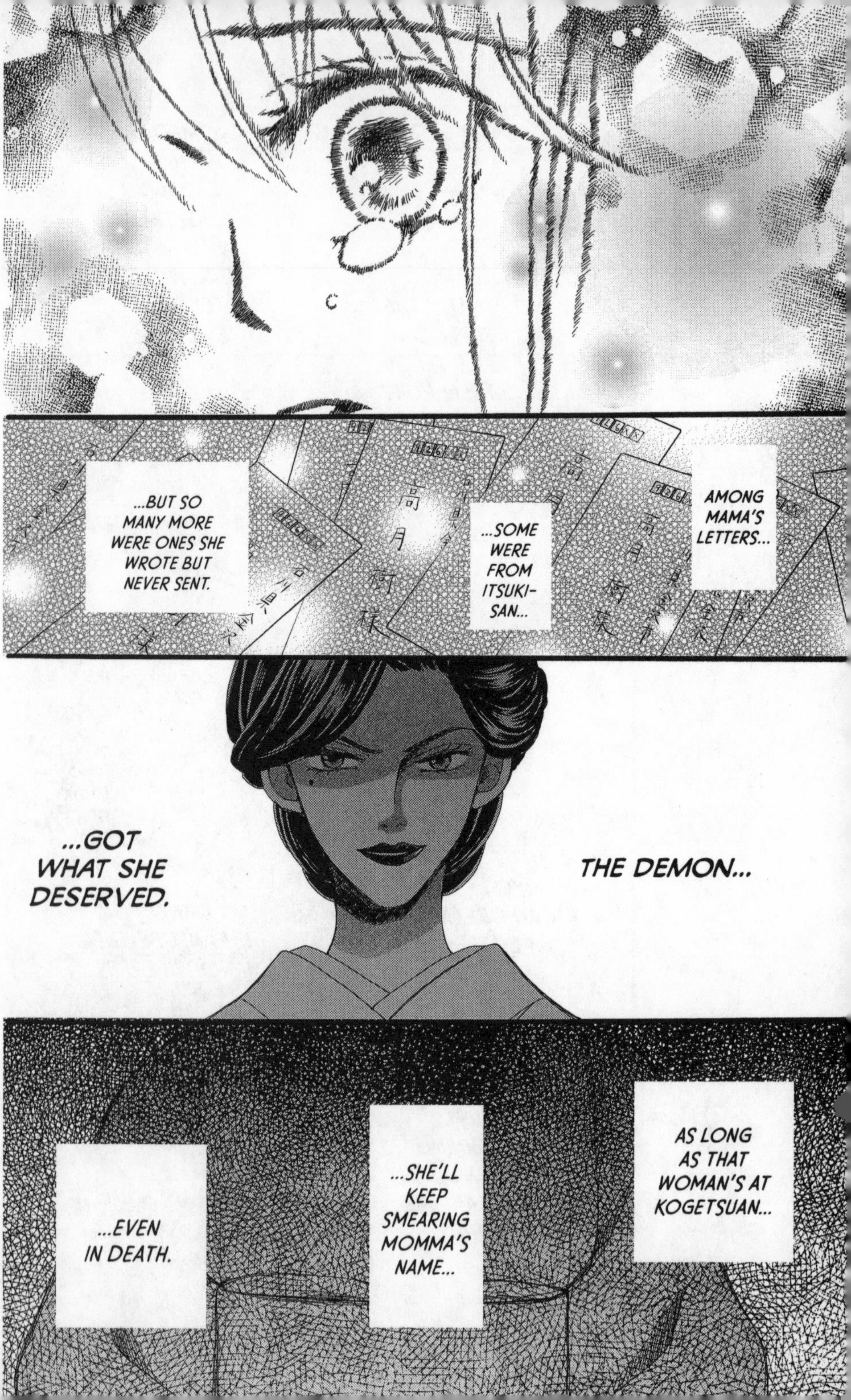
AMONG MAMA'S LETTERS...
...SOME WERE FROM ITSUKI-SAN...
...BUT SO MANY MORE WERE ONES SHE WROTE BUT NEVER SENT.
THE DEMON...
...GOT WHAT SHE DESERVED.
AS LONG AS THAT WOMAN'S AT KOGETSUAN...
...SHE'LL KEEP SMEARING MOMMA'S NAME...
...EVEN IN DEATH.

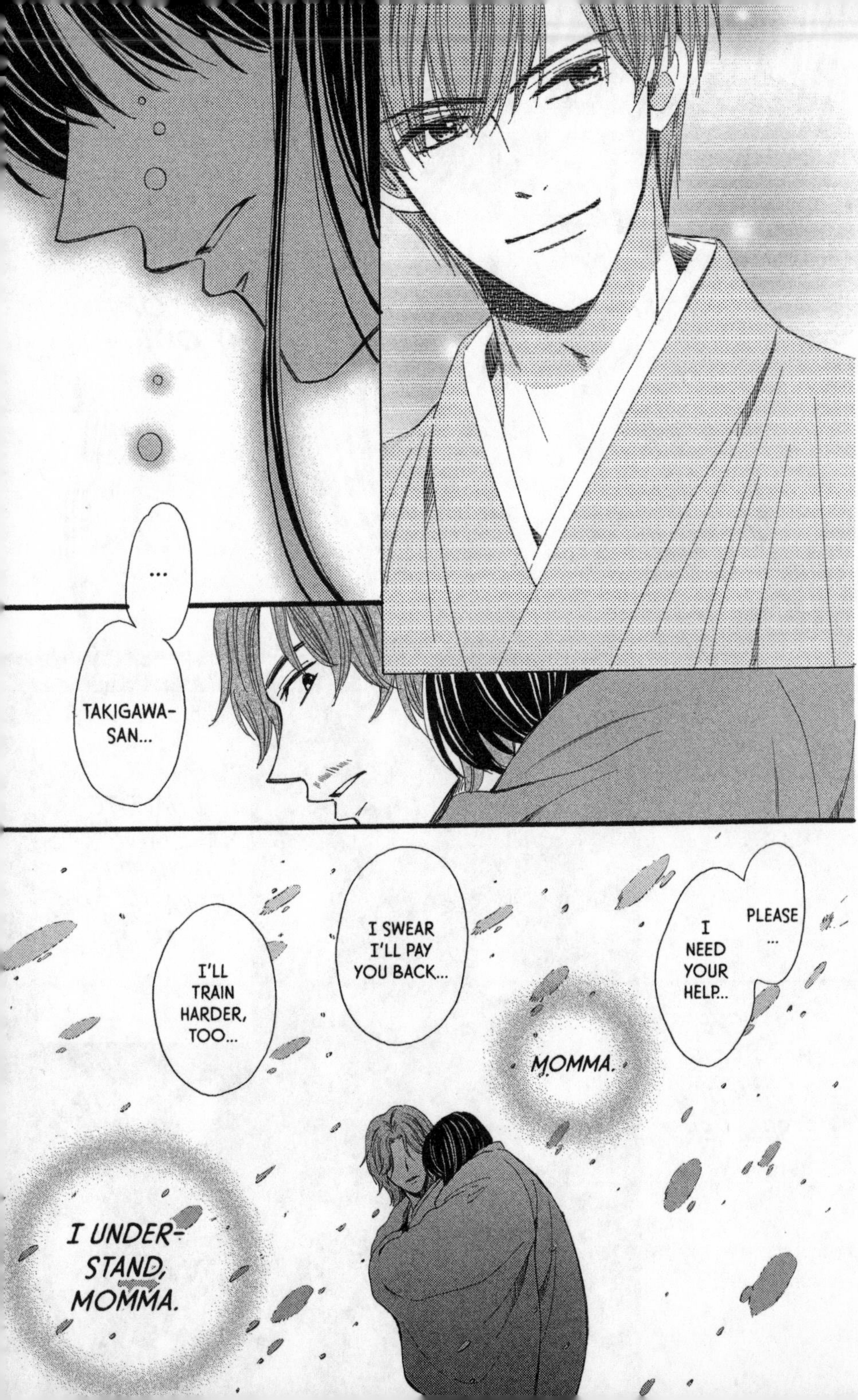
...
TAKIGAWA-SAN...
PLEASE...
I NEED YOUR HELP...
I SWEAR I'LL PAY YOU BACK...
I'LL TRAIN HARDER, TOO...
MOMMA.
I UNDER-STAND, MOMMA.

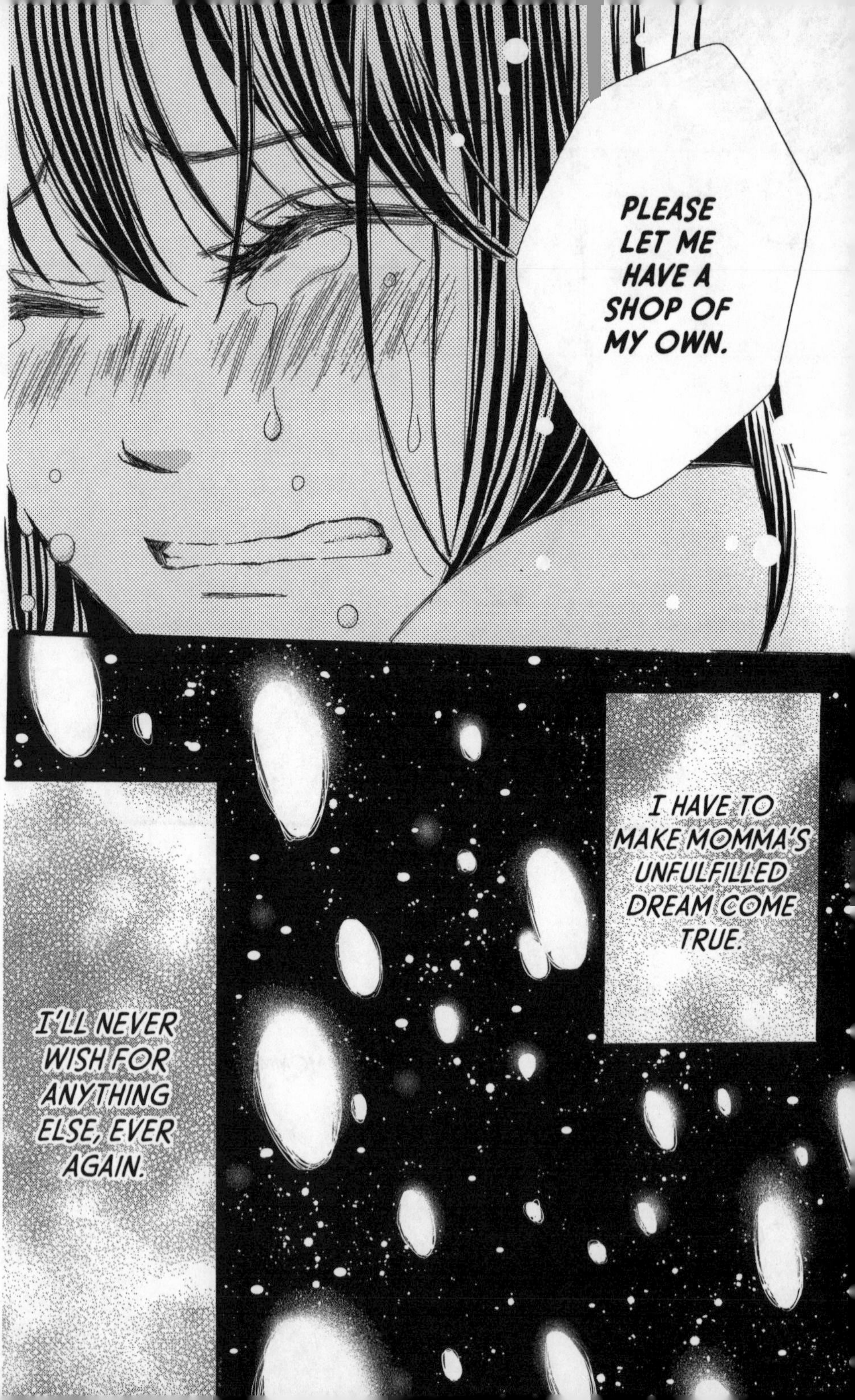
PLEASE LET ME HAVE A SHOP OF MY OWN.
I HAVE TO MAKE MOMMA'S UNFULFILLED DREAM COME TRUE.
I'LL NEVER WISH FOR ANYTHING ELSE, EVER AGAIN.

Chapter 43 *Determination*

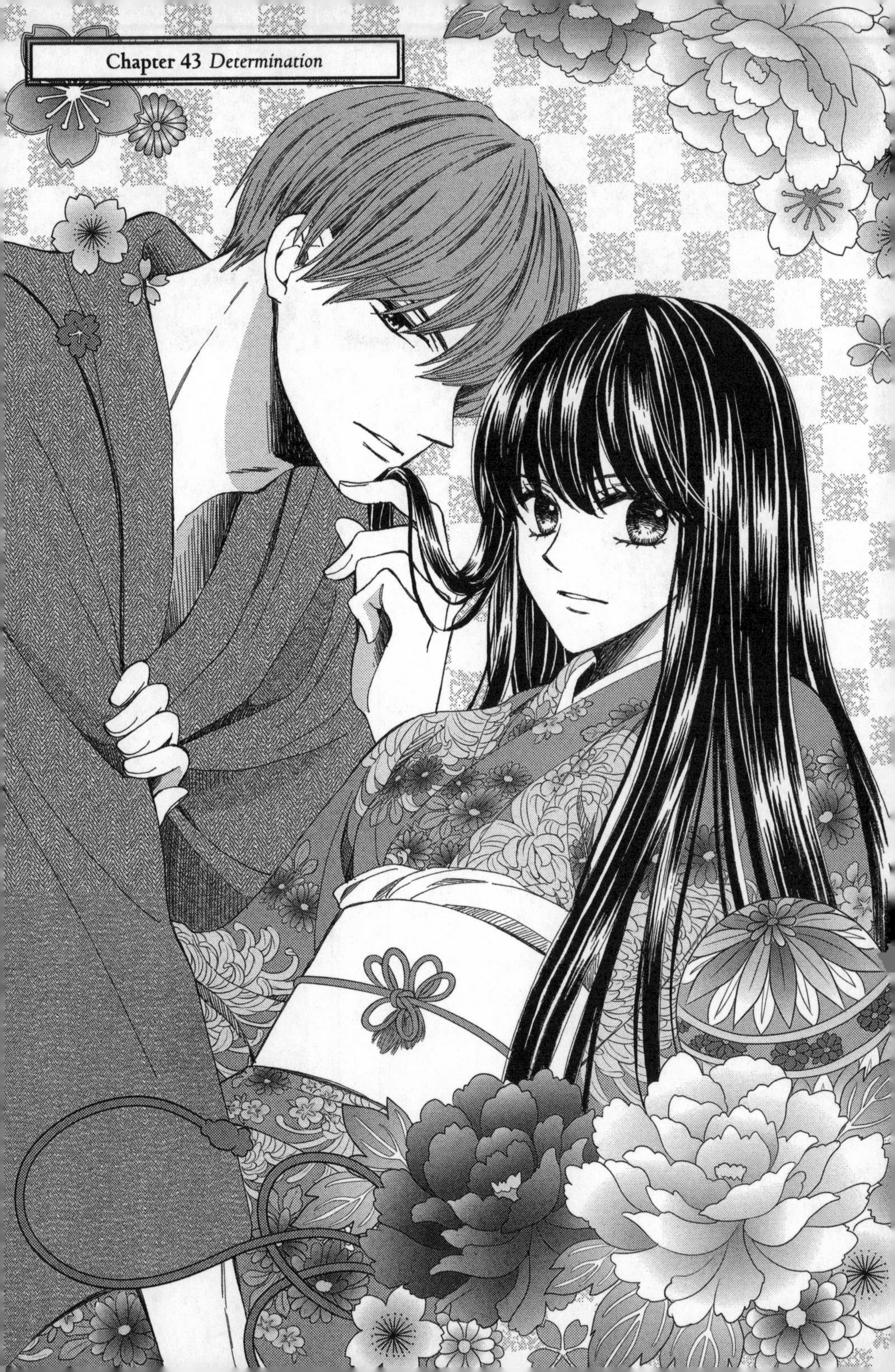

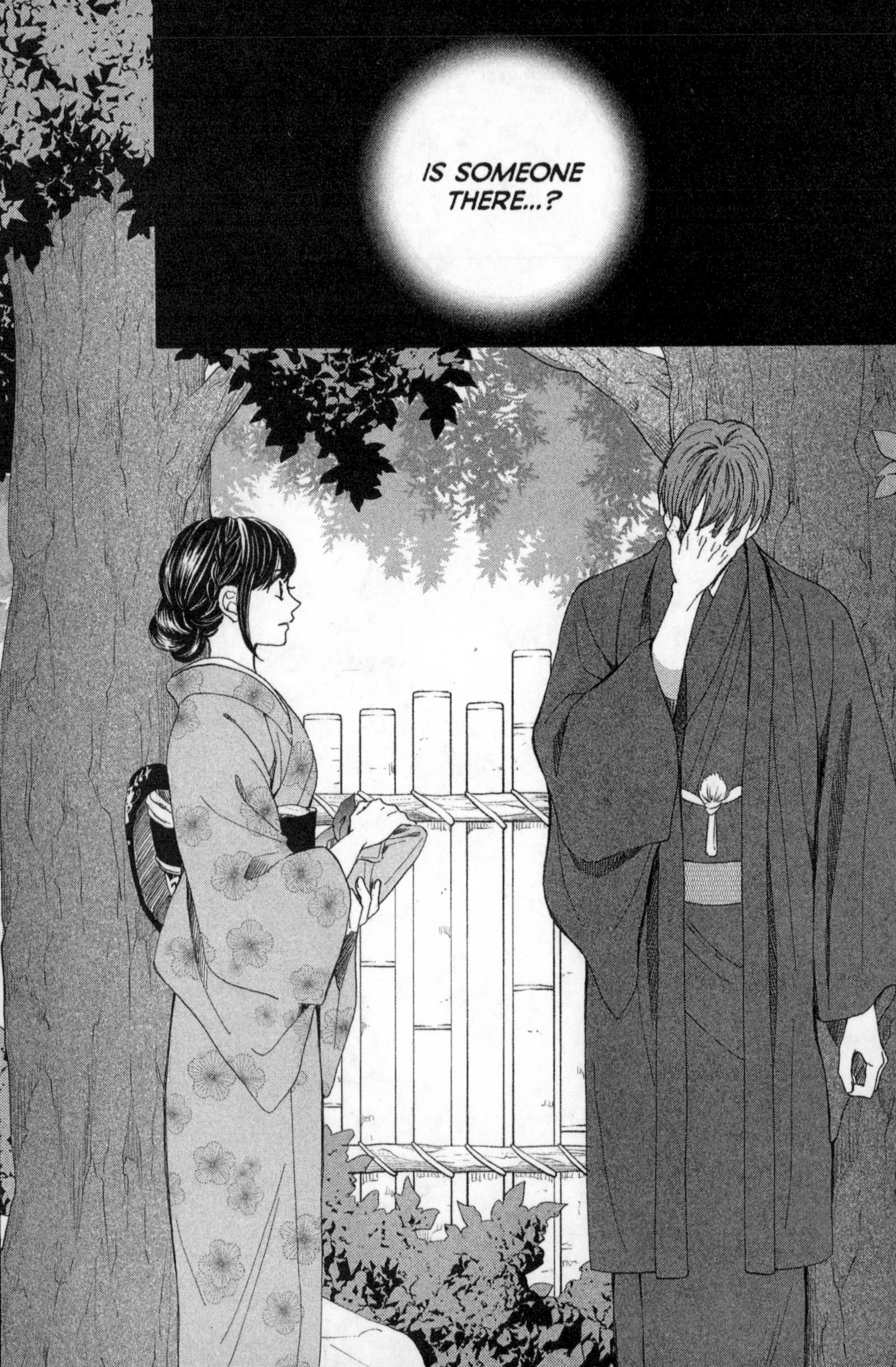
IS SOMEONE THERE...?

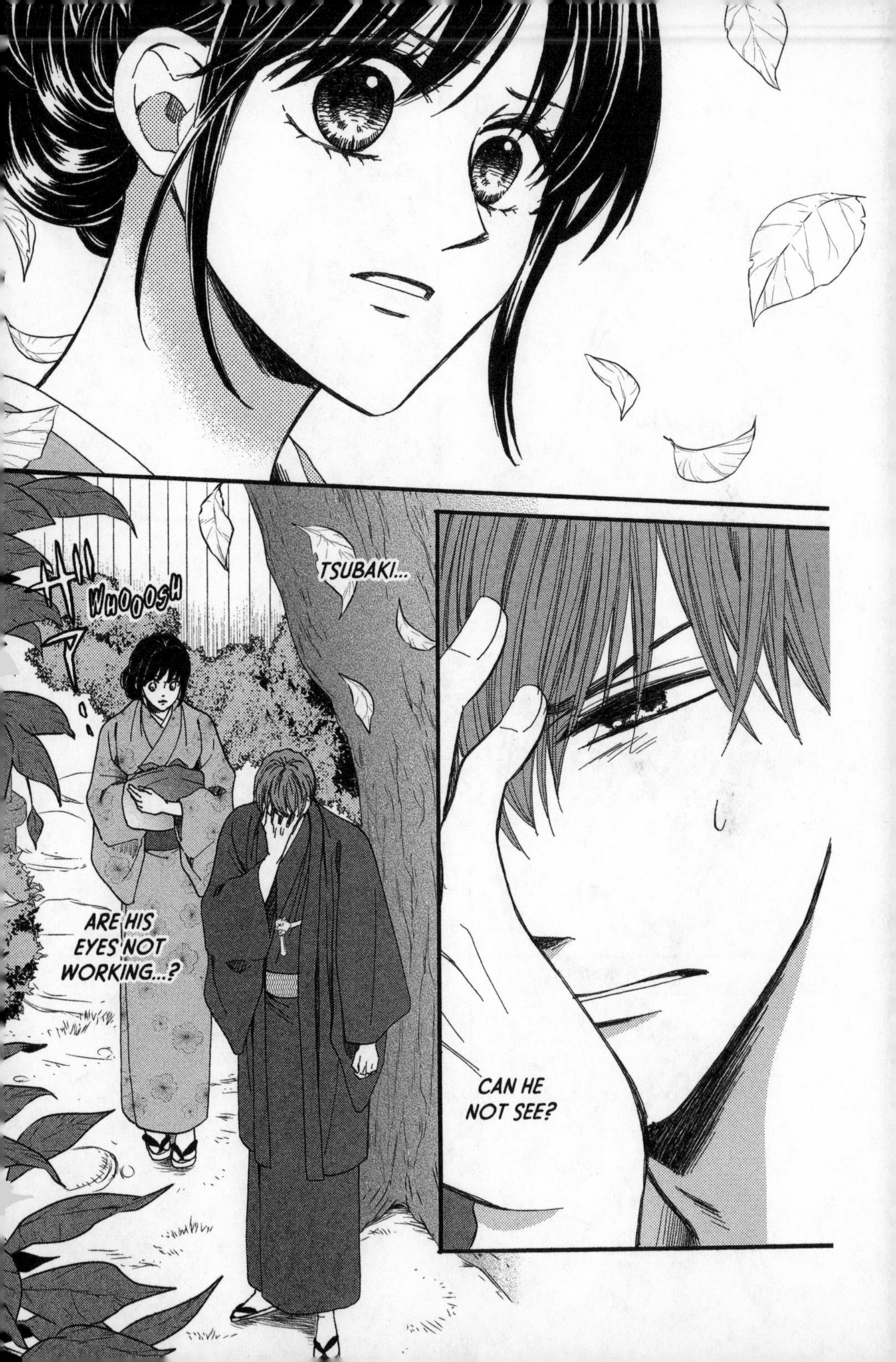
CAN HE
NOT SEE?
WHOOOSH
TSUBAKI...
ARE HIS
EYES NOT
WORKING...?

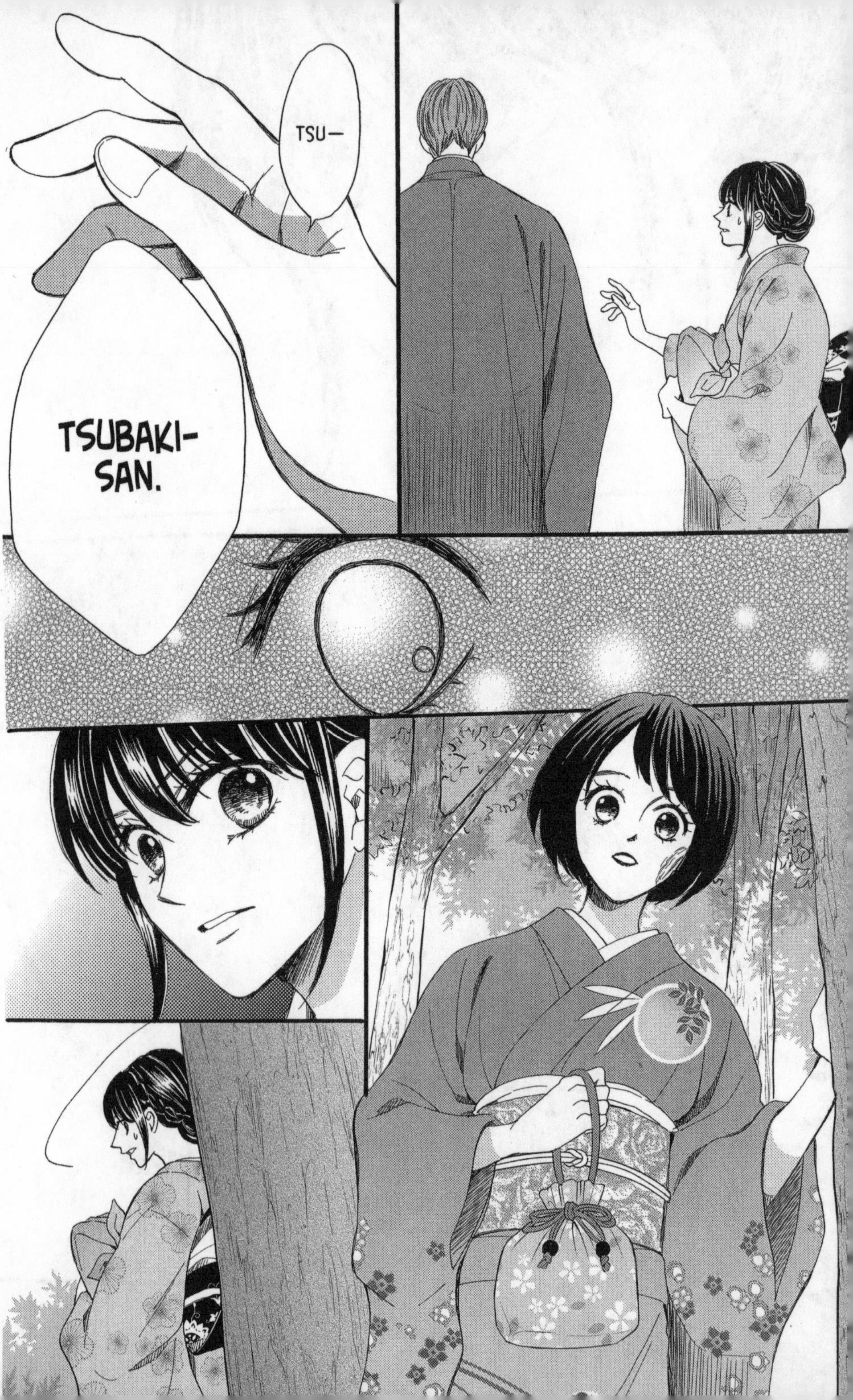
TSU—
TSUBAKI-SAN.

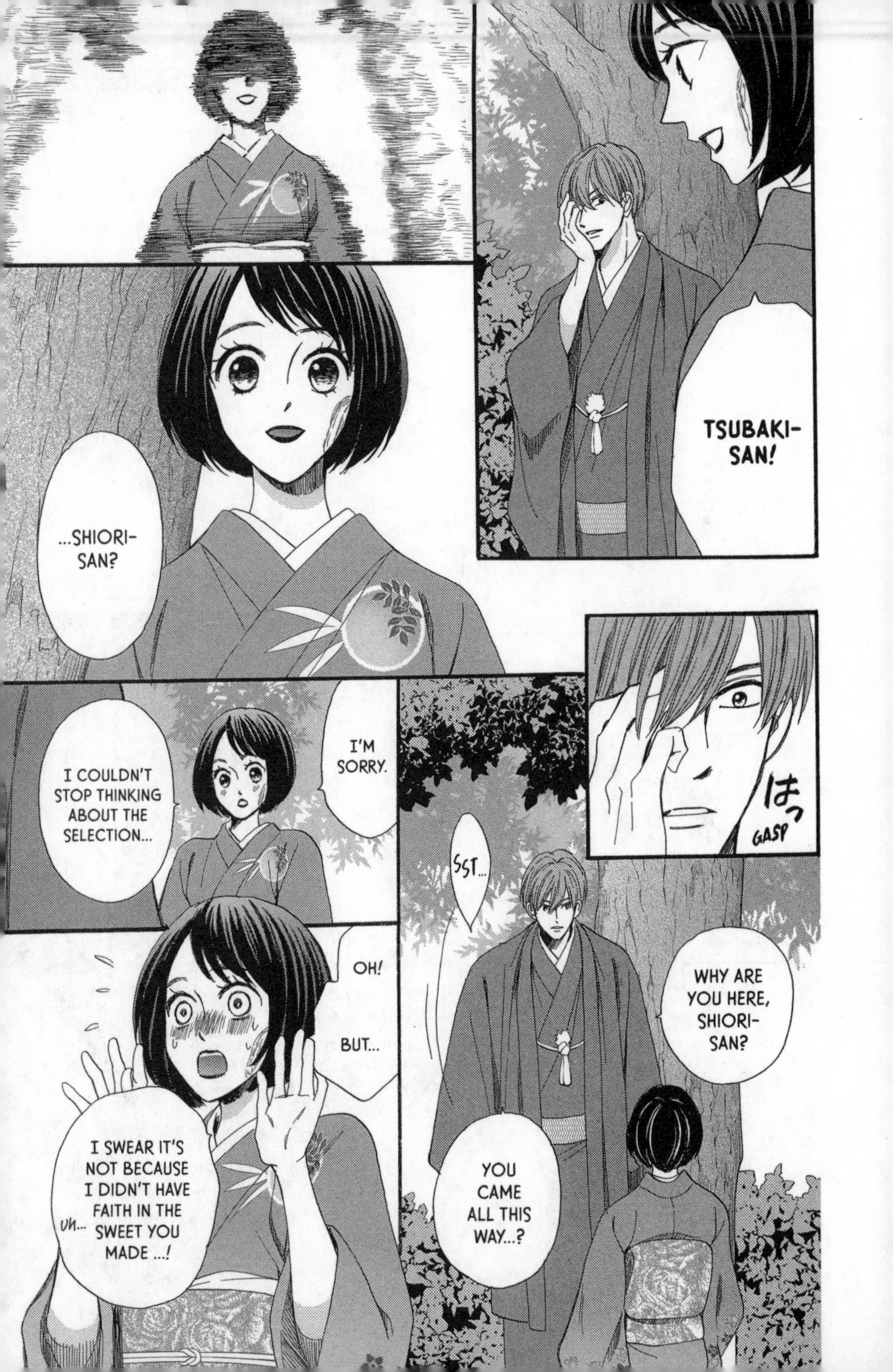
TSUBAKI-SAN!
...SHIORI-SAN?
はっ
GASP
SST...
WHY ARE YOU HERE, SHIORI-SAN?
YOU CAME ALL THIS WAY...?
I'M SORRY.
I COULDN'T STOP THINKING ABOUT THE SELECTION...
OH!
BUT...
I SWEAR IT'S NOT BECAUSE I DIDN'T HAVE FAITH IN THE SWEET YOU MADE ...!
uh...

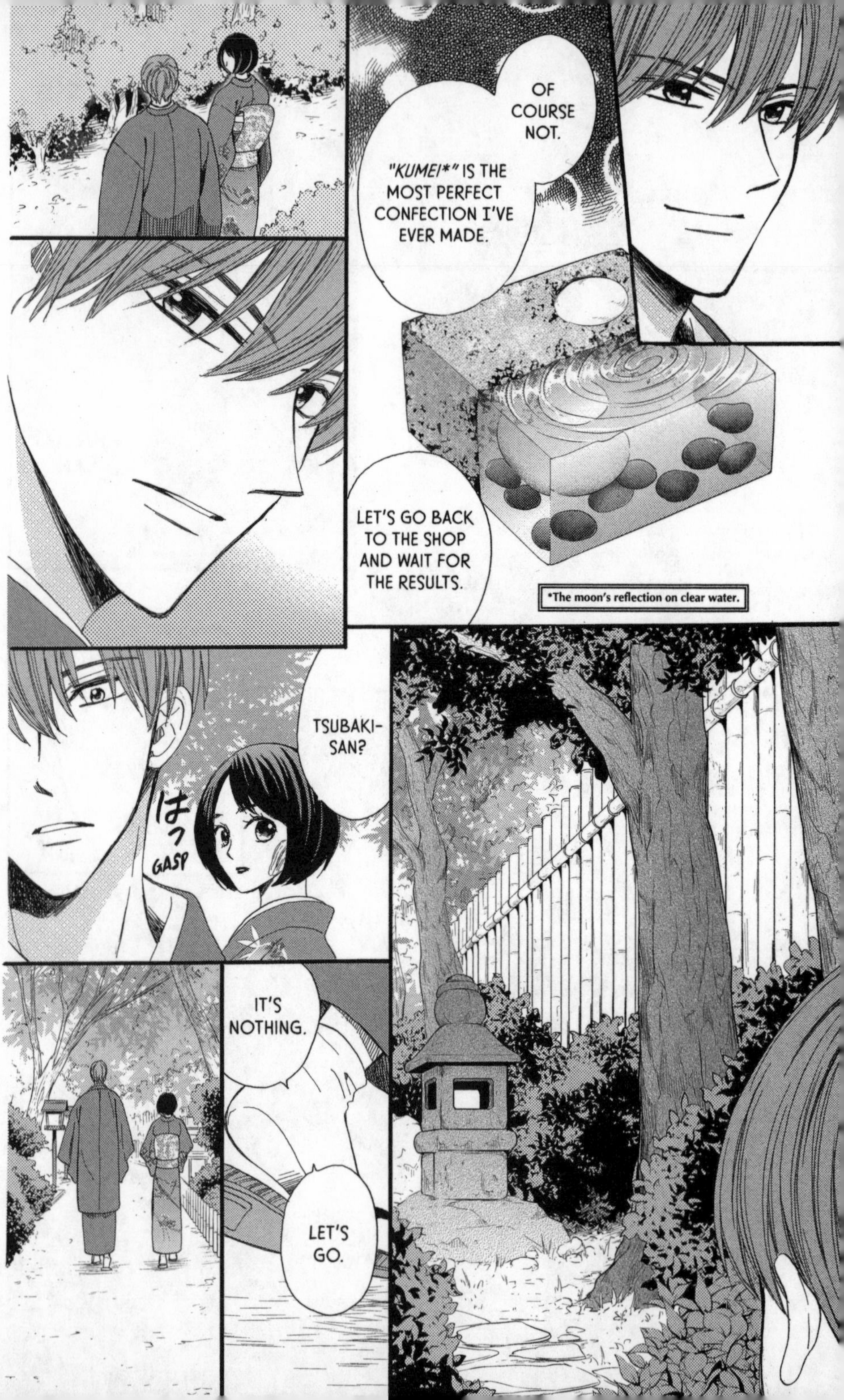
OF COURSE NOT.
"KUMEI*" IS THE MOST PERFECT CONFECTION I'VE EVER MADE.
LET'S GO BACK TO THE SHOP AND WAIT FOR THE RESULTS.
*The moon's reflection on clear water.
TSUBAKI-SAN?
はっ GASP
IT'S NOTHING.
LET'S GO.

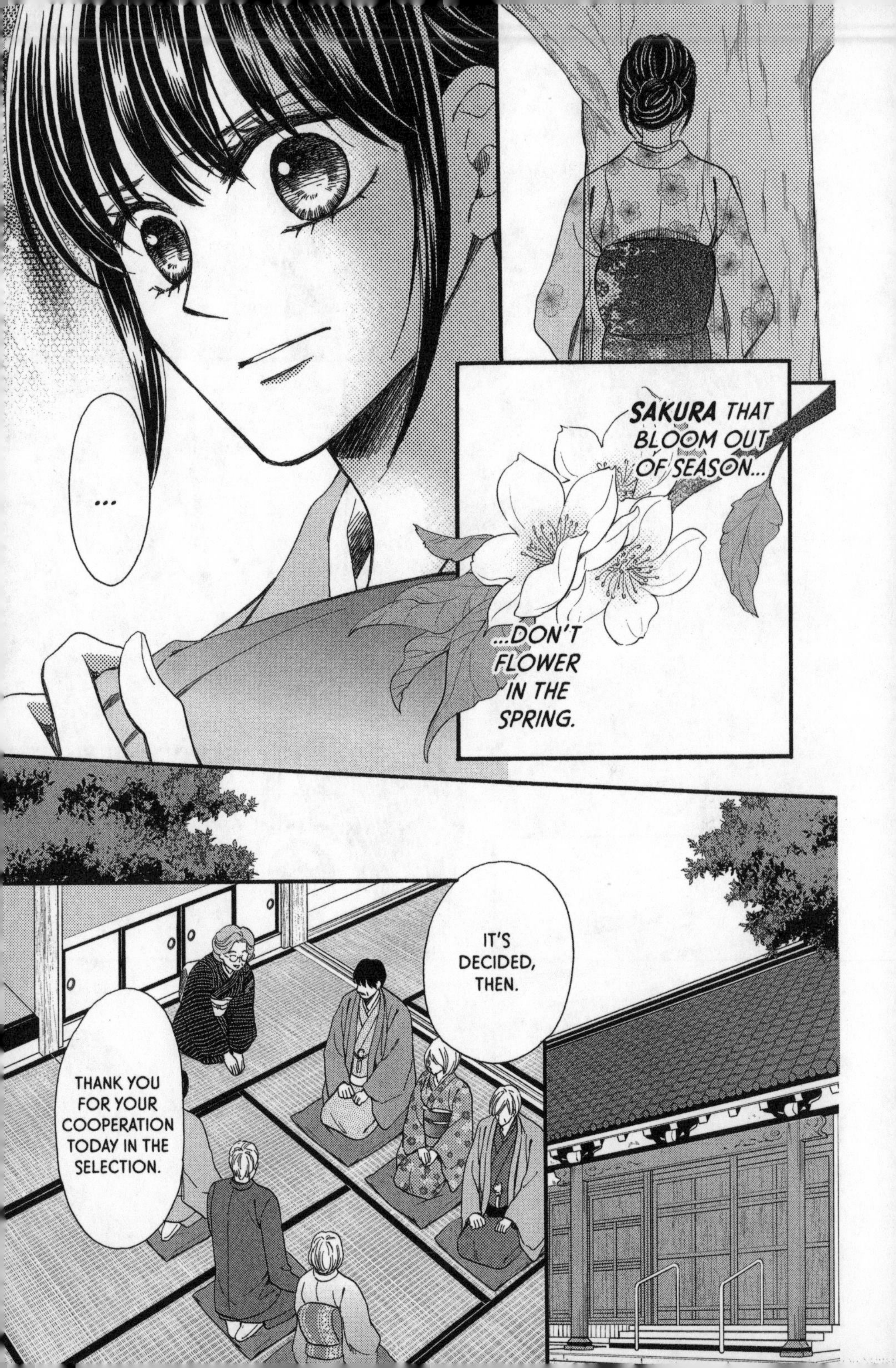
SAKURA THAT BLOOM OUT OF SEASON...
...DON'T FLOWER IN THE SPRING.
...
IT'S DECIDED, THEN.
THANK YOU FOR YOUR COOPERATION TODAY IN THE SELECTION.

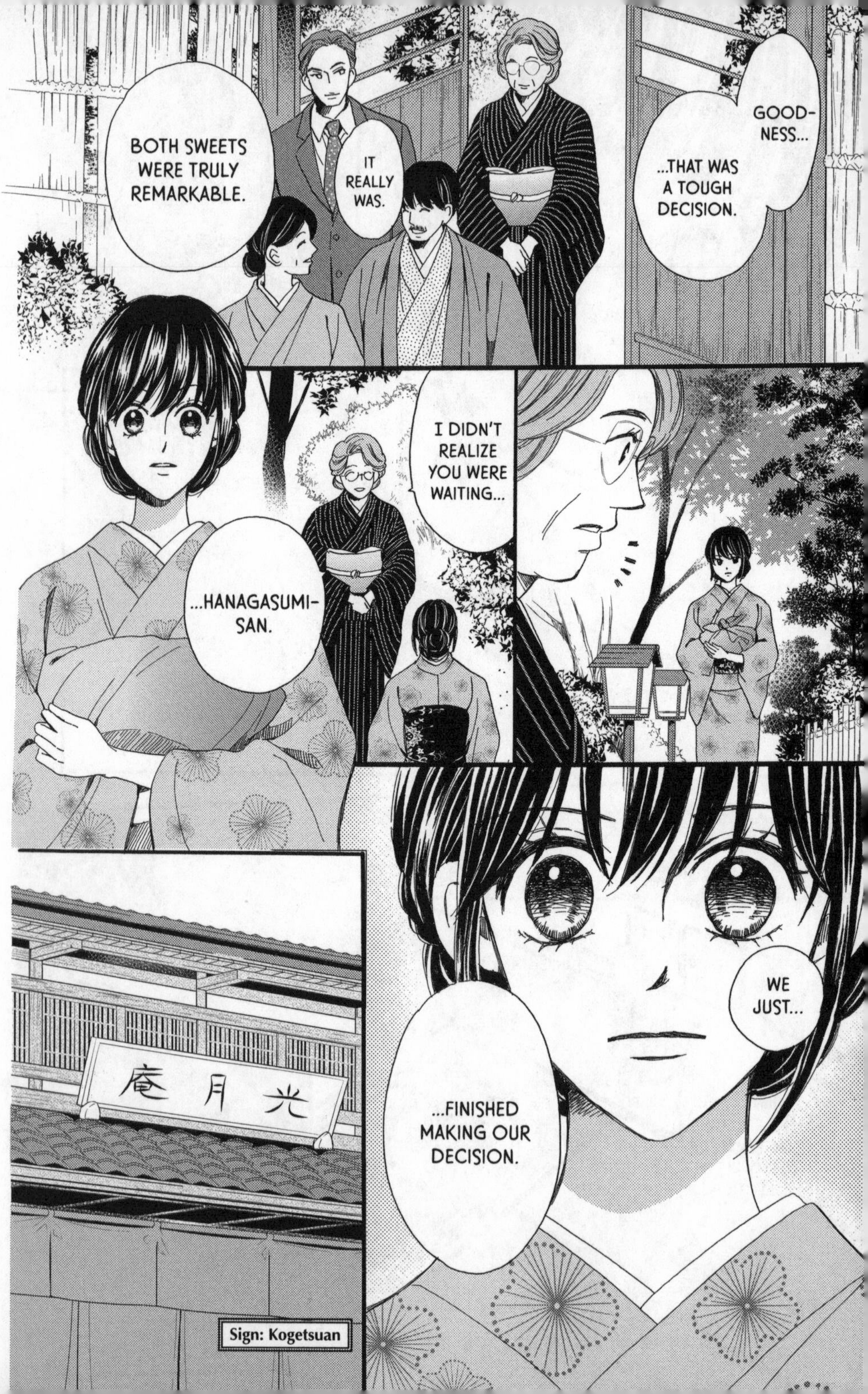
GOOD-NESS...
...THAT WAS A TOUGH DECISION.
IT REALLY WAS.
BOTH SWEETS WERE TRULY REMARKABLE.
I DIDN'T REALIZE YOU WERE WAITING...
...HANAGASUMI-SAN.
WE JUST...
...FINISHED MAKING OUR DECISION.
光月庵
Sign: Kogetsuan

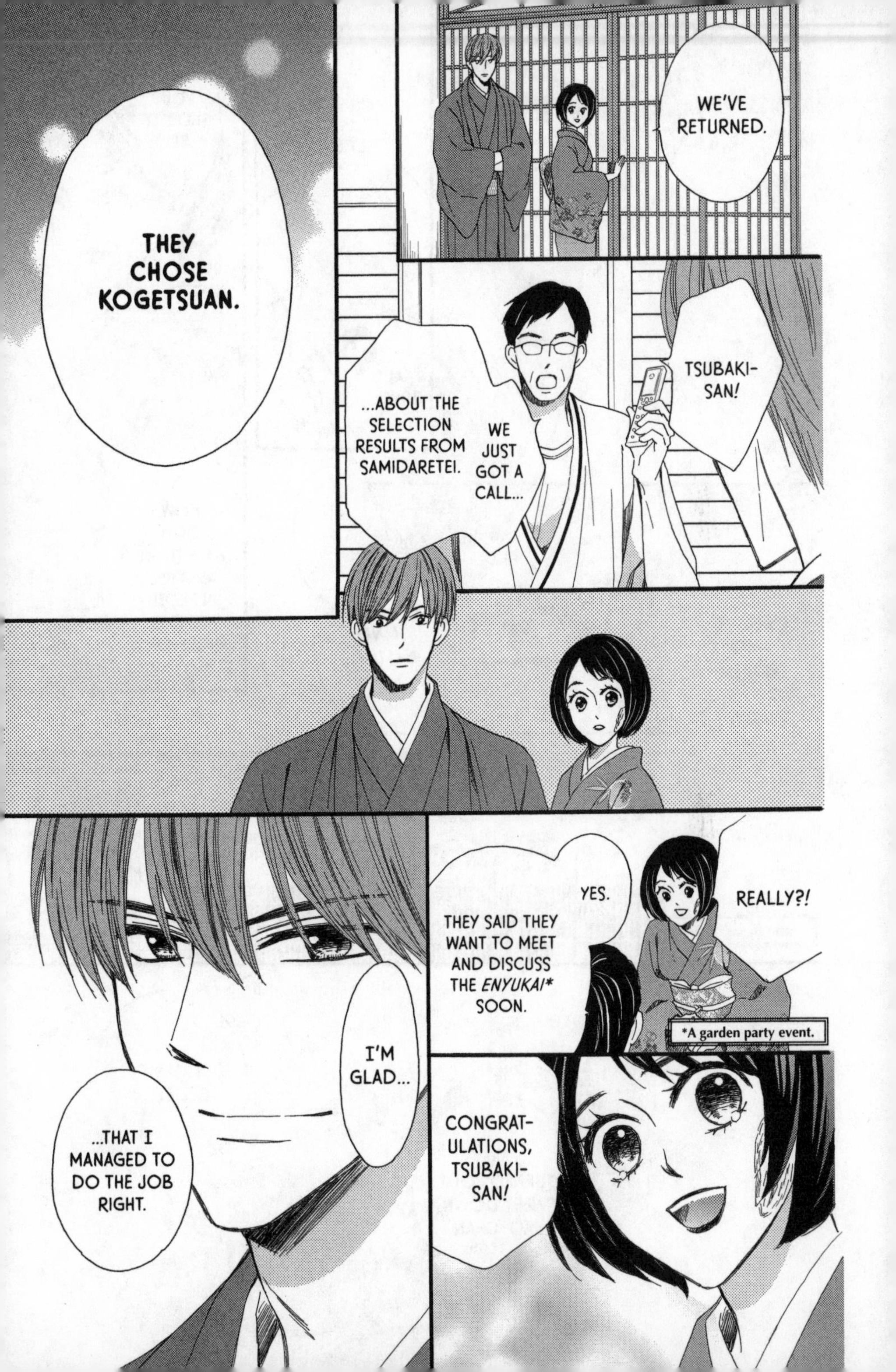
WE'VE RETURNED.
TSUBAKI-SAN!
WE JUST GOT A CALL...
...ABOUT THE SELECTION RESULTS FROM SAMIDARETEI.
THEY CHOSE KOGETSUAN.
REALLY?!
YES.
THEY SAID THEY WANT TO MEET AND DISCUSS THE *ENYUKAI** SOON.
*A garden party event.
CONGRATULATIONS, TSUBAKI-SAN!
I'M GLAD...
...THAT I MANAGED TO DO THE JOB RIGHT.

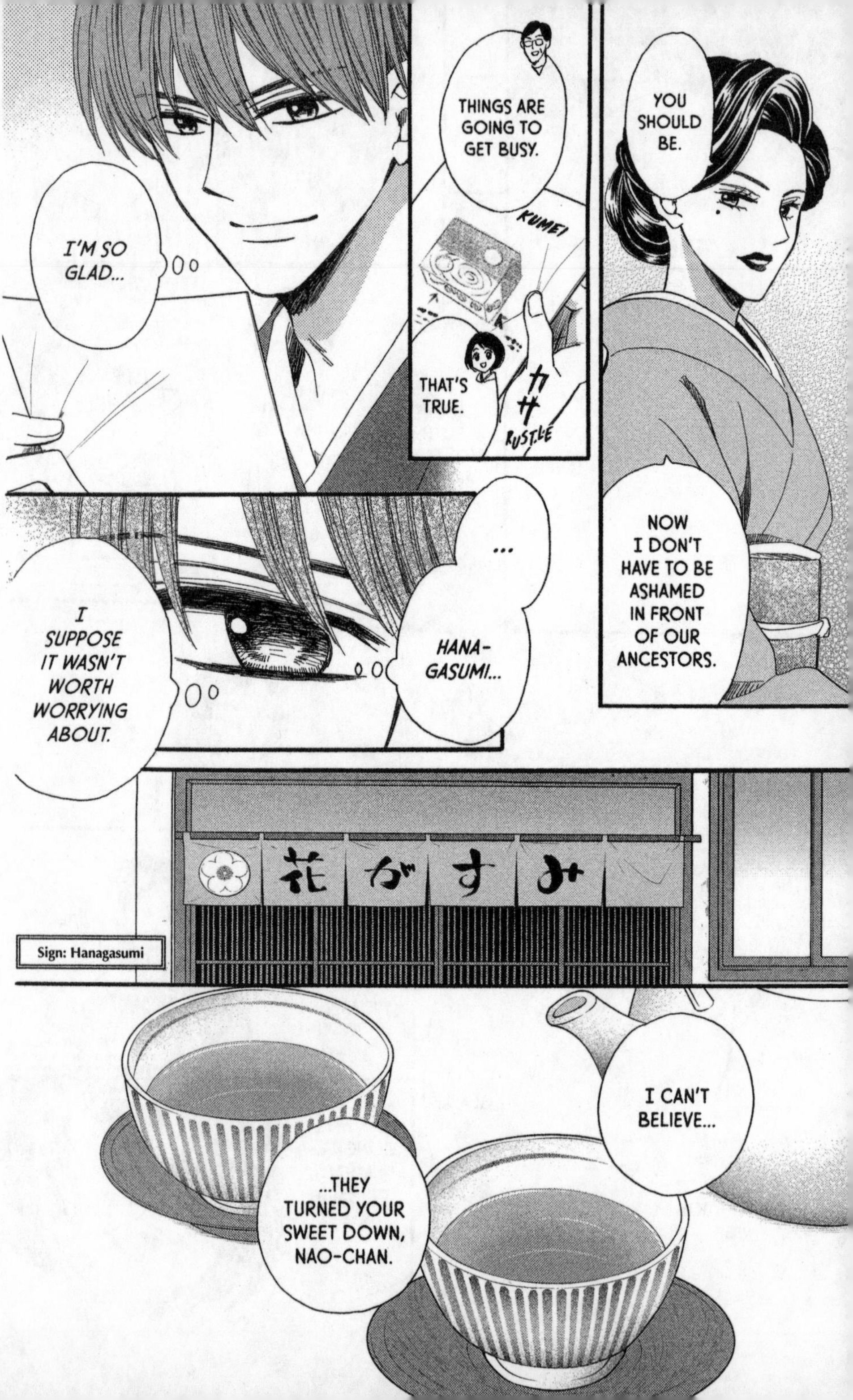
YOU SHOULD BE.
NOW I DON'T HAVE TO BE ASHAMED IN FRONT OF OUR ANCESTORS.
THINGS ARE GOING TO GET BUSY.
KUMEI
THAT'S TRUE.
カサ
RUSTLE
I'M SO GLAD...
...
HANA-GASUMI...
I SUPPOSE IT WASN'T WORTH WORRYING ABOUT.
花がすみ
Sign: Hanagasumi
I CAN'T BELIEVE...
...THEY TURNED YOUR SWEET DOWN, NAO-CHAN.

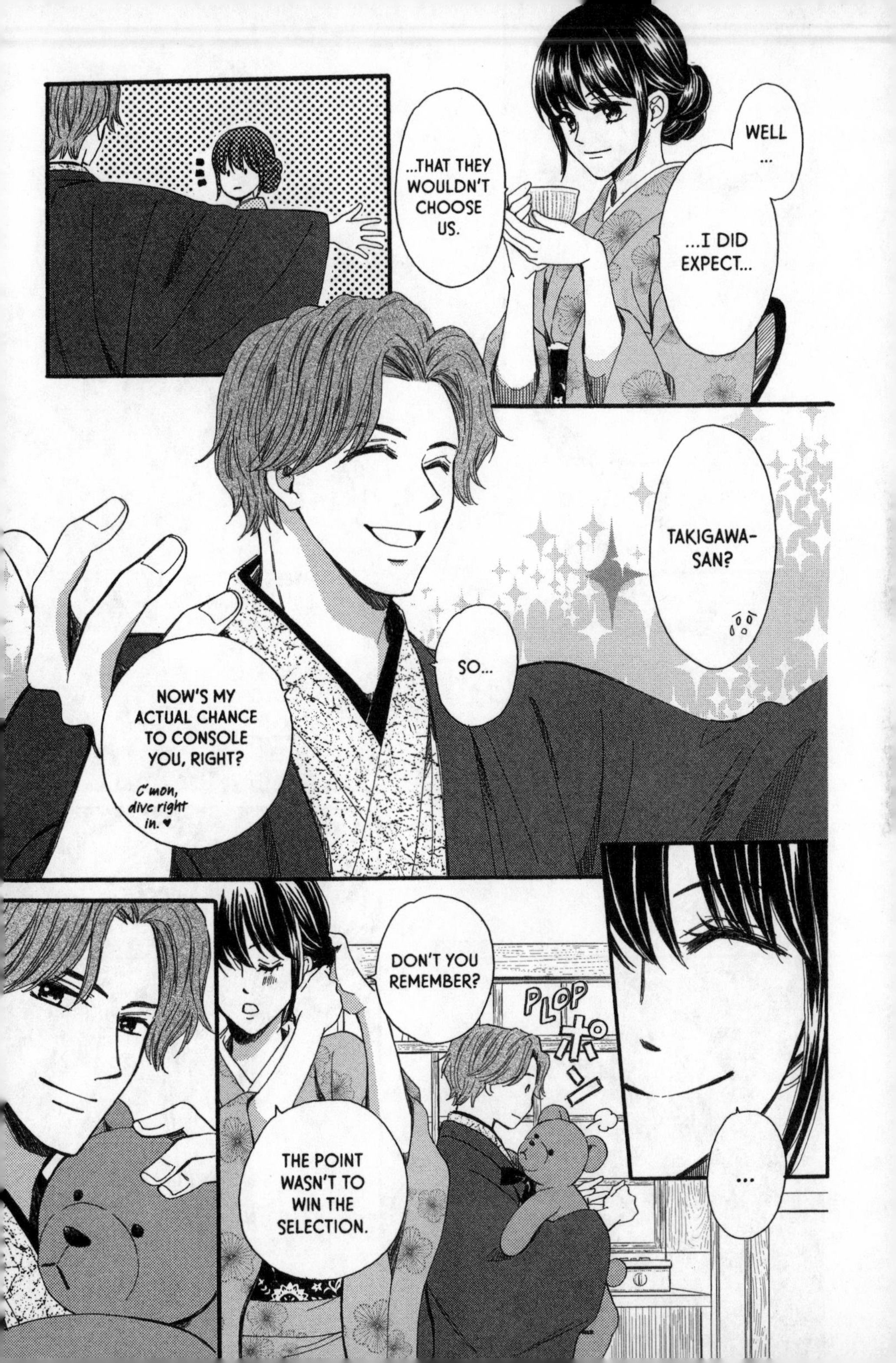
WELL ...
...I DID EXPECT...
...THAT THEY WOULDN'T CHOOSE US.
TAKIGAWA-SAN?
SO...
NOW'S MY ACTUAL CHANCE TO CONSOLE YOU, RIGHT?
C'mon, dive right in. ♥
...
DON'T YOU REMEMBER?
PLOP
THE POINT WASN'T TO WIN THE SELECTION.

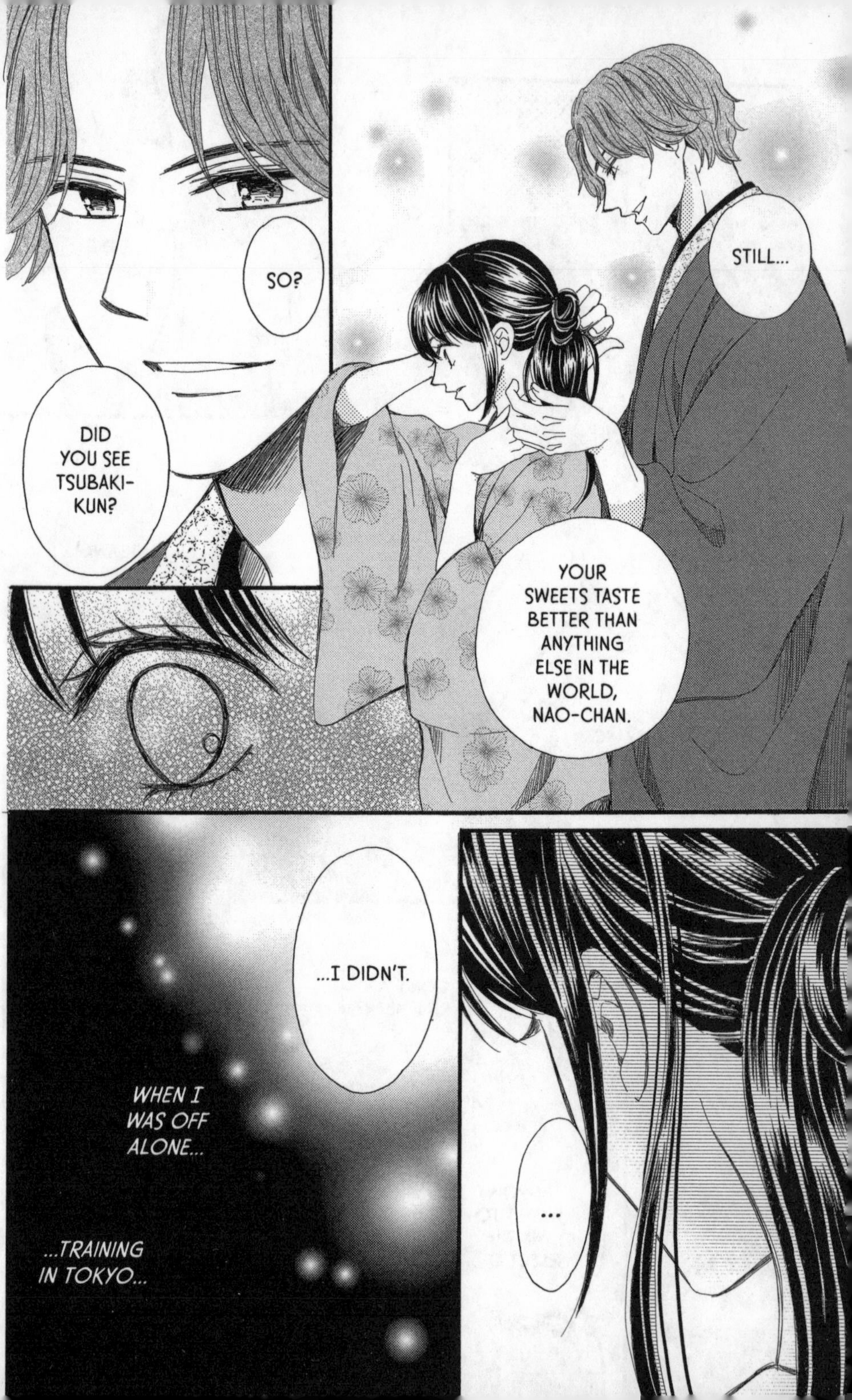
STILL...
YOUR SWEETS TASTE BETTER THAN ANYTHING ELSE IN THE WORLD, NAO-CHAN.
SO?
DID YOU SEE TSUBAKI-KUN?
...
...I DIDN'T.
WHEN I WAS OFF ALONE...
...TRAINING IN TOKYO...

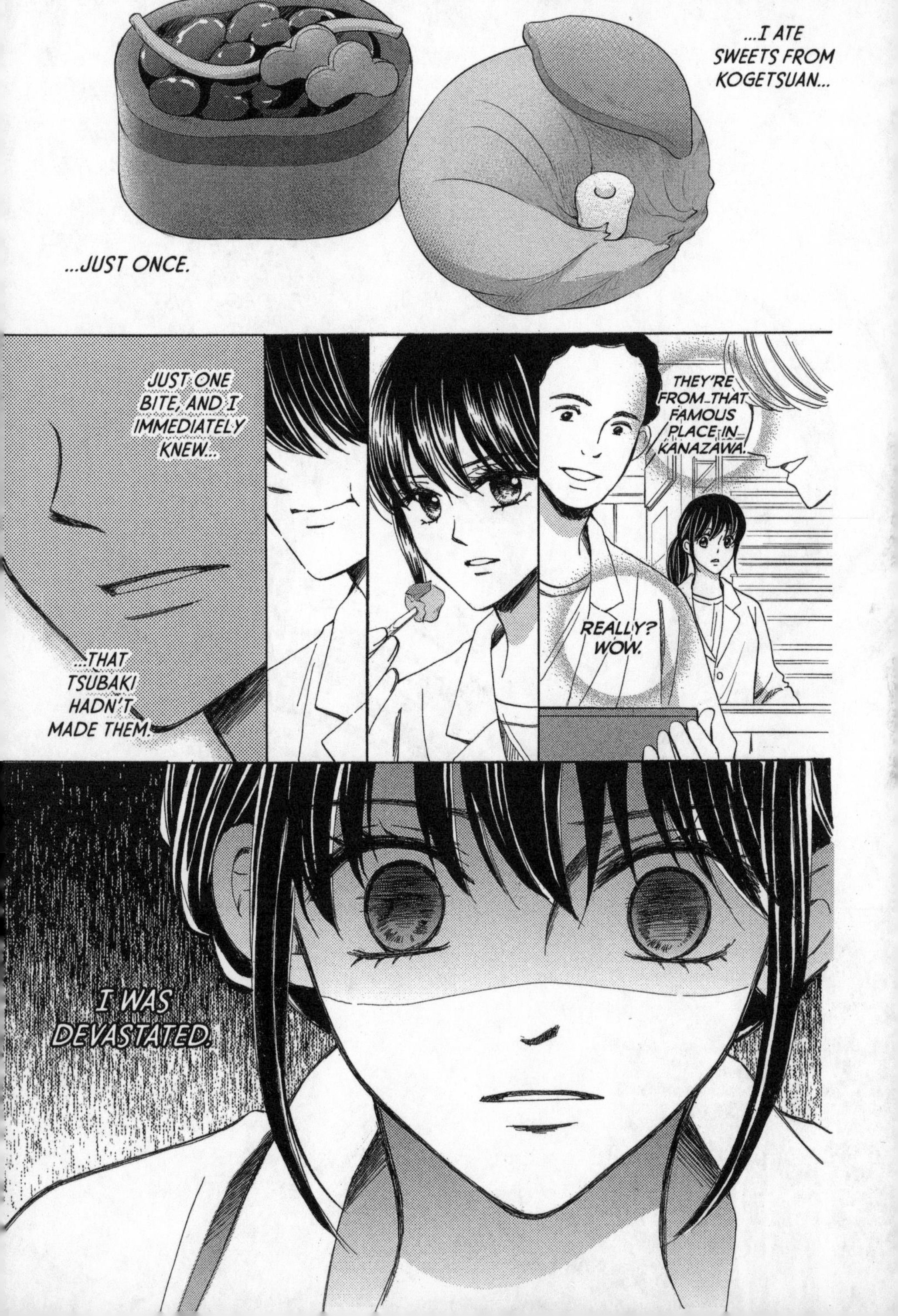
...I ATE SWEETS FROM KOGETSUAN...
...JUST ONCE.
THEY'RE FROM THAT FAMOUS PLACE IN KANAZAWA.
REALLY? WOW.
JUST ONE BITE, AND I IMMEDIATELY KNEW...
...THAT TSUBAKI HADN'T MADE THEM.
I WAS DEVASTATED.

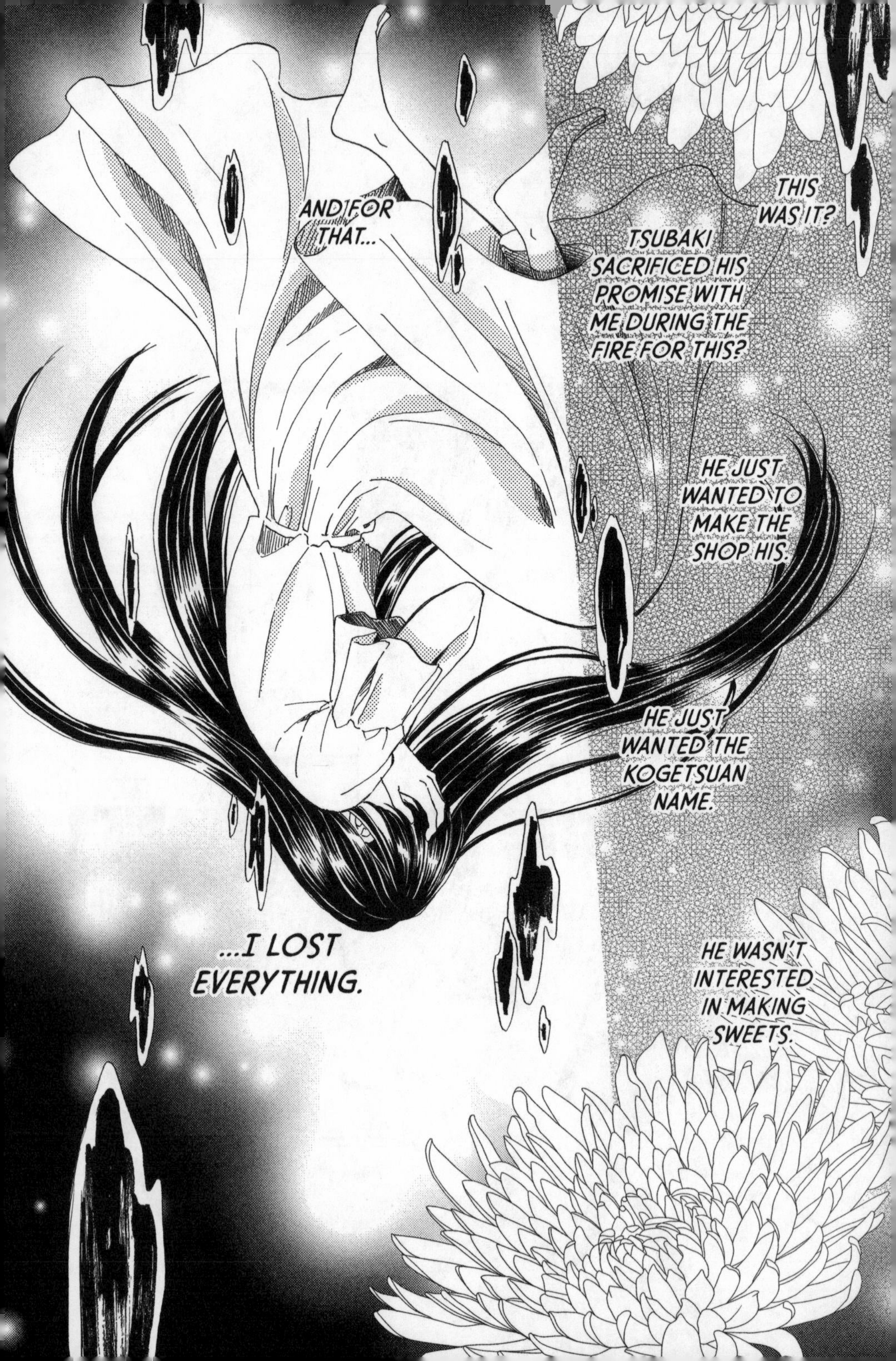
THIS WAS IT?
TSUBAKI SACRIFICED HIS PROMISE WITH ME DURING THE FIRE FOR THIS?
HE JUST WANTED TO MAKE THE SHOP HIS.
HE JUST WANTED THE KOGETSUAN NAME.
HE WASN'T INTERESTED IN MAKING SWEETS.
AND FOR THAT...
...I LOST EVERYTHING.

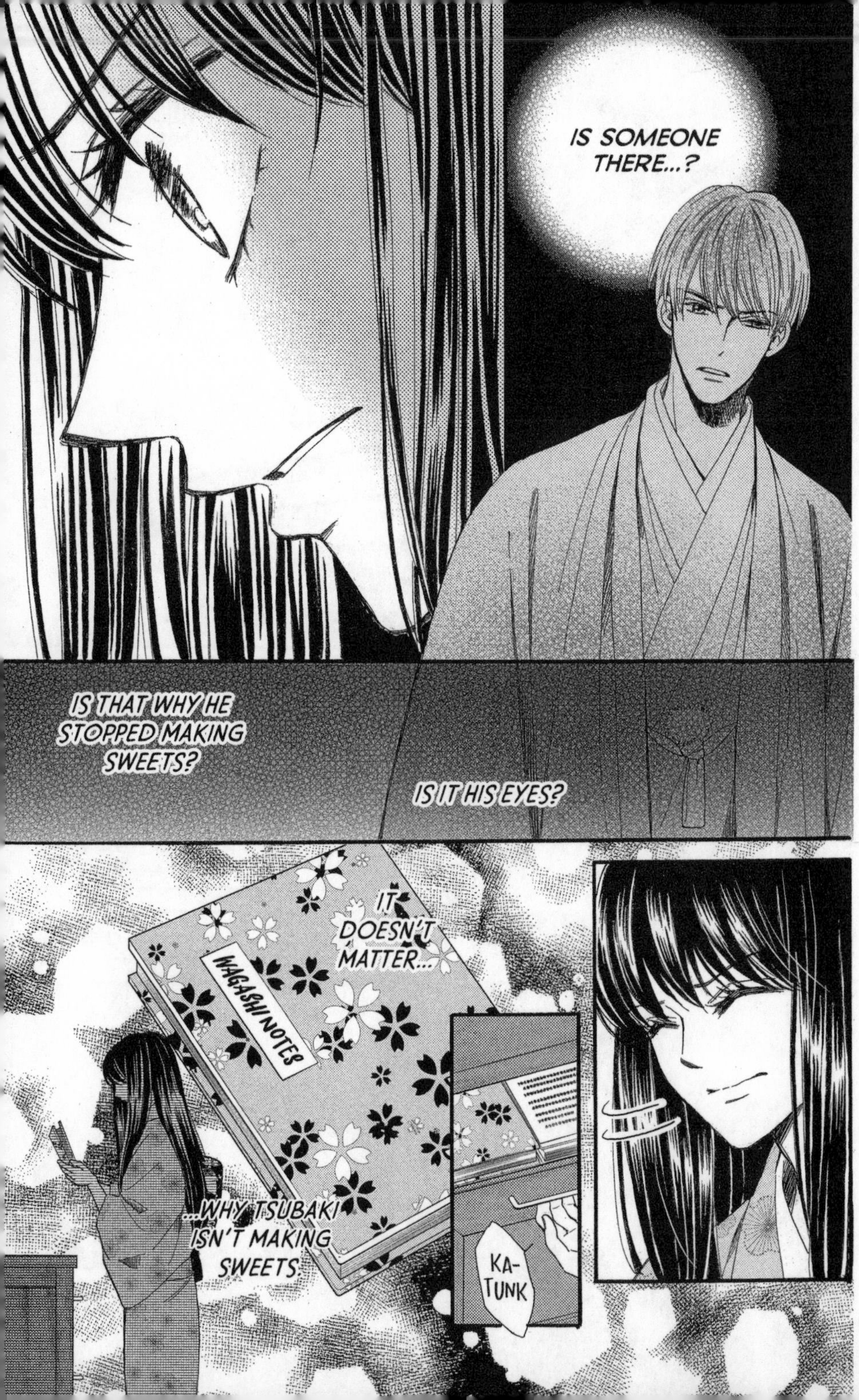
IS SOMEONE THERE...?
IS IT HIS EYES?
IS THAT WHY HE STOPPED MAKING SWEETS?
KA-TUNK
IT DOESN'T MATTER...
WAGASHI NOTES
...WHY TSUBAKI ISN'T MAKING SWEETS.

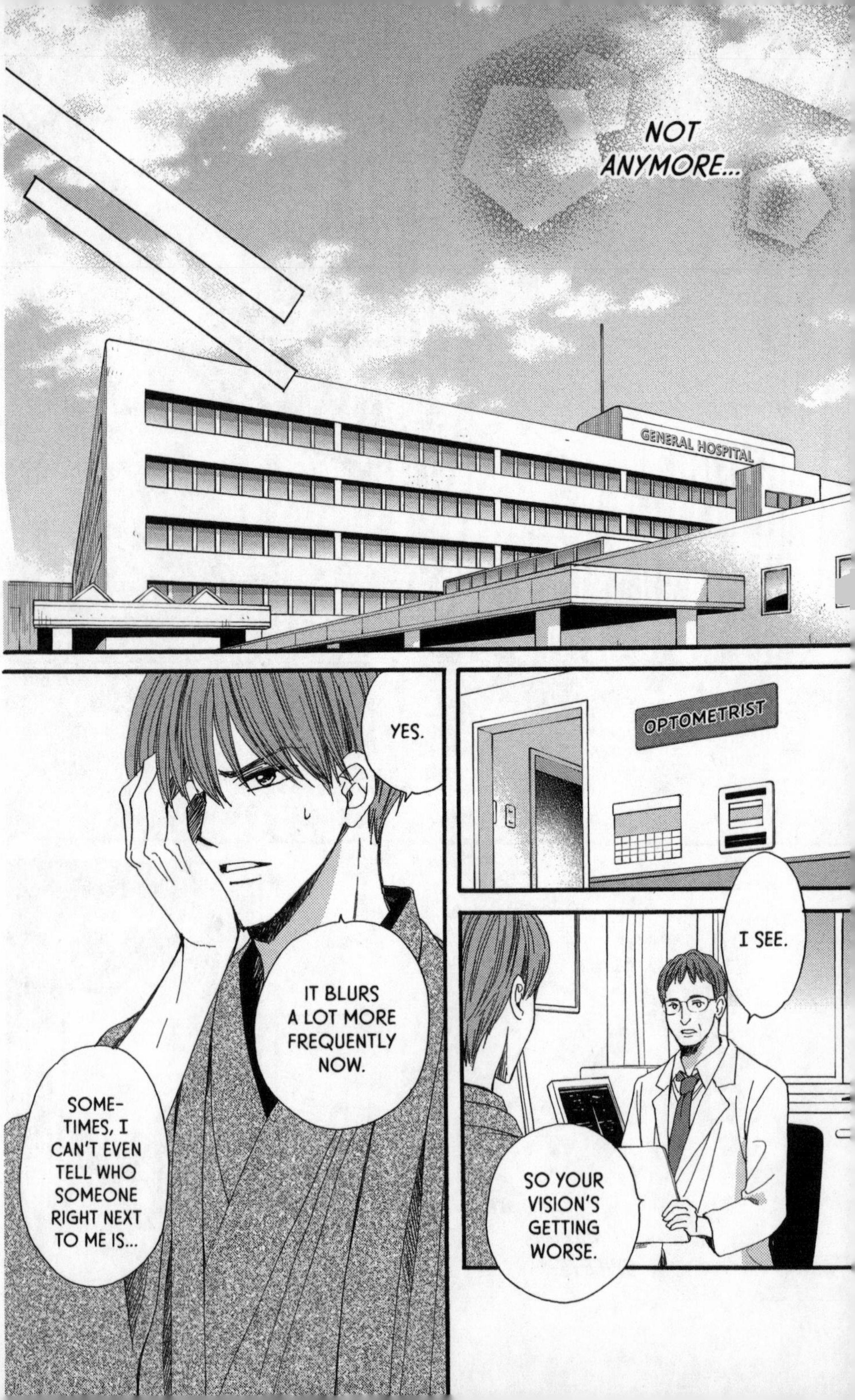
NOT ANYMORE...
GENERAL HOSPITAL
OPTOMETRIST
I SEE.
SO YOUR VISION'S GETTING WORSE.
YES.
IT BLURS A LOT MORE FREQUENTLY NOW.
SOMETIMES, I CAN'T EVEN TELL WHO SOMEONE RIGHT NEXT TO ME IS...

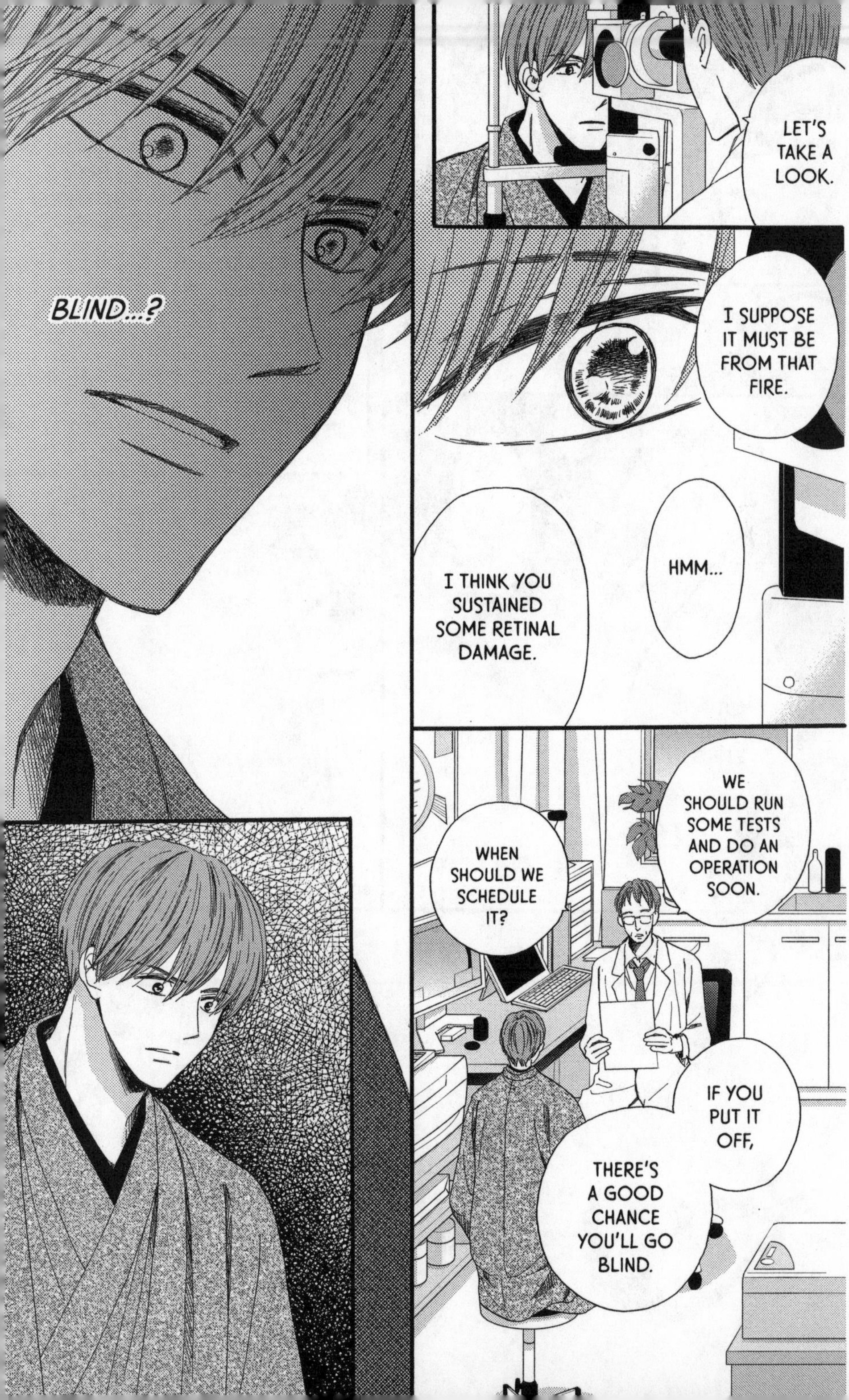
LET'S TAKE A LOOK.
I SUPPOSE IT MUST BE FROM THAT FIRE.
HMM...
I THINK YOU SUSTAINED SOME RETINAL DAMAGE.
WE SHOULD RUN SOME TESTS AND DO AN OPERATION SOON.
WHEN SHOULD WE SCHEDULE IT?
IF YOU PUT IT OFF,
THERE'S A GOOD CHANCE YOU'LL GO BLIND.
BLIND...?

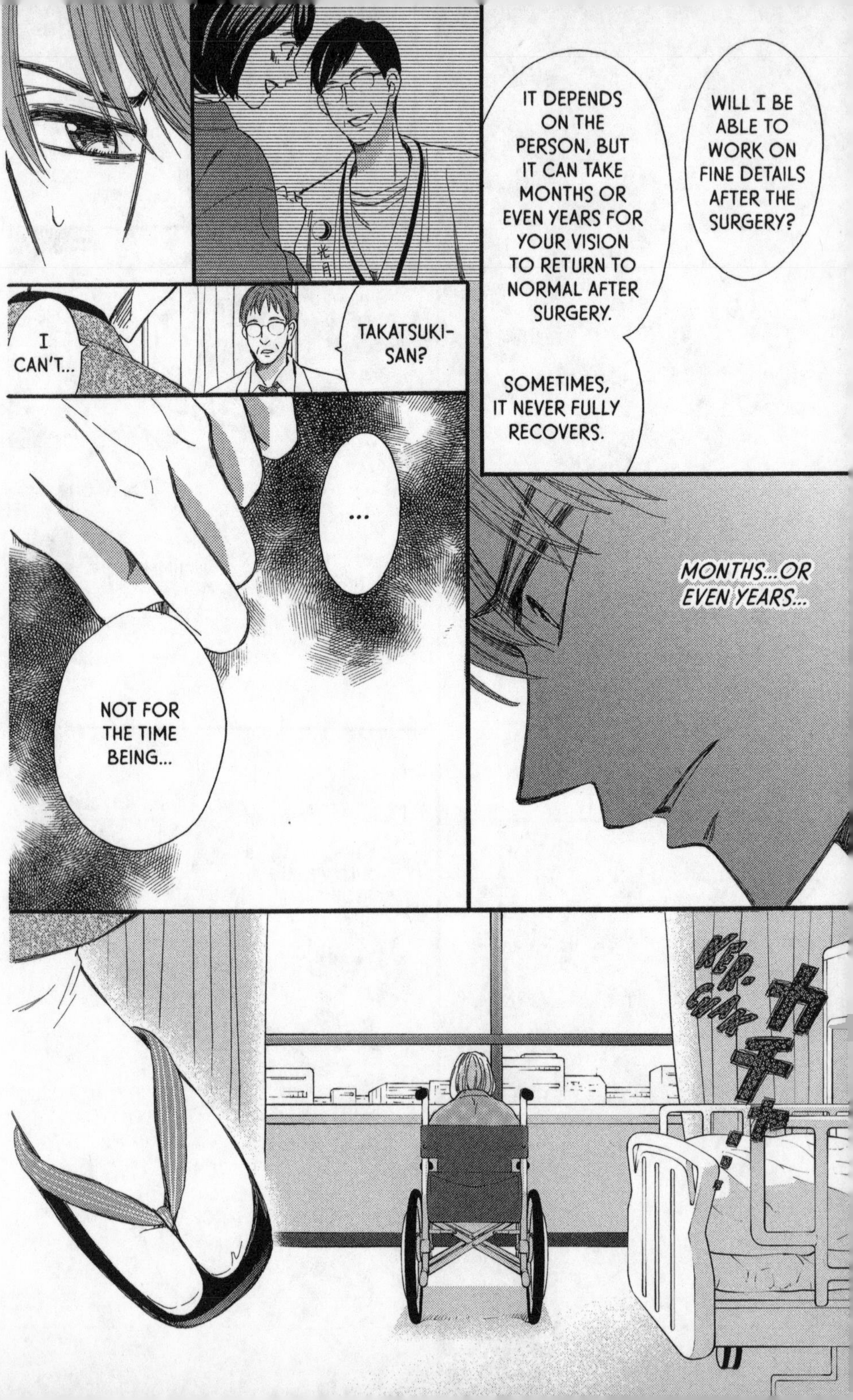
WILL I BE ABLE TO WORK ON FINE DETAILS AFTER THE SURGERY?
IT DEPENDS ON THE PERSON, BUT IT CAN TAKE MONTHS OR EVEN YEARS FOR YOUR VISION TO RETURN TO NORMAL AFTER SURGERY.
SOMETIMES, IT NEVER FULLY RECOVERS.
TAKATSUKI-SAN?
I CAN'T...
MONTHS...OR EVEN YEARS...
...
NOT FOR THE TIME BEING...
KER-CHAK

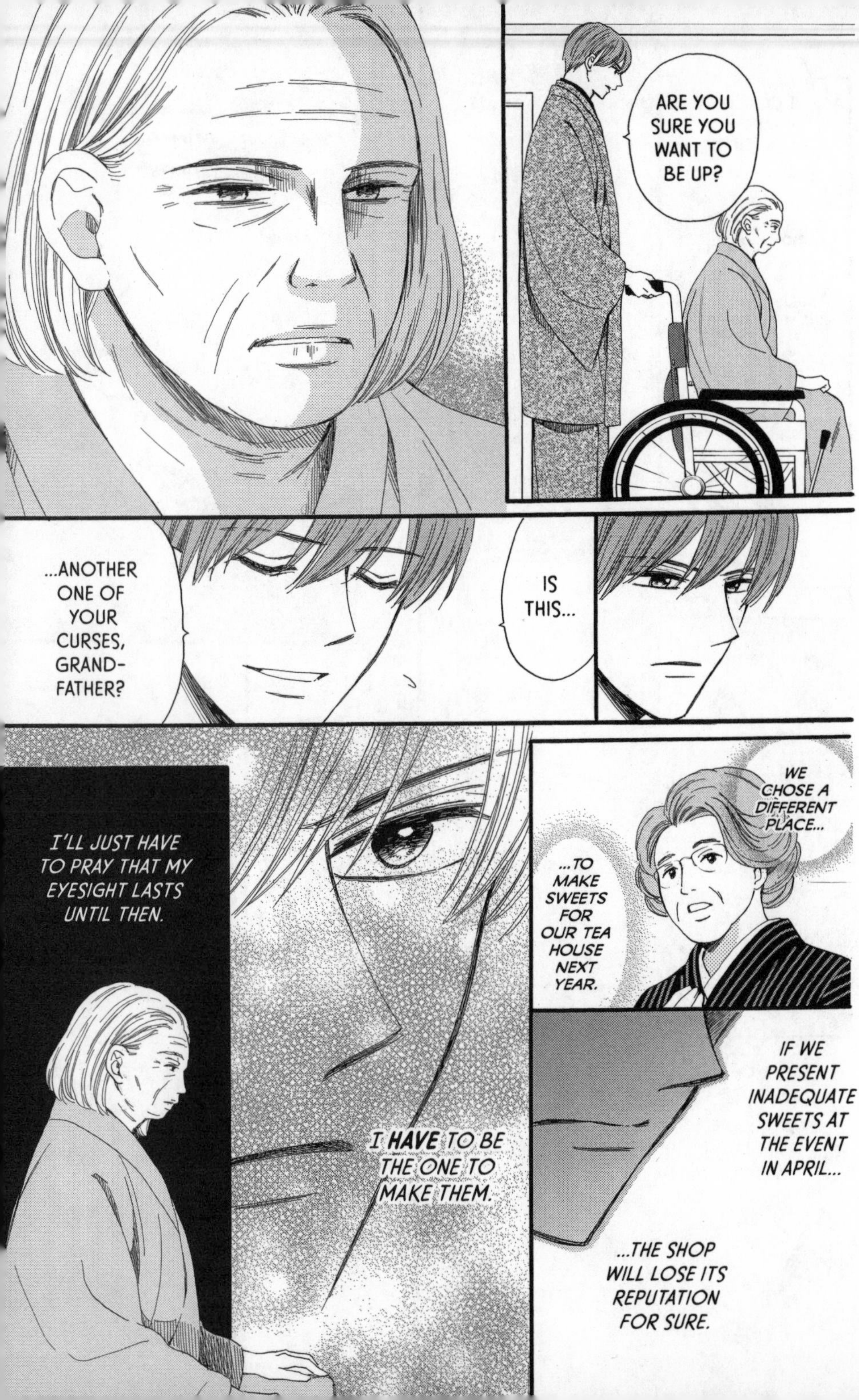
ARE YOU SURE YOU WANT TO BE UP?
IS THIS...
...ANOTHER ONE OF YOUR CURSES, GRAND-FATHER?
WE CHOSE A DIFFERENT PLACE...
...TO MAKE SWEETS FOR OUR TEA HOUSE NEXT YEAR.
IF WE PRESENT INADEQUATE SWEETS AT THE EVENT IN APRIL...
...THE SHOP WILL LOSE ITS REPUTATION FOR SURE.
I **HAVE** TO BE THE ONE TO MAKE THEM.
I'LL JUST HAVE TO PRAY THAT MY EYESIGHT LASTS UNTIL THEN.

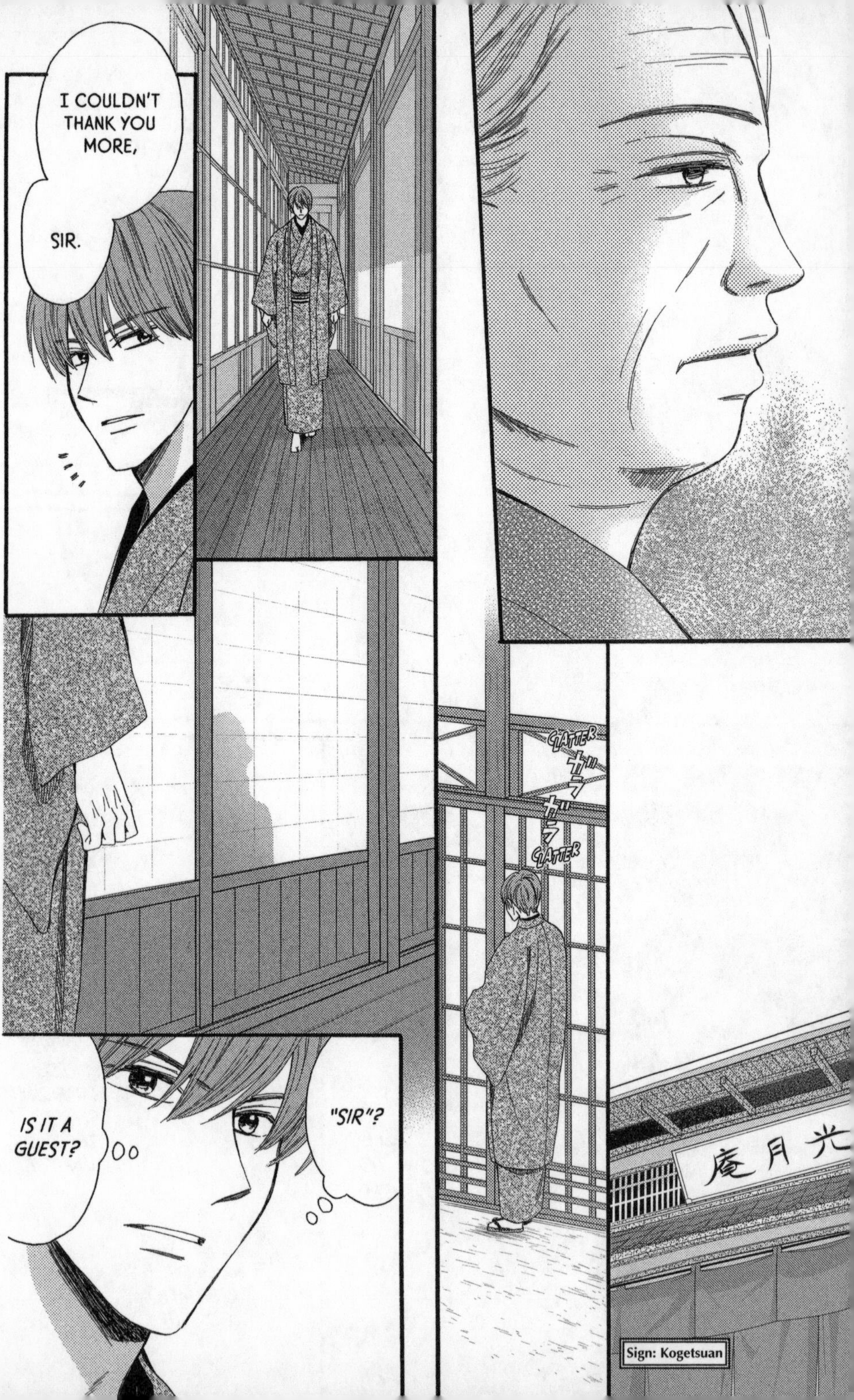
I COULDN'T THANK YOU MORE,
SIR.
光月庵
Sign: Kogetsuan
CLATTER
ガラ
ガラ
CLATTER
"SIR"?
IS IT A GUEST?

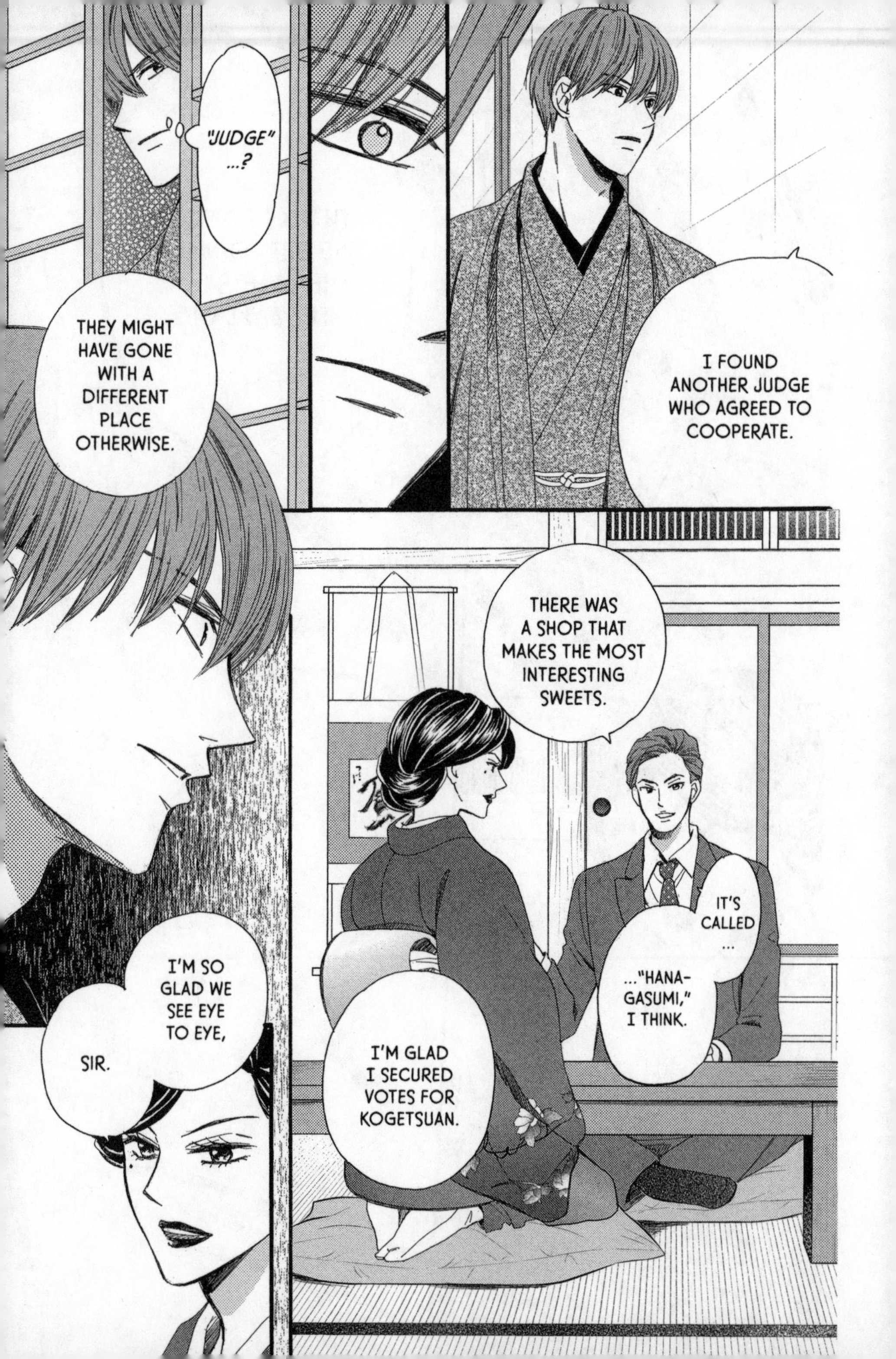
I FOUND ANOTHER JUDGE WHO AGREED TO COOPERATE.
"JUDGE" ...?
THEY MIGHT HAVE GONE WITH A DIFFERENT PLACE OTHERWISE.
THERE WAS A SHOP THAT MAKES THE MOST INTERESTING SWEETS.
IT'S CALLED ...
..."HANA-GASUMI," I THINK.
I'M GLAD I SECURED VOTES FOR KOGETSUAN.
I'M SO GLAD WE SEE EYE TO EYE,
SIR.

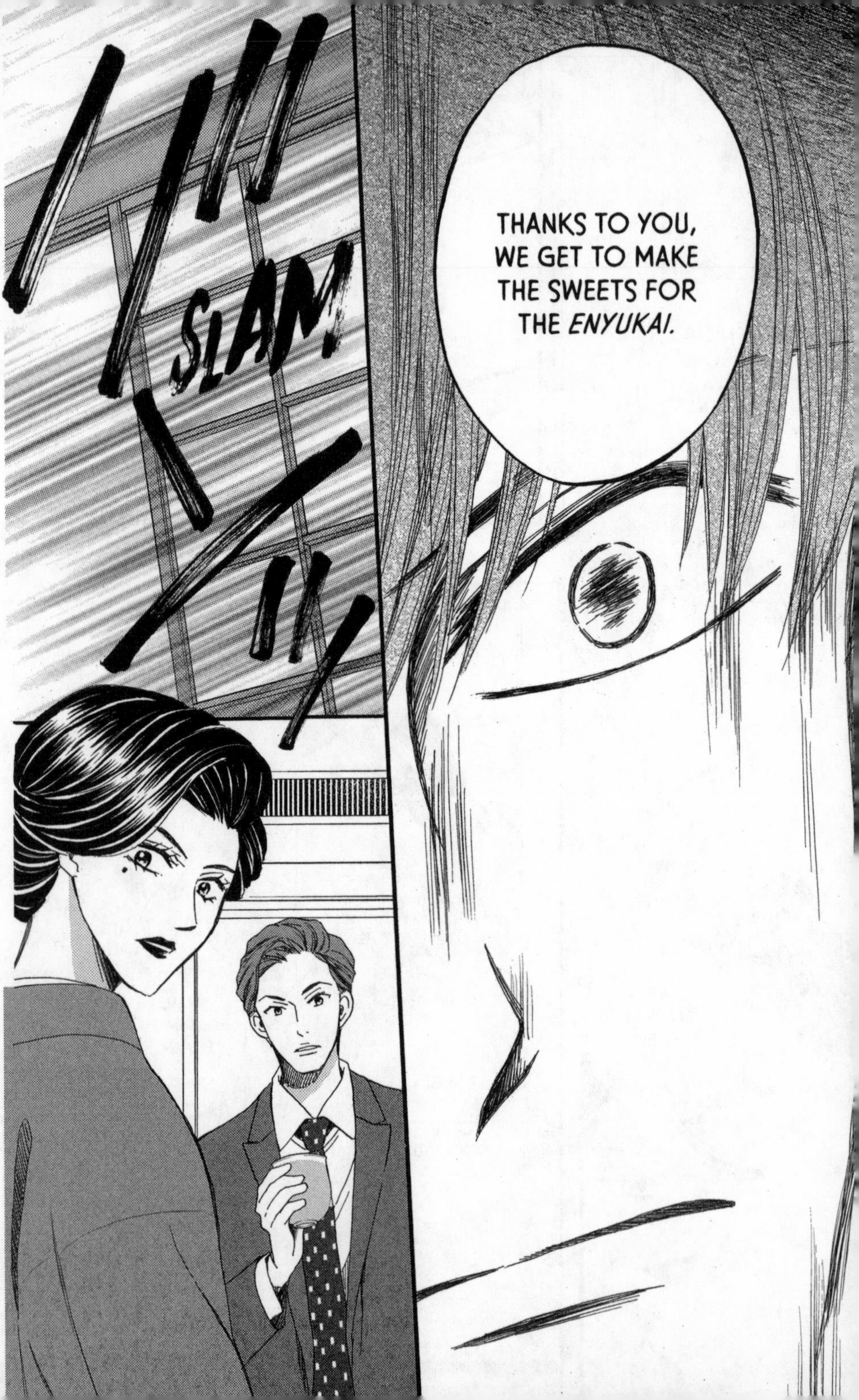
THANKS TO YOU, WE GET TO MAKE THE SWEETS FOR THE *ENYUKAI.*
SLAM!

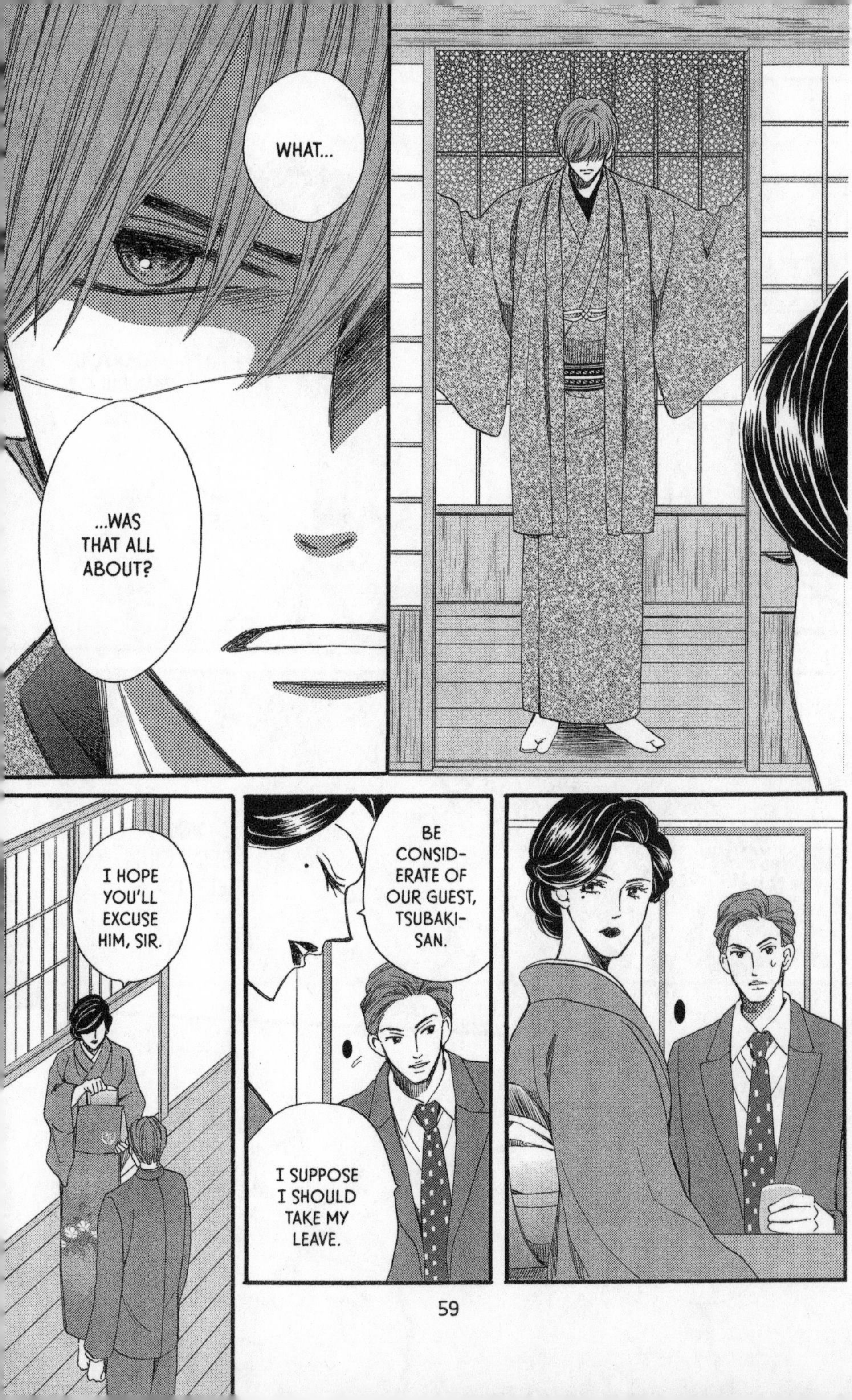
WHAT...
...WAS THAT ALL ABOUT?
BE CONSIDERATE OF OUR GUEST, TSUBAKI-SAN.
I SUPPOSE I SHOULD TAKE MY LEAVE.
I HOPE YOU'LL EXCUSE HIM, SIR.

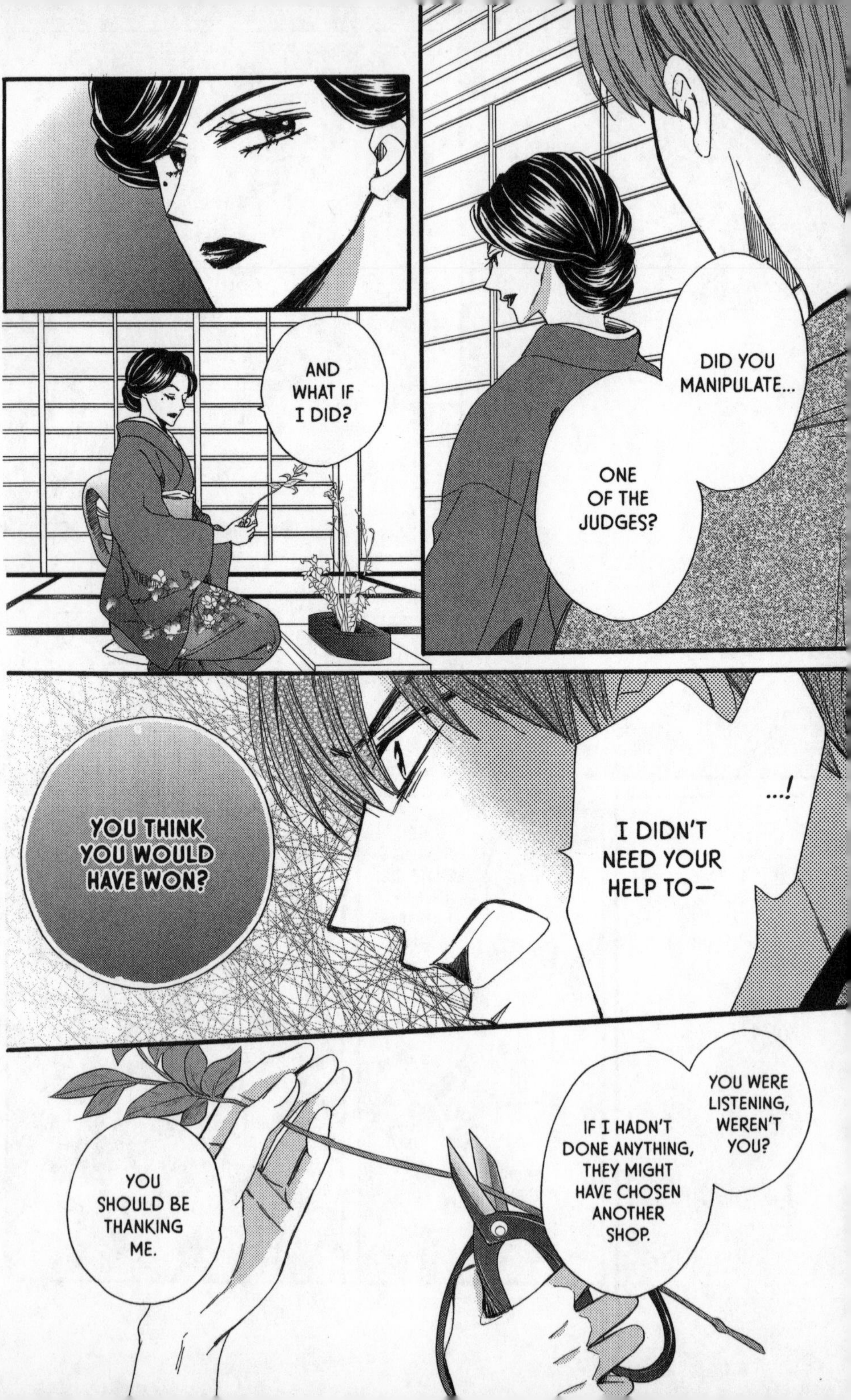
DID YOU MANIPULATE...
ONE OF THE JUDGES?
AND WHAT IF I DID?
...!
I DIDN'T NEED YOUR HELP TO—
YOU THINK YOU WOULD HAVE WON?
YOU WERE LISTENING, WEREN'T YOU?
IF I HADN'T DONE ANYTHING, THEY MIGHT HAVE CHOSEN ANOTHER SHOP.
YOU SHOULD BE THANKING ME.

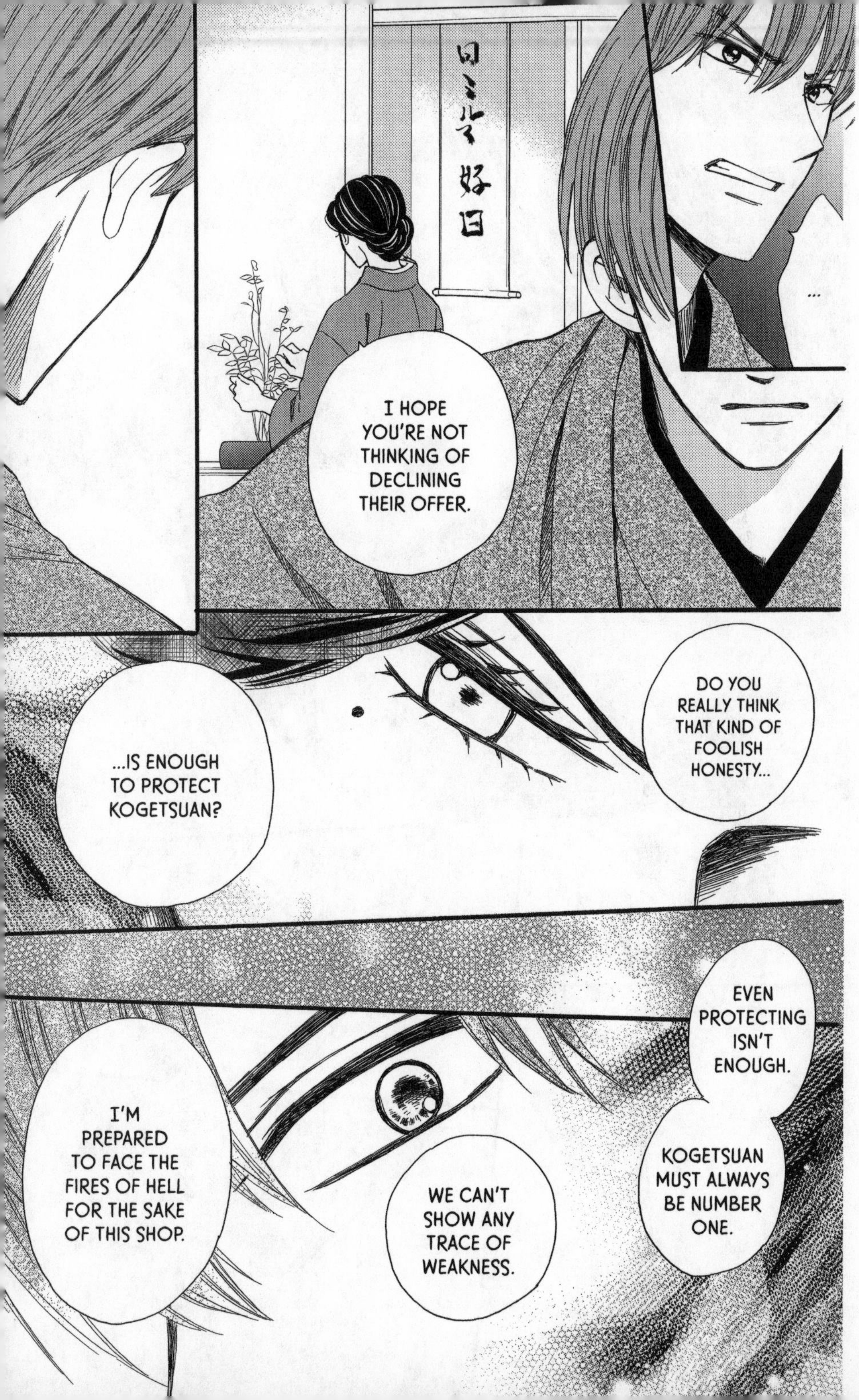
...
I HOPE YOU'RE NOT THINKING OF DECLINING THEIR OFFER.
DO YOU REALLY THINK THAT KIND OF FOOLISH HONESTY...
...IS ENOUGH TO PROTECT KOGETSUAN?
EVEN PROTECTING ISN'T ENOUGH.
KOGETSUAN MUST ALWAYS BE NUMBER ONE.
WE CAN'T SHOW ANY TRACE OF WEAKNESS.
I'M PREPARED TO FACE THE FIRES OF HELL FOR THE SAKE OF THIS SHOP.

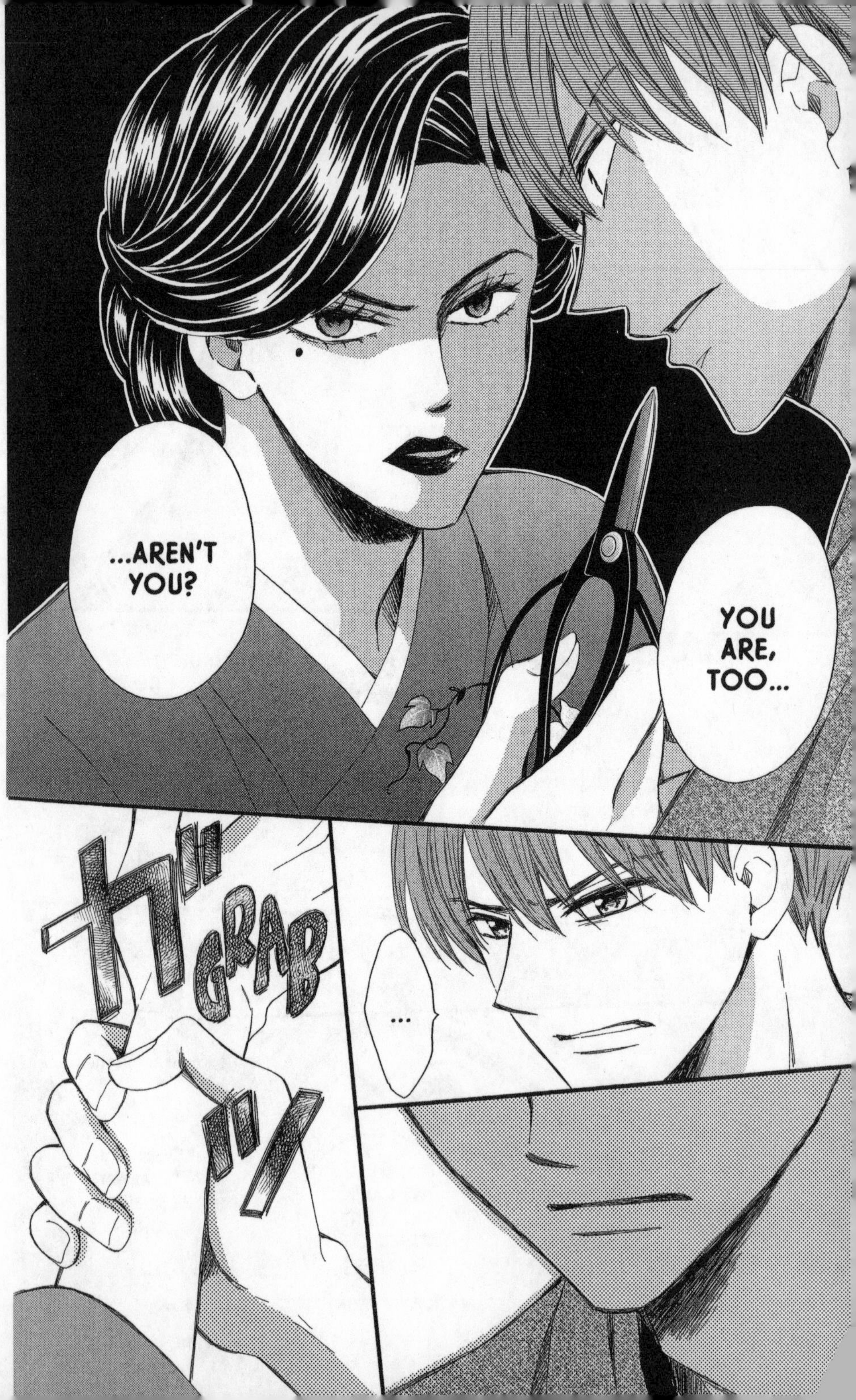
YOU ARE, TOO...
...AREN'T YOU?
...
ガッ
GRAB

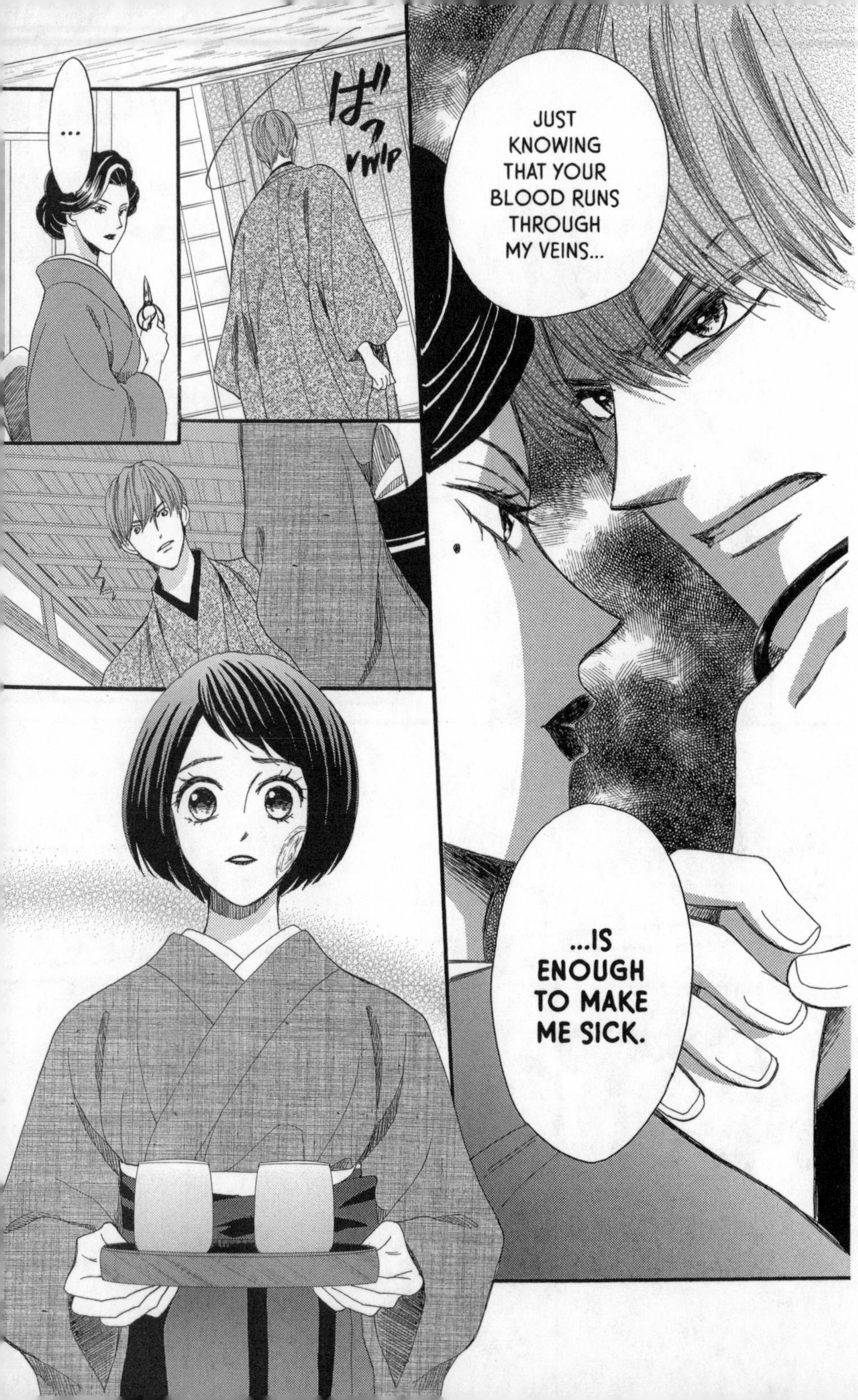
JUST KNOWING THAT YOUR BLOOD RUNS THROUGH MY VEINS...
...IS ENOUGH TO MAKE ME SICK.
ばっ
VWIP
...

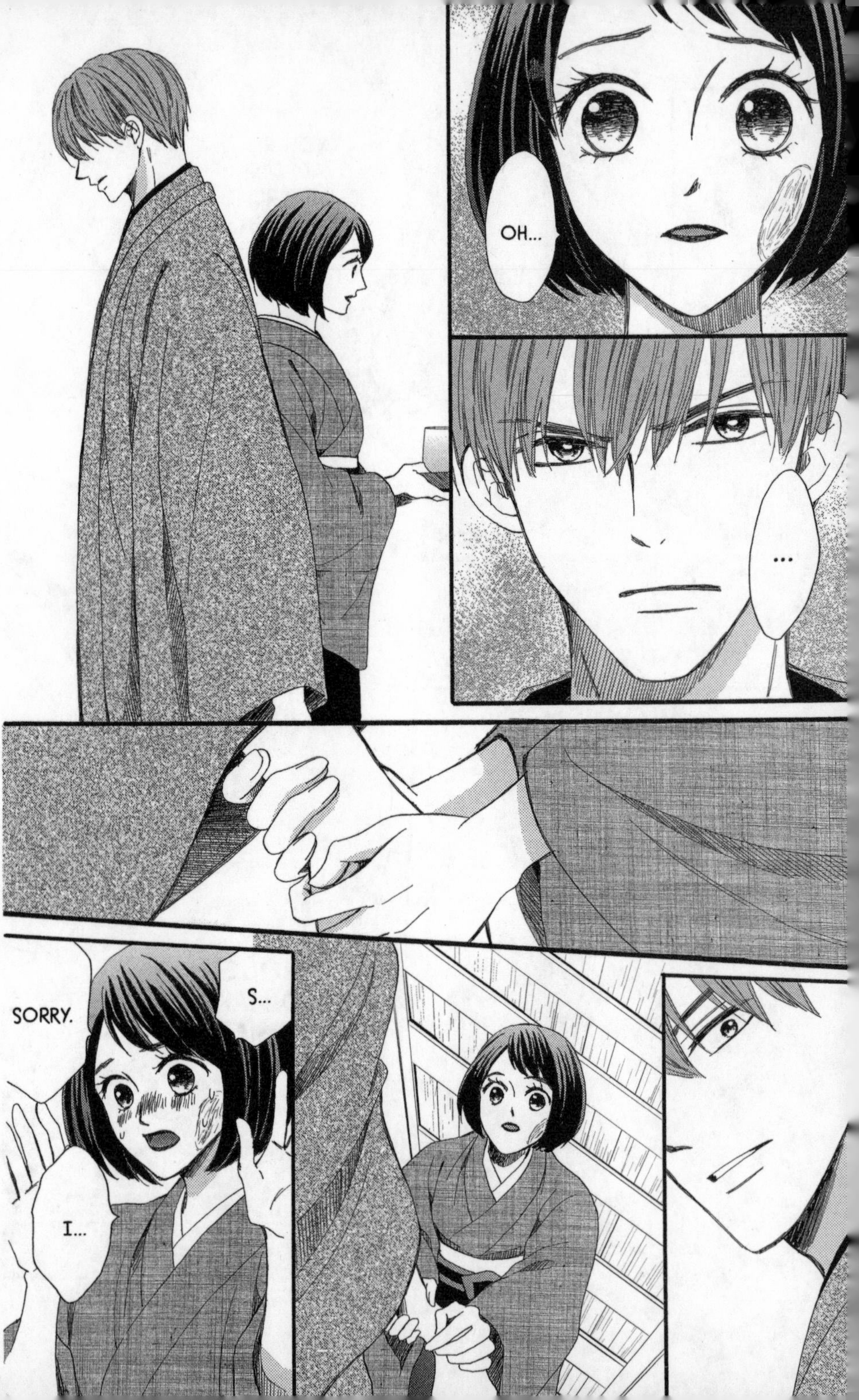
OH...
...
S...
SORRY.
I...

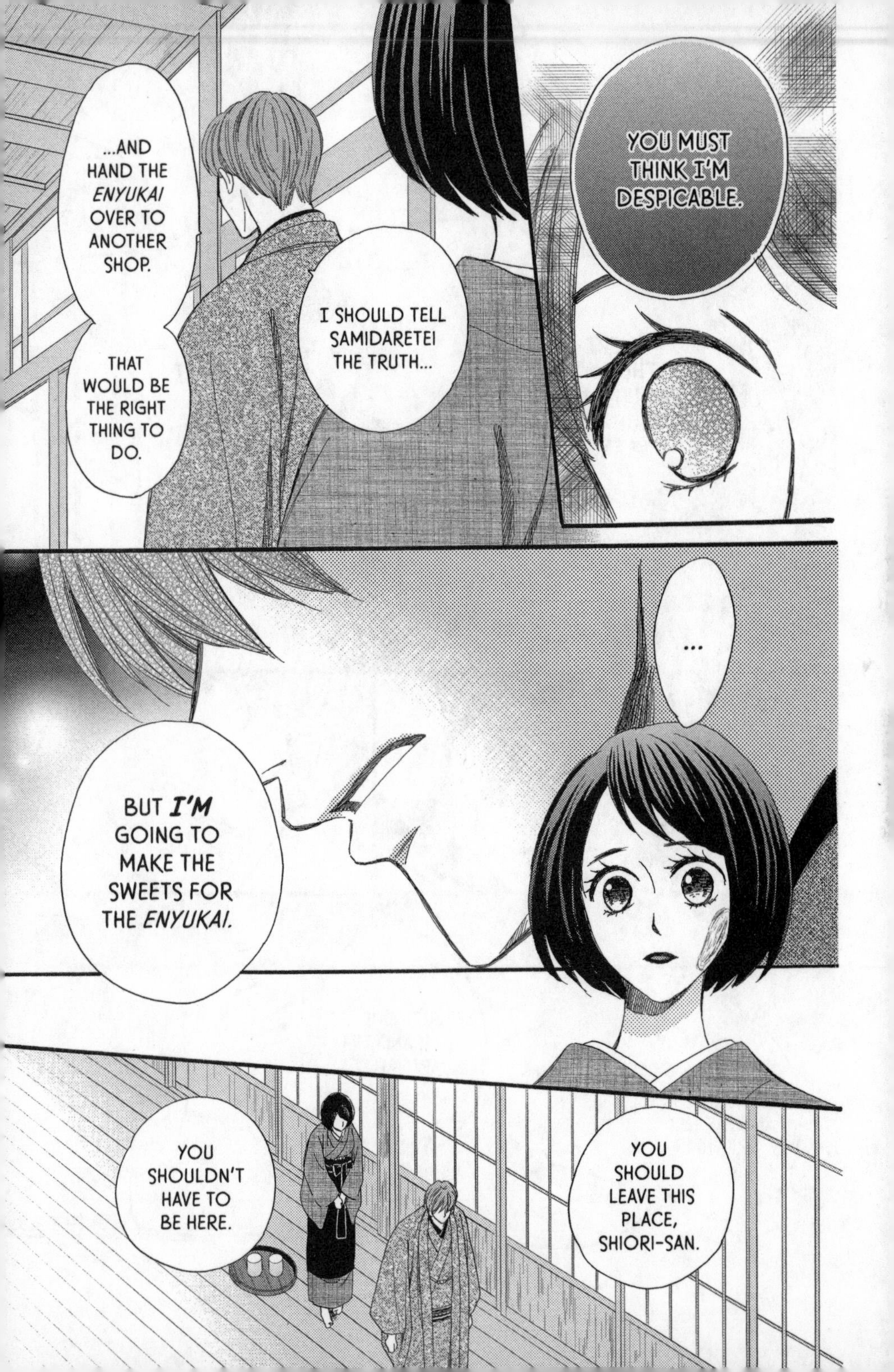
YOU MUST THINK I'M DESPICABLE.
I SHOULD TELL SAMIDARETEI THE TRUTH...
...AND HAND THE *ENYUKAI* OVER TO ANOTHER SHOP.
THAT WOULD BE THE RIGHT THING TO DO.
...
BUT ***I'M*** GOING TO MAKE THE SWEETS FOR THE *ENYUKAI.*
YOU SHOULD LEAVE THIS PLACE, SHIORI-SAN.
YOU SHOULDN'T HAVE TO BE HERE.

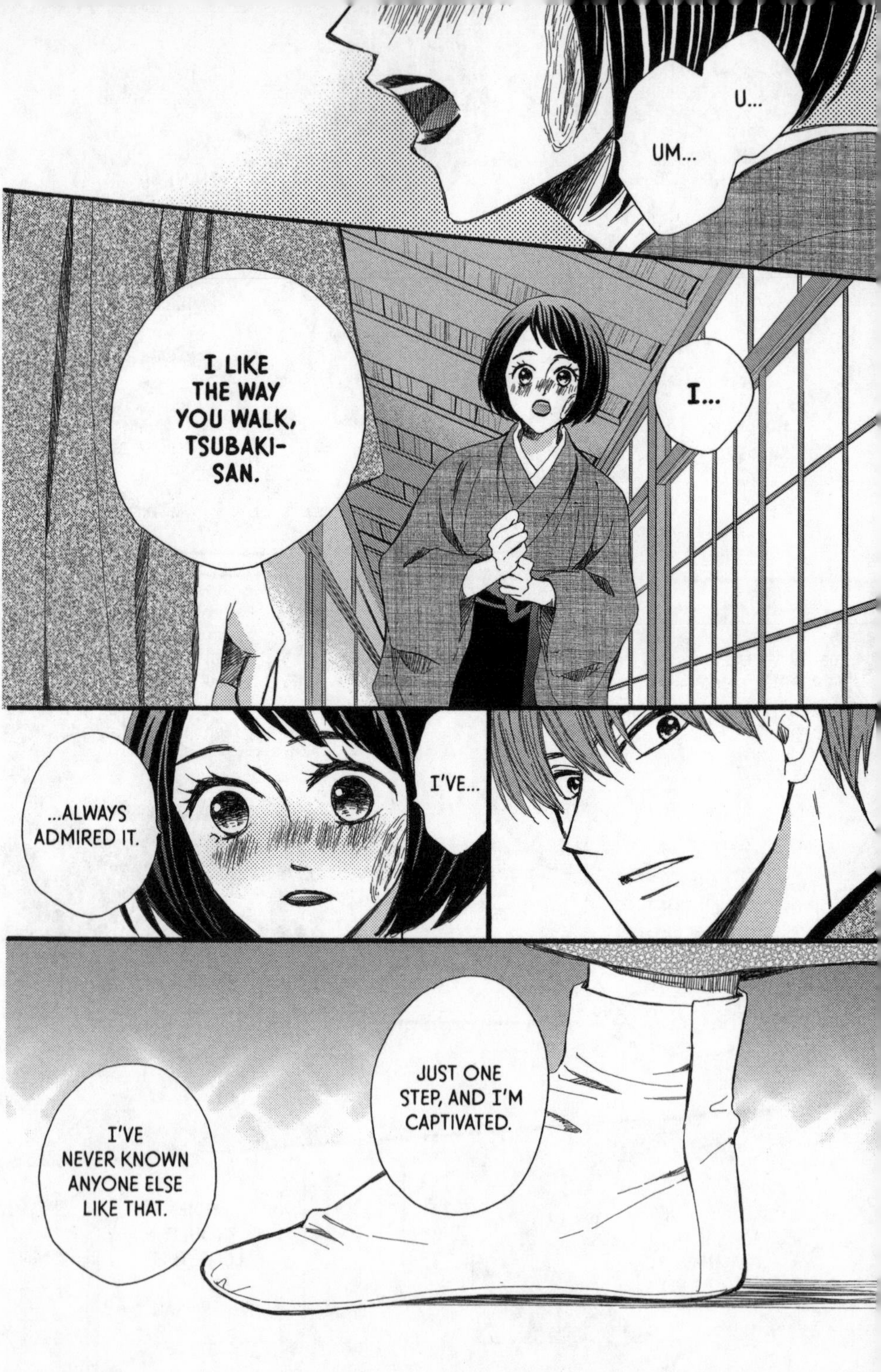
U...
UM...
I...
I LIKE THE WAY YOU WALK, TSUBAKI-SAN.
I'VE...
...ALWAYS ADMIRED IT.
JUST ONE STEP, AND I'M CAPTIVATED.
I'VE NEVER KNOWN ANYONE ELSE LIKE THAT.

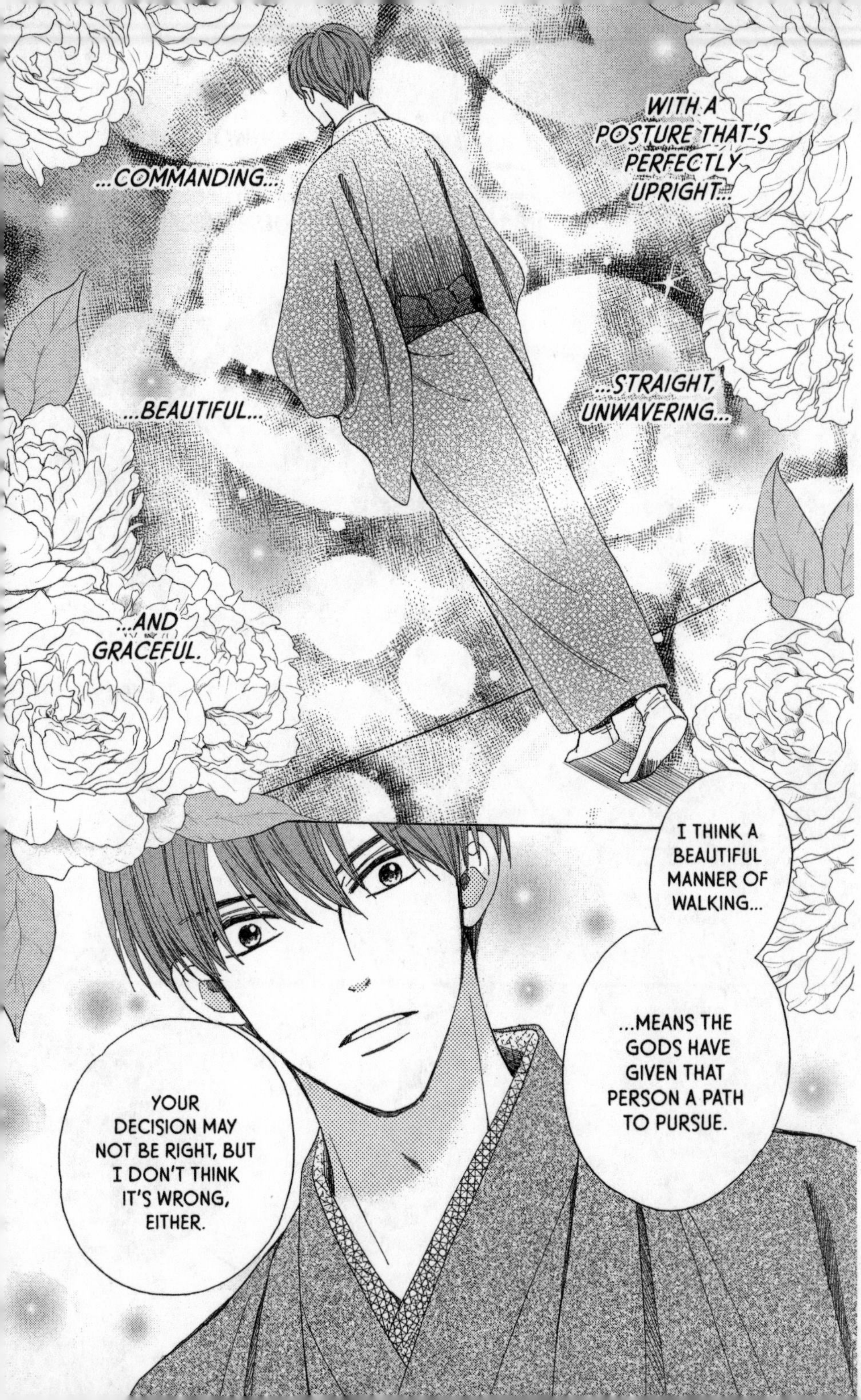
WITH A POSTURE THAT'S PERFECTLY UPRIGHT...
...COMMANDING...
...STRAIGHT, UNWAVERING...
...BEAUTIFUL...
...AND GRACEFUL.
I THINK A BEAUTIFUL MANNER OF WALKING...
...MEANS THE GODS HAVE GIVEN THAT PERSON A PATH TO PURSUE.
YOUR DECISION MAY NOT BE RIGHT, BUT I DON'T THINK IT'S WRONG, EITHER.

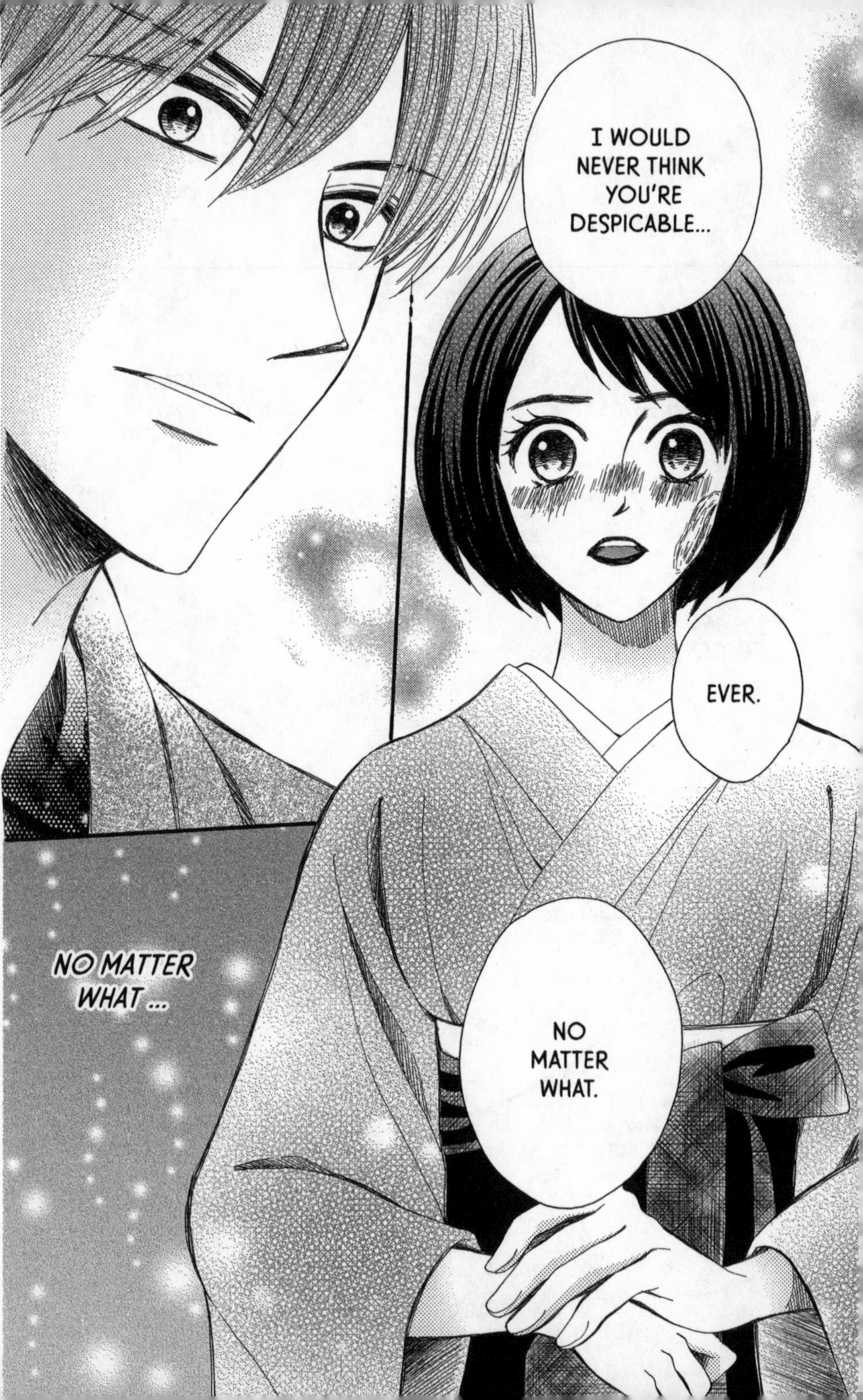
I WOULD NEVER THINK YOU'RE DESPICABLE...
EVER.
NO MATTER WHAT.
NO MATTER WHAT ...

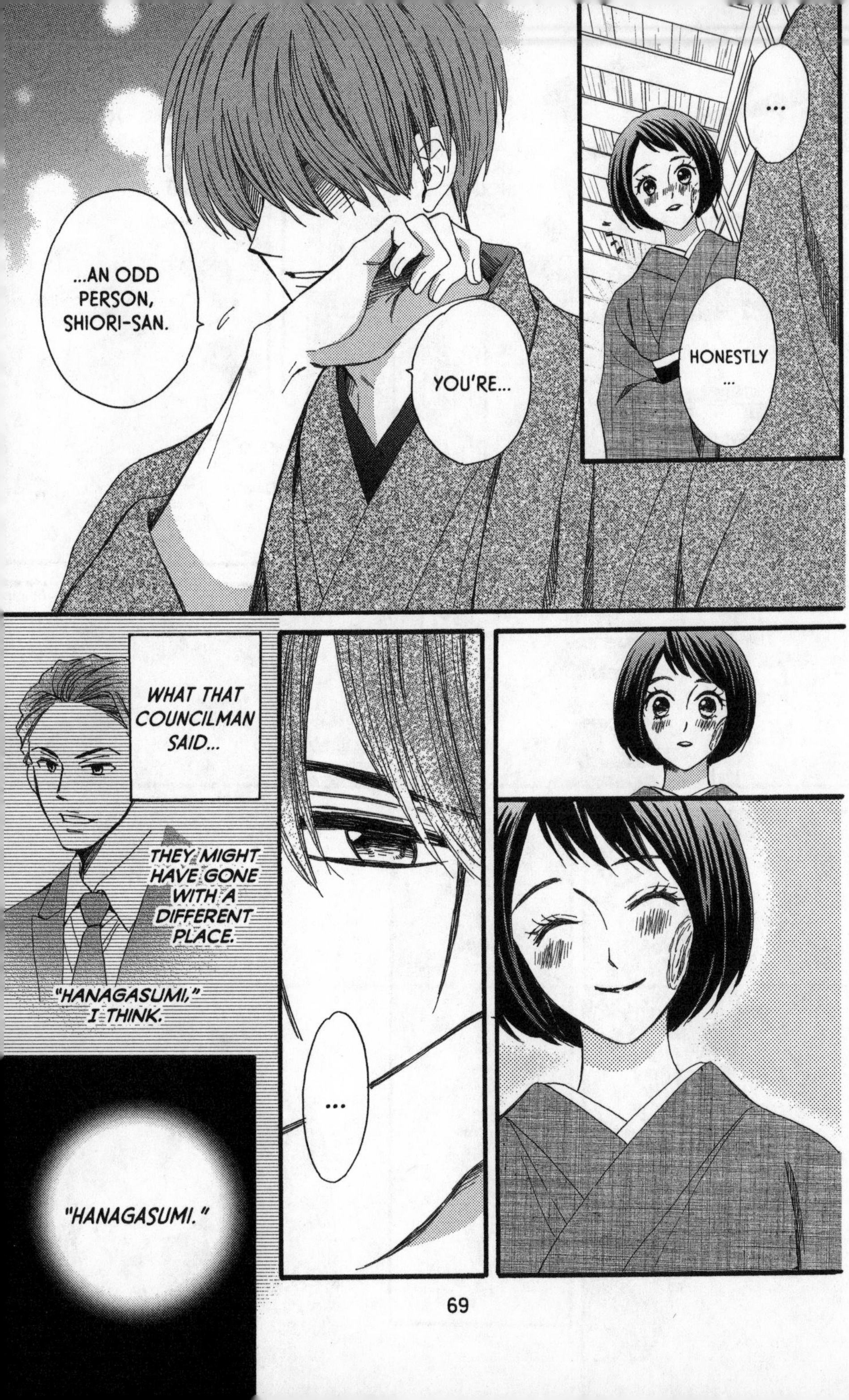
...
HONESTLY ...
YOU'RE...
...AN ODD PERSON, SHIORI-SAN.
...
WHAT THAT COUNCILMAN SAID...
THEY MIGHT HAVE GONE WITH A DIFFERENT PLACE.
"HANAGASUMI," I THINK.
"HANAGASUMI."

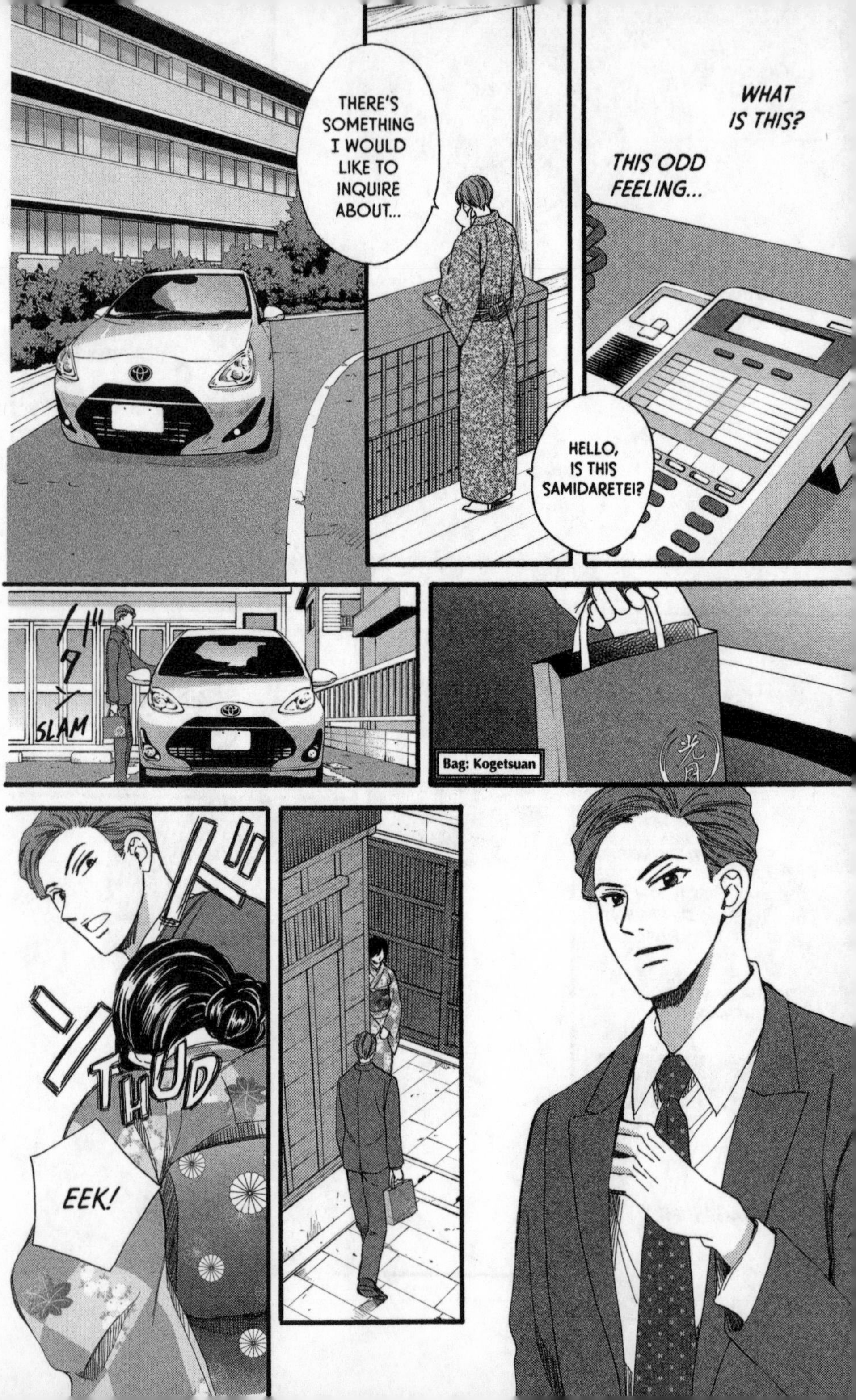
WHAT IS THIS?
THIS ODD FEELING...
HELLO, IS THIS SAMIDARETEI?
THERE'S SOMETHING I WOULD LIKE TO INQUIRE ABOUT...
Bag: Kogetsuan
バタン
SLAM
THUD
EEK!

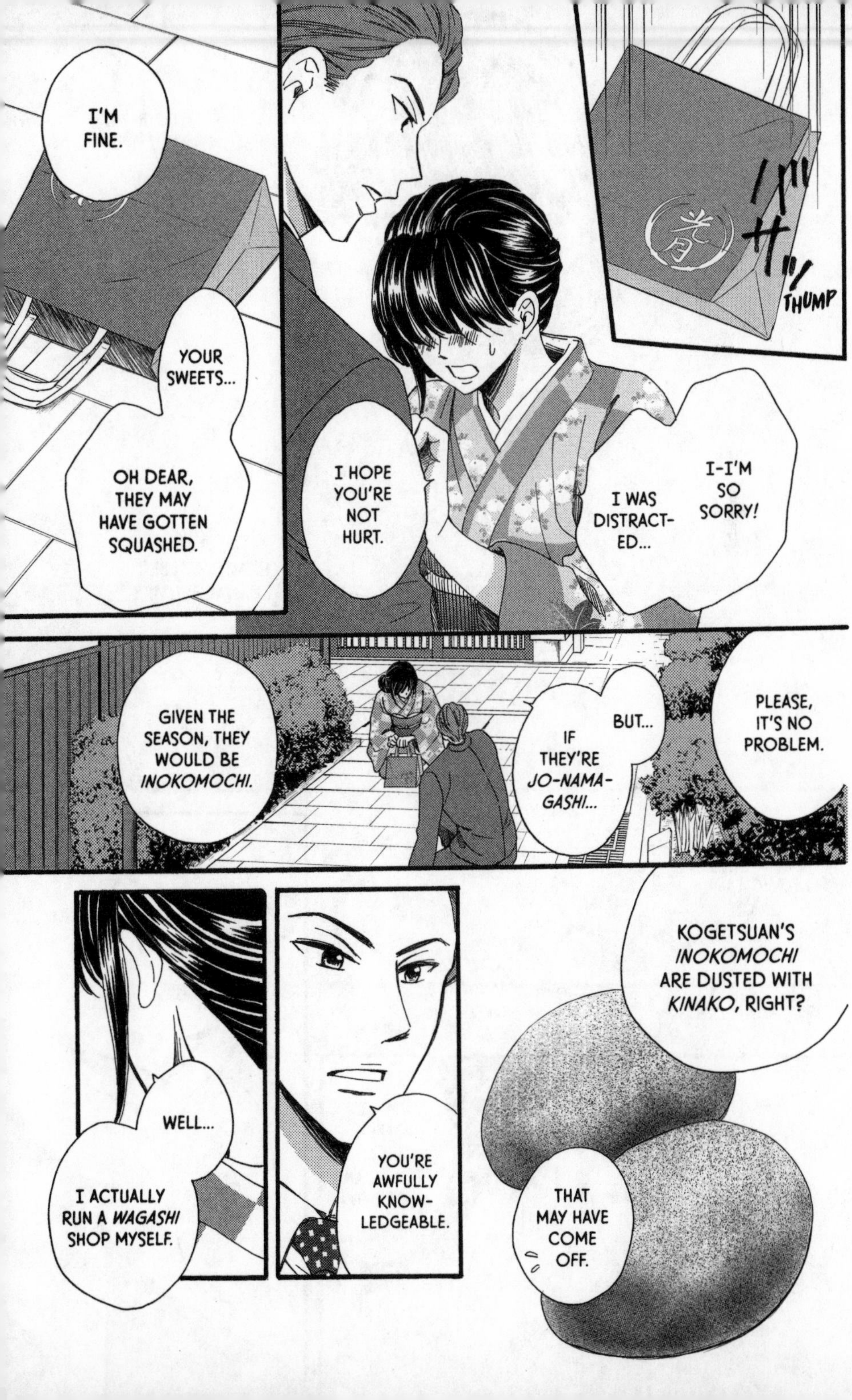
THUMP
I-I'M SO SORRY!
I WAS DISTRACT-ED...
I HOPE YOU'RE NOT HURT.
I'M FINE.
YOUR SWEETS...
OH DEAR, THEY MAY HAVE GOTTEN SQUASHED.
PLEASE, IT'S NO PROBLEM.
BUT...
IF THEY'RE *JO-NAMA-GASHI*...
GIVEN THE SEASON, THEY WOULD BE *INOKOMOCHI.*
KOGETSUAN'S *INOKOMOCHI* ARE DUSTED WITH *KINAKO*, RIGHT?
THAT MAY HAVE COME OFF.
YOU'RE AWFULLY KNOW-LEDGEABLE.
WELL...
I ACTUALLY RUN A *WAGASHI* SHOP MYSELF.

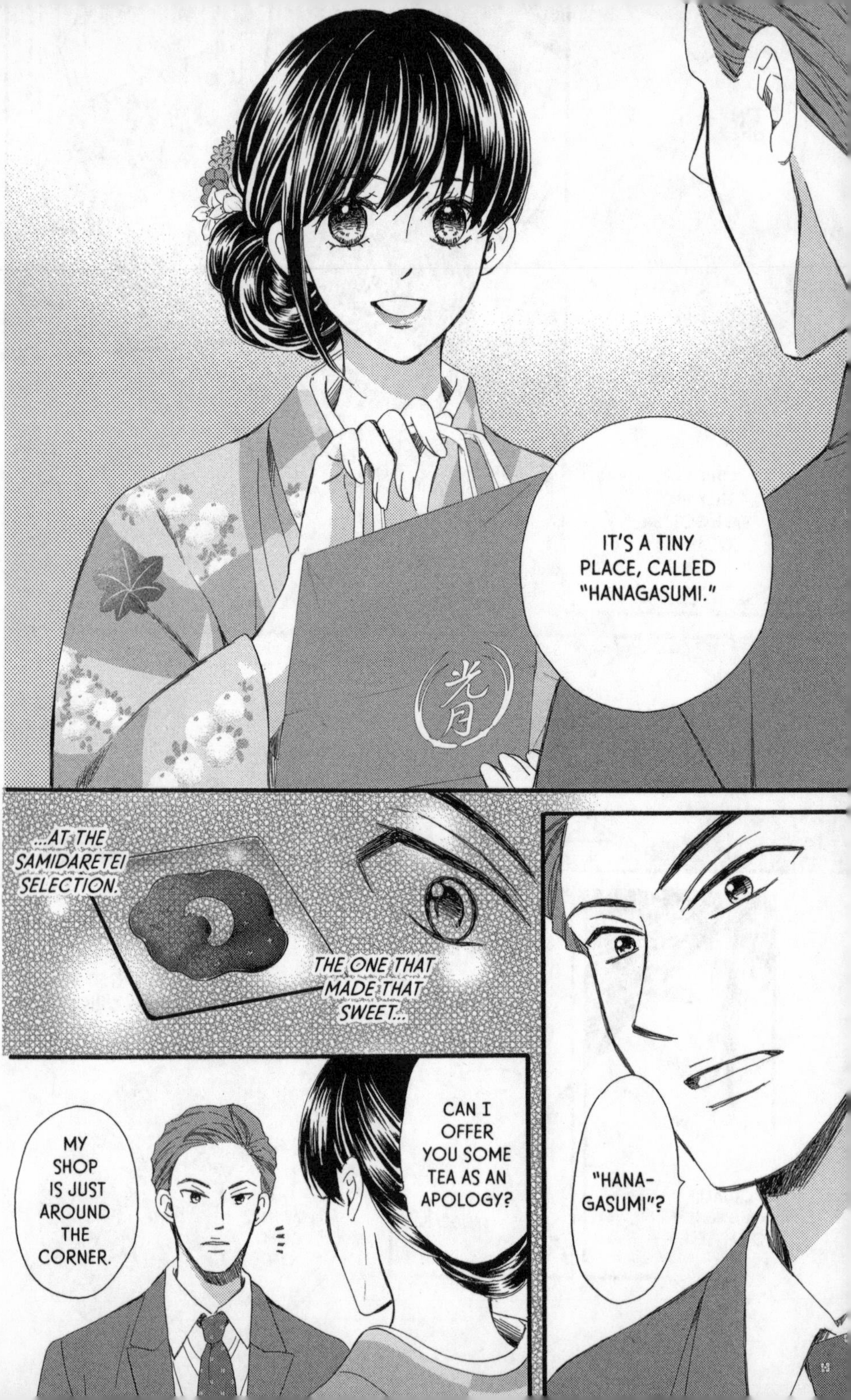
IT'S A TINY PLACE, CALLED "HANAGASUMI."
"HANA-GASUMI"?
...AT THE SAMIDARETEI SELECTION.
THE ONE THAT MADE THAT SWEET...
CAN I OFFER YOU SOME TEA AS AN APOLOGY?
MY SHOP IS JUST AROUND THE CORNER.

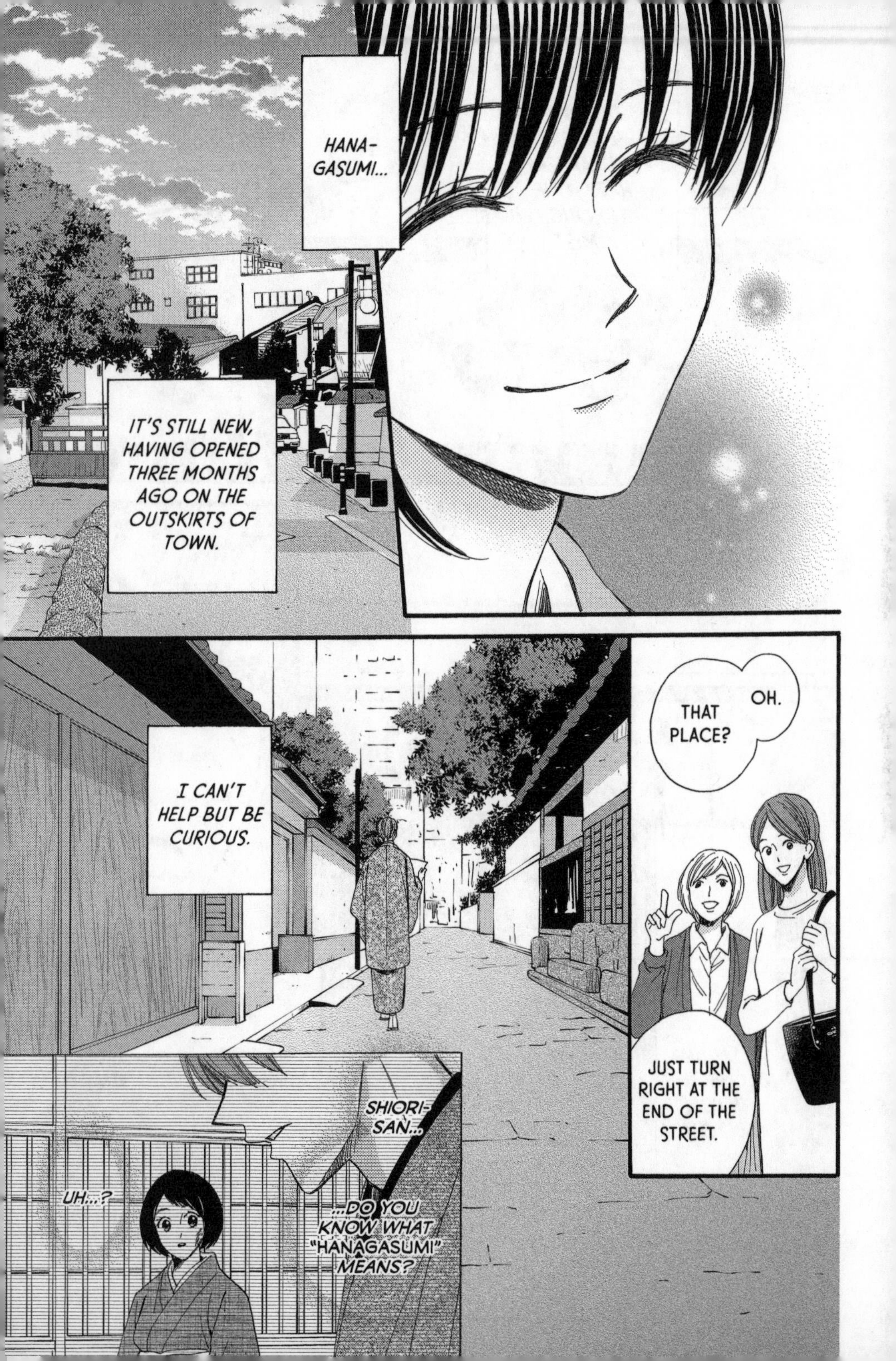
HANA-GASUMI...
IT'S STILL NEW, HAVING OPENED THREE MONTHS AGO ON THE OUTSKIRTS OF TOWN.
OH. THAT PLACE?
JUST TURN RIGHT AT THE END OF THE STREET.
I CAN'T HELP BUT BE CURIOUS.
SHIORI-SAN...
...DO YOU KNOW WHAT "HANAGASUMI" MEANS?
UH...?

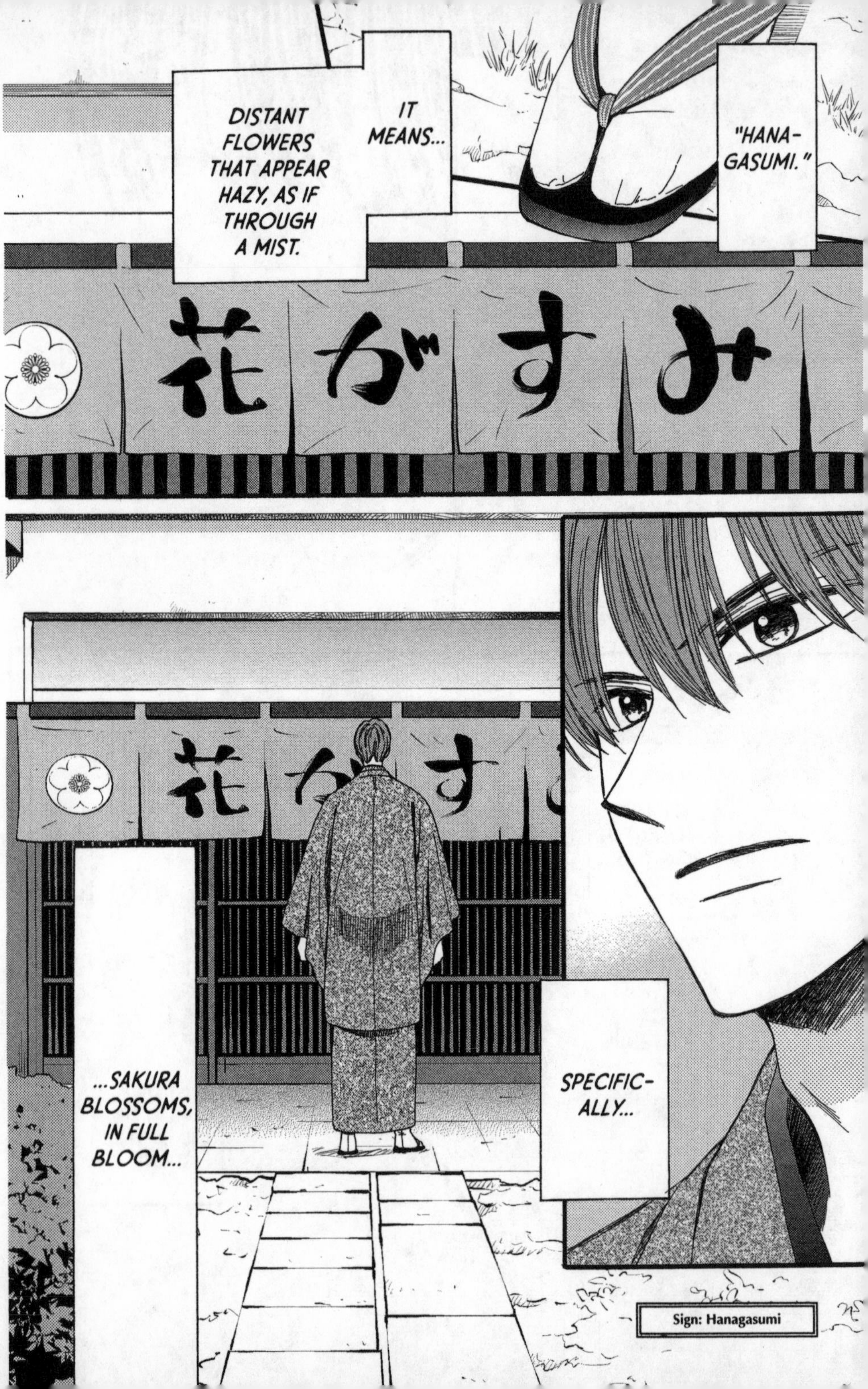
"HANA-GASUMI."
IT MEANS...
DISTANT FLOWERS THAT APPEAR HAZY, AS IF THROUGH A MIST.
花がすみ
SPECIFIC-ALLY...
...SAKURA BLOSSOMS, IN FULL BLOOM...
Sign: Hanagasumi

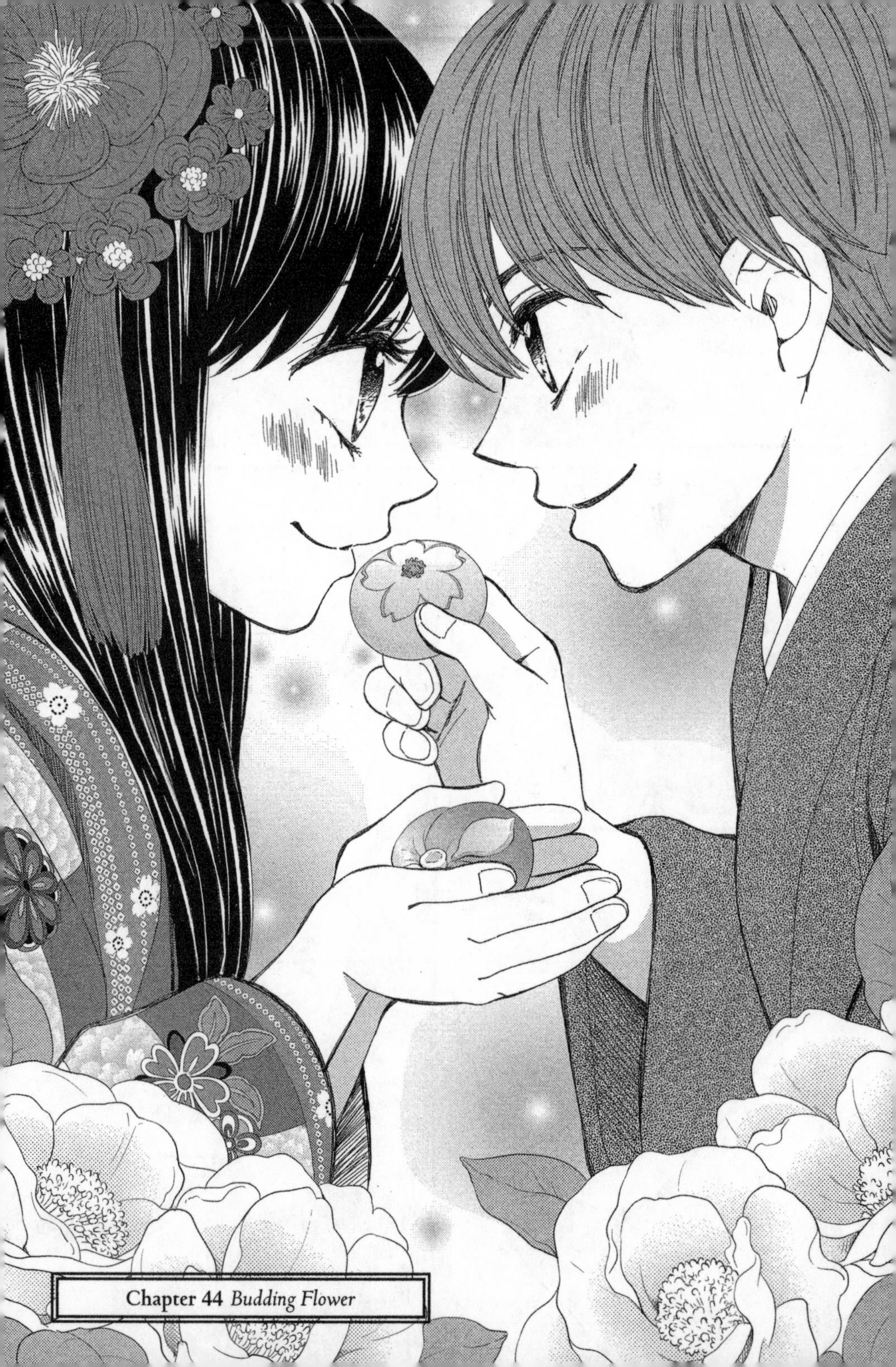

Chapter 44 *Budding Flower*

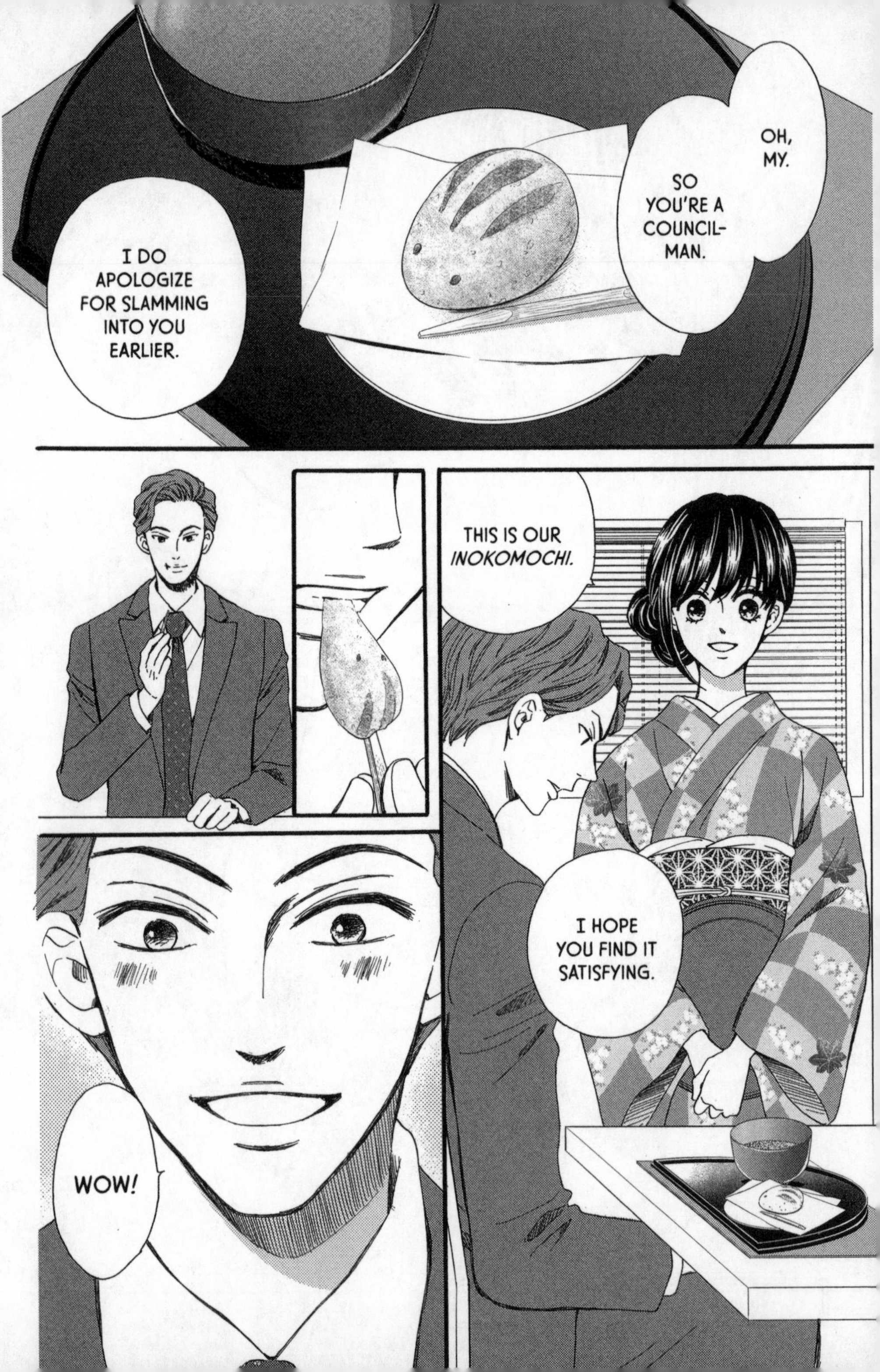
OH, MY.
SO YOU'RE A COUNCIL-MAN.
I DO APOLOGIZE FOR SLAMMING INTO YOU EARLIER.
THIS IS OUR *INOKOMOCHI.*
I HOPE YOU FIND IT SATISFYING.
WOW!

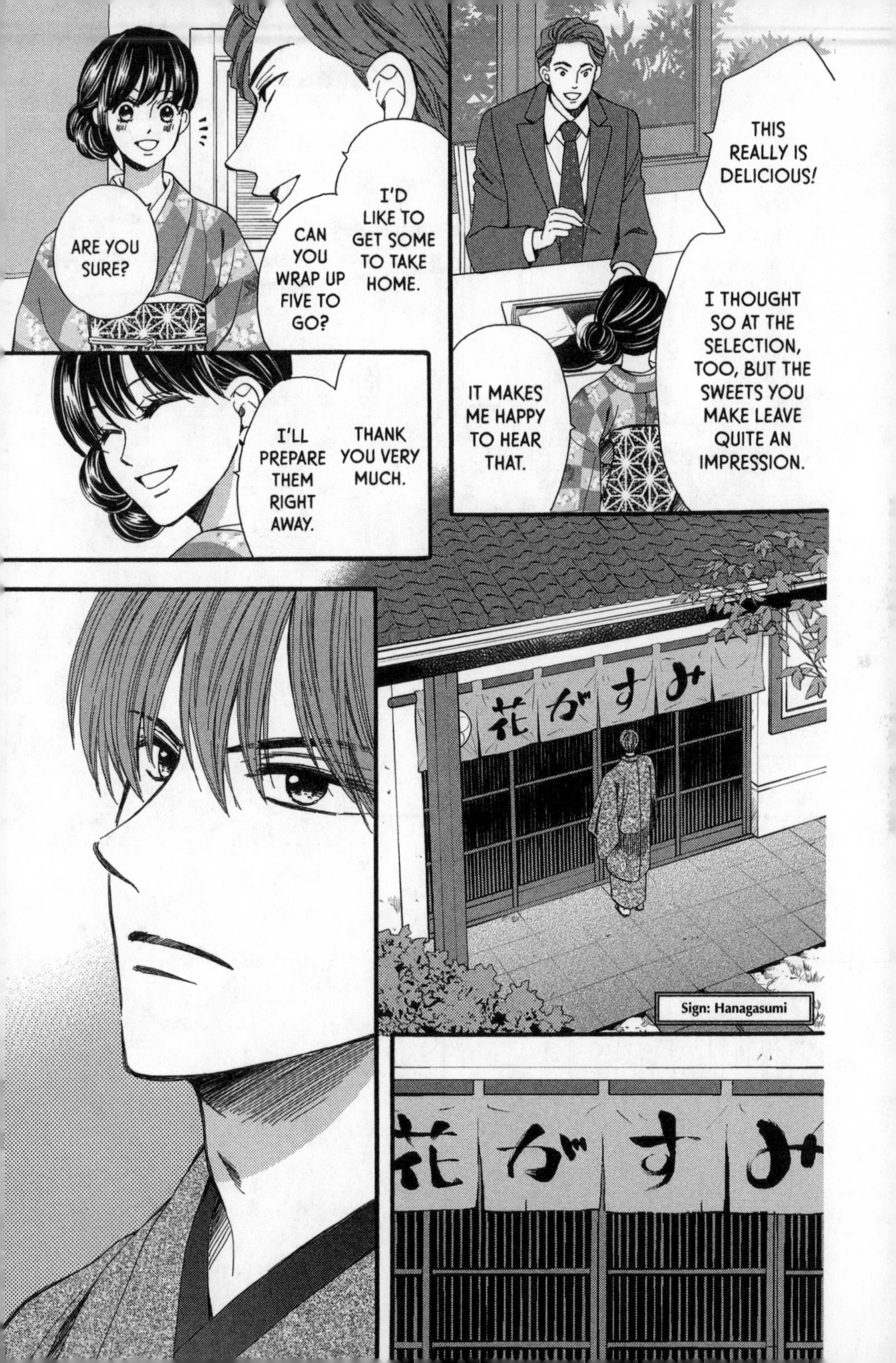
THIS REALLY IS DELICIOUS!
I THOUGHT SO AT THE SELECTION, TOO, BUT THE SWEETS YOU MAKE LEAVE QUITE AN IMPRESSION.
IT MAKES ME HAPPY TO HEAR THAT.
I'D LIKE TO GET SOME TO TAKE HOME.
CAN YOU WRAP UP FIVE TO GO?
ARE YOU SURE?
THANK YOU VERY MUCH.
I'LL PREPARE THEM RIGHT AWAY.
花がすみ
Sign: Hanagasumi
花がすみ

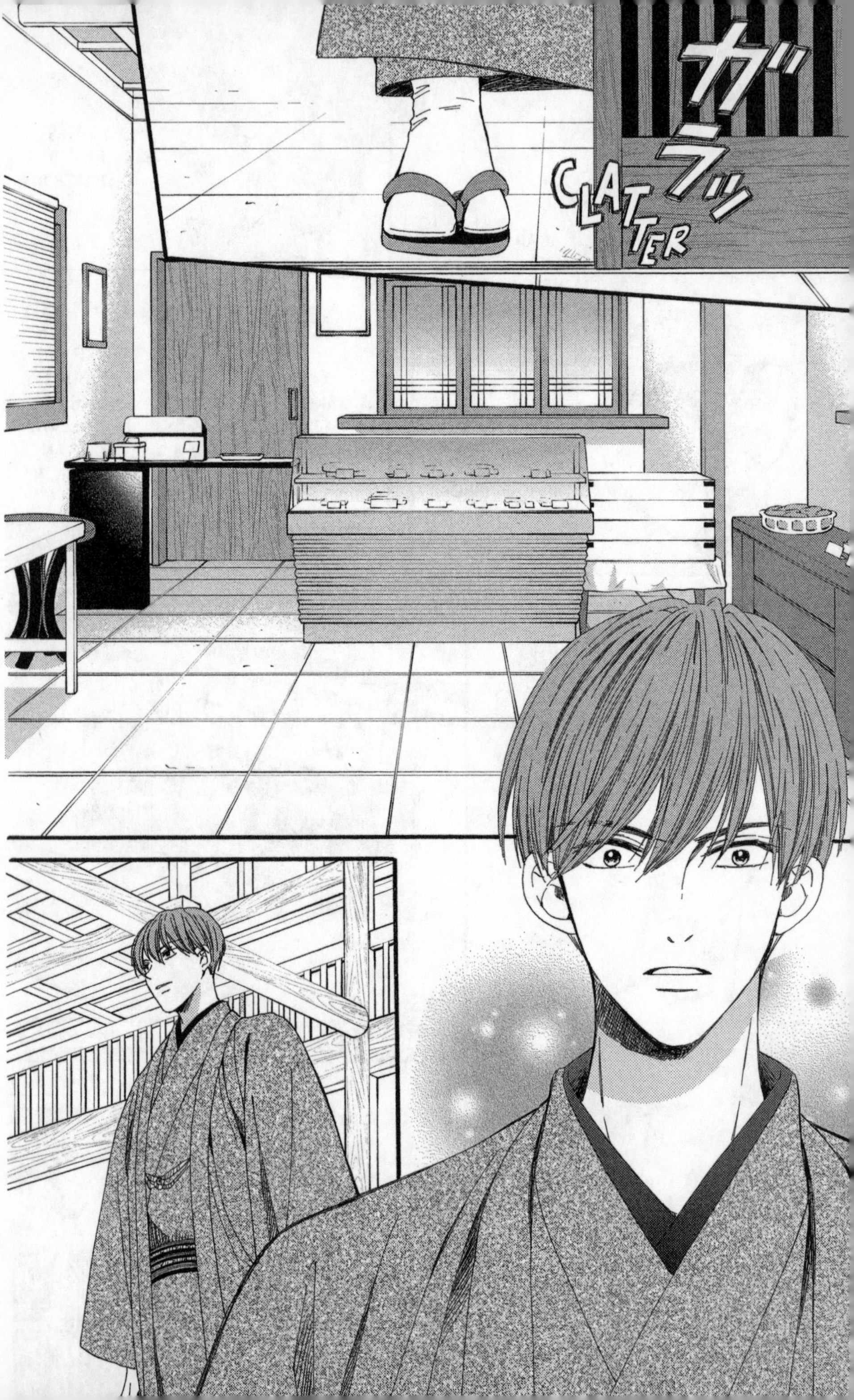
ガラッ
CLATTER

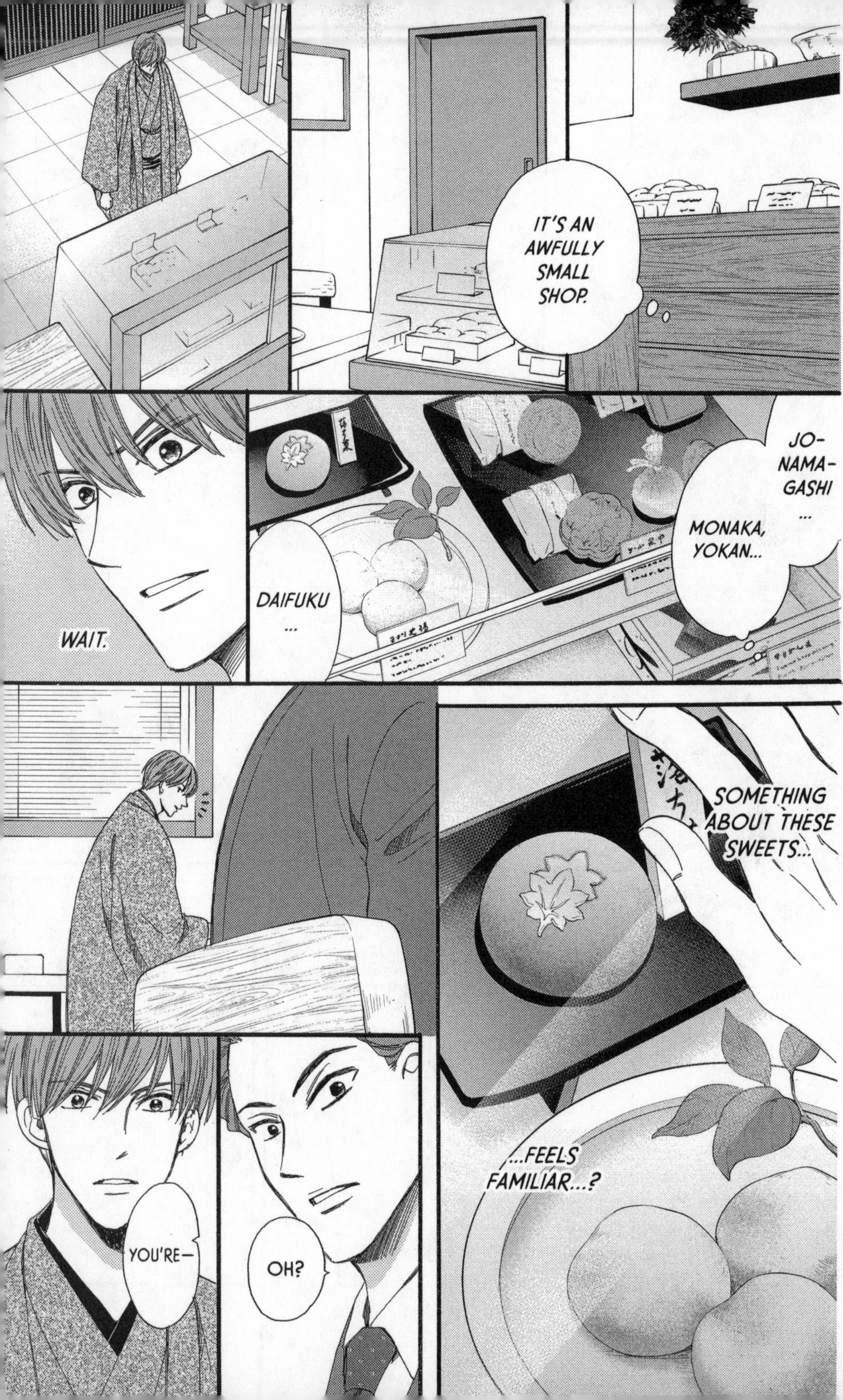
IT'S AN AWFULLY SMALL SHOP.
JO-NAMA-GASHI ...
MONAKA, YOKAN...
DAIFUKU ...
WAIT.
SOMETHING ABOUT THESE SWEETS...
...FEELS FAMILIAR...?
OH?
YOU'RE—

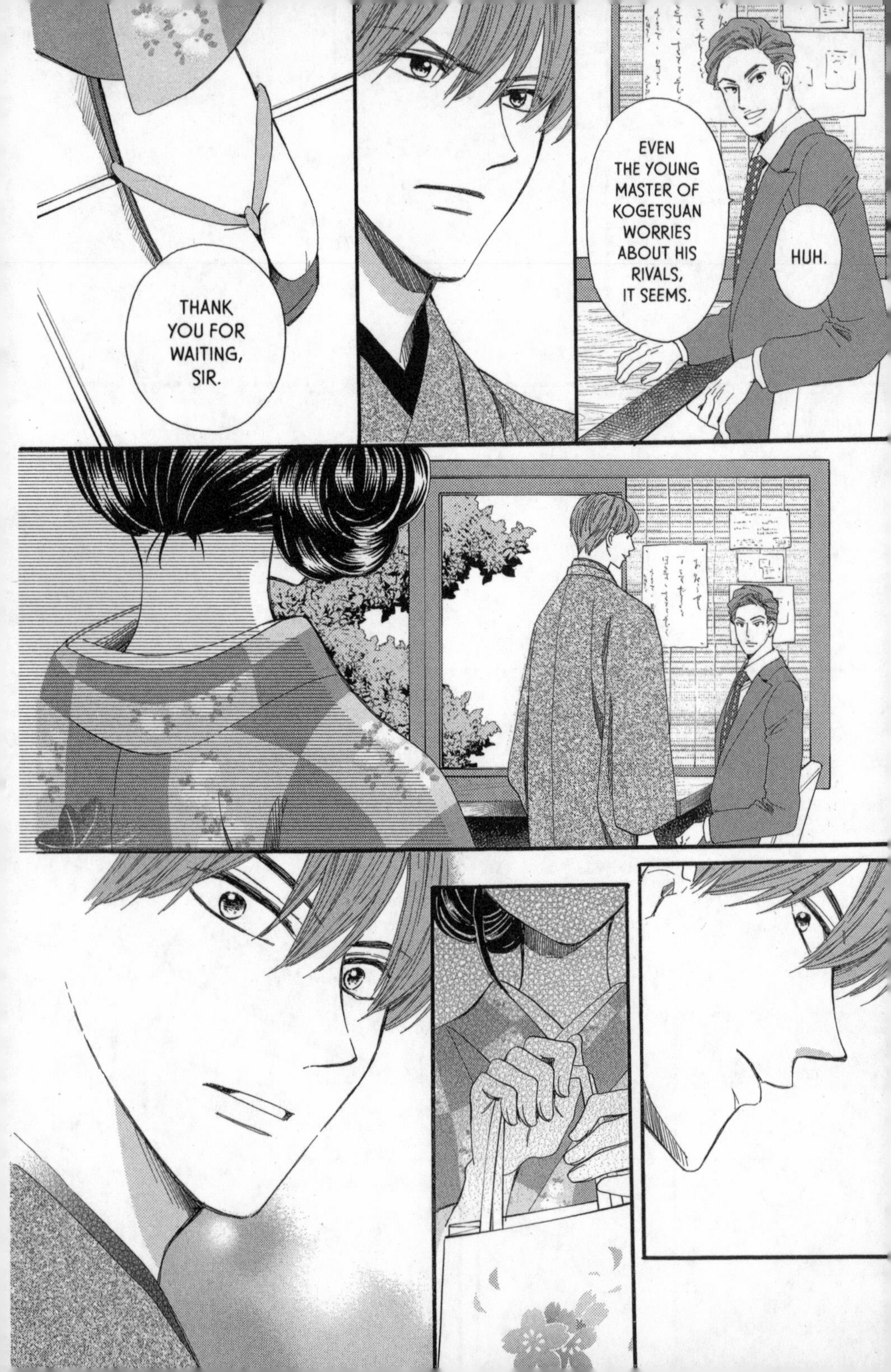
HUH.
EVEN THE YOUNG MASTER OF KOGETSUAN WORRIES ABOUT HIS RIVALS, IT SEEMS.
THANK YOU FOR WAITING, SIR.

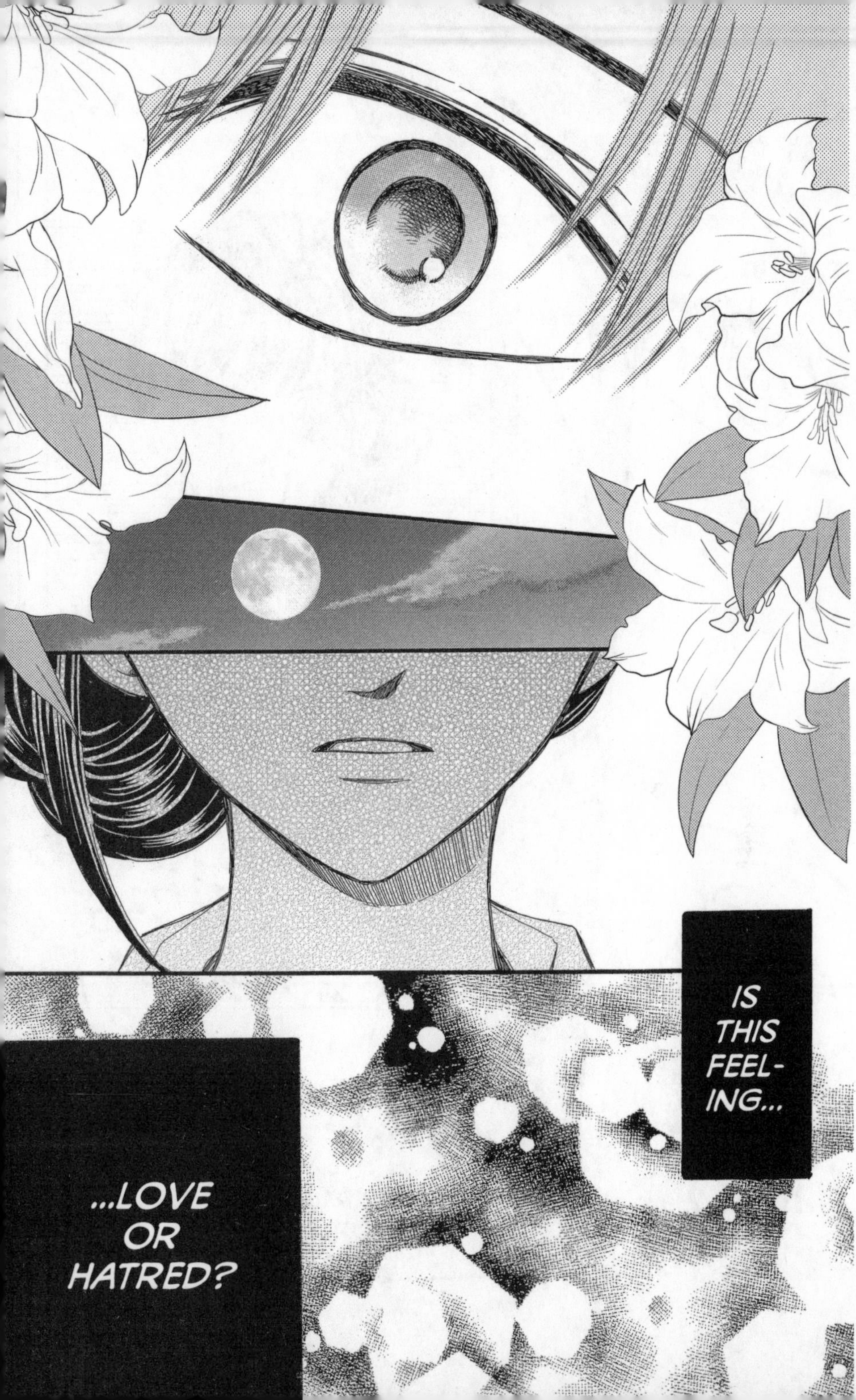
IS THIS FEEL-ING...
...LOVE OR HATRED?

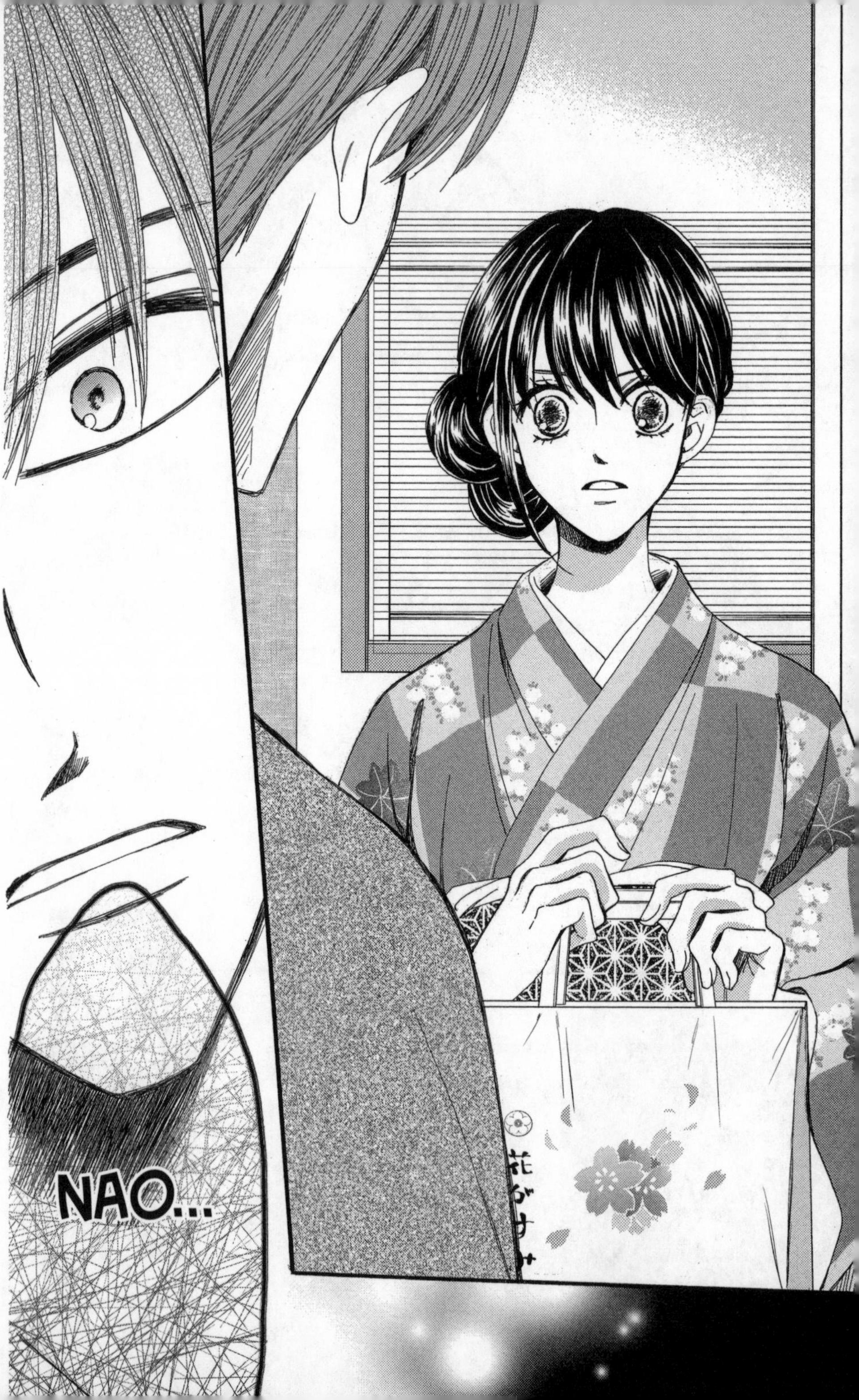
花がす
NAO...

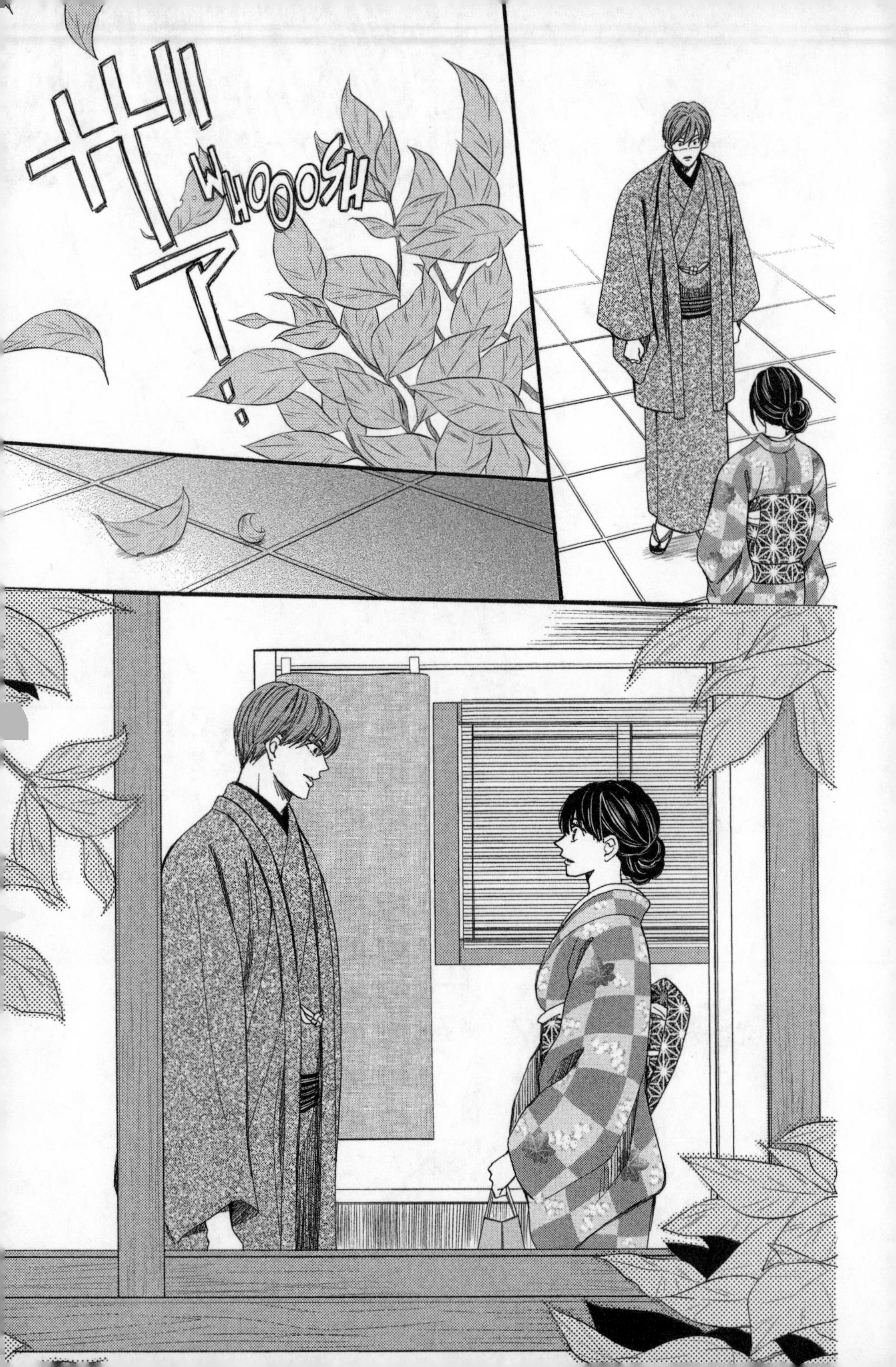
WHOOOSH

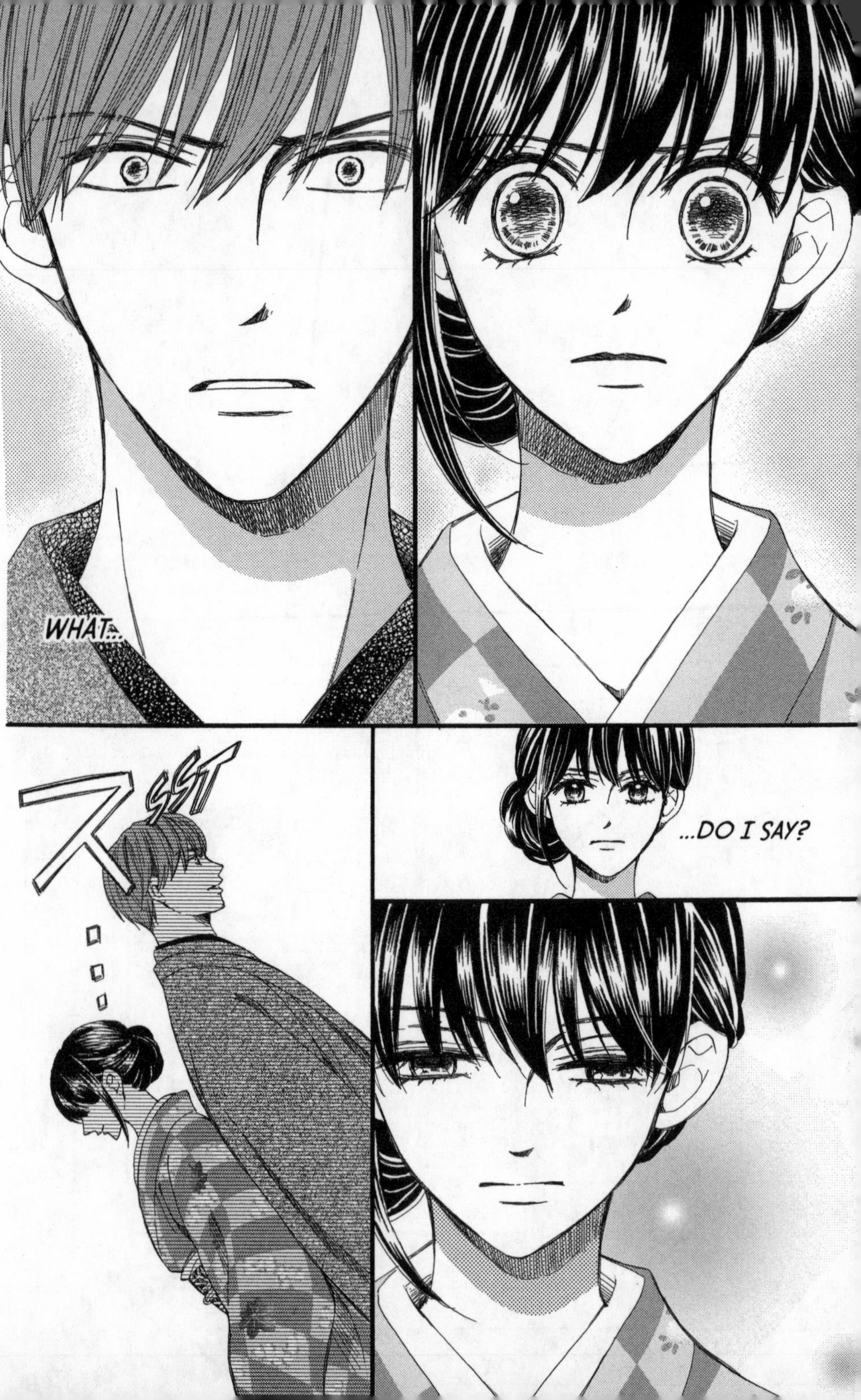
WHAT...
...DO I SAY?
スSST
...

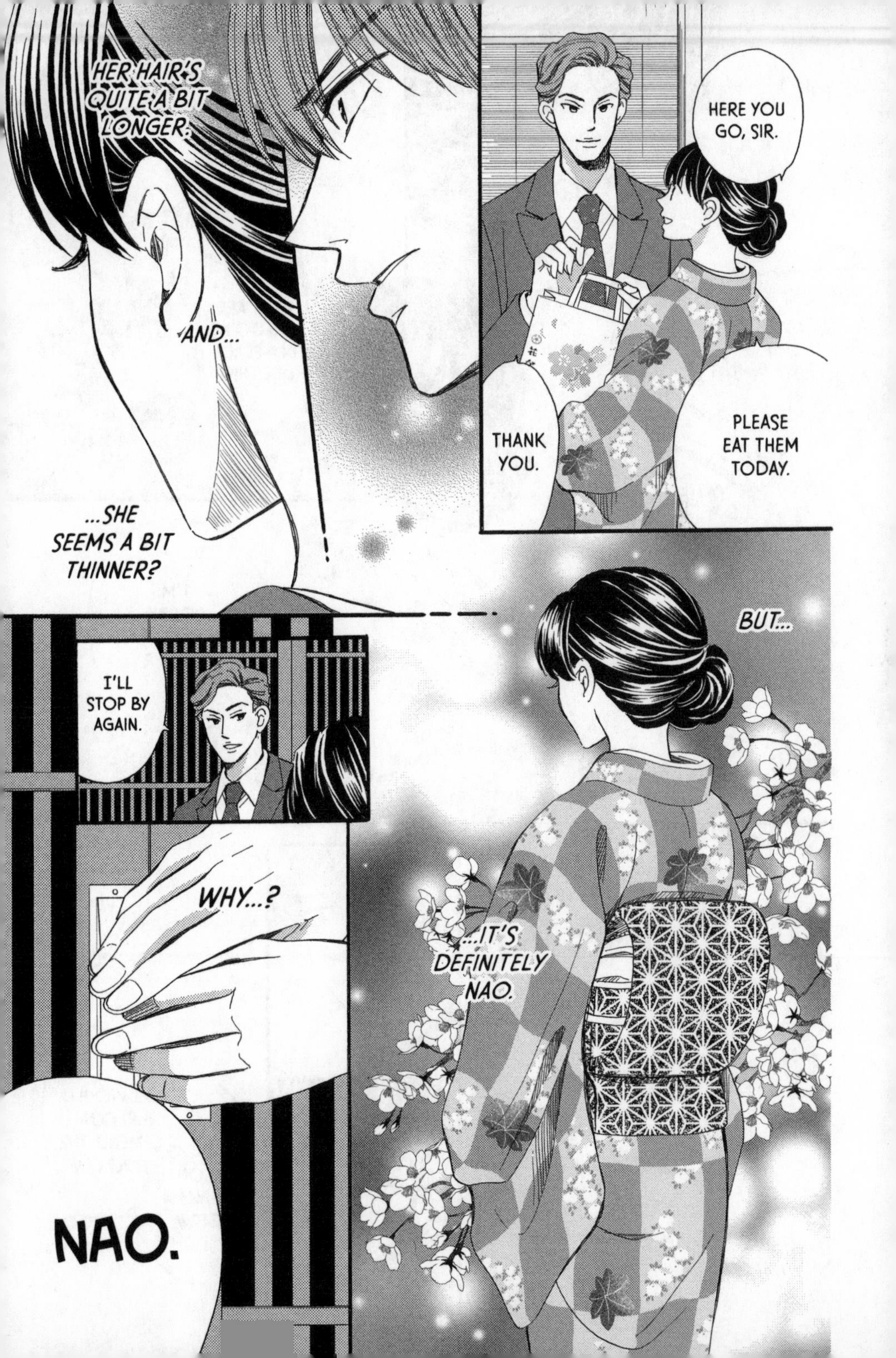
HERE YOU GO, SIR.
PLEASE EAT THEM TODAY.
THANK YOU.
HER HAIR'S QUITE A BIT LONGER.
AND...
...SHE SEEMS A BIT THINNER?
BUT...
...IT'S DEFINITELY NAO.
I'LL STOP BY AGAIN.
WHY...?
NAO.

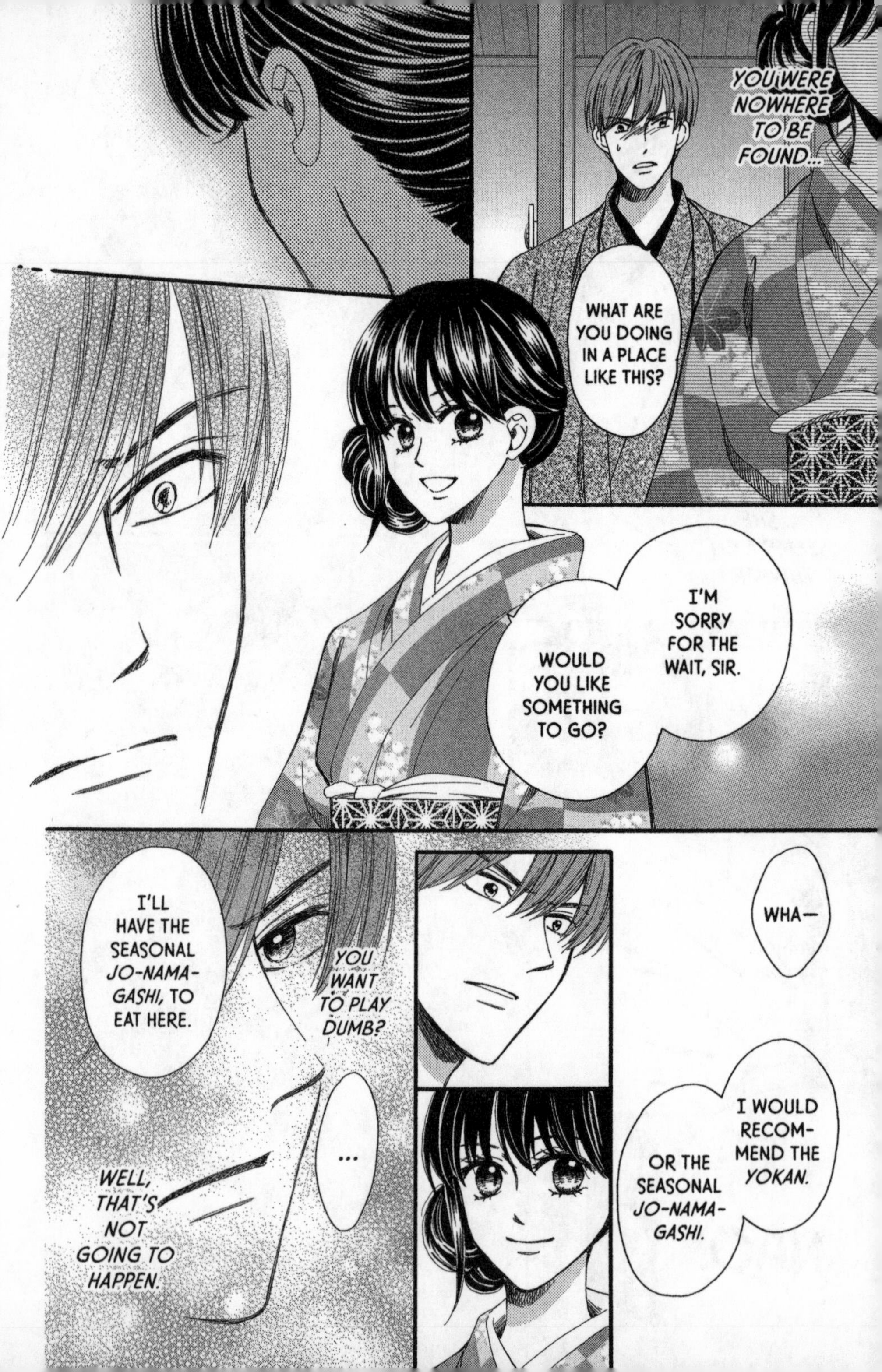
YOU WERE NOWHERE TO BE FOUND...
WHAT ARE YOU DOING IN A PLACE LIKE THIS?
I'M SORRY FOR THE WAIT, SIR.
WOULD YOU LIKE SOMETHING TO GO?
WHA—
I WOULD RECOMMEND THE *YOKAN.*
OR THE SEASONAL *JO-NAMAGASHI.*
I'LL HAVE THE SEASONAL *JO-NAMAGASHI,* TO EAT HERE.
YOU WANT TO PLAY DUMB?
...
WELL, THAT'S NOT GOING TO HAPPEN.

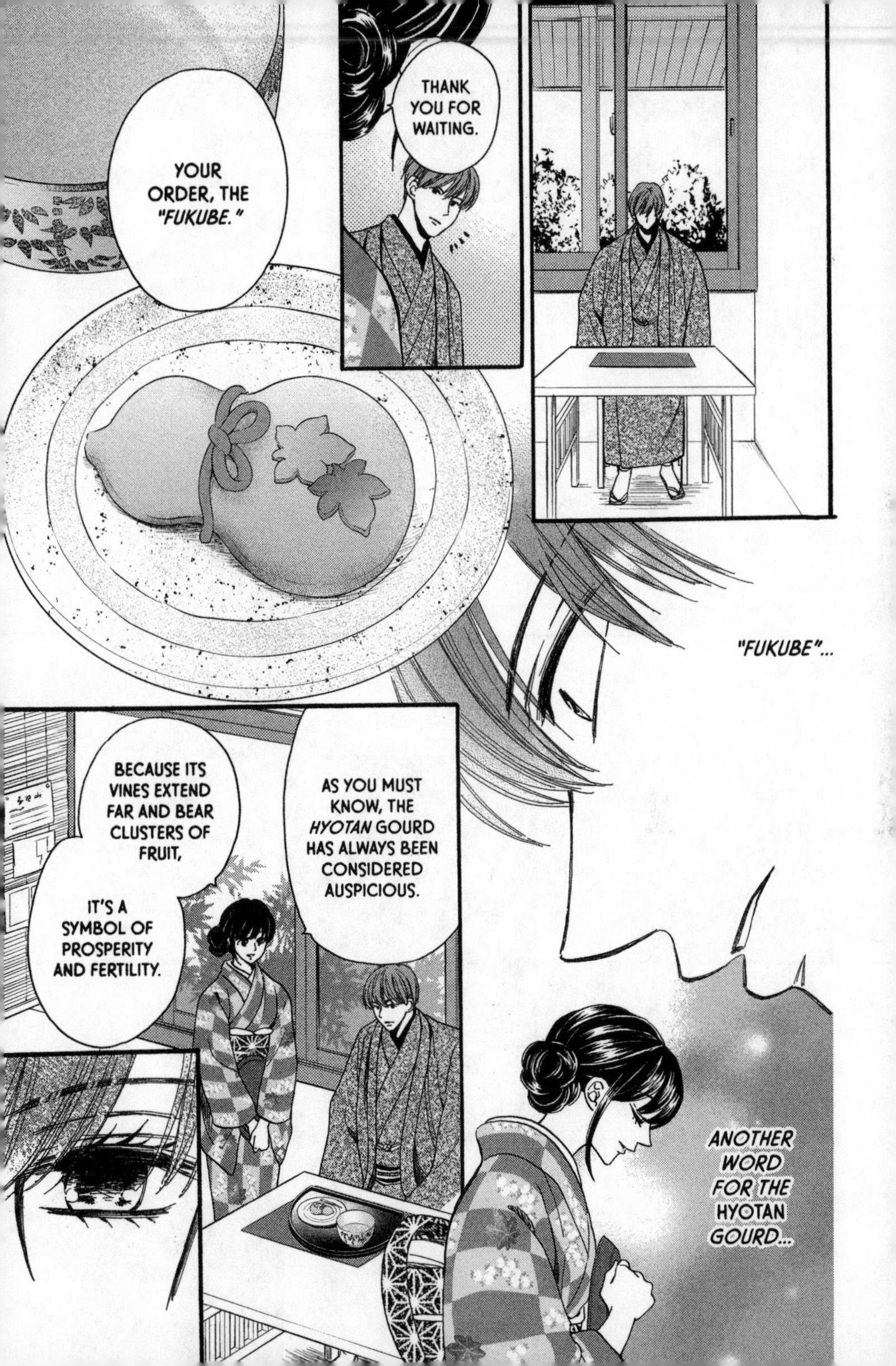
THANK YOU FOR WAITING.
YOUR ORDER, THE *"FUKUBE."*
"FUKUBE"...
ANOTHER WORD FOR THE HYOTAN GOURD...
AS YOU MUST KNOW, THE *HYOTAN* GOURD HAS ALWAYS BEEN CONSIDERED AUSPICIOUS.
BECAUSE ITS VINES EXTEND FAR AND BEAR CLUSTERS OF FRUIT,
IT'S A SYMBOL OF PROSPERITY AND FERTILITY.

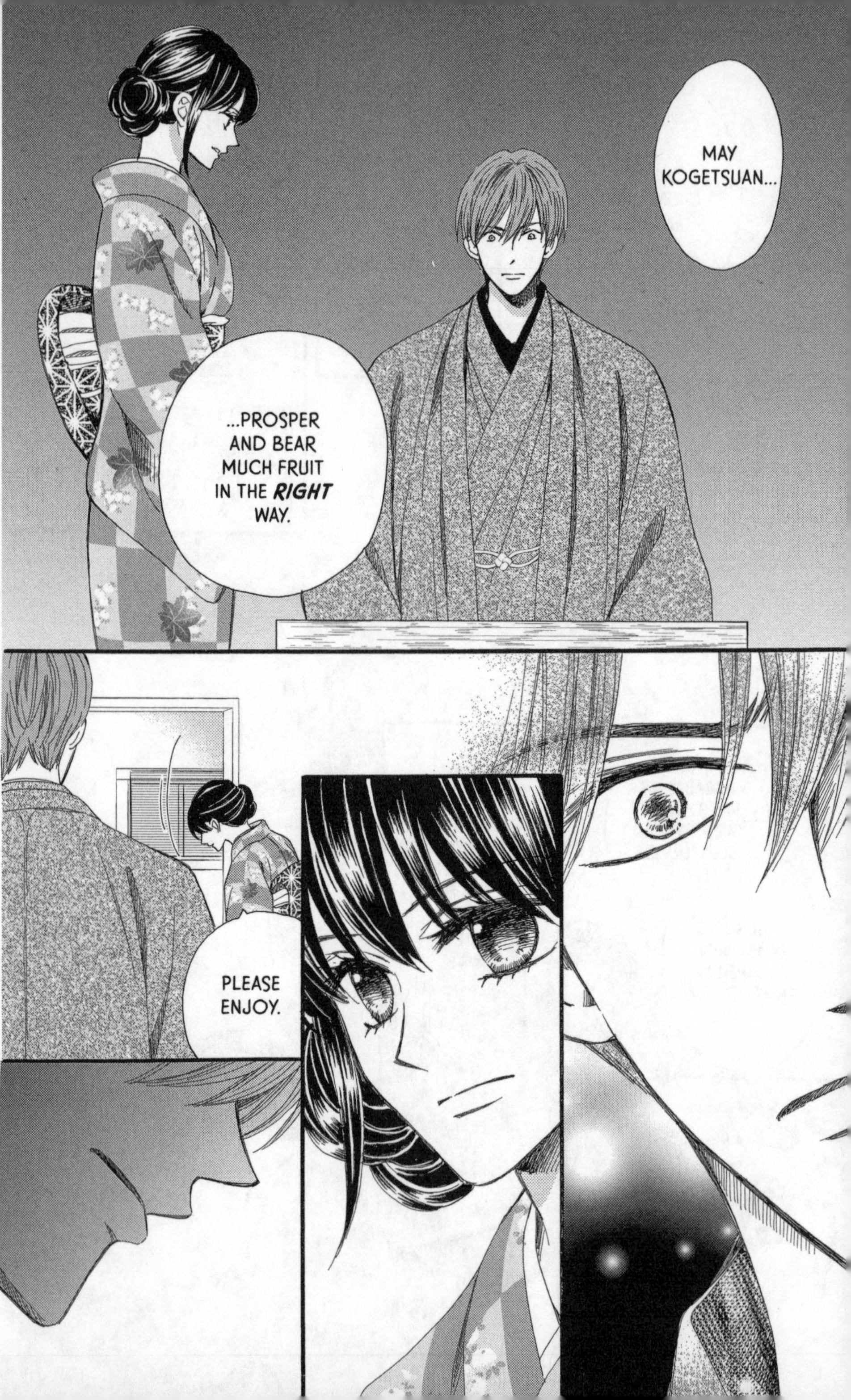
MAY KOGETSUAN...
...PROSPER AND BEAR MUCH FRUIT IN THE ***RIGHT*** WAY.
PLEASE ENJOY.

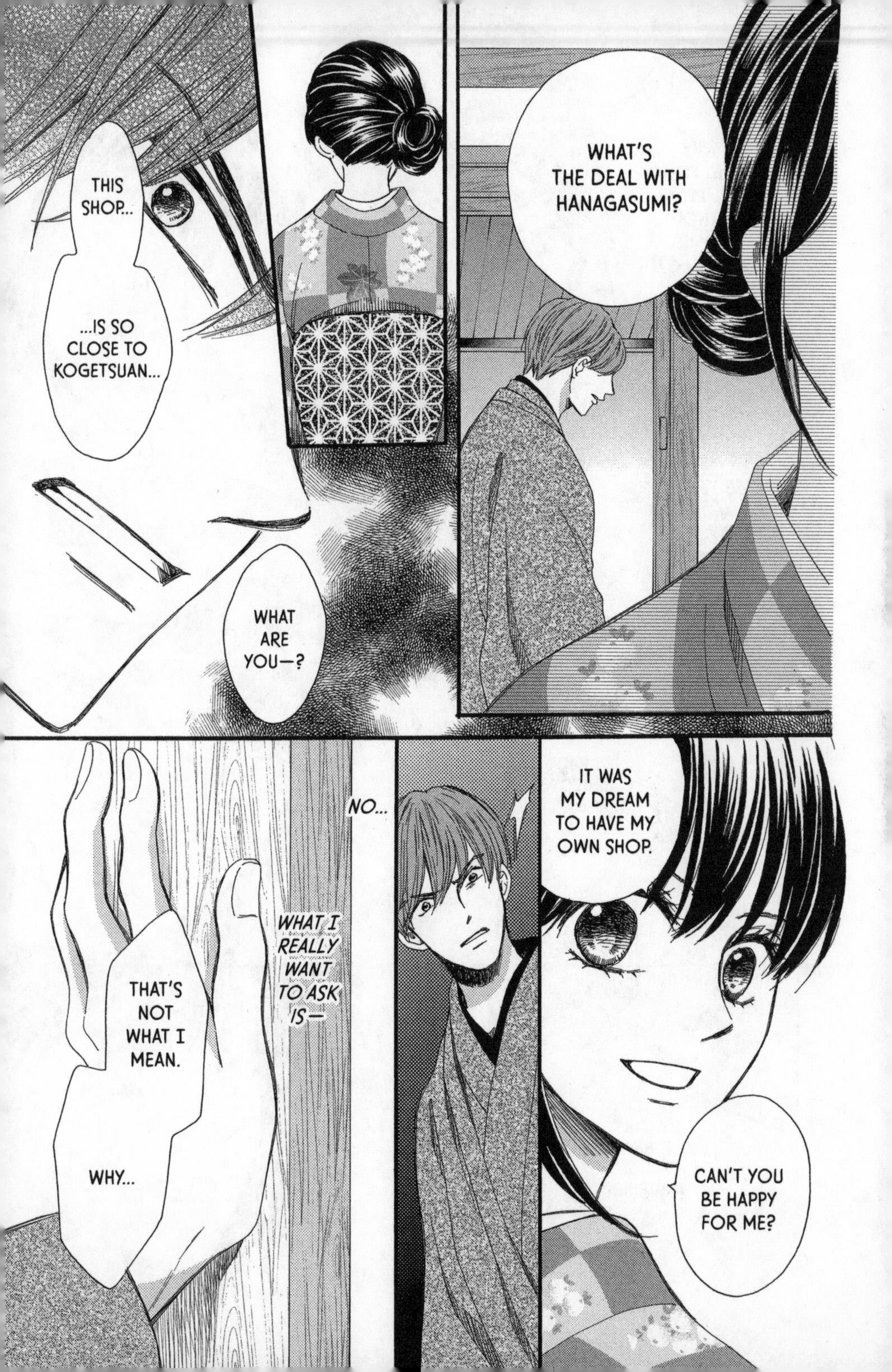
WHAT'S THE DEAL WITH HANAGASUMI?
THIS SHOP...
...IS SO CLOSE TO KOGETSUAN...
WHAT ARE YOU—?
IT WAS MY DREAM TO HAVE MY OWN SHOP.
CAN'T YOU BE HAPPY FOR ME?
NO...
WHAT I REALLY WANT TO ASK IS—
THAT'S NOT WHAT I MEAN.
WHY...

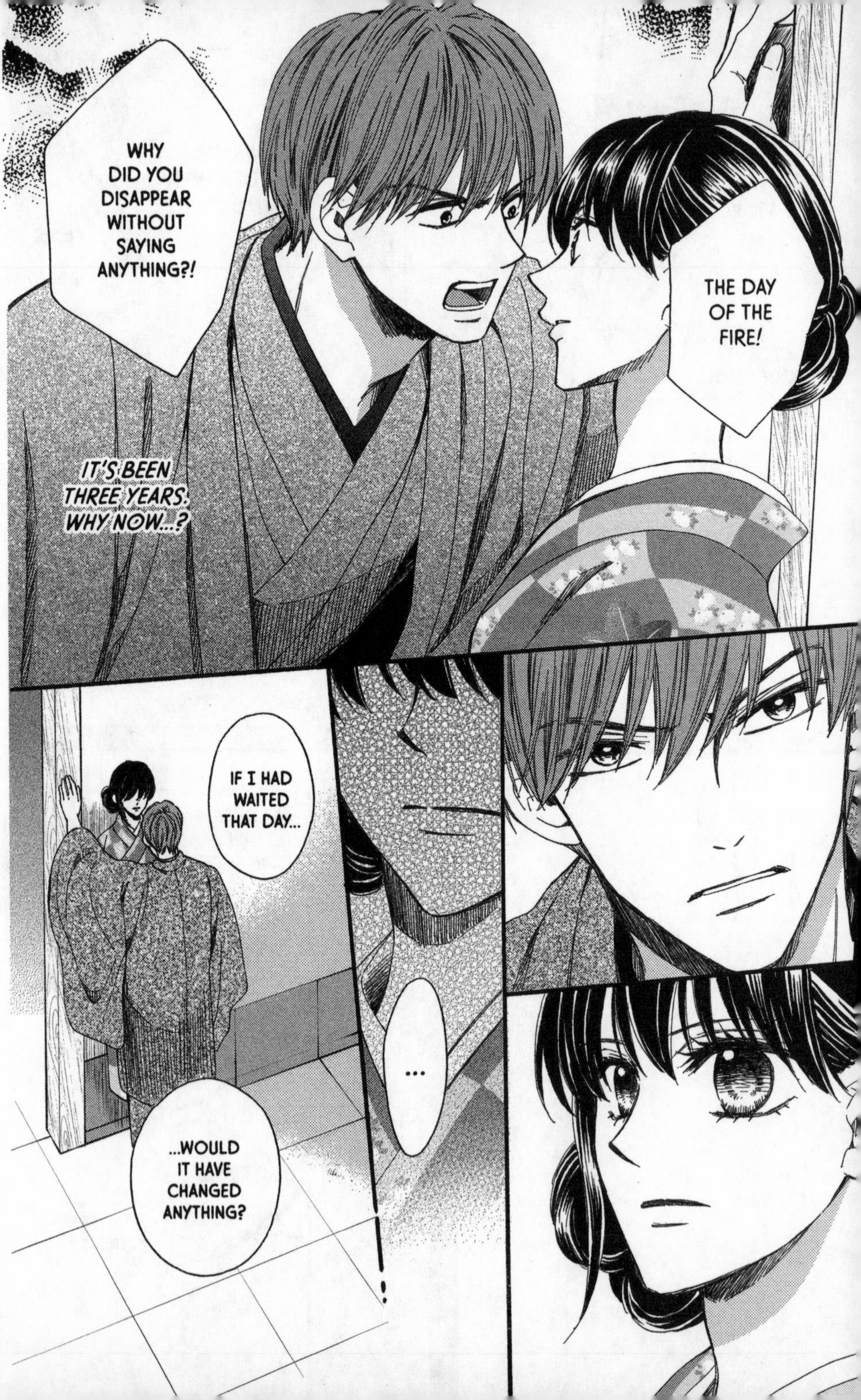
WHY DID YOU DISAPPEAR WITHOUT SAYING ANYTHING?!
THE DAY OF THE FIRE!
IT'S BEEN THREE YEARS. WHY NOW...?
...
IF I HAD WAITED THAT DAY...
...WOULD IT HAVE CHANGED ANYTHING?

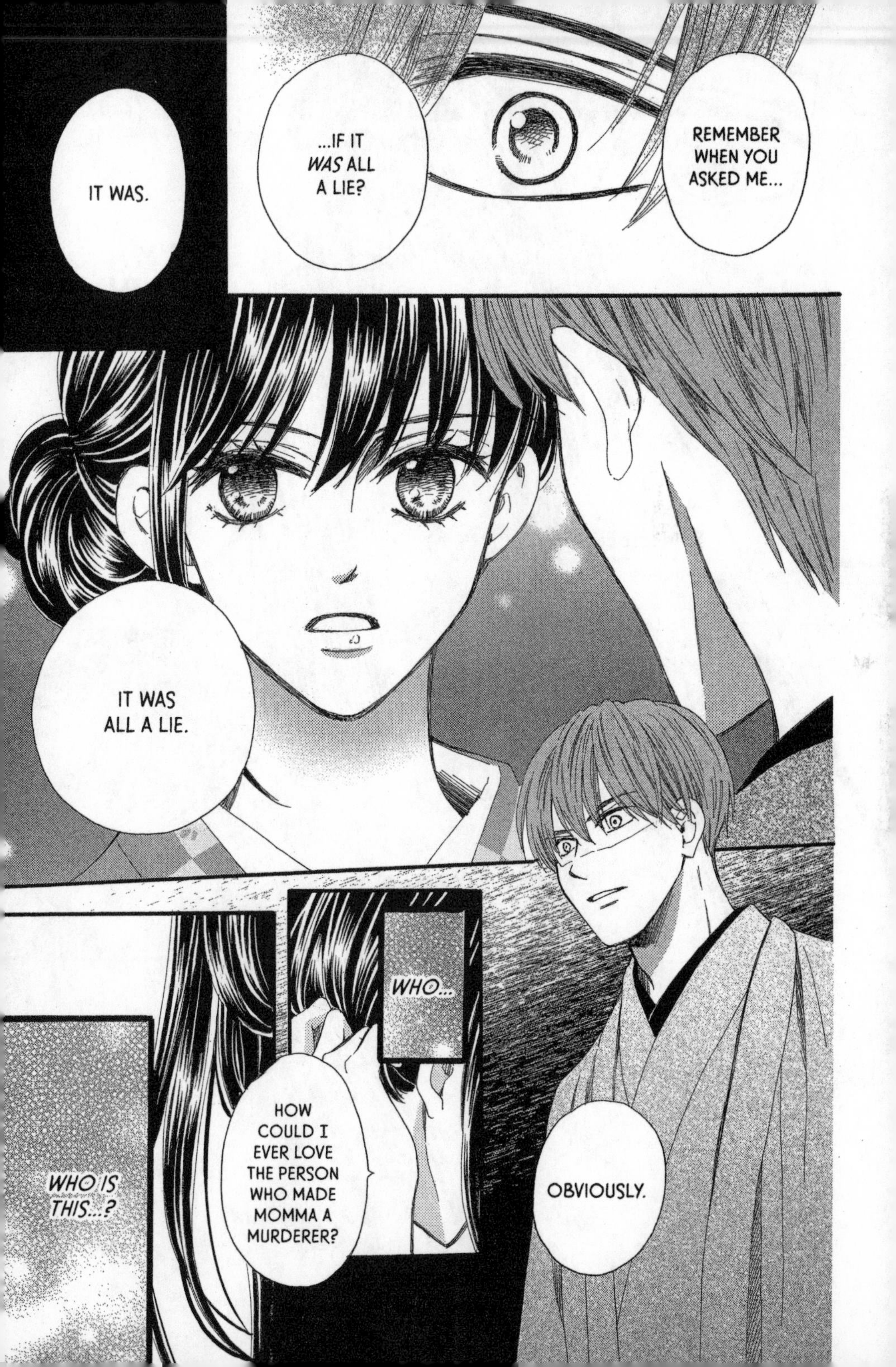
REMEMBER WHEN YOU ASKED ME...
...IF IT *WAS* ALL A LIE?
IT WAS.
IT WAS ALL A LIE.
WHO...
HOW COULD I EVER LOVE THE PERSON WHO MADE MOMMA A MURDERER?
OBVIOUSLY.
WHO IS THIS...?

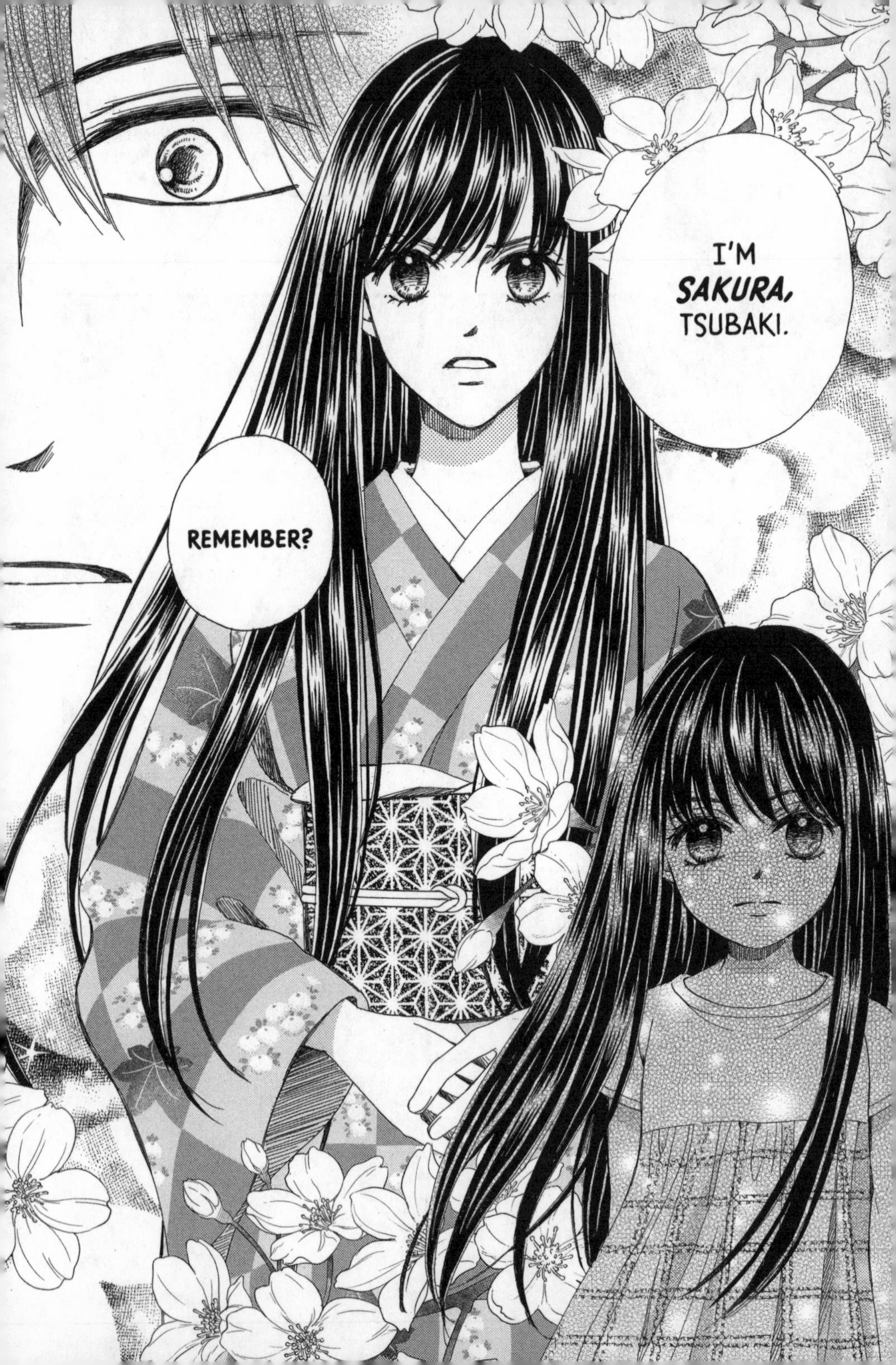
I'M *SAKURA,* TSUBAKI.
REMEMBER?

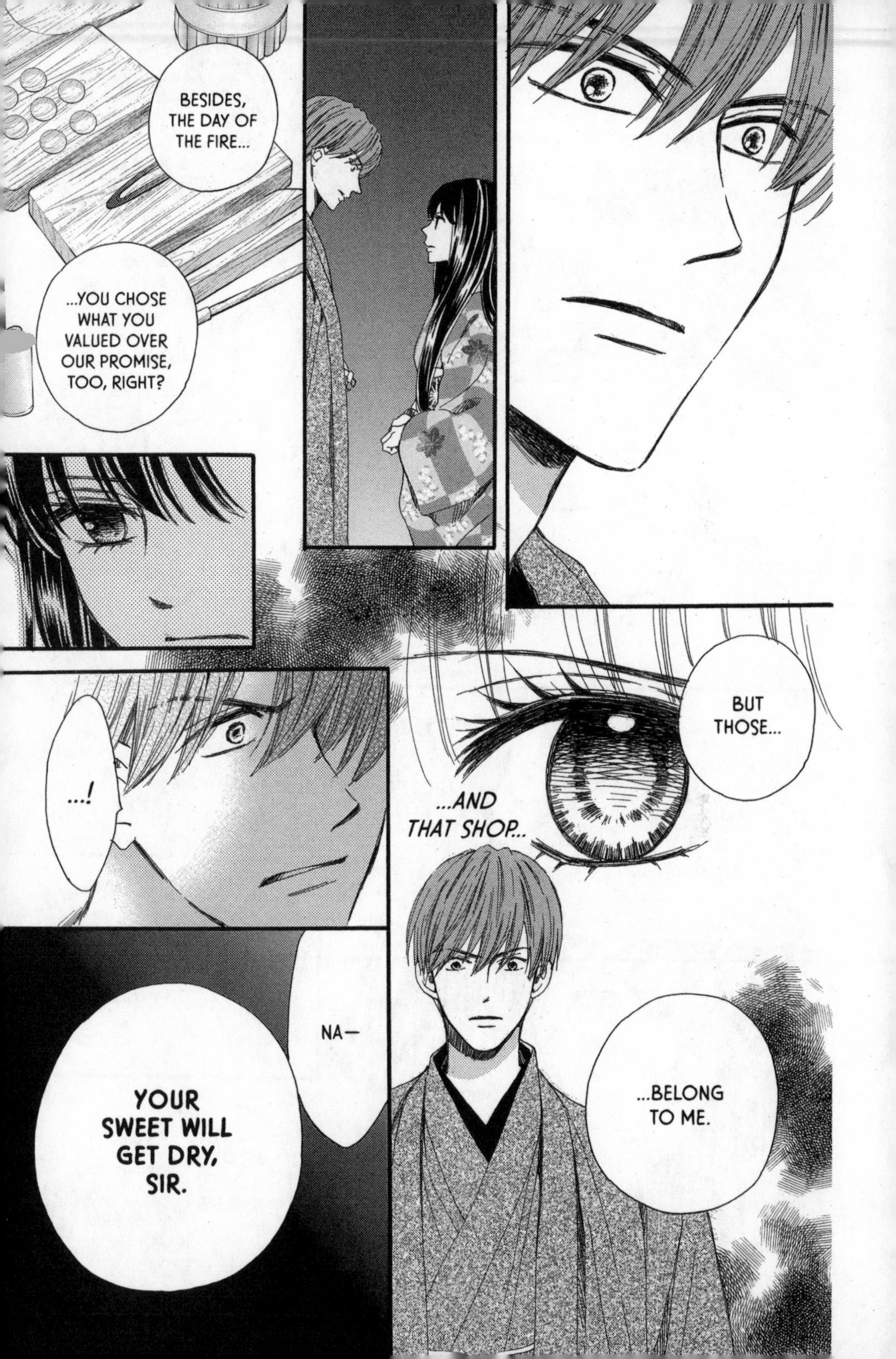
BESIDES, THE DAY OF THE FIRE...
...YOU CHOSE WHAT YOU VALUED OVER OUR PROMISE, TOO, RIGHT?
BUT THOSE...
...AND THAT SHOP...
...BELONG TO ME.
...!
NA—
YOUR SWEET WILL GET DRY, SIR.

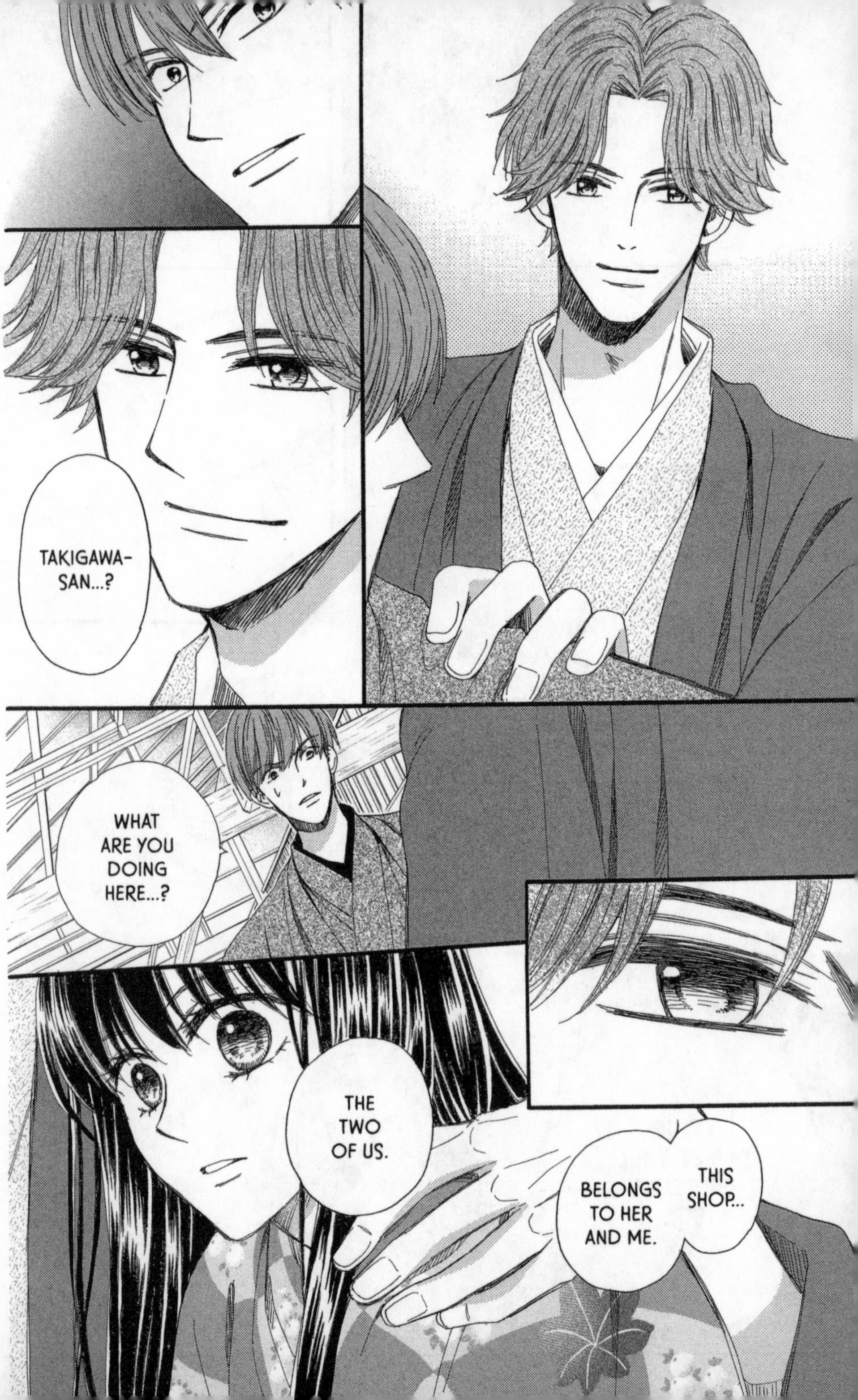

TAKIGAWA-SAN...?
WHAT ARE YOU DOING HERE...?
THIS SHOP...
BELONGS TO HER AND ME.
THE TWO OF US.

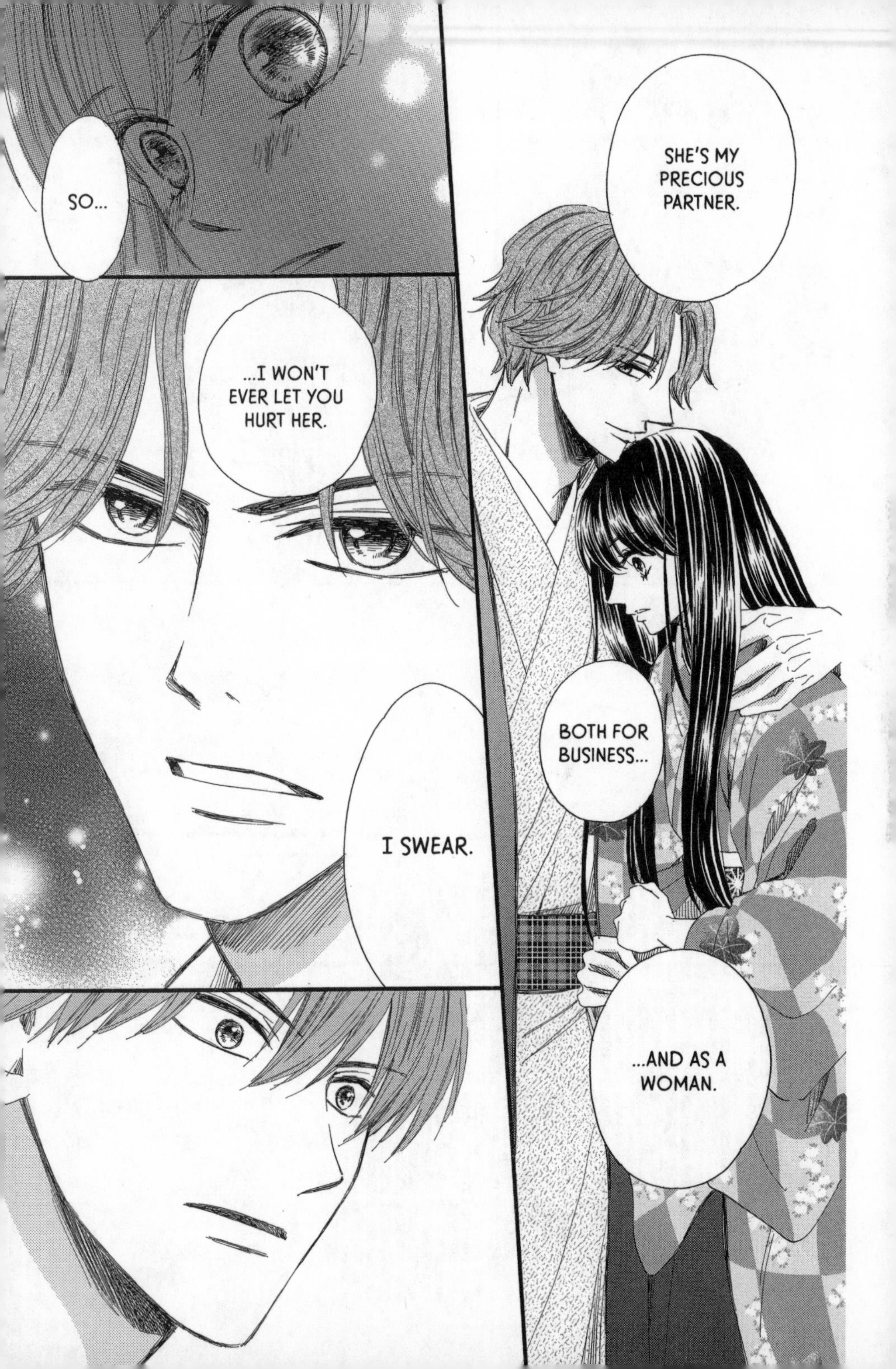
SHE'S MY PRECIOUS PARTNER.
BOTH FOR BUSINESS...
...AND AS A WOMAN.
SO...
...I WON'T EVER LET YOU HURT HER.
I SWEAR.

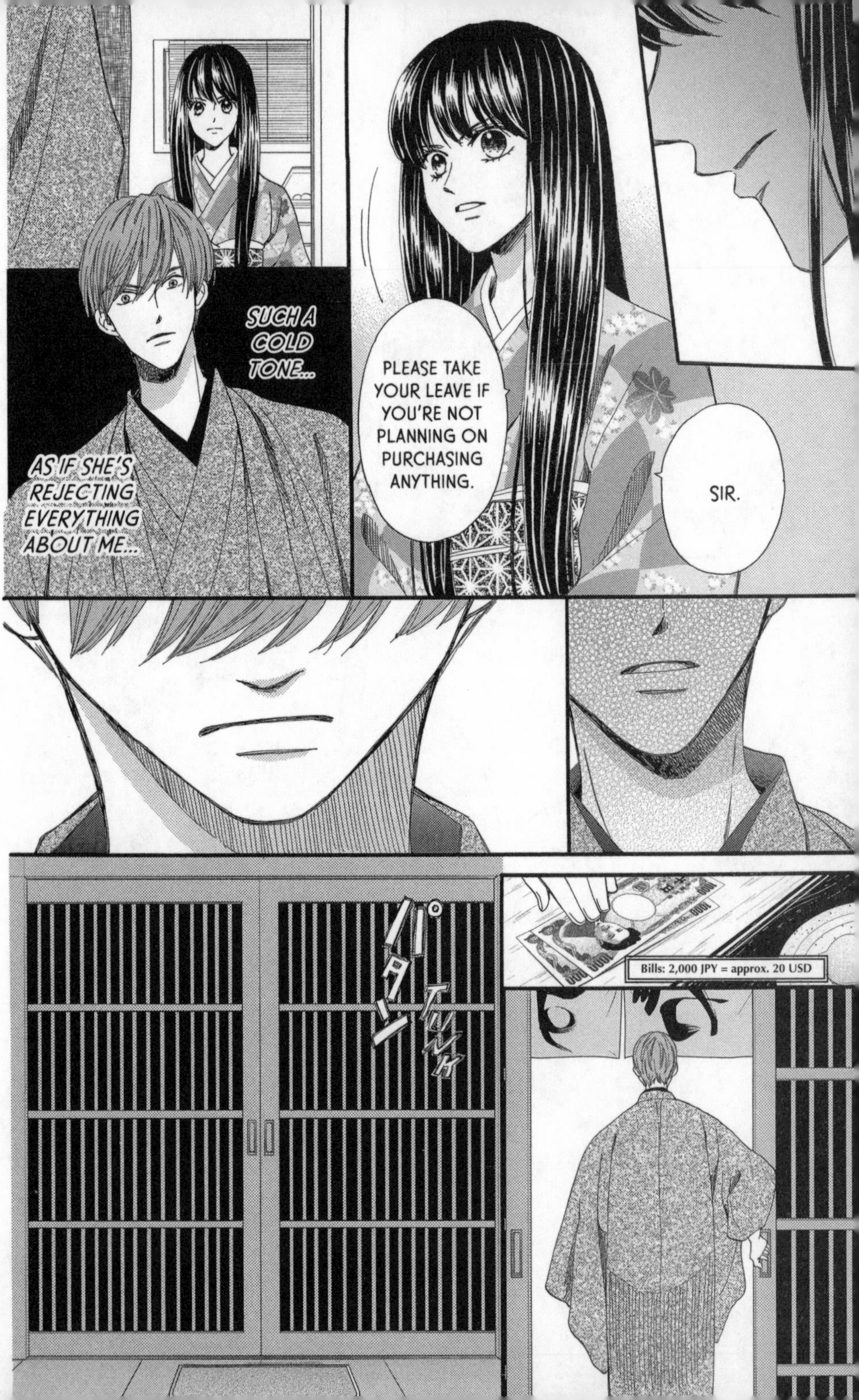
PLEASE TAKE YOUR LEAVE IF YOU'RE NOT PLANNING ON PURCHASING ANYTHING.
SIR.
SUCH A COLD TONE...
AS IF SHE'S REJECTING EVERYTHING ABOUT ME...
Bills: 2,000 JPY = approx. 20 USD
パタン
TINK

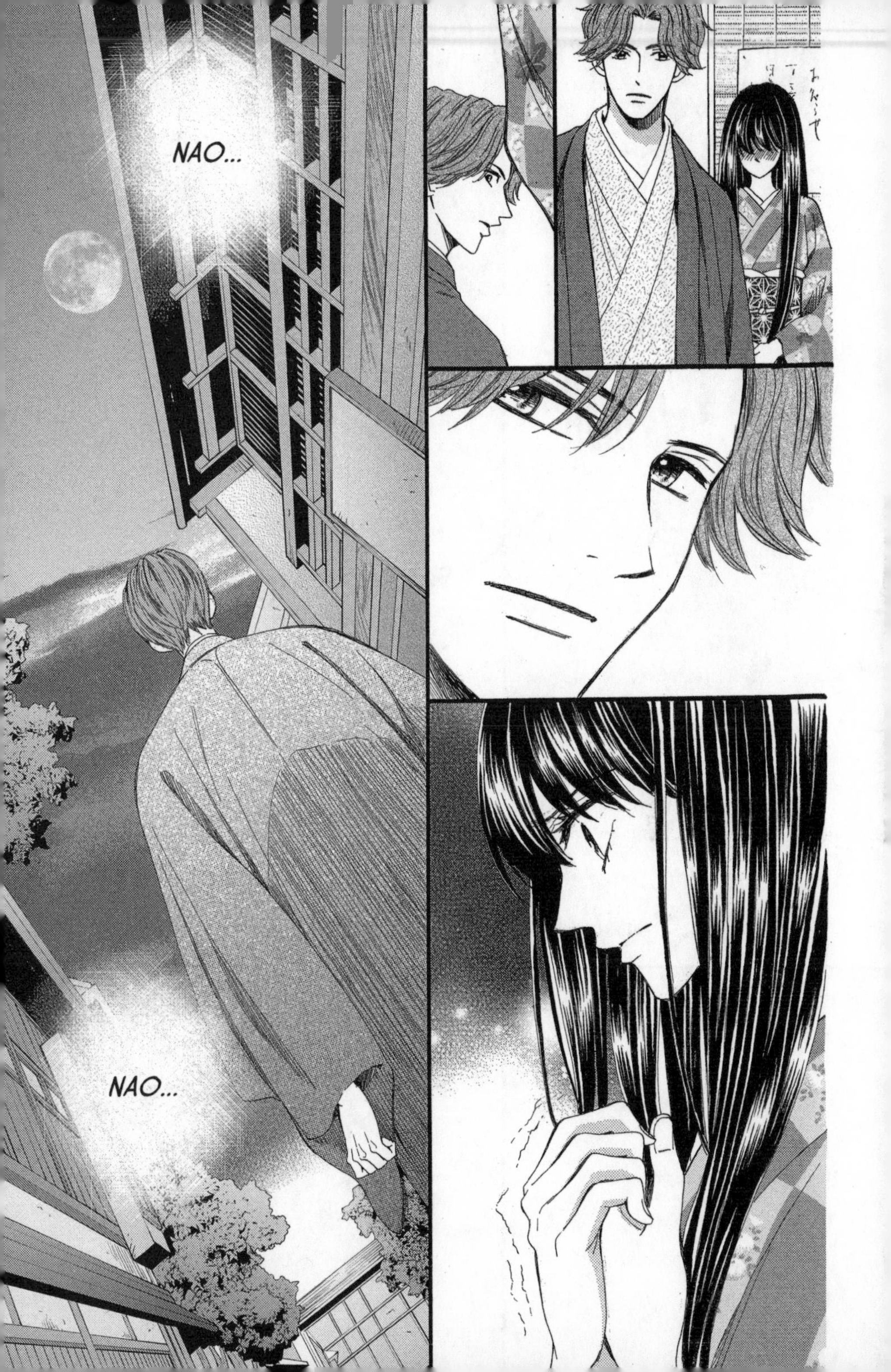
NAO...
NAO...

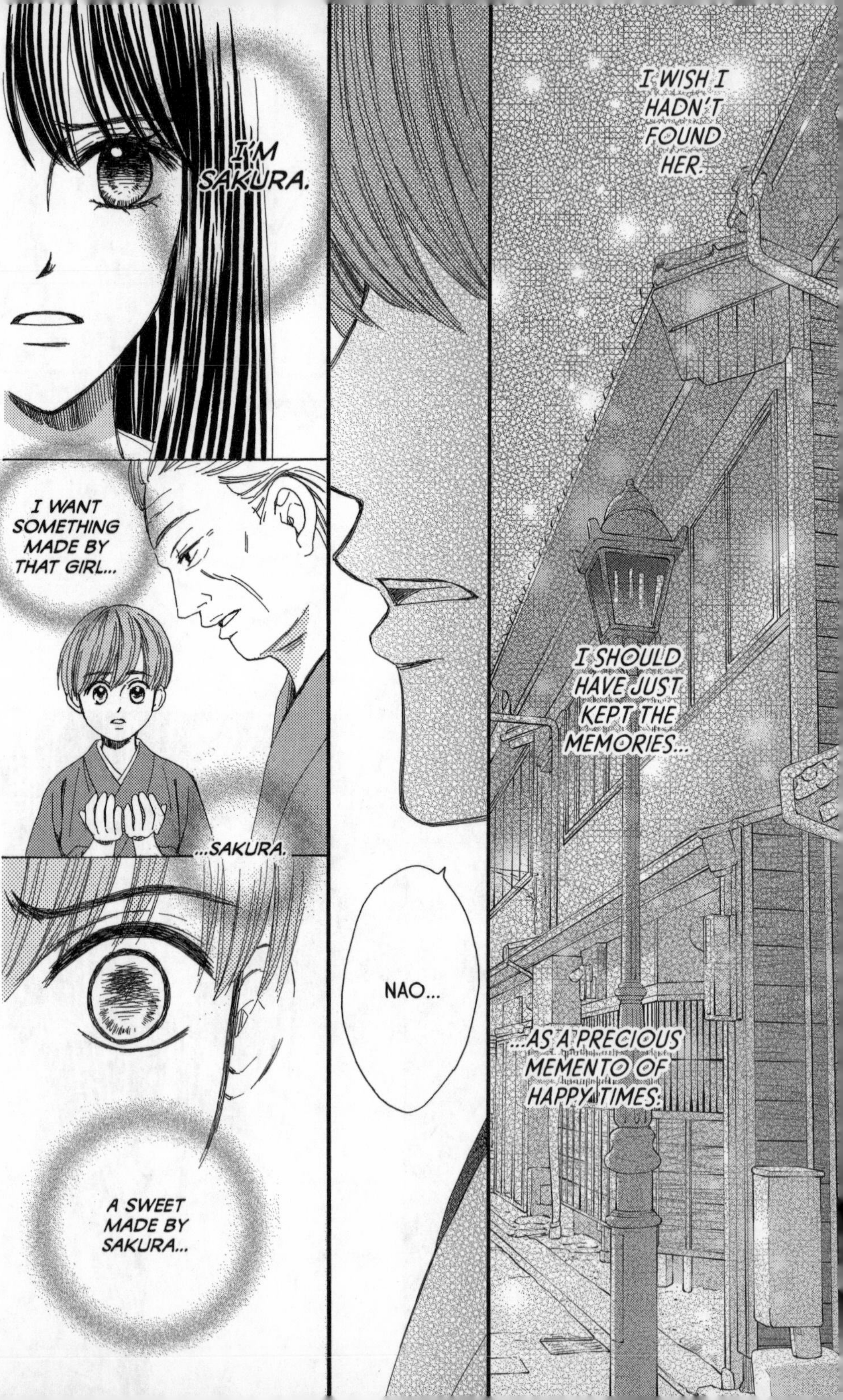
I WISH I HADN'T FOUND HER.
I SHOULD HAVE JUST KEPT THE MEMORIES...
...AS A PRECIOUS MEMENTO OF HAPPY TIMES.
NAO...
I'M SAKURA.
I WANT SOMETHING MADE BY THAT GIRL...
...SAKURA.
A SWEET MADE BY SAKURA...

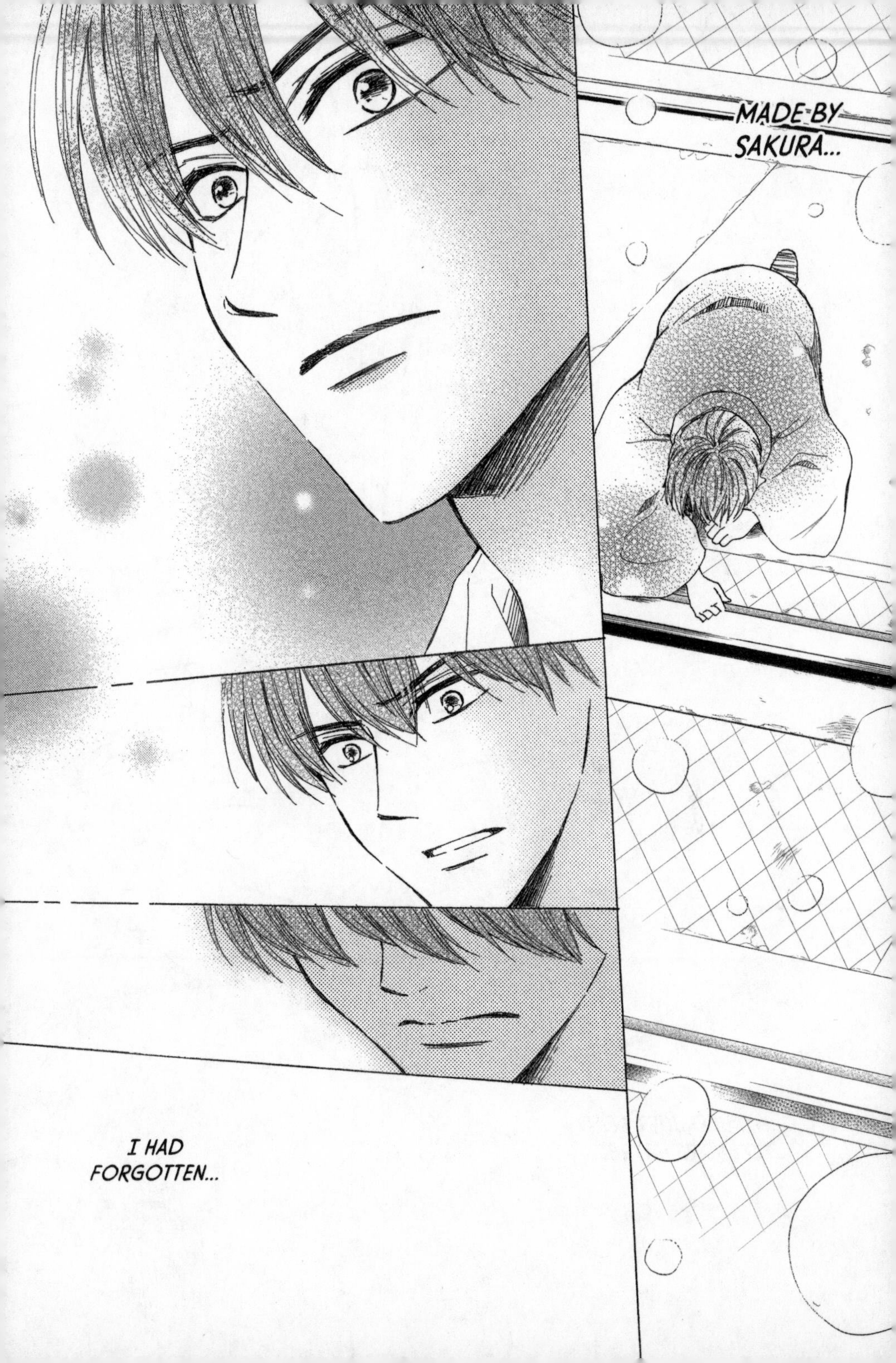
MADE BY SAKURA...
I HAD FORGOTTEN...

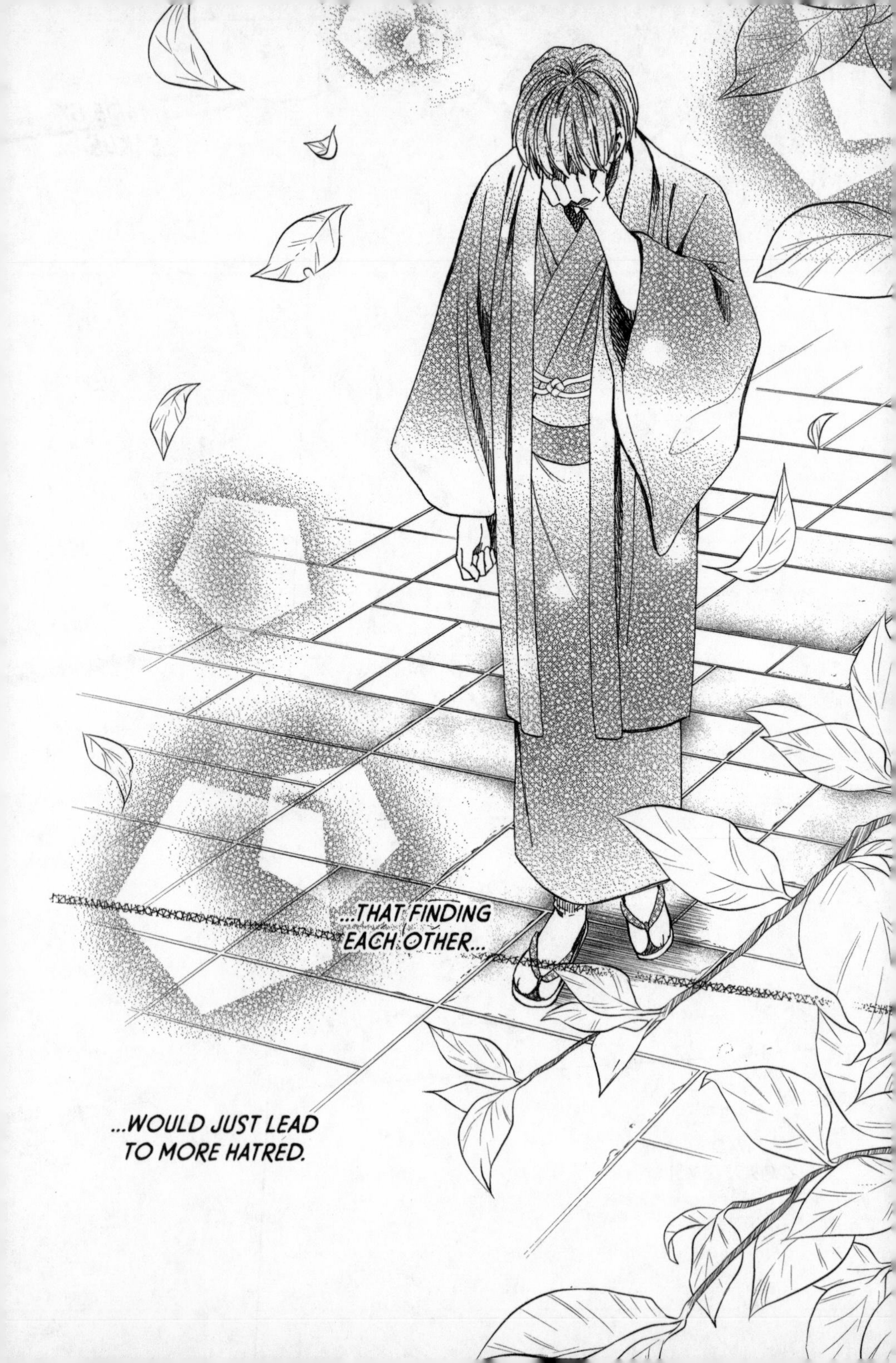
...THAT FINDING EACH OTHER...
...WOULD JUST LEAD TO MORE HATRED.

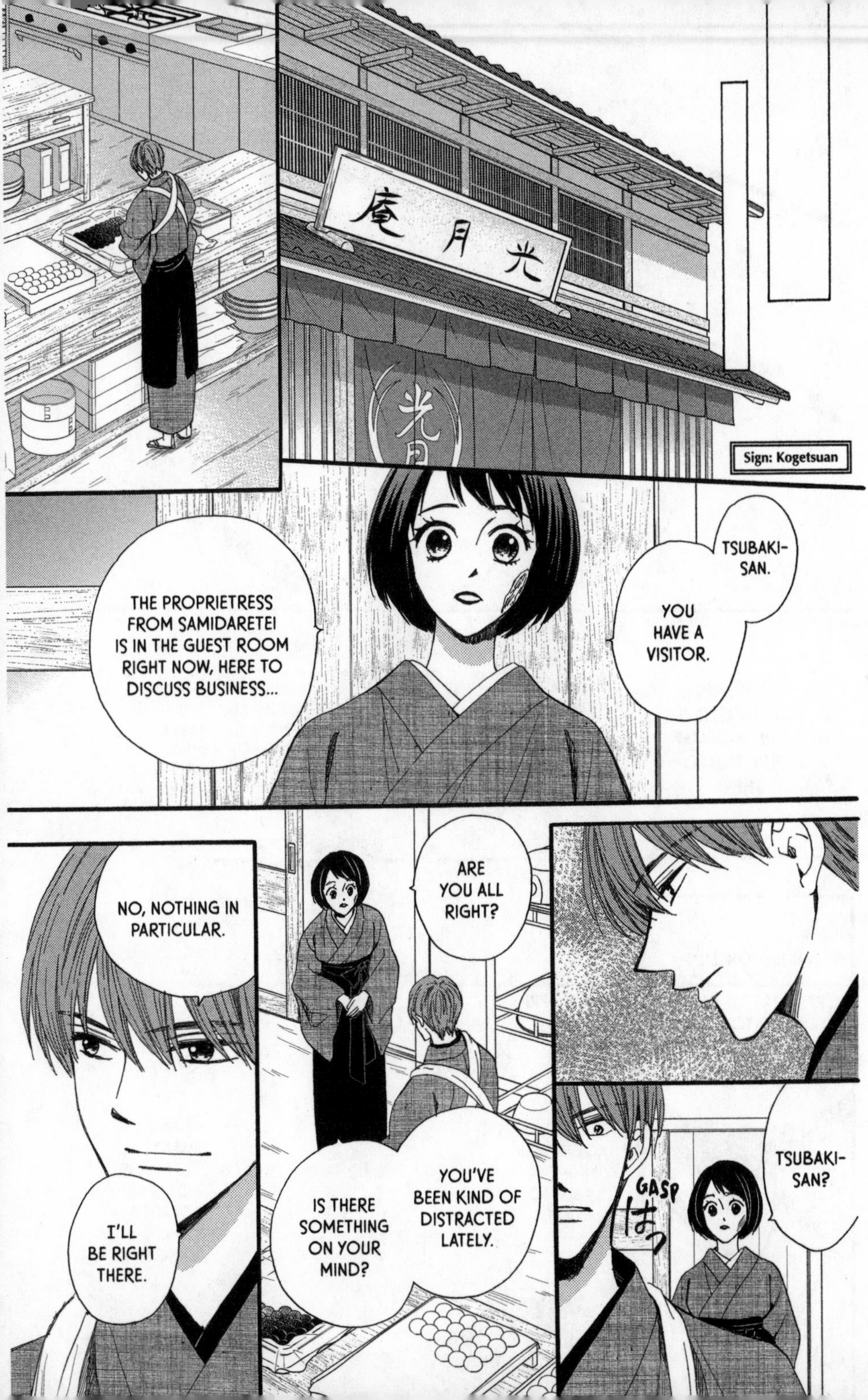
Sign: Kogetsuan
TSUBAKI-SAN.
YOU HAVE A VISITOR.
THE PROPRIETRESS FROM SAMIDARETEI IS IN THE GUEST ROOM RIGHT NOW, HERE TO DISCUSS BUSINESS...
TSUBAKI-SAN?
GASP
はっ
ARE YOU ALL RIGHT?
YOU'VE BEEN KIND OF DISTRACTED LATELY.
IS THERE SOMETHING ON YOUR MIND?
NO, NOTHING IN PARTICULAR.
I'LL BE RIGHT THERE.

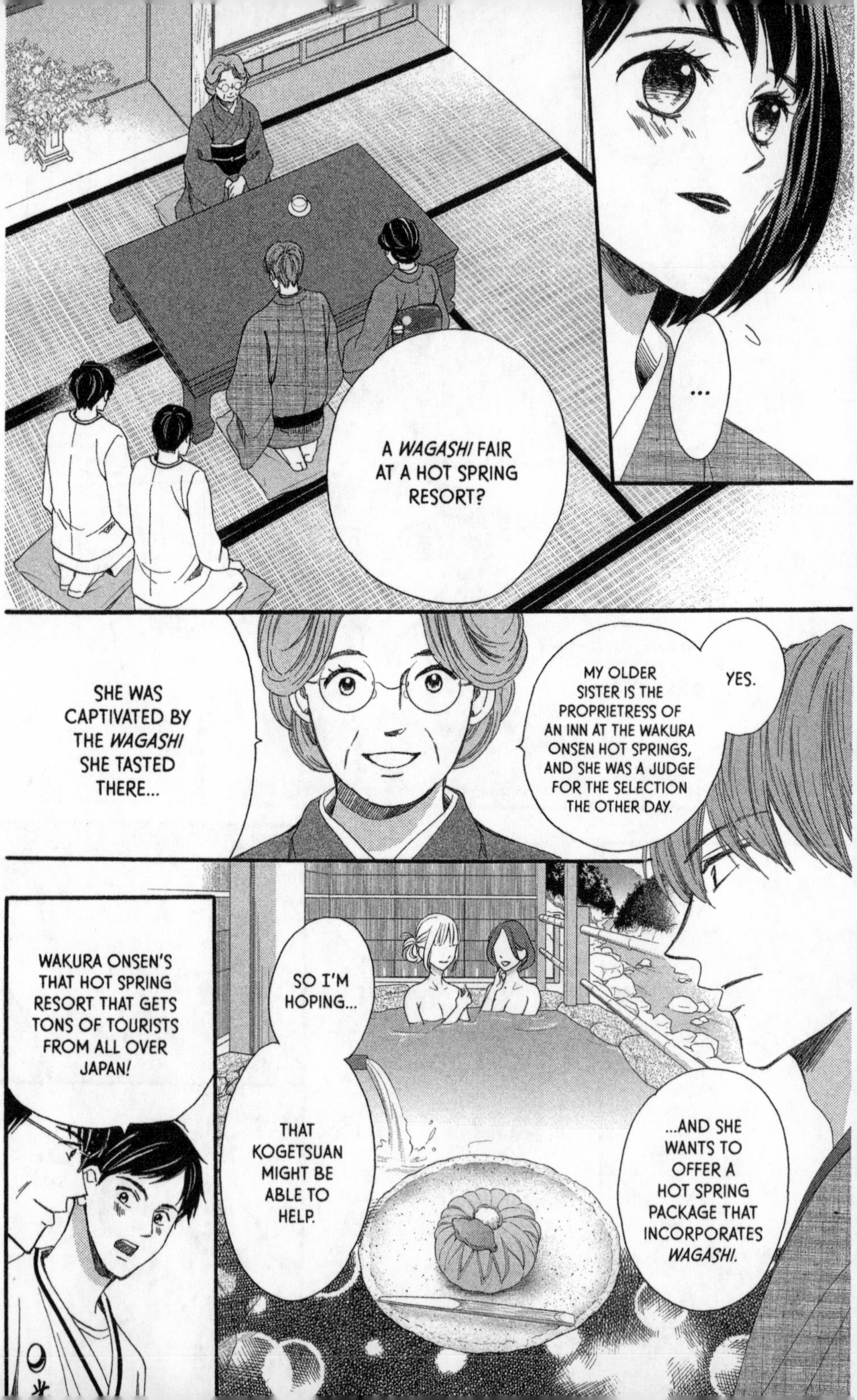
...
A *WAGASHI* FAIR AT A HOT SPRING RESORT?
YES.
MY OLDER SISTER IS THE PROPRIETRESS OF AN INN AT THE WAKURA ONSEN HOT SPRINGS, AND SHE WAS A JUDGE FOR THE SELECTION THE OTHER DAY.
SHE WAS CAPTIVATED BY THE *WAGASHI* SHE TASTED THERE...
...AND SHE WANTS TO OFFER A HOT SPRING PACKAGE THAT INCORPORATES *WAGASHI*.
SO I'M HOPING...
THAT KOGETSUAN MIGHT BE ABLE TO HELP.
WAKURA ONSEN'S THAT HOT SPRING RESORT THAT GETS TONS OF TOURISTS FROM ALL OVER JAPAN!

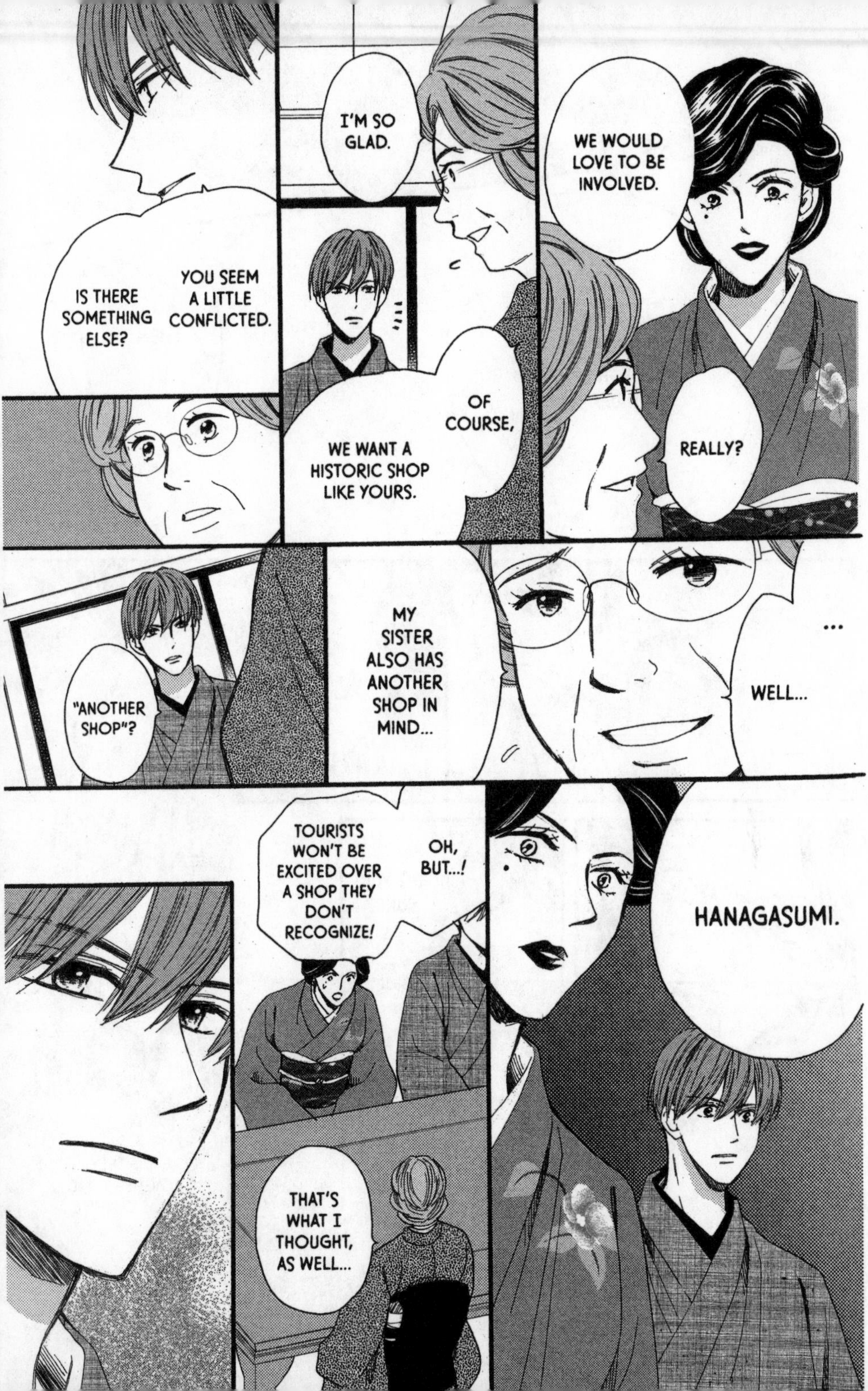

WE WOULD LOVE TO BE INVOLVED.
REALLY?
I'M SO GLAD.
OF COURSE,
WE WANT A HISTORIC SHOP LIKE YOURS.
YOU SEEM A LITTLE CONFLICTED.
IS THERE SOMETHING ELSE?
...
WELL...
MY SISTER ALSO HAS ANOTHER SHOP IN MIND...
"ANOTHER SHOP"?
HANAGASUMI.
OH, BUT...!
TOURISTS WON'T BE EXCITED OVER A SHOP THEY DON'T RECOGNIZE!
THAT'S WHAT I THOUGHT, AS WELL...

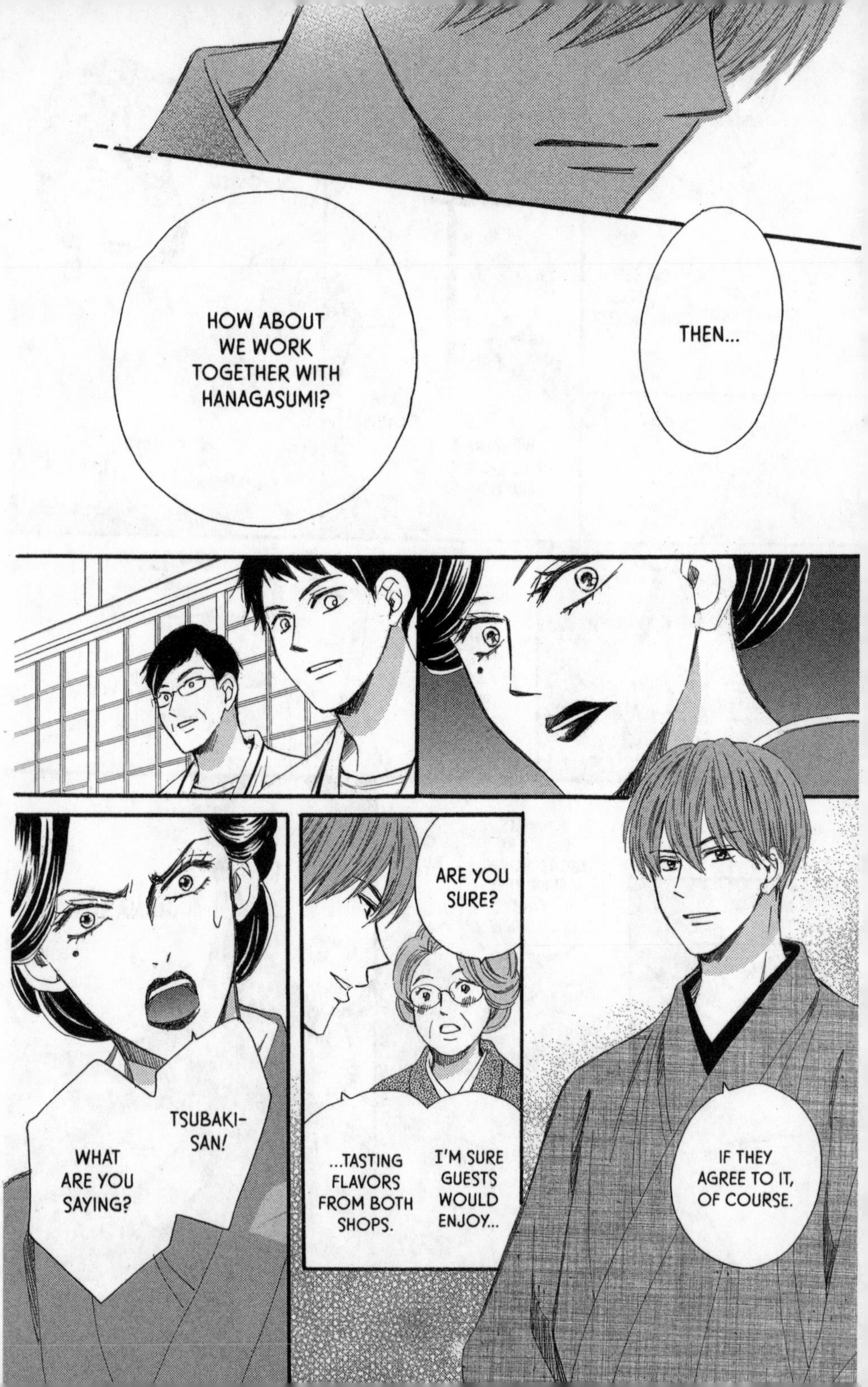
THEN...
HOW ABOUT WE WORK TOGETHER WITH HANAGASUMI?
IF THEY AGREE TO IT, OF COURSE.
ARE YOU SURE?
I'M SURE GUESTS WOULD ENJOY...
...TASTING FLAVORS FROM BOTH SHOPS.
TSUBAKI-SAN!
WHAT ARE YOU SAYING?

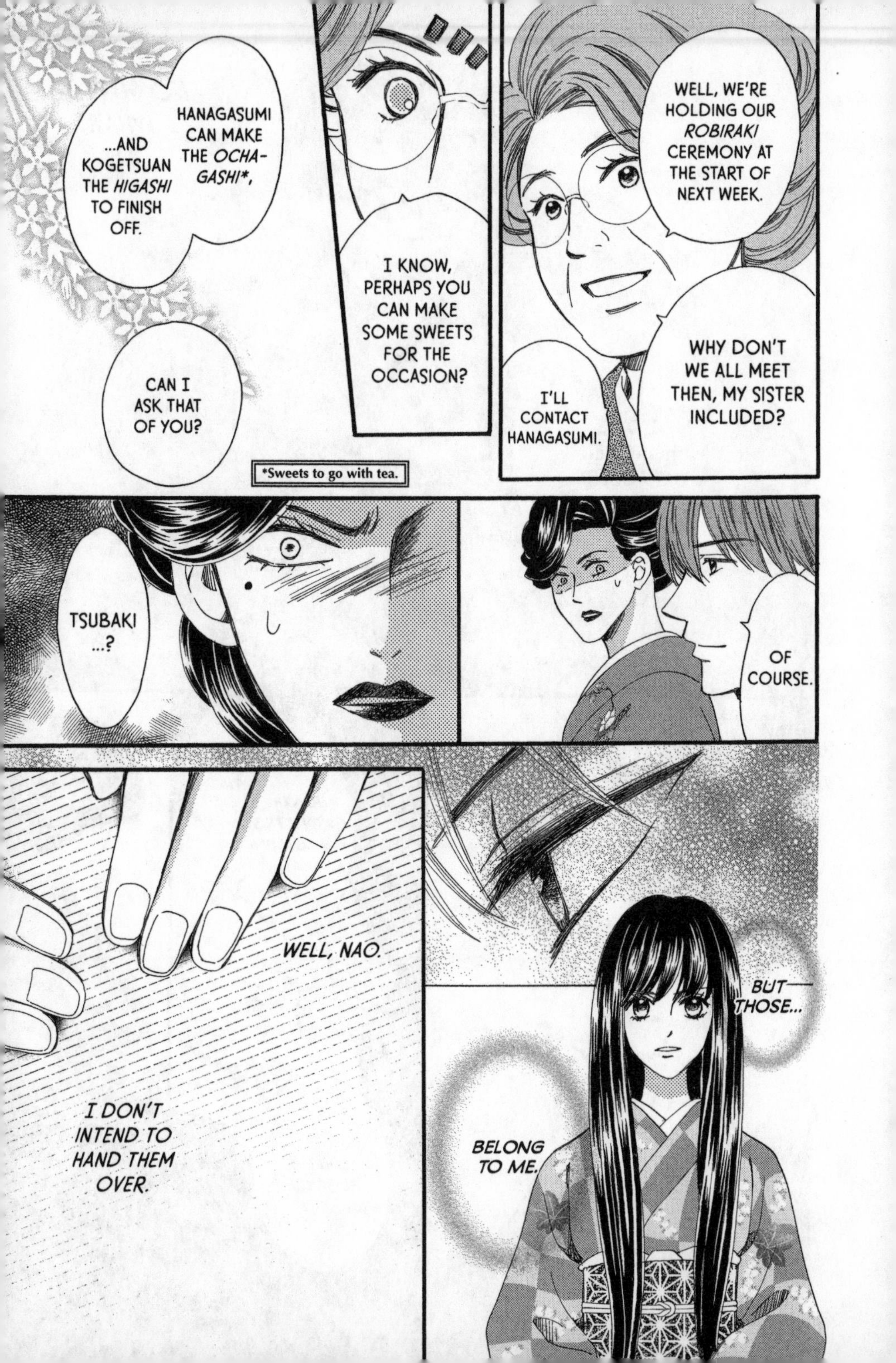
WELL, WE'RE HOLDING OUR *ROBIRAKI* CEREMONY AT THE START OF NEXT WEEK.
WHY DON'T WE ALL MEET THEN, MY SISTER INCLUDED?
I'LL CONTACT HANAGASUMI.
I KNOW, PERHAPS YOU CAN MAKE SOME SWEETS FOR THE OCCASION?
HANAGASUMI CAN MAKE THE *OCHA-GASHI**,
...AND KOGETSUAN THE *HIGASHI* TO FINISH OFF.
CAN I ASK THAT OF YOU?
OF COURSE.
TSUBAKI ...?
BUT— THOSE...
BELONG TO ME.
WELL, NAO.
I DON'T INTEND TO HAND THEM OVER.

*Sweets to go with tea.

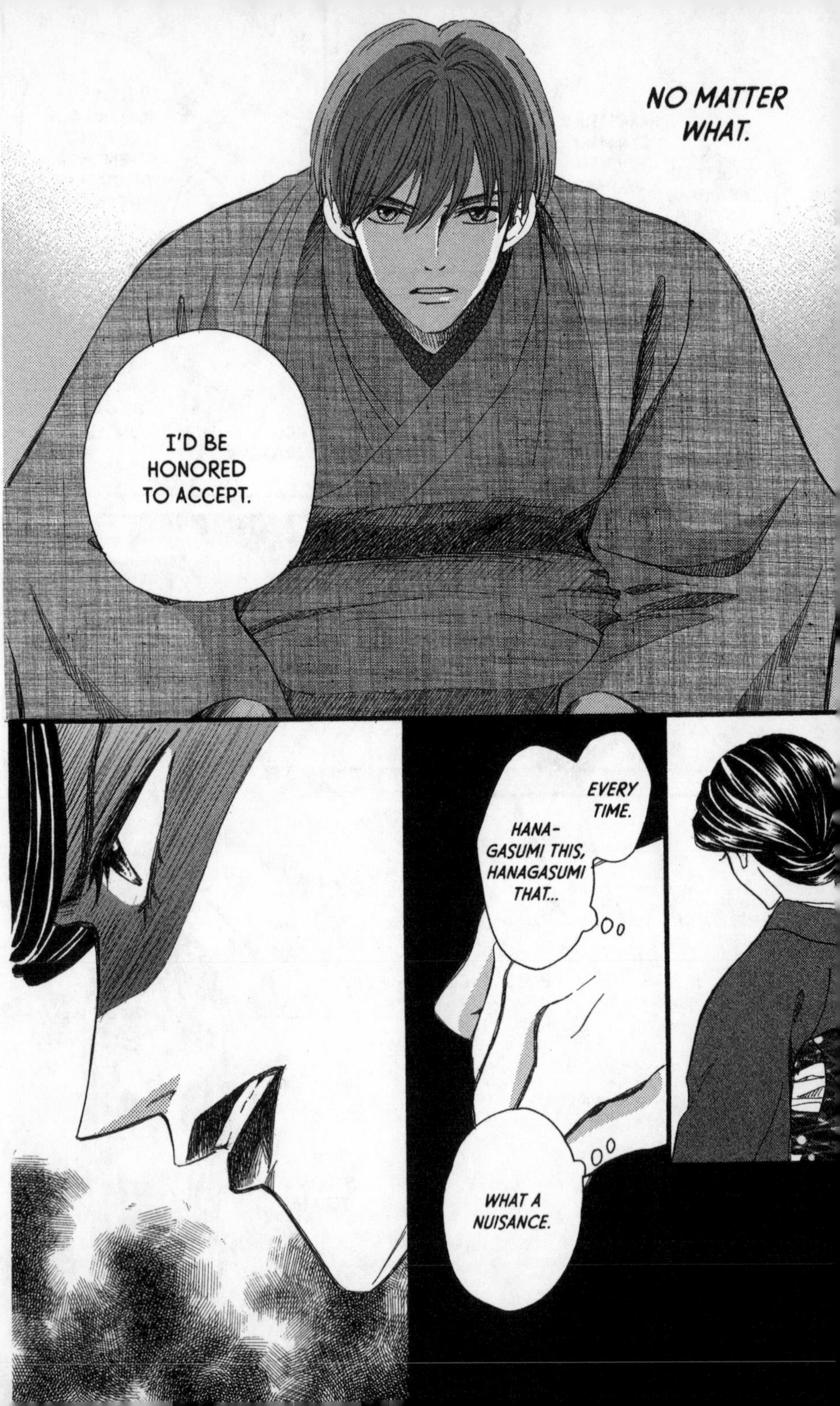
NO MATTER WHAT.
I'D BE HONORED TO ACCEPT.
EVERY TIME.
HANA-GASUMI THIS, HANAGASUMI THAT...
WHAT A NUISANCE.

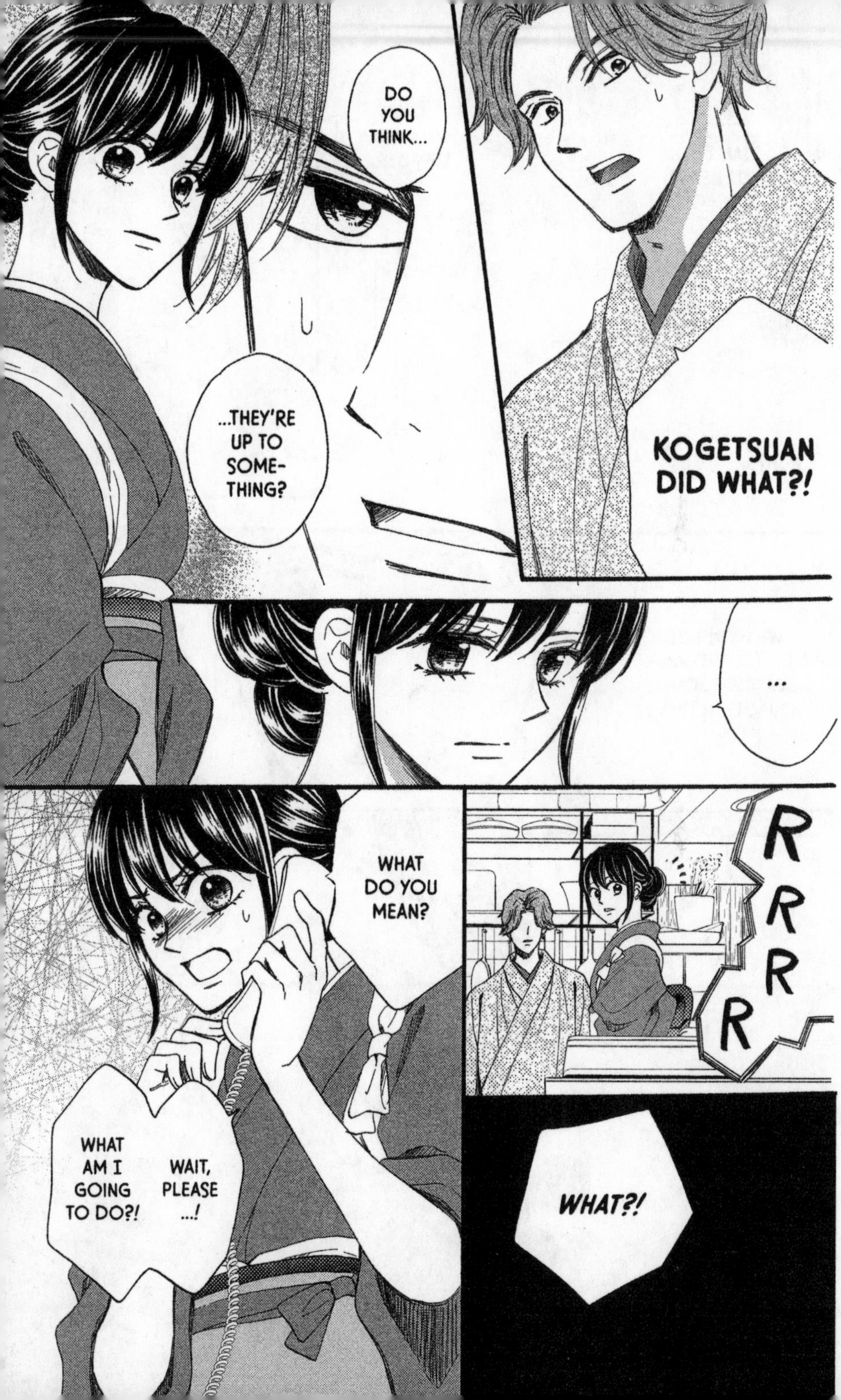
KOGETSUAN DID WHAT?!
DO YOU THINK...
...THEY'RE UP TO SOME-THING?
...
RRRR
WHAT?!
WHAT DO YOU MEAN?
WAIT, PLEASE ...!
WHAT AM I GOING TO DO?!

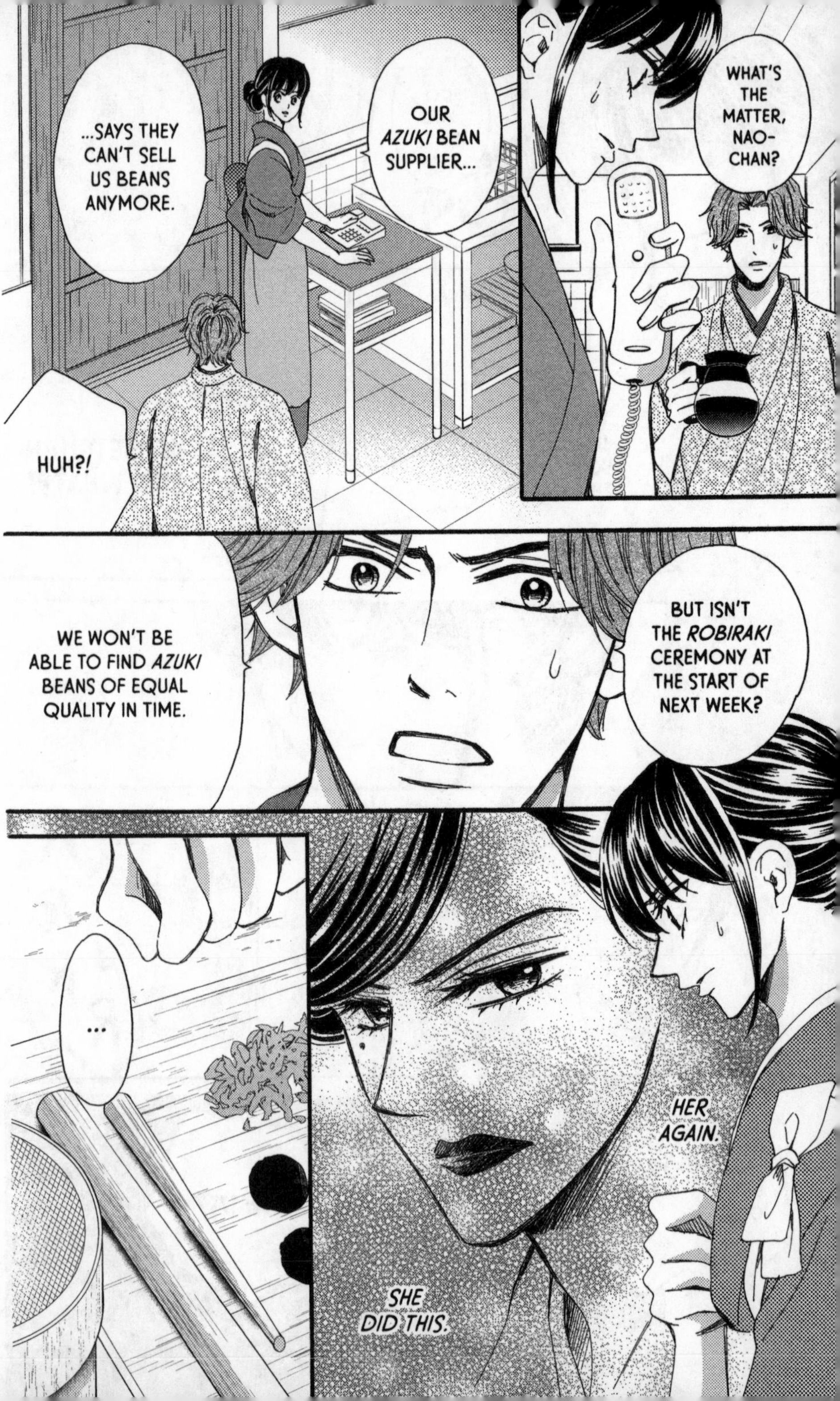
WHAT'S THE MATTER, NAO-CHAN?
OUR AZUKI BEAN SUPPLIER...
...SAYS THEY CAN'T SELL US BEANS ANYMORE.
HUH?!
BUT ISN'T THE ROBIRAKI CEREMONY AT THE START OF NEXT WEEK?
WE WON'T BE ABLE TO FIND AZUKI BEANS OF EQUAL QUALITY IN TIME.
HER AGAIN.
SHE DID THIS.
...

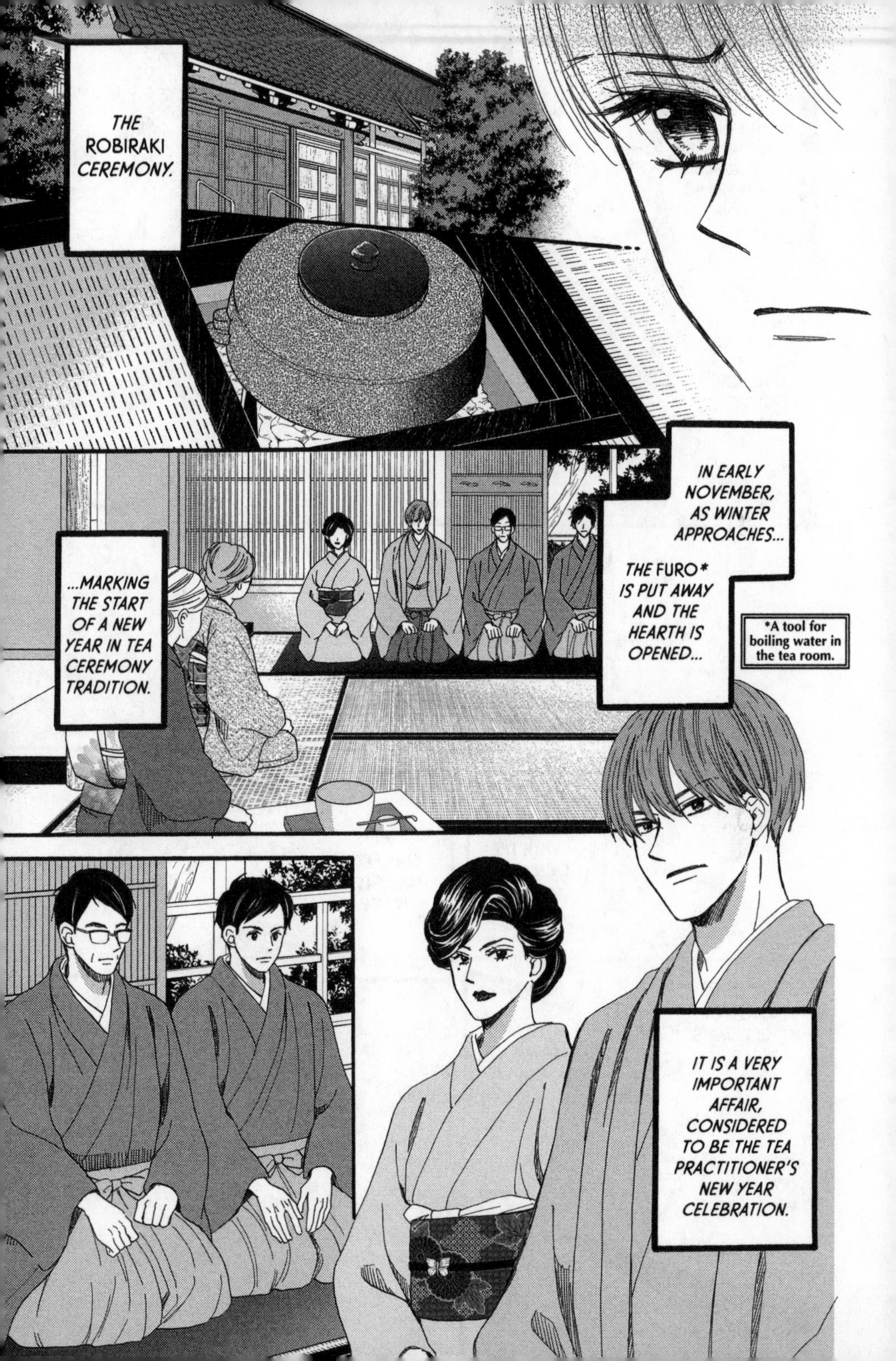
THE ROBIRAKI CEREMONY.
IN EARLY NOVEMBER, AS WINTER APPROACHES...
THE FURO* IS PUT AWAY AND THE HEARTH IS OPENED...
*A tool for boiling water in the tea room.
...MARKING THE START OF A NEW YEAR IN TEA CEREMONY TRADITION.
IT IS A VERY IMPORTANT AFFAIR, CONSIDERED TO BE THE TEA PRACTITIONER'S NEW YEAR CELEBRATION.

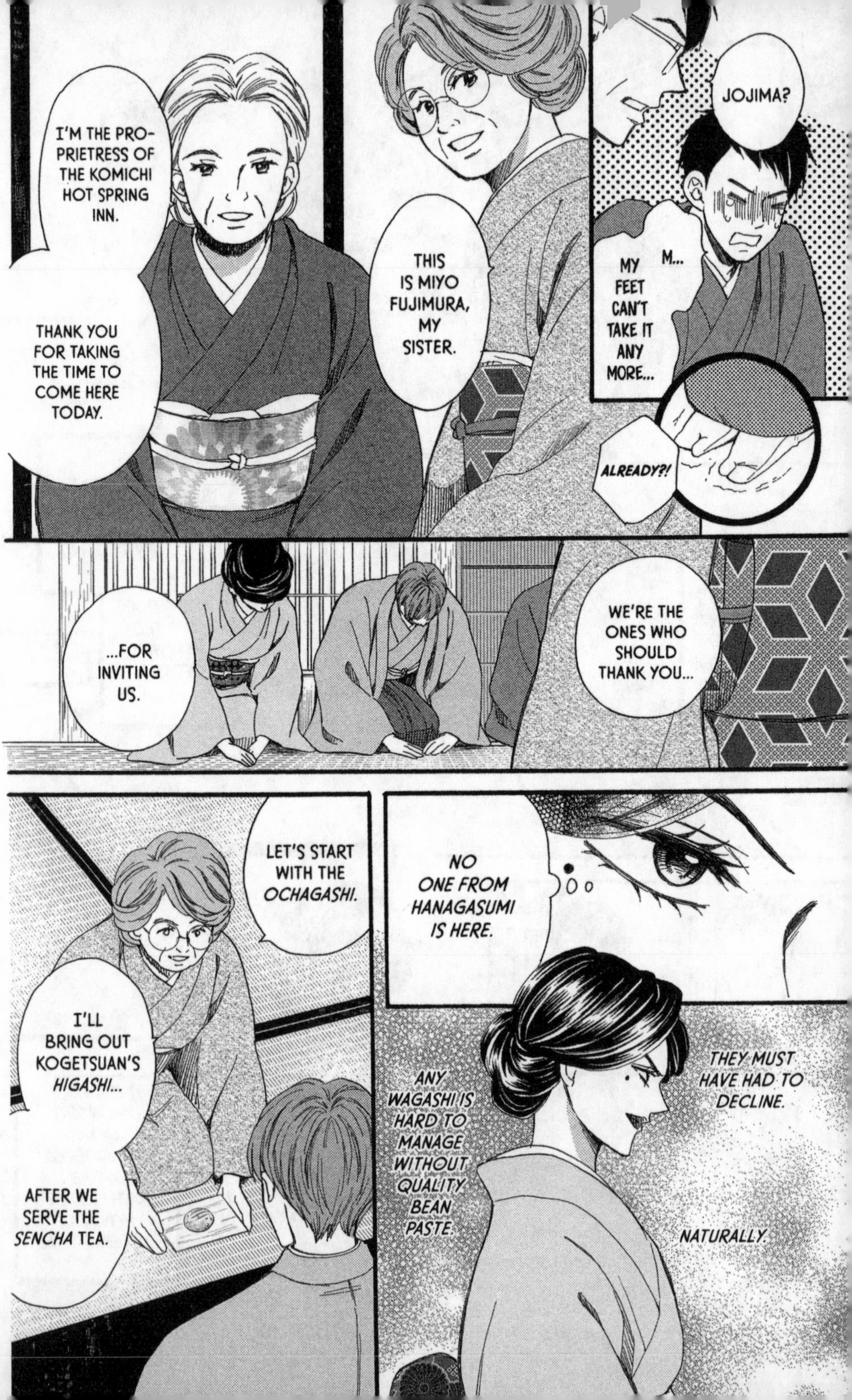
JOJIMA?
M...
MY FEET CAN'T TAKE IT ANY MORE...
ALREADY?!
THIS IS MIYO FUJIMURA, MY SISTER.
I'M THE PRO-PRIETRESS OF THE KOMICHI HOT SPRING INN.
THANK YOU FOR TAKING THE TIME TO COME HERE TODAY.
WE'RE THE ONES WHO SHOULD THANK YOU...
...FOR INVITING US.
NO ONE FROM HANAGASUMI IS HERE.
THEY MUST HAVE HAD TO DECLINE.
ANY WAGASHI IS HARD TO MANAGE WITHOUT QUALITY BEAN PASTE.
NATURALLY.
LET'S START WITH THE *OCHAGASHI*.
I'LL BRING OUT KOGETSUAN'S *HIGASHI*...
AFTER WE SERVE THE *SENCHA* TEA.

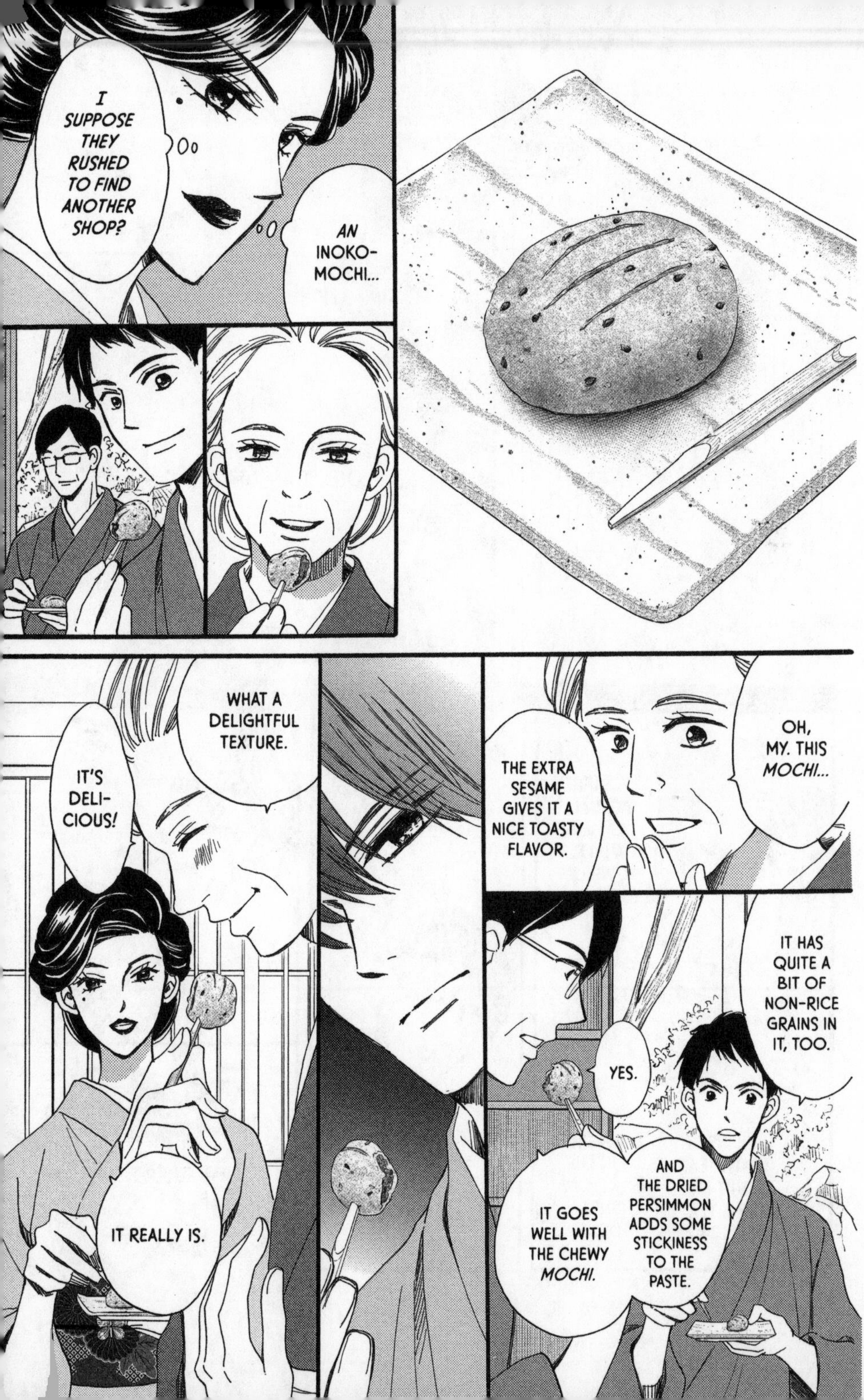

AN INOKO-MOCHI...
I SUPPOSE THEY RUSHED TO FIND ANOTHER SHOP?
OH, MY. THIS *MOCHI*...
THE EXTRA SESAME GIVES IT A NICE TOASTY FLAVOR.
IT HAS QUITE A BIT OF NON-RICE GRAINS IN IT, TOO.
YES.
AND THE DRIED PERSIMMON ADDS SOME STICKINESS TO THE PASTE.
IT GOES WELL WITH THE CHEWY *MOCHI*.
WHAT A DELIGHTFUL TEXTURE.
IT'S DELI-CIOUS!
IT REALLY IS.

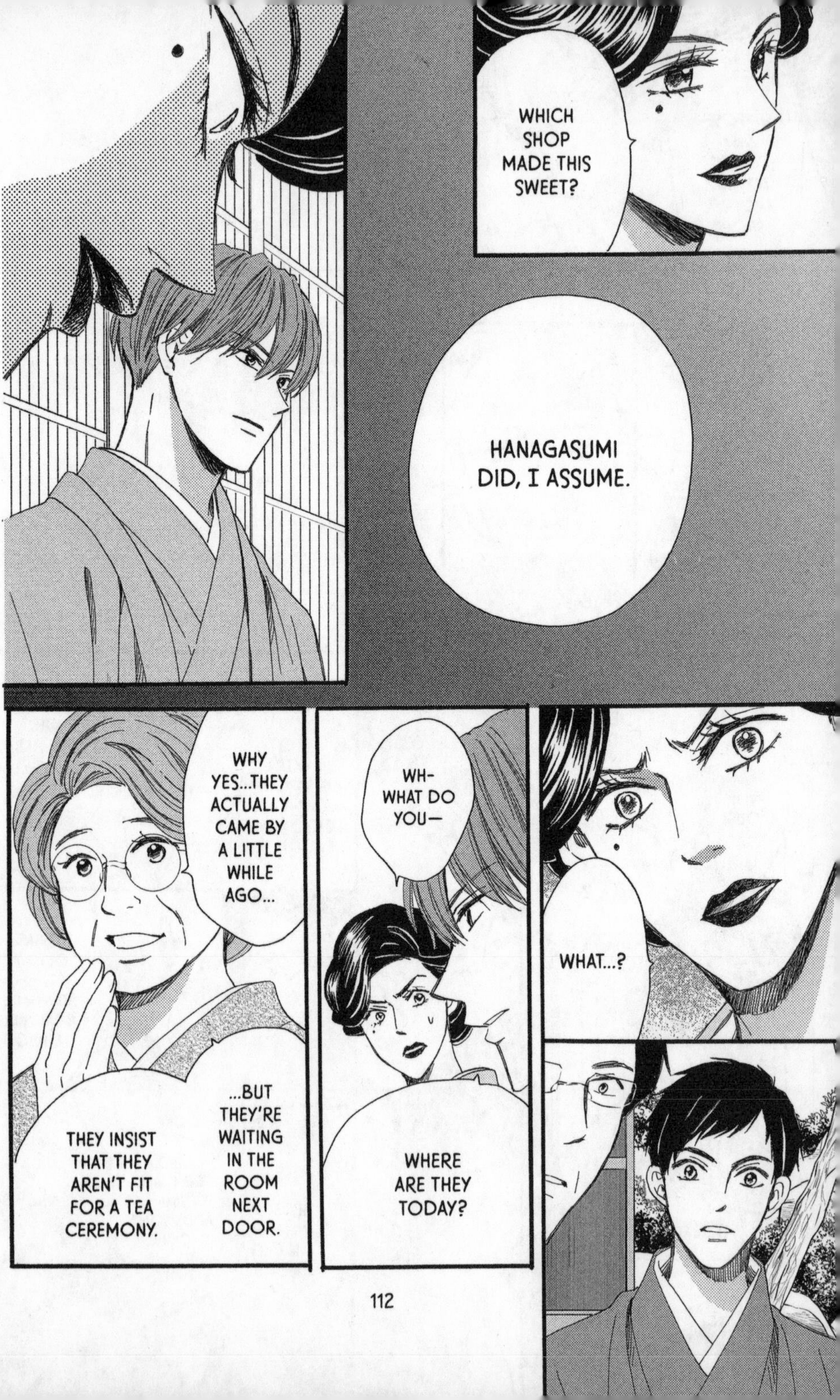
WHICH SHOP MADE THIS SWEET?
HANAGASUMI DID, I ASSUME.
WHAT...?
WH- WHAT DO YOU—
WHERE ARE THEY TODAY?
WHY YES...THEY ACTUALLY CAME BY A LITTLE WHILE AGO...
...BUT THEY'RE WAITING IN THE ROOM NEXT DOOR.
THEY INSIST THAT THEY AREN'T FIT FOR A TEA CEREMONY.

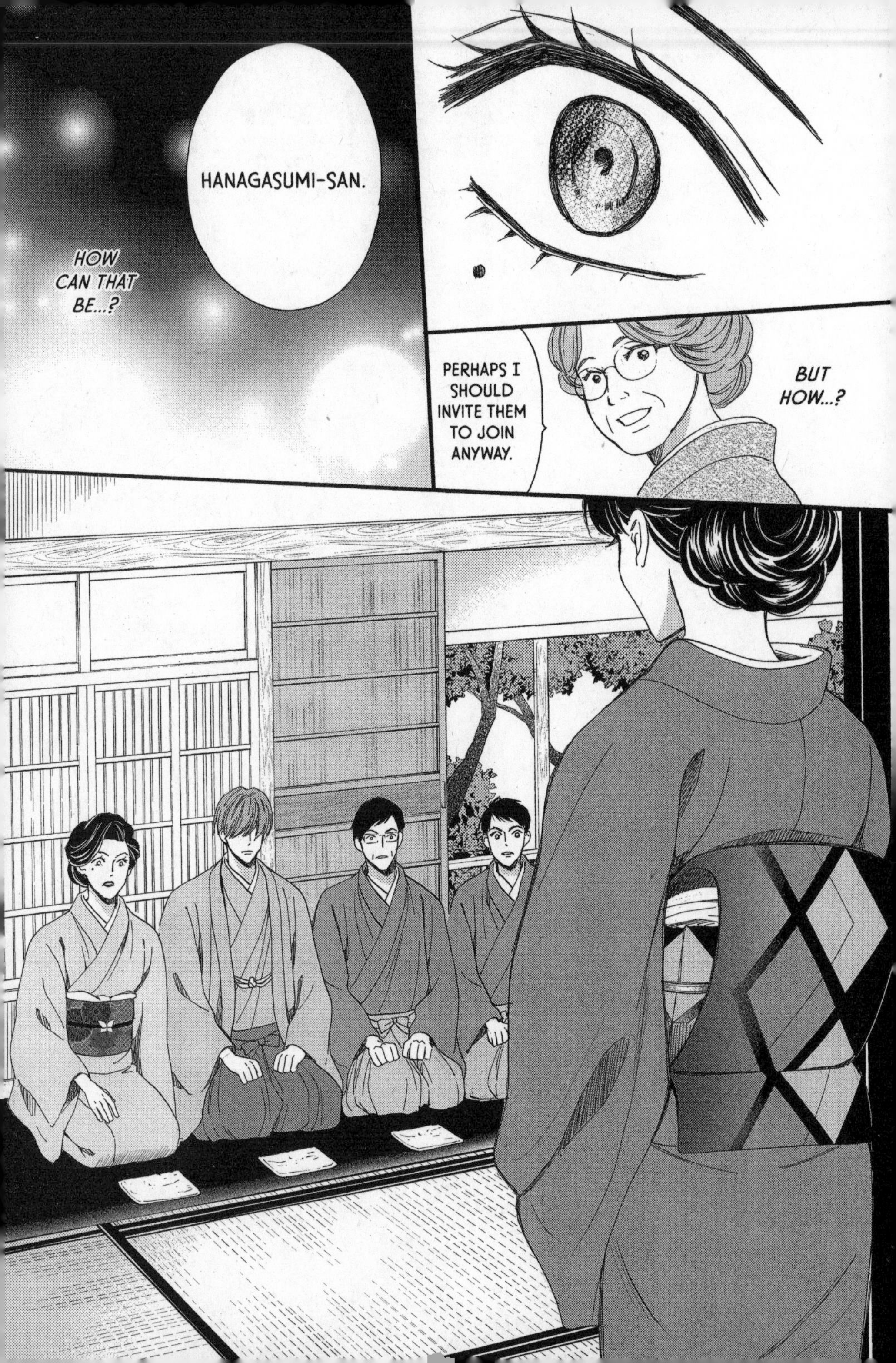
BUT HOW...?
PERHAPS I SHOULD INVITE THEM TO JOIN ANYWAY.
HANAGASUMI-SAN.
HOW CAN THAT BE...?

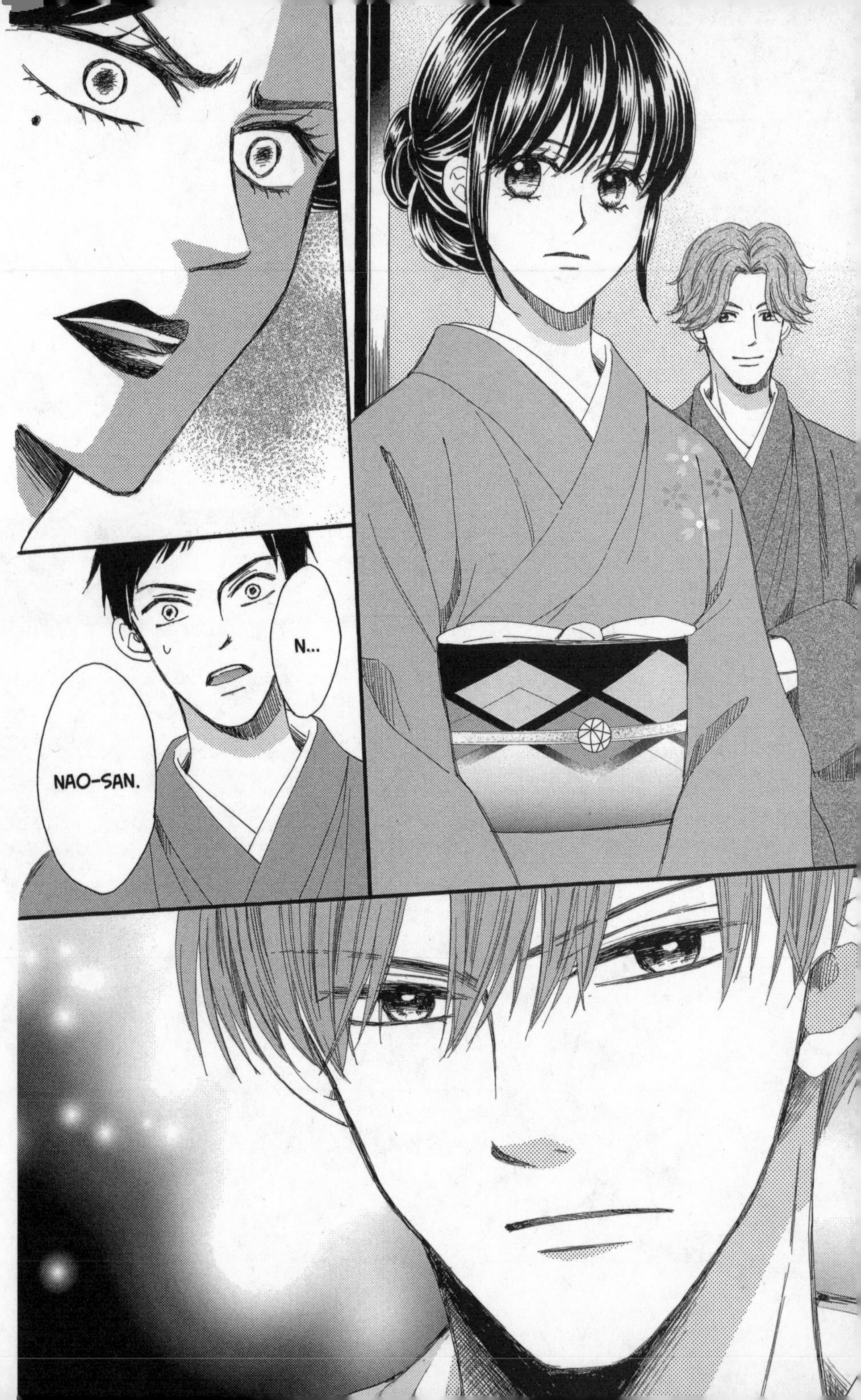
N...
NAO-SAN.

Chapter 45 *Wakura Onsen*

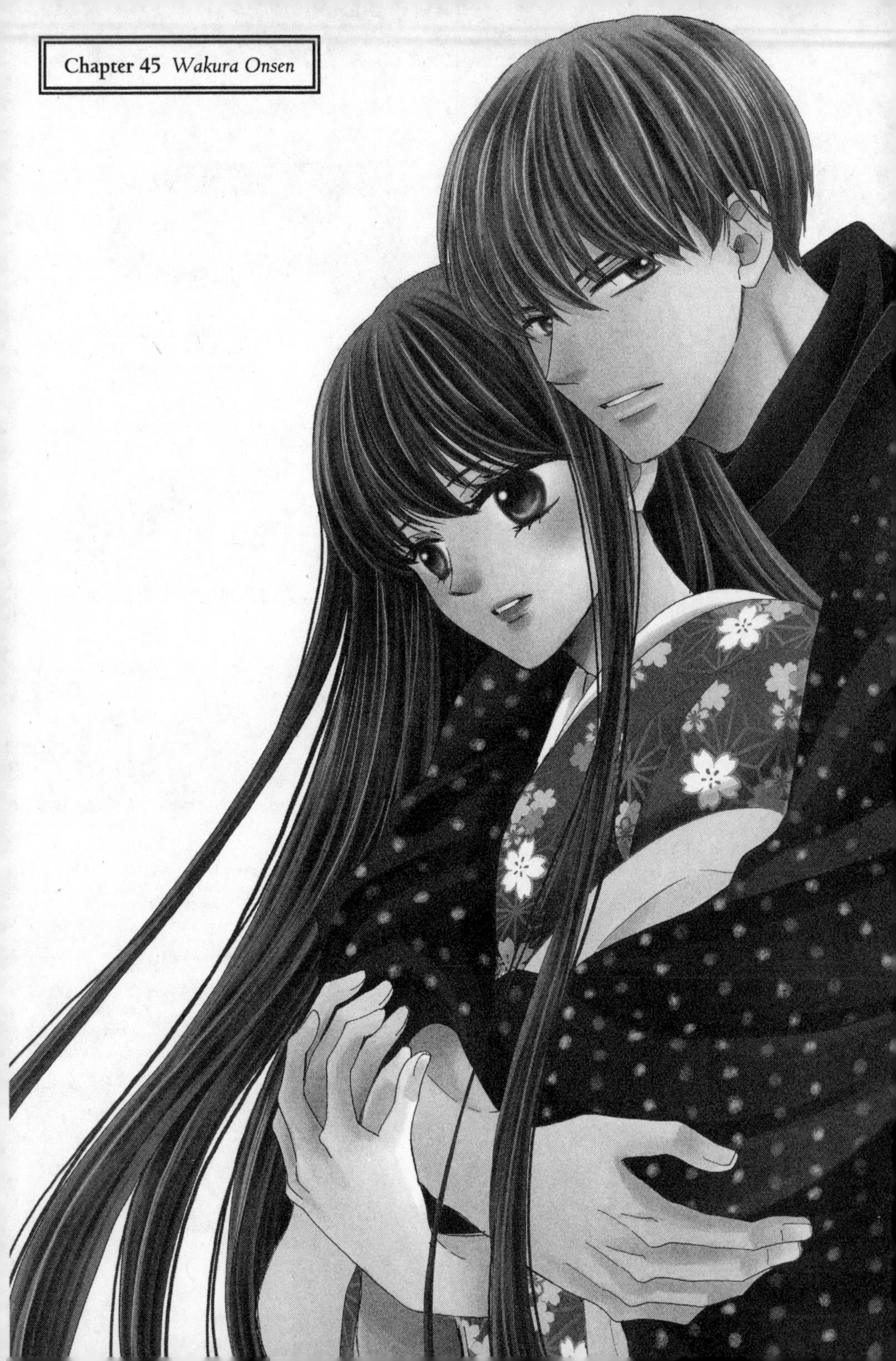

Tracing Something's Wrong With Us

on

A Tour Around KANAZAWA 🌸

Here are some of the many, many photos I took when scoping out Kanazawa.

Kanazawa's "gateway," the Tsuzumi-mon. What a sight! Understandably chosen as one of the 14 most beautiful train stations in the world.

Ishikawa-mon gate of the Kanazawa Castle. It was sakura season and a row of sakura trees stretch beyond the gate.

The Kazue-machi Chaya District. I used it in volume 2 in the scene where Tsubaki holds Nao's hand to "act like a married couple."

The Asano River that runs near the Higashi Chaya District. Shiori slept on these banks after she left home.

The 21st Century Museum of Contemporary Art. I haven't been in yet, so I want to check it out the next time I go!

Gold leaf soft-serve ice cream, Kanazawa's specialty, and the wagashi I got to eat at the Hyakumangoku Festival in June.

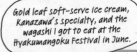

The must-visit tourist spot, Kenrokuen Garden. There are a few tea houses on the grounds that always draw me in!

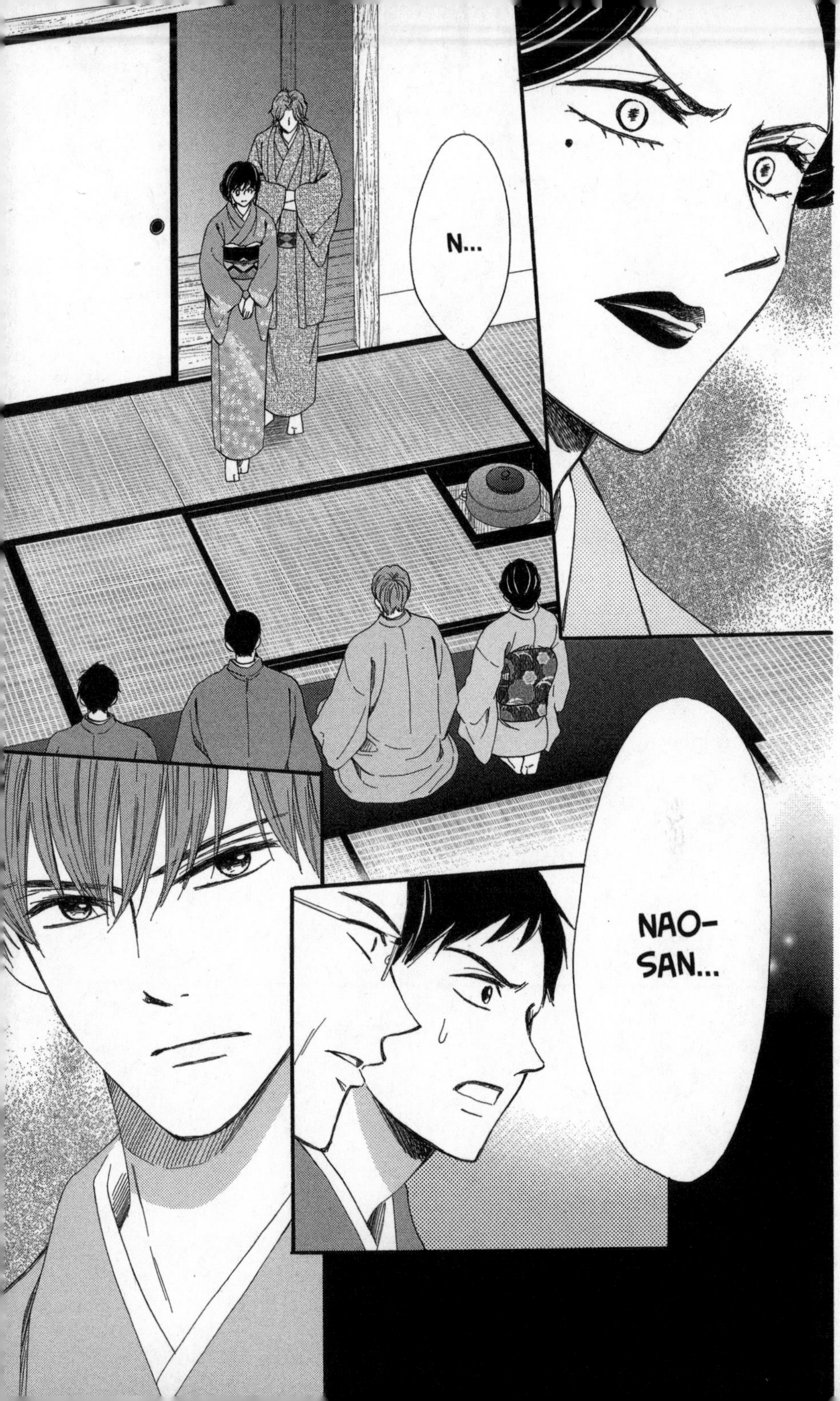
N...
NAO-SAN...

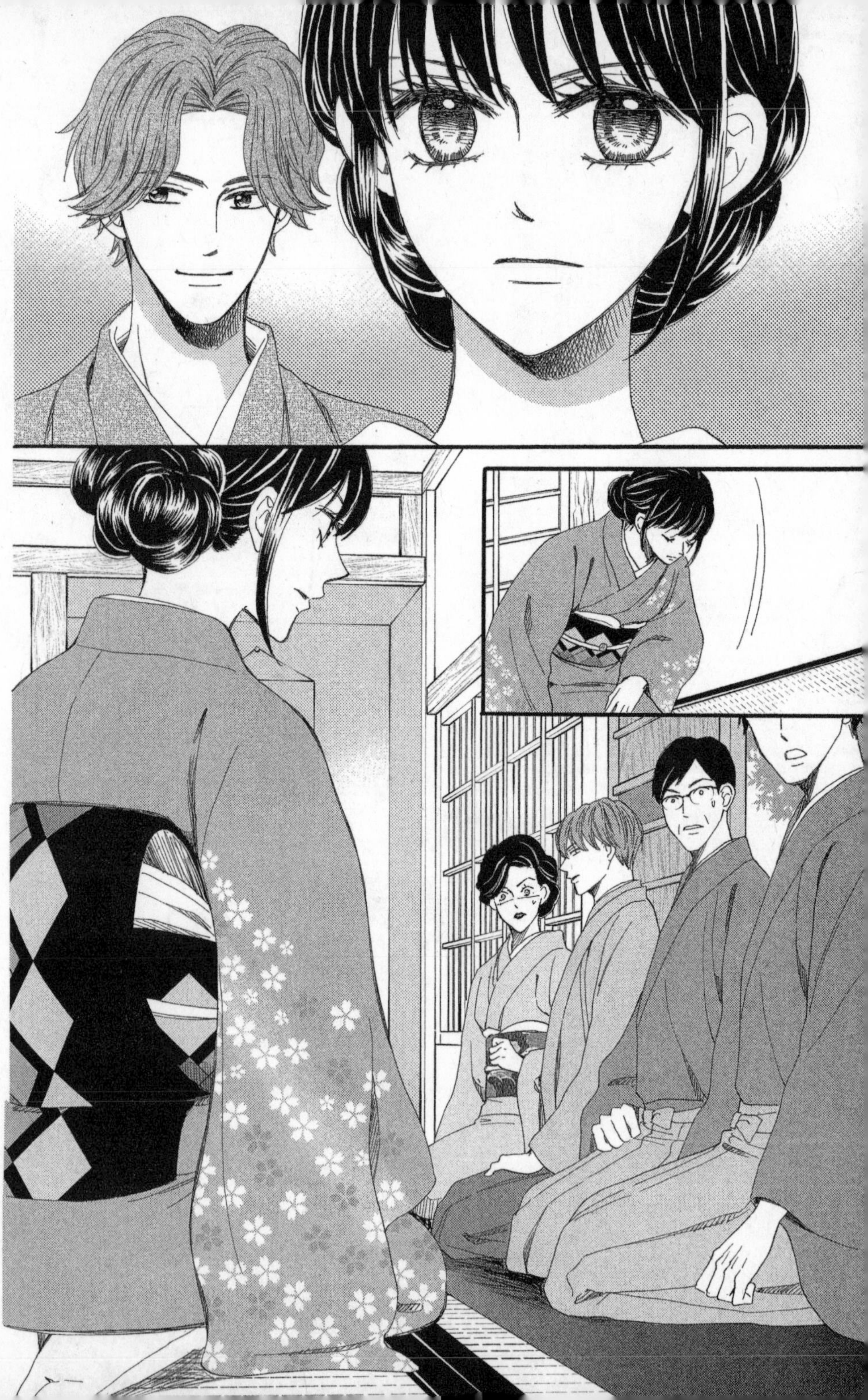

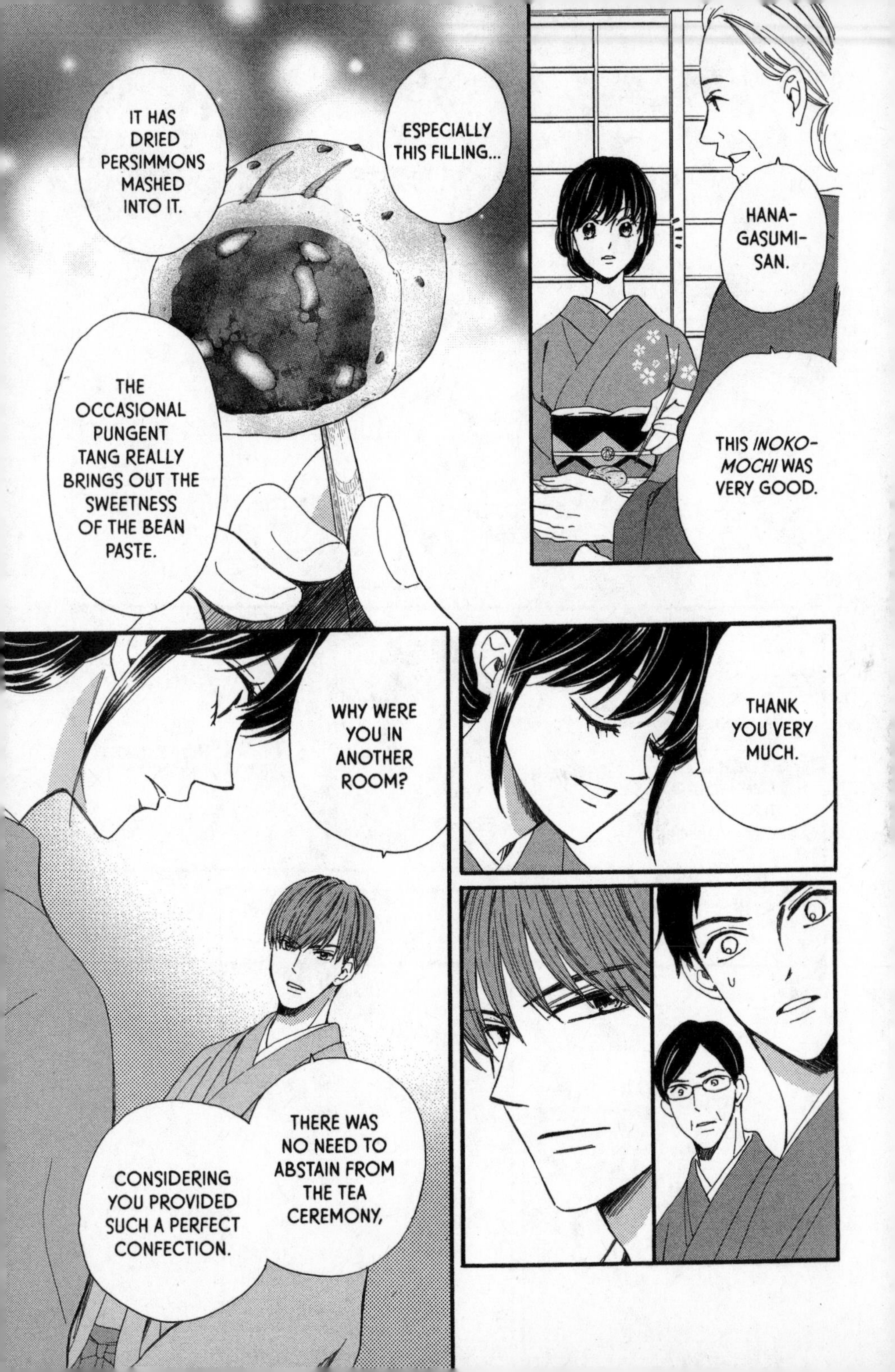
HANA-GASUMI-SAN.
THIS INOKO-MOCHI WAS VERY GOOD.
ESPECIALLY THIS FILLING...
IT HAS DRIED PERSIMMONS MASHED INTO IT.
THE OCCASIONAL PUNGENT TANG REALLY BRINGS OUT THE SWEETNESS OF THE BEAN PASTE.
THANK YOU VERY MUCH.
WHY WERE YOU IN ANOTHER ROOM?
THERE WAS NO NEED TO ABSTAIN FROM THE TEA CEREMONY,
CONSIDERING YOU PROVIDED SUCH A PERFECT CONFECTION.

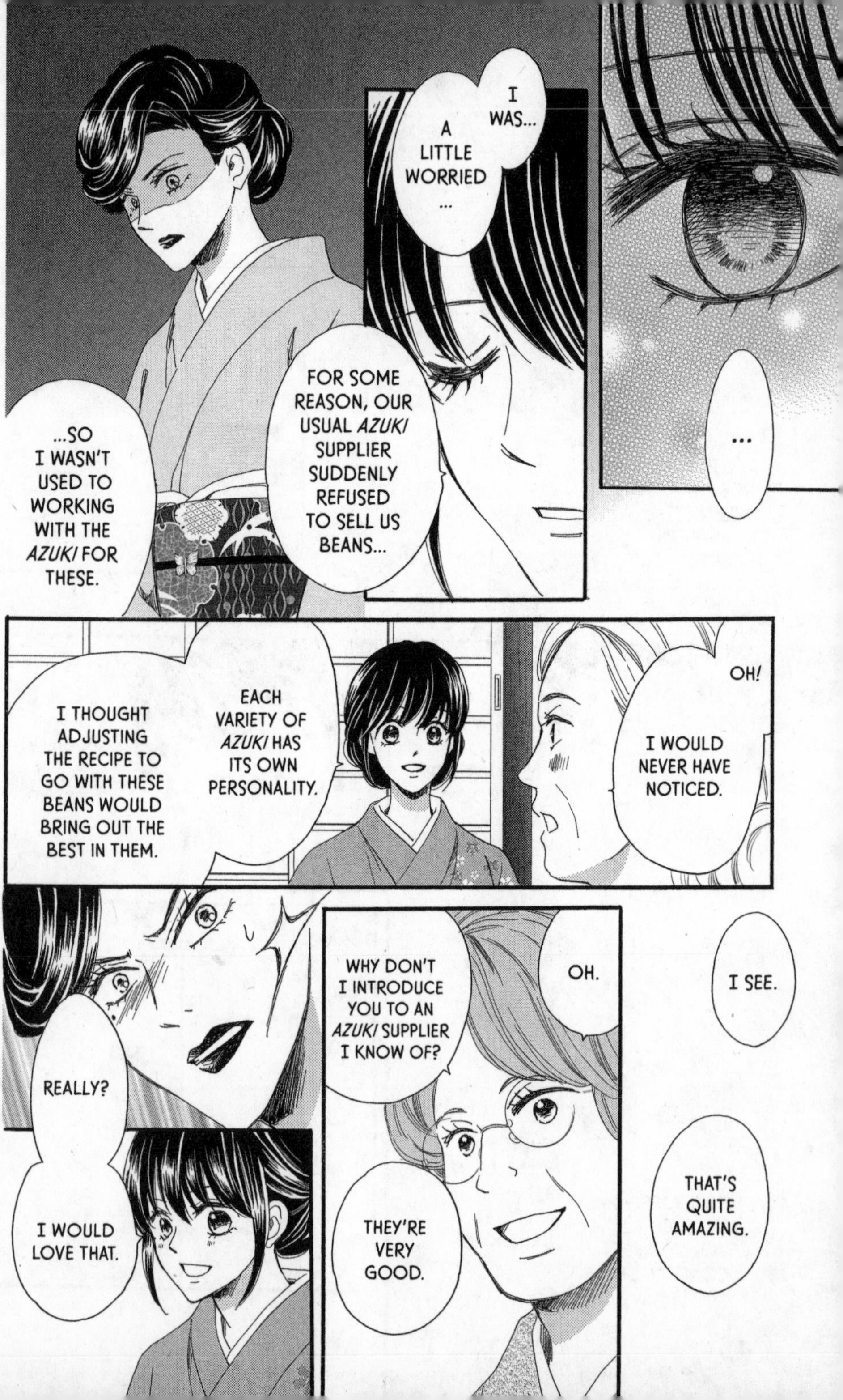
...
I WAS... A LITTLE WORRIED ...
FOR SOME REASON, OUR USUAL *AZUKI* SUPPLIER SUDDENLY REFUSED TO SELL US BEANS...
...SO I WASN'T USED TO WORKING WITH THE *AZUKI* FOR THESE.
OH!
I WOULD NEVER HAVE NOTICED.
EACH VARIETY OF *AZUKI* HAS ITS OWN PERSONALITY.
I THOUGHT ADJUSTING THE RECIPE TO GO WITH THESE BEANS WOULD BRING OUT THE BEST IN THEM.
I SEE.
THAT'S QUITE AMAZING.
THEY'RE VERY GOOD.
OH.
WHY DON'T I INTRODUCE YOU TO AN *AZUKI* SUPPLIER I KNOW OF?
REALLY?
I WOULD LOVE THAT.

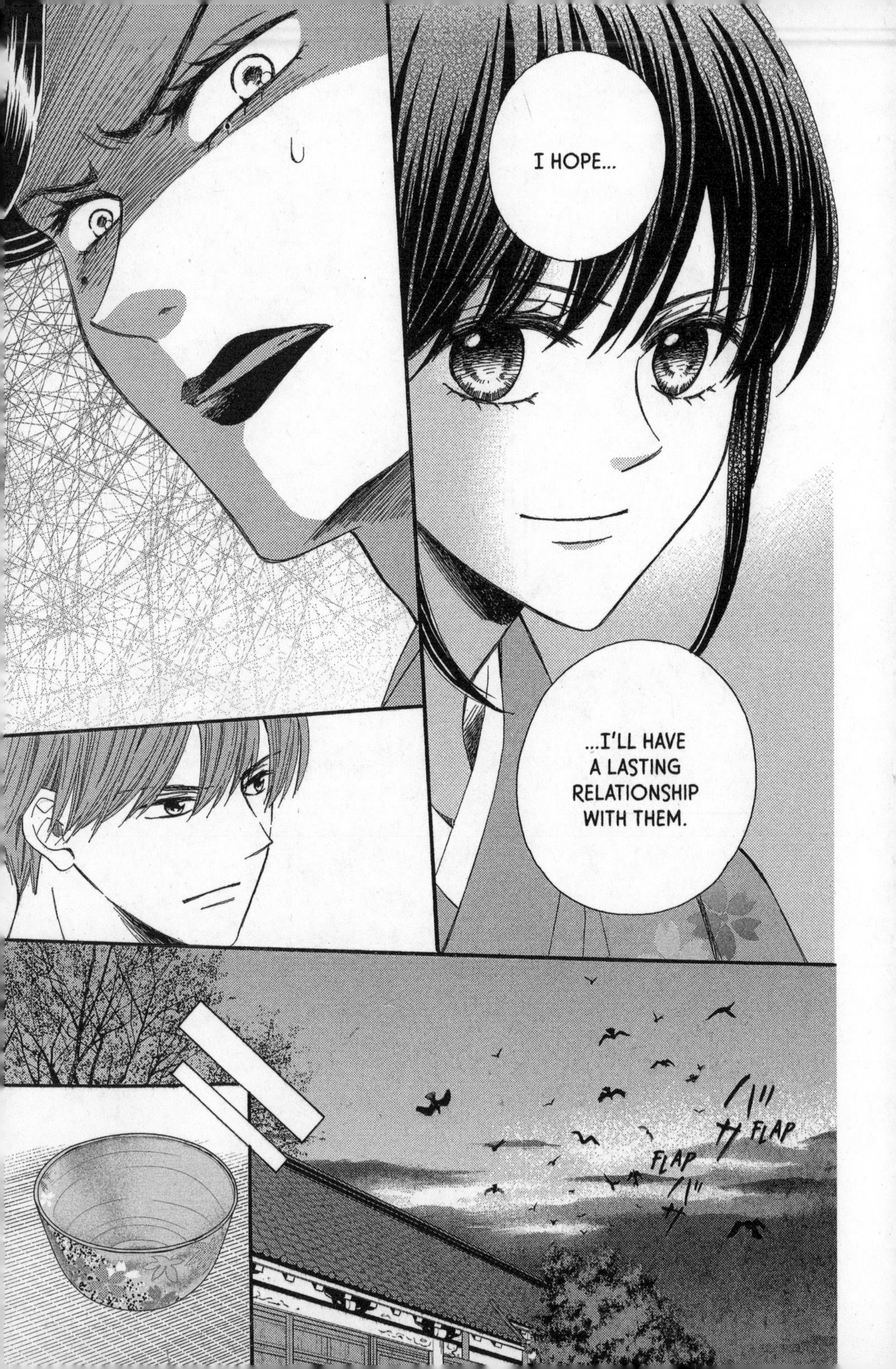
I HOPE...
...I'LL HAVE A LASTING RELATIONSHIP WITH THEM.
FLAP
FLAP

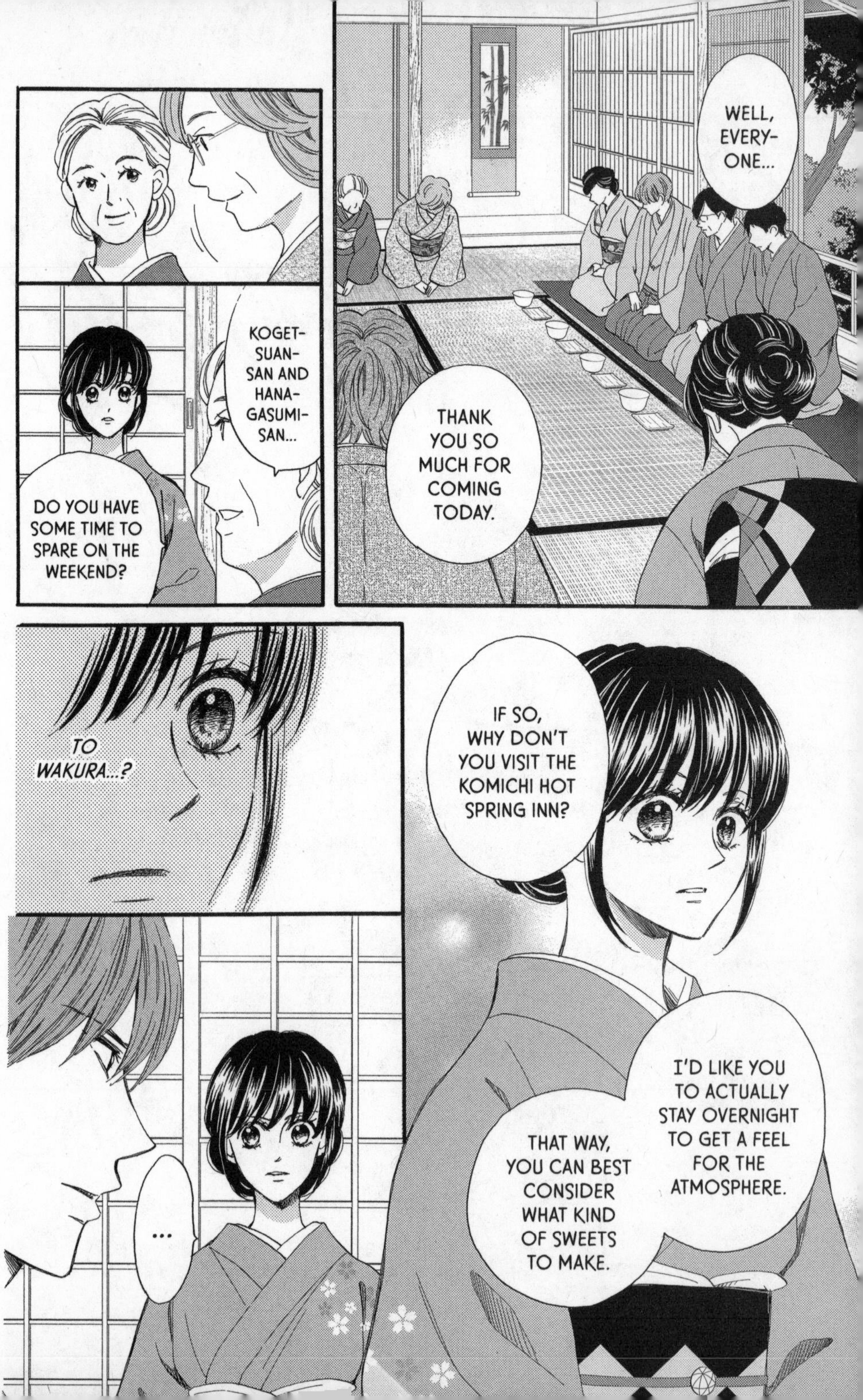
WELL, EVERY-ONE...
THANK YOU SO MUCH FOR COMING TODAY.
KOGET-SUAN-SAN AND HANA-GASUMI-SAN...
DO YOU HAVE SOME TIME TO SPARE ON THE WEEKEND?
IF SO, WHY DON'T YOU VISIT THE KOMICHI HOT SPRING INN?
I'D LIKE YOU TO ACTUALLY STAY OVERNIGHT TO GET A FEEL FOR THE ATMOSPHERE.
THAT WAY, YOU CAN BEST CONSIDER WHAT KIND OF SWEETS TO MAKE.
TO WAKURA...?
...

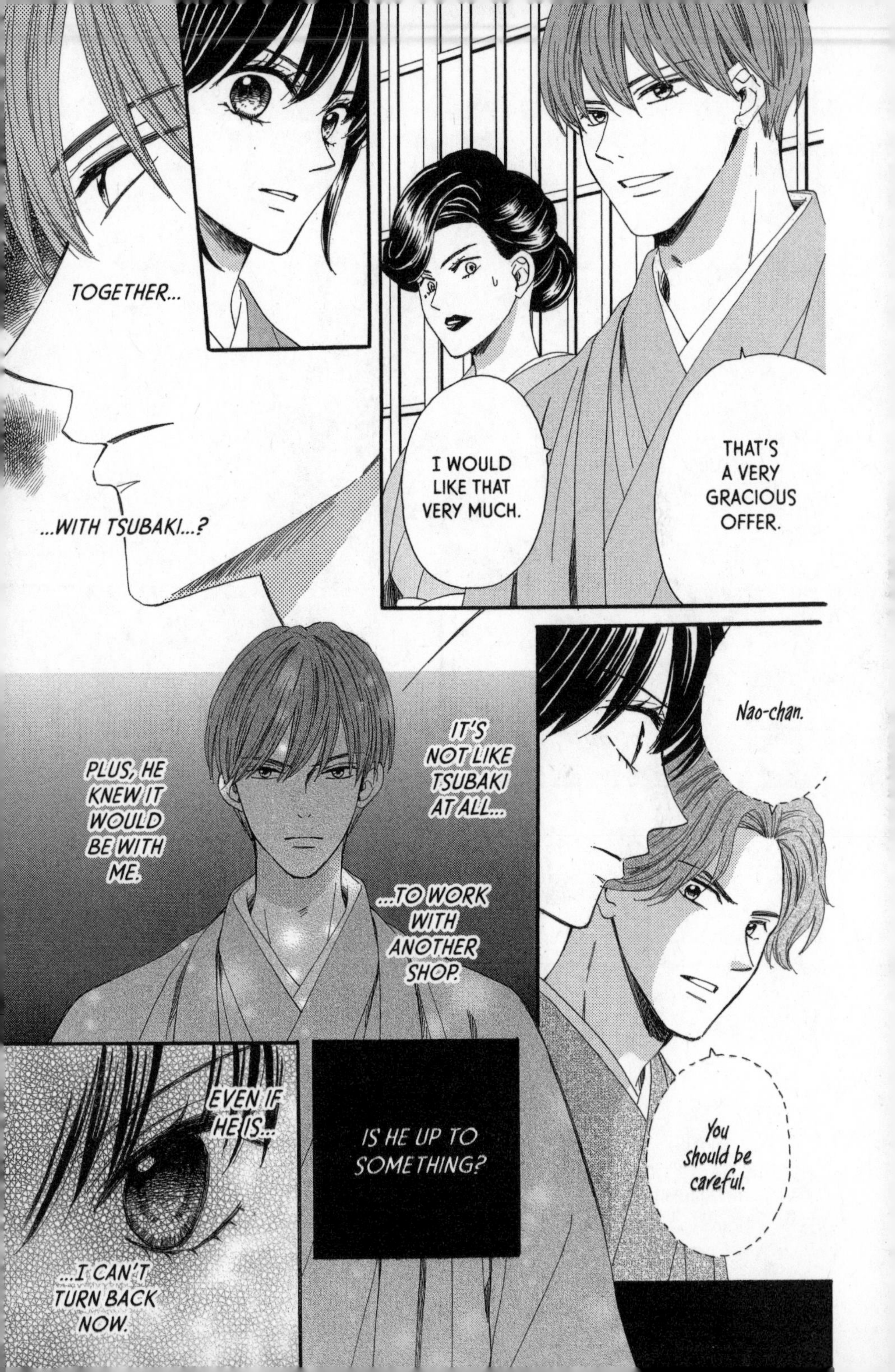
THAT'S A VERY GRACIOUS OFFER.
I WOULD LIKE THAT VERY MUCH.
TOGETHER...
...WITH TSUBAKI...?
Nao-chan.
You should be careful.
IT'S NOT LIKE TSUBAKI AT ALL...
...TO WORK WITH ANOTHER SHOP.
PLUS, HE KNEW IT WOULD BE WITH ME.
IS HE UP TO SOMETHING?
EVEN IF HE IS...
...I CAN'T TURN BACK NOW.

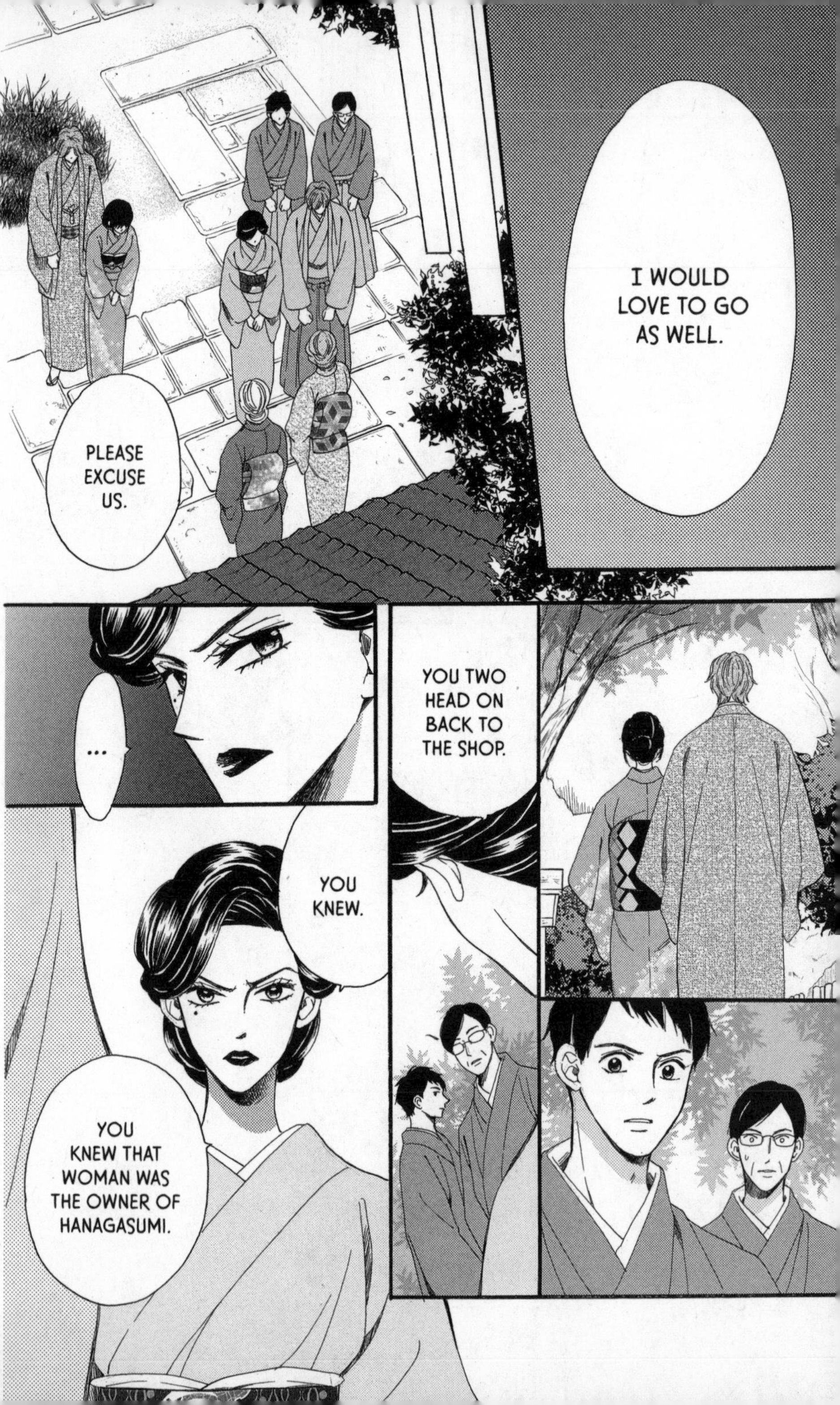
I WOULD LOVE TO GO AS WELL.
PLEASE EXCUSE US.
YOU TWO HEAD ON BACK TO THE SHOP.
...
YOU KNEW.
YOU KNEW THAT WOMAN WAS THE OWNER OF HANAGASUMI.

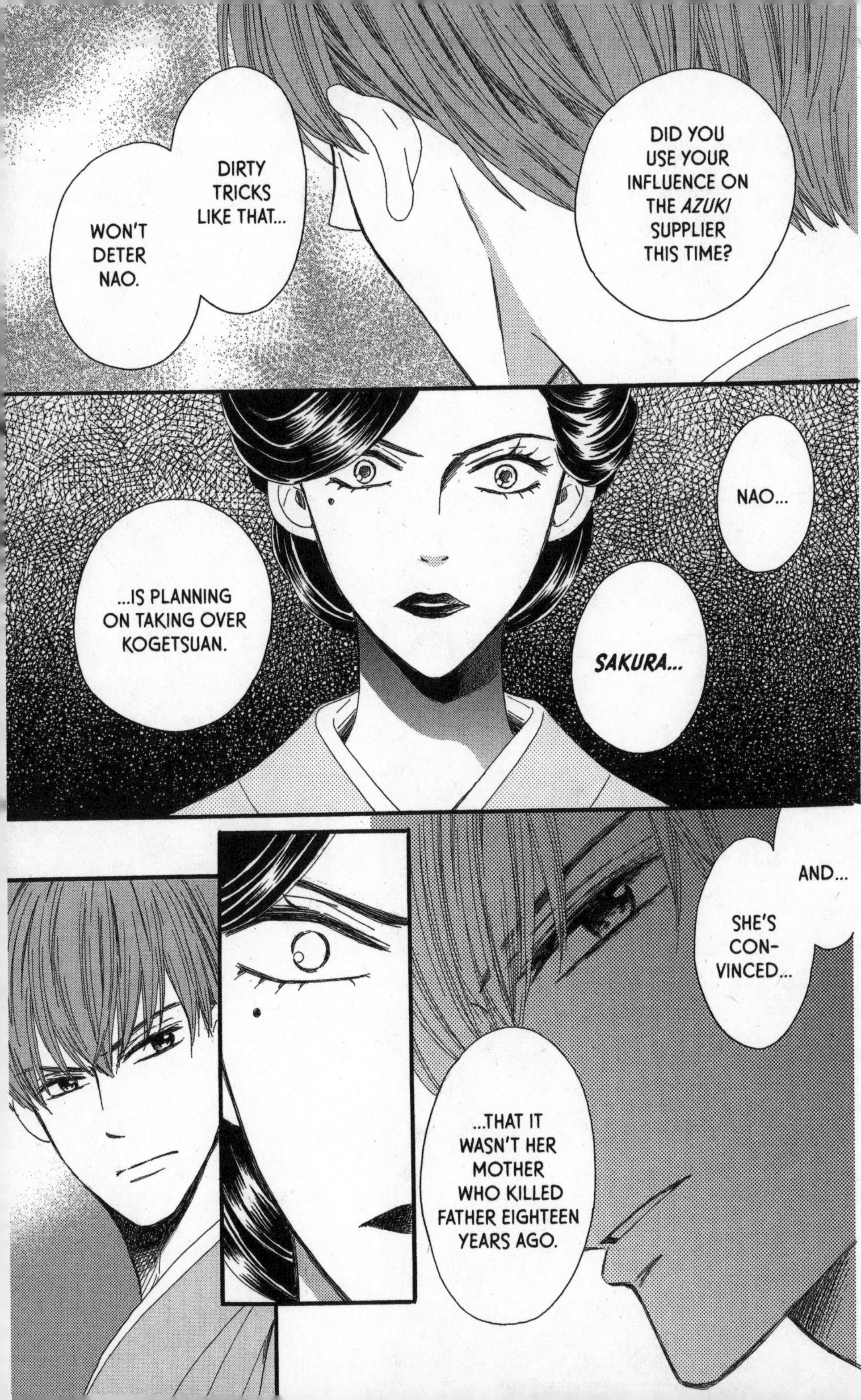

DID YOU USE YOUR INFLUENCE ON THE *AZUKI* SUPPLIER THIS TIME?
DIRTY TRICKS LIKE THAT...
WON'T DETER NAO.
NAO...
SAKURA...
...IS PLANNING ON TAKING OVER KOGETSUAN.
AND...
SHE'S CON-VINCED...
...THAT IT WASN'T HER MOTHER WHO KILLED FATHER EIGHTEEN YEARS AGO.

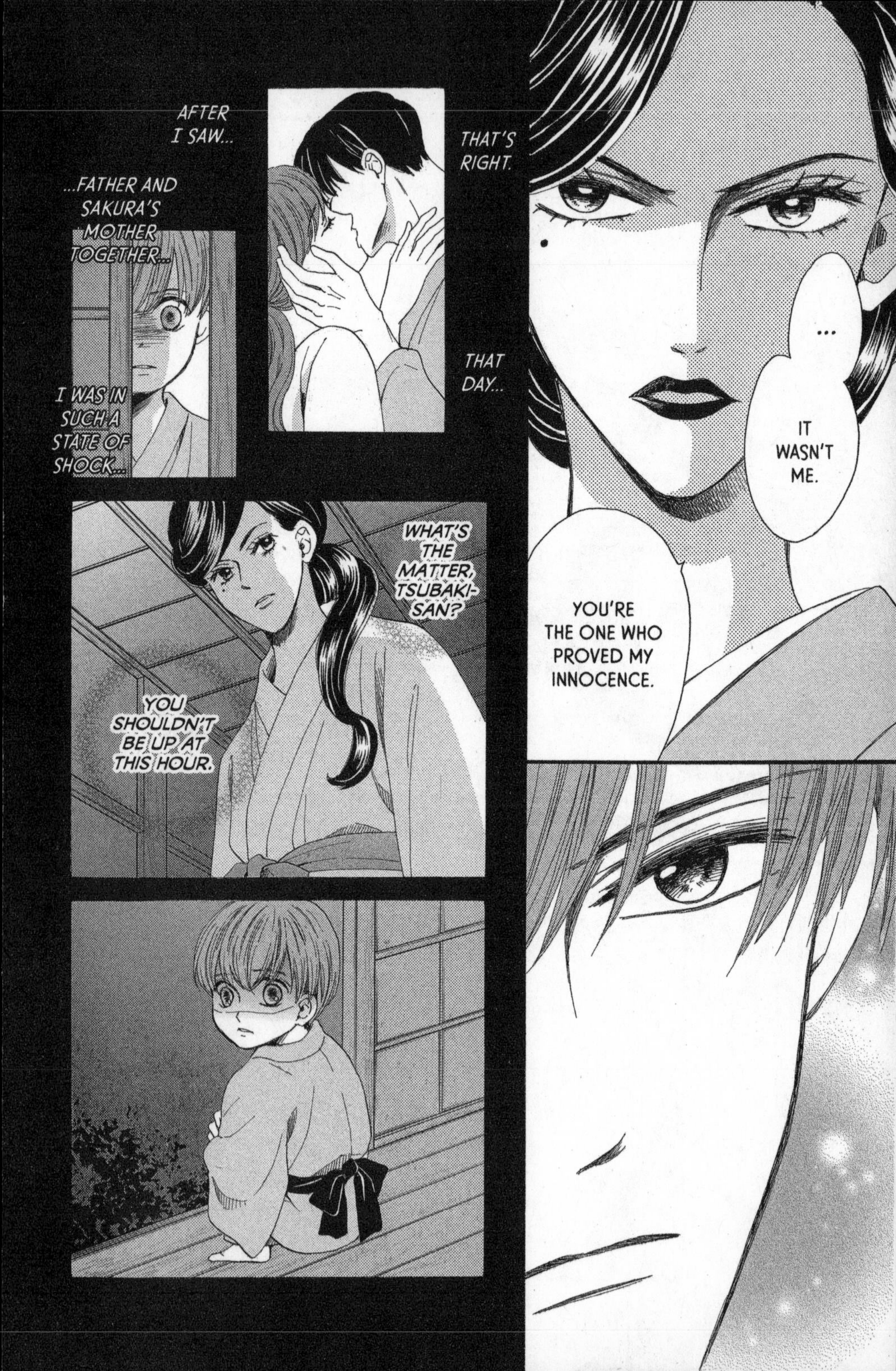
...
IT WASN'T ME.
YOU'RE THE ONE WHO PROVED MY INNOCENCE.
THAT'S RIGHT.
THAT DAY...
AFTER I SAW...
...FATHER AND SAKURA'S MOTHER TOGETHER...
I WAS IN SUCH A STATE OF SHOCK...
WHAT'S THE MATTER, TSUBAKI-SAN?
YOU SHOULDN'T BE UP AT THIS HOUR.

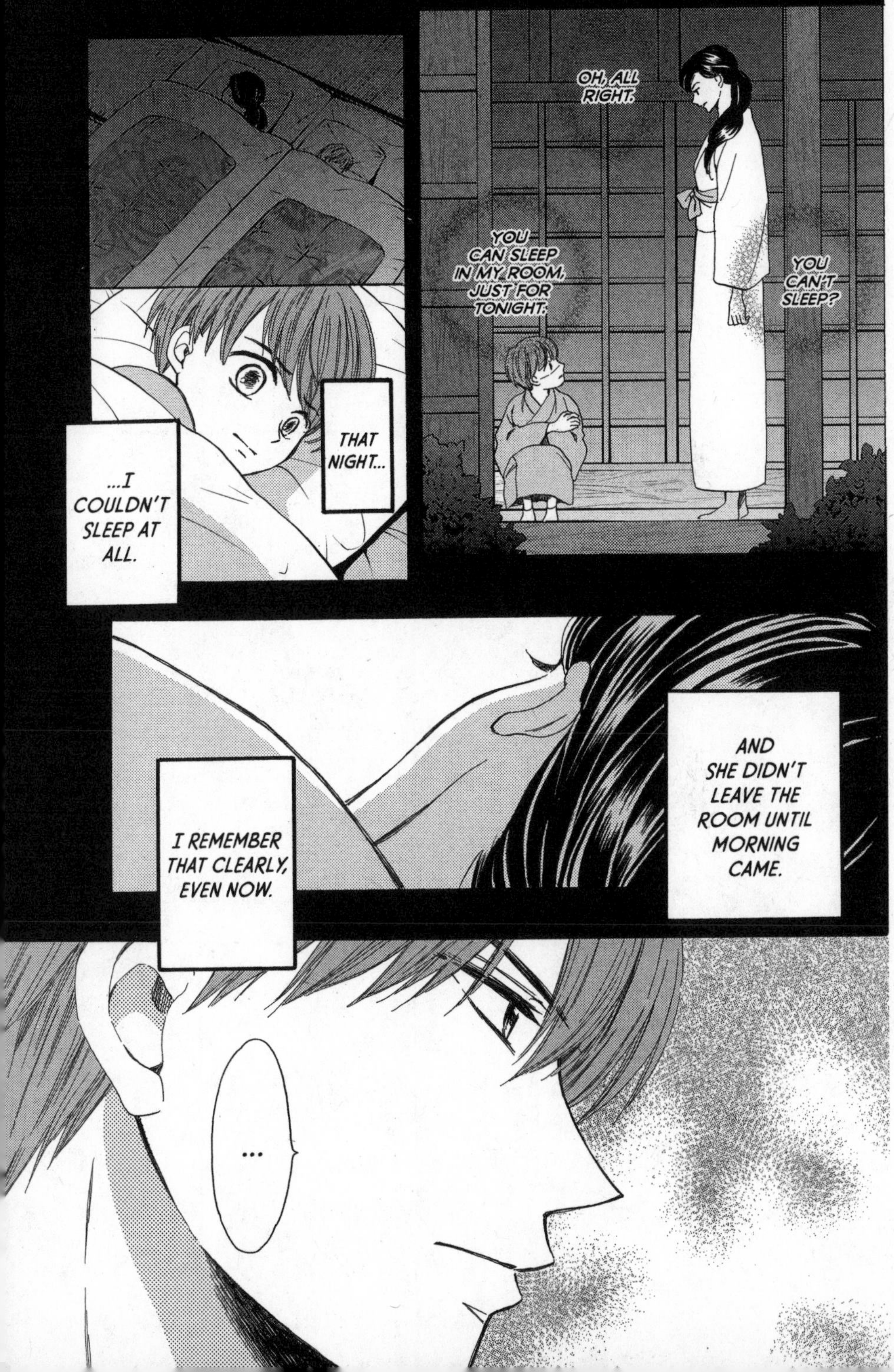
YOU CAN'T SLEEP?
YOU CAN SLEEP IN MY ROOM, JUST FOR TONIGHT.
OH, ALL RIGHT.
THAT NIGHT...
...I COULDN'T SLEEP AT ALL.
AND SHE DIDN'T LEAVE THE ROOM UNTIL MORNING CAME.
I REMEMBER THAT CLEARLY, EVEN NOW.
...

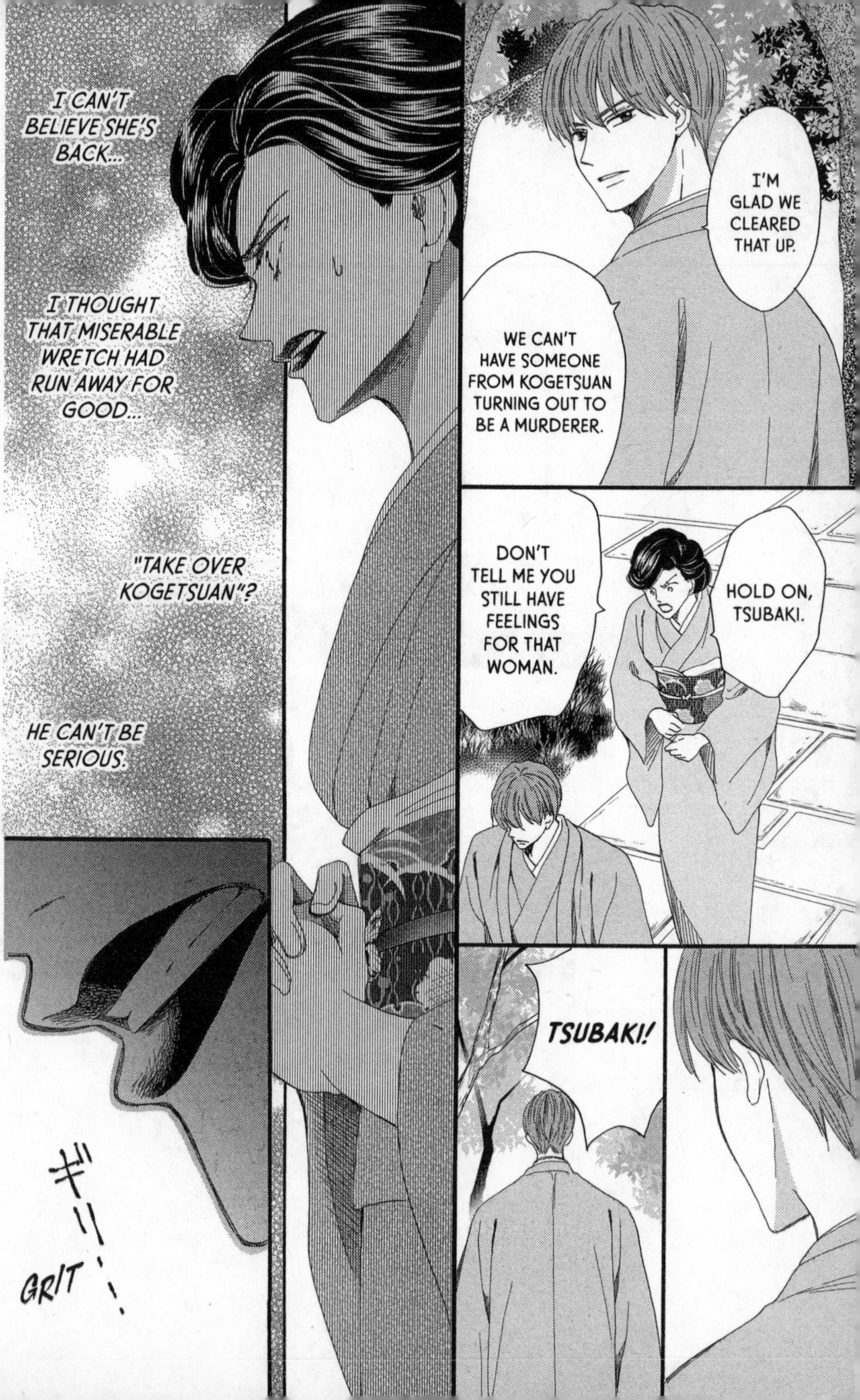
I'M GLAD WE CLEARED THAT UP.
WE CAN'T HAVE SOMEONE FROM KOGETSUAN TURNING OUT TO BE A MURDERER.
HOLD ON, TSUBAKI.
DON'T TELL ME YOU STILL HAVE FEELINGS FOR THAT WOMAN.
TSUBAKI!
I CAN'T BELIEVE SHE'S BACK...
I THOUGHT THAT MISERABLE WRETCH HAD RUN AWAY FOR GOOD...
"TAKE OVER KOGETSUAN"?
HE CAN'T BE SERIOUS.
ギリ…
GRIT

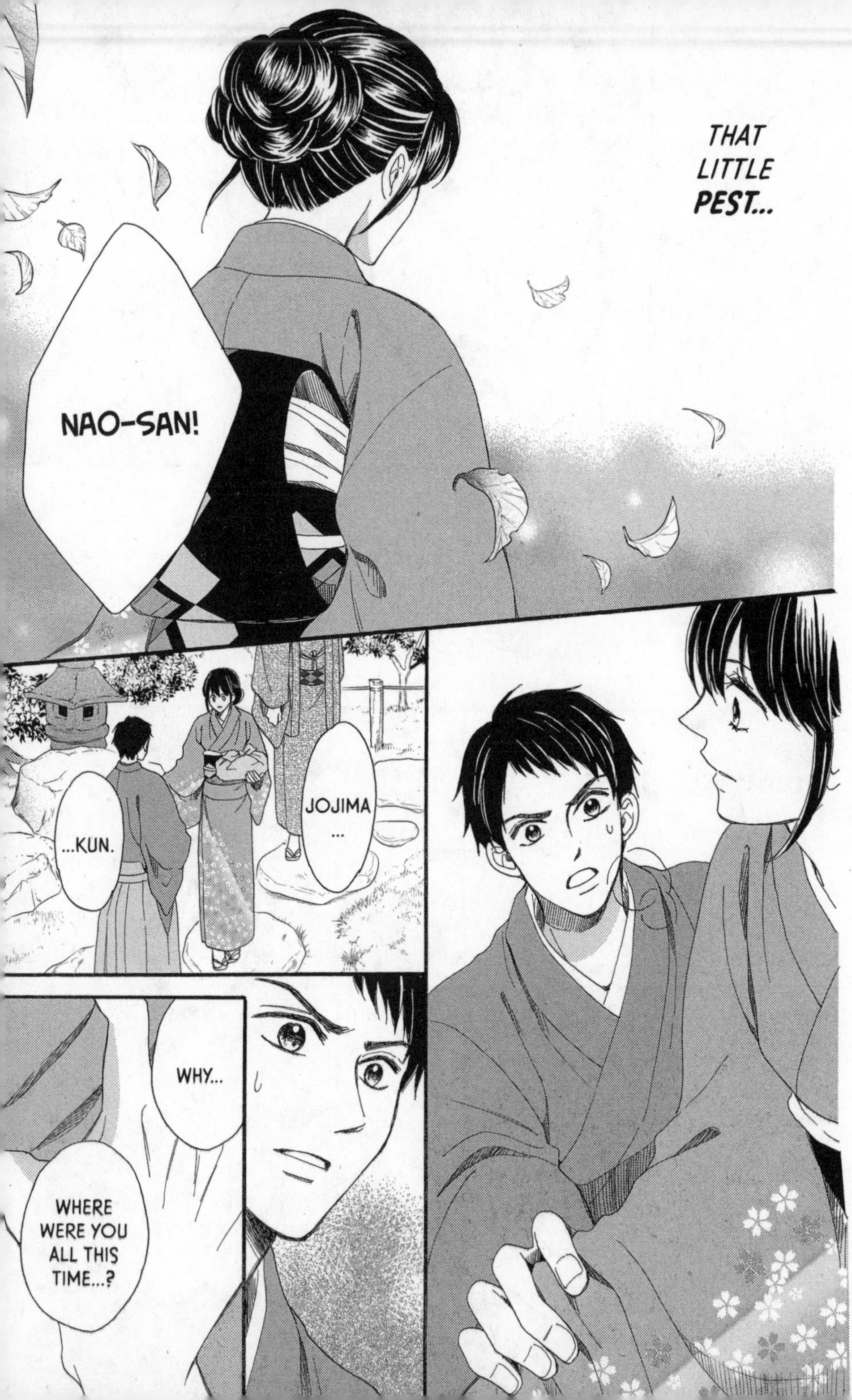
THAT LITTLE PEST...
NAO-SAN!
JOJIMA ...
...KUN.
WHY...
WHERE WERE YOU ALL THIS TIME...?

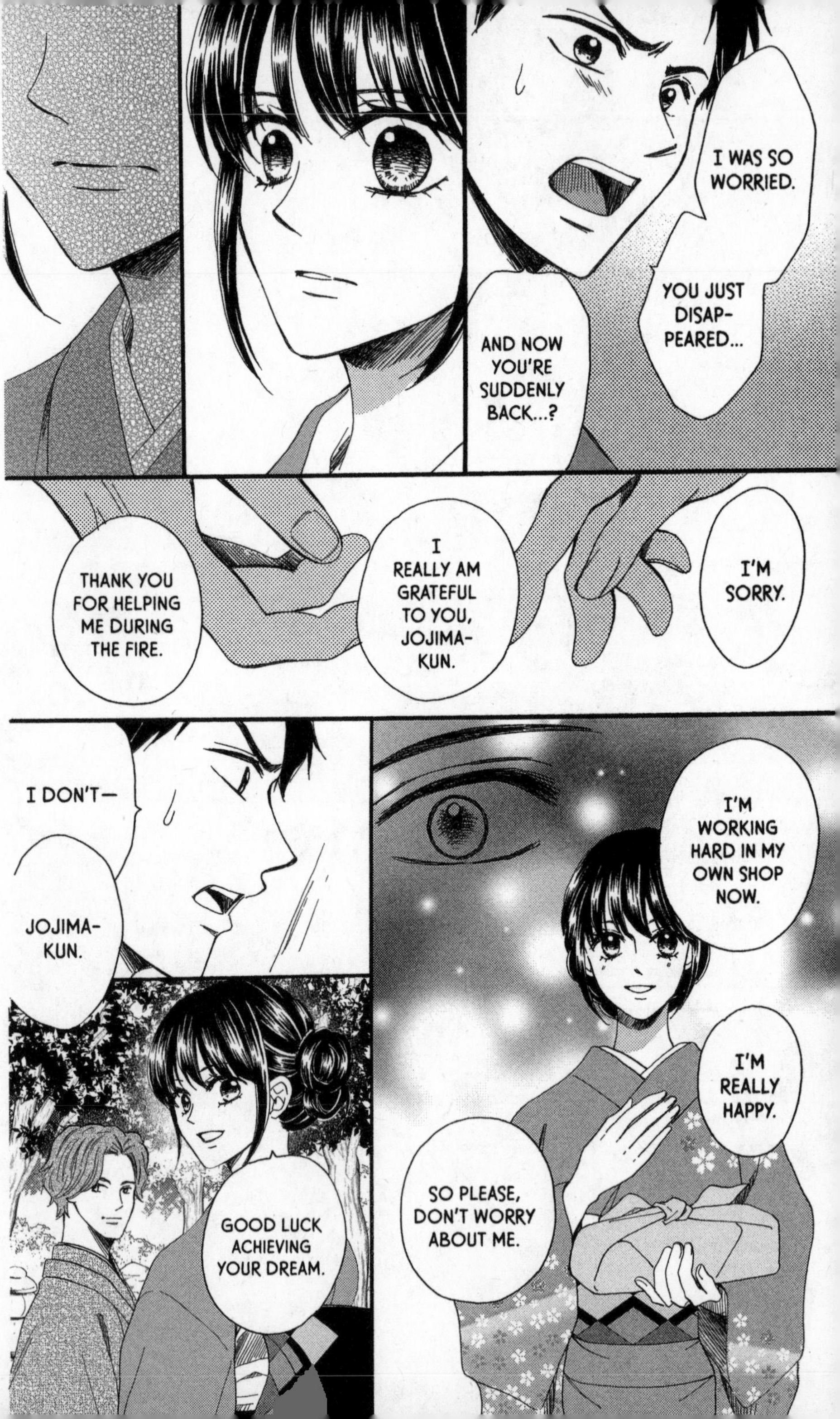
I WAS SO WORRIED.
YOU JUST DISAP-PEARED...
AND NOW YOU'RE SUDDENLY BACK...?
I'M SORRY.
I REALLY AM GRATEFUL TO YOU, JOJIMA-KUN.
THANK YOU FOR HELPING ME DURING THE FIRE.
I'M WORKING HARD IN MY OWN SHOP NOW.
I'M REALLY HAPPY.
SO PLEASE, DON'T WORRY ABOUT ME.
I DON'T—
JOJIMA-KUN.
GOOD LUCK ACHIEVING YOUR DREAM.

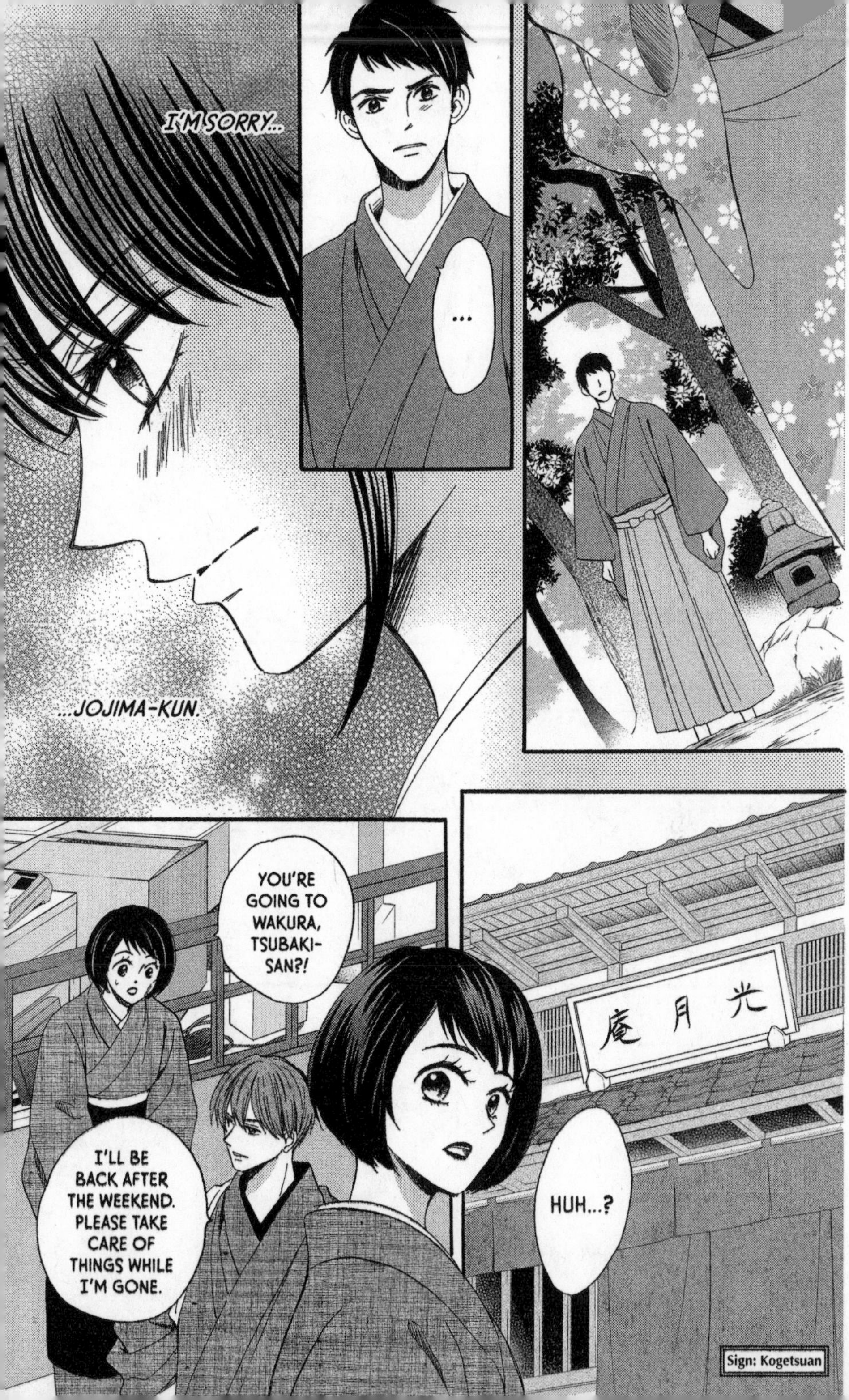
...
I'M SORRY...
...JOJIMA-KUN.
光月庵
Sign: Kogetsuan
YOU'RE GOING TO WAKURA, TSUBAKI-SAN?!
HUH...?
I'LL BE BACK AFTER THE WEEKEND. PLEASE TAKE CARE OF THINGS WHILE I'M GONE.

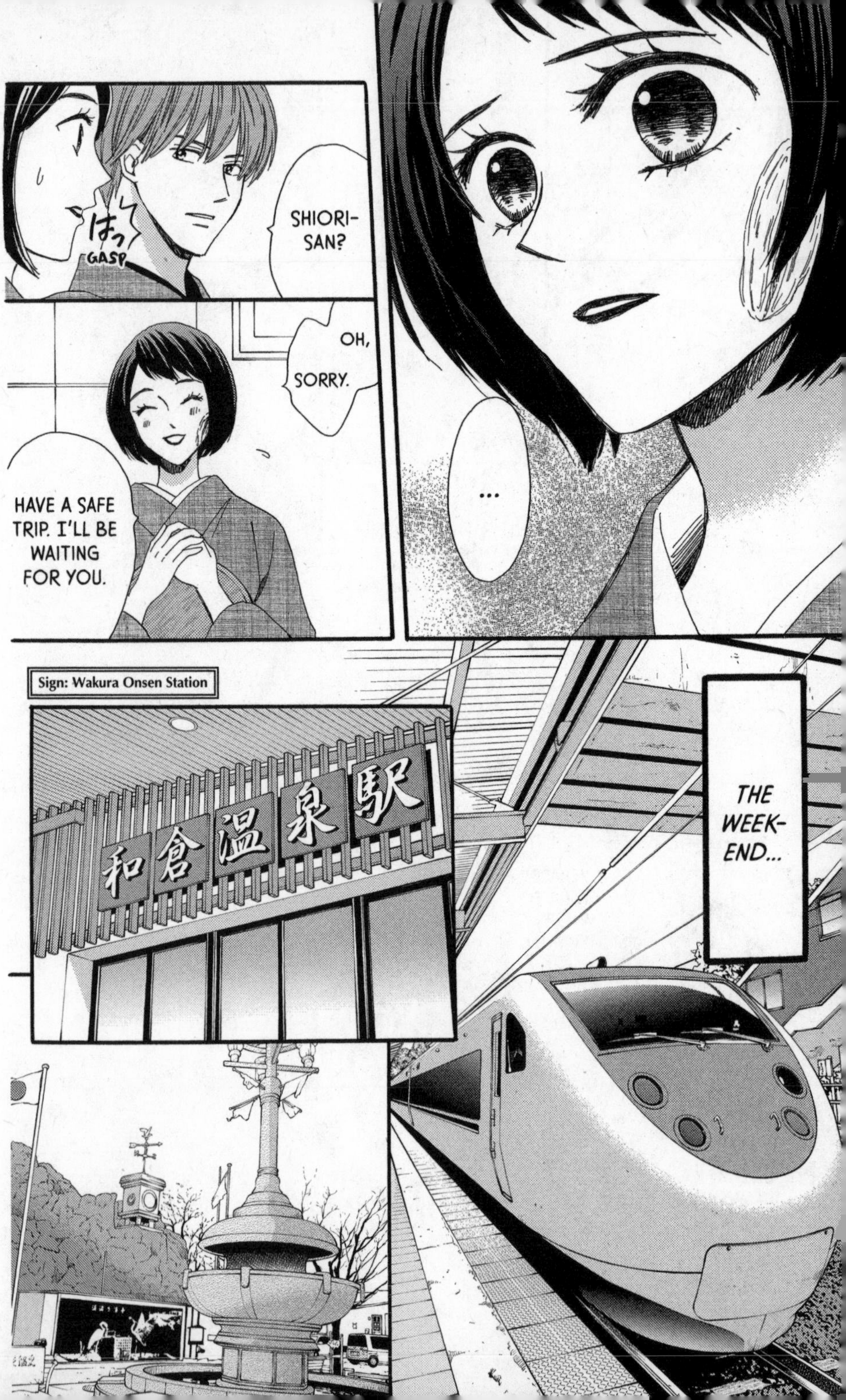
...
SHIORI-SAN?
はっ GASP
OH, SORRY.
HAVE A SAFE TRIP. I'LL BE WAITING FOR YOU.
THE WEEK-END...
Sign: Wakura Onsen Station
和倉温泉駅

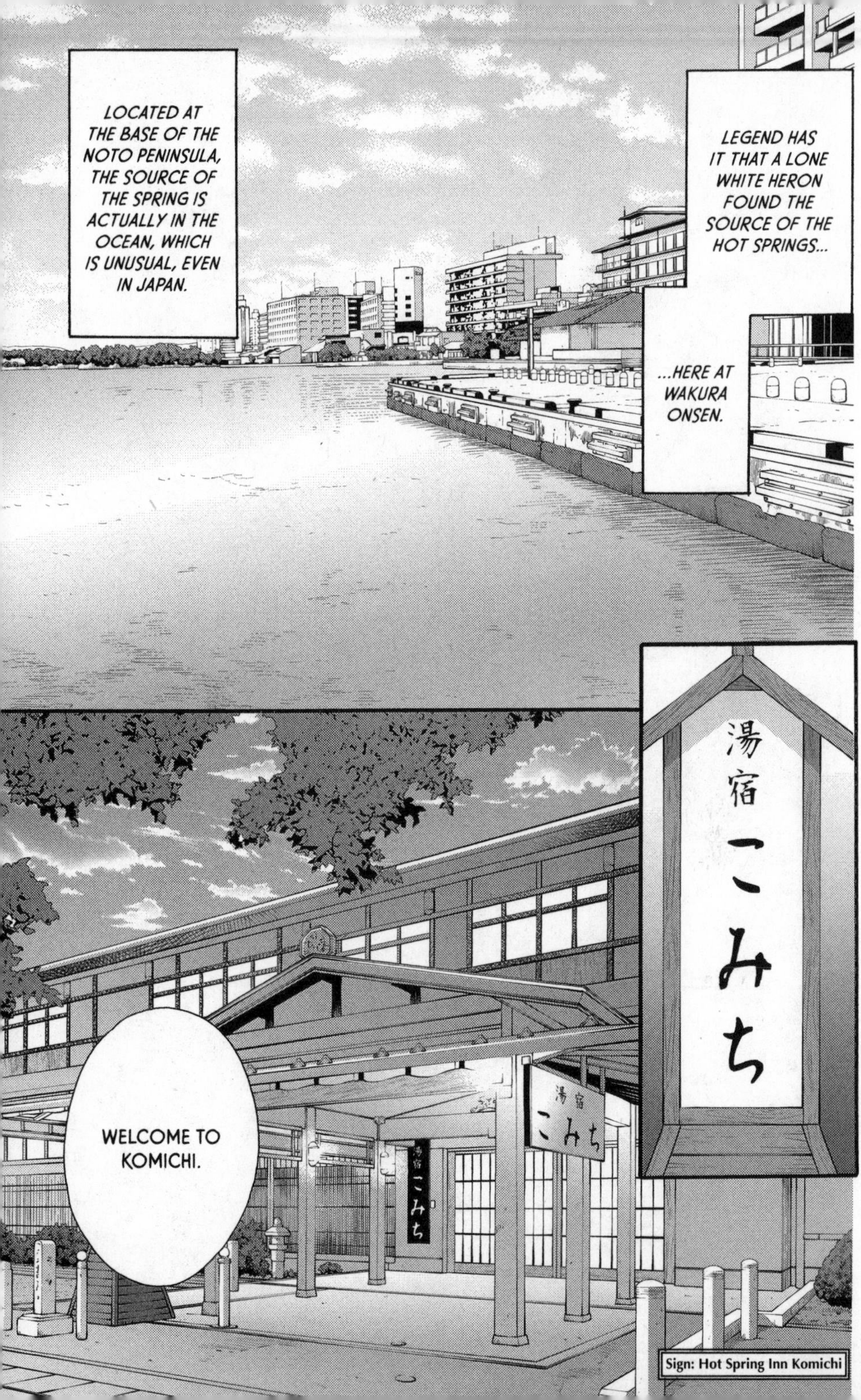
LEGEND HAS IT THAT A LONE WHITE HERON FOUND THE SOURCE OF THE HOT SPRINGS...
...HERE AT WAKURA ONSEN.
LOCATED AT THE BASE OF THE NOTO PENINSULA, THE SOURCE OF THE SPRING IS ACTUALLY IN THE OCEAN, WHICH IS UNUSUAL, EVEN IN JAPAN.
湯宿こみち
WELCOME TO KOMICHI.
湯宿こみち
湯宿こみち
Sign: Hot Spring Inn Komichi

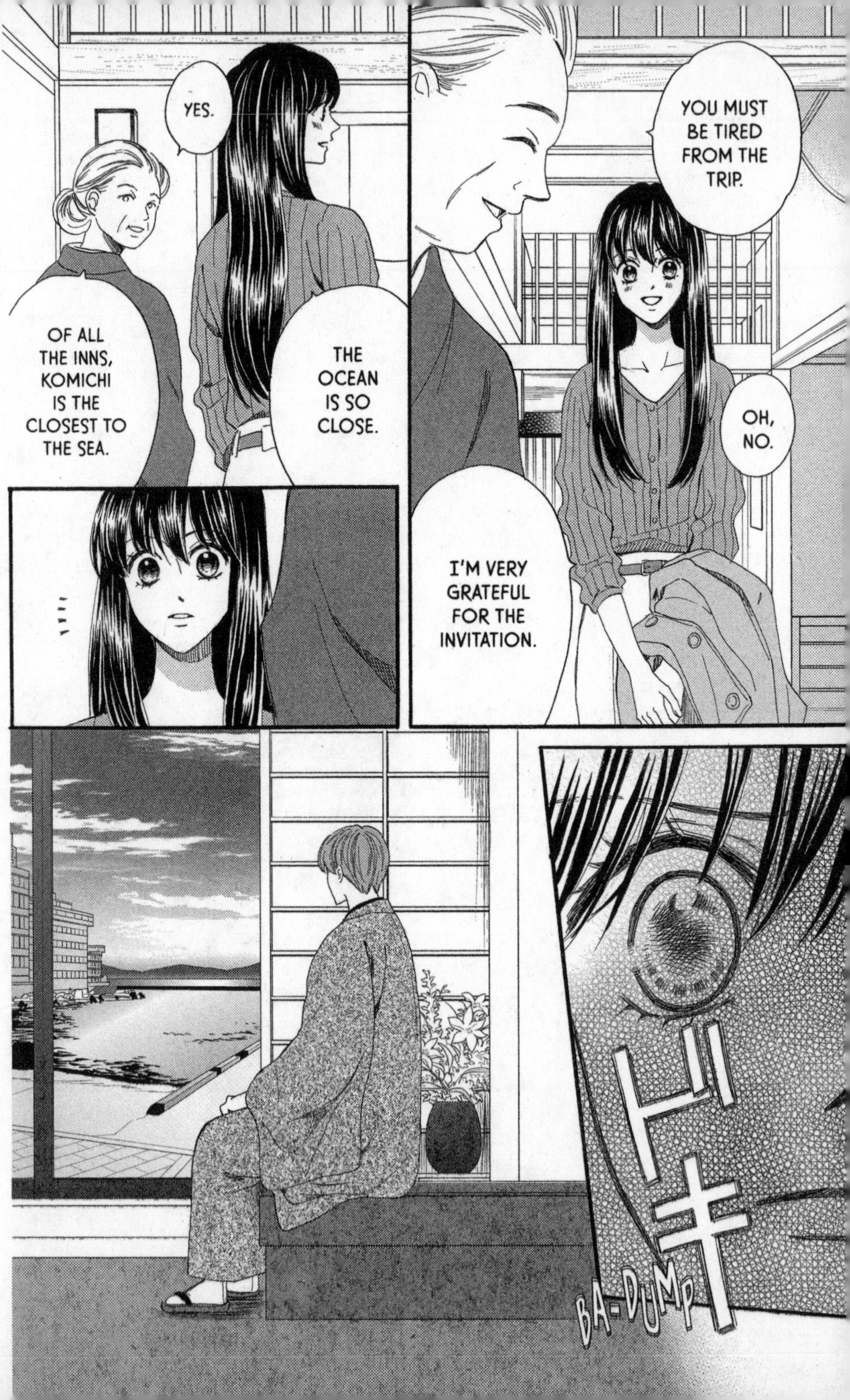

YOU MUST BE TIRED FROM THE TRIP.
OH, NO.
I'M VERY GRATEFUL FOR THE INVITATION.
YES.
THE OCEAN IS SO CLOSE.
OF ALL THE INNS, KOMICHI IS THE CLOSEST TO THE SEA.
ドキ
BA-DUMP

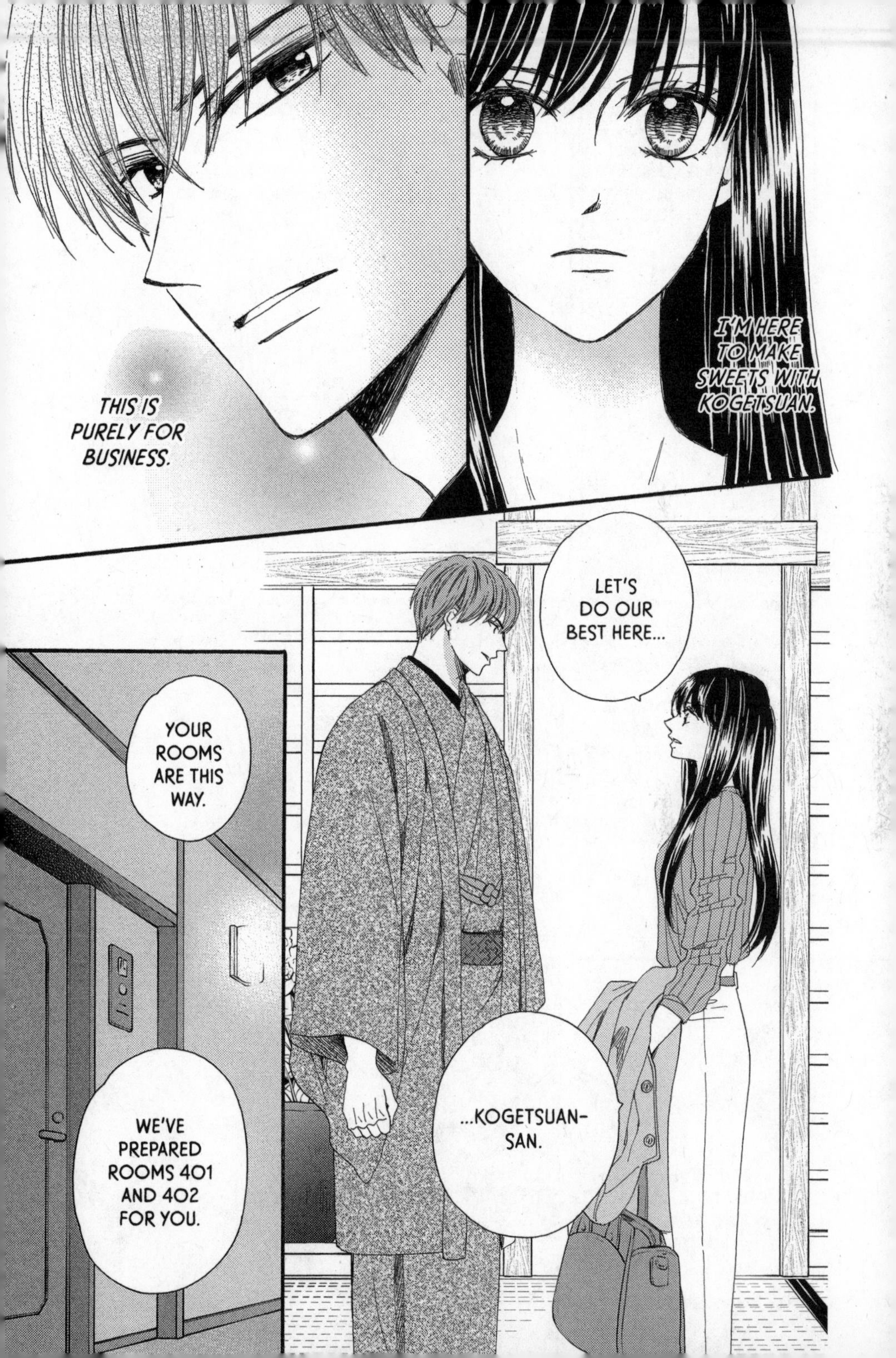
I'M HERE TO MAKE SWEETS WITH KOGETSUAN.
THIS IS PURELY FOR BUSINESS.
LET'S DO OUR BEST HERE...
...KOGETSUAN-SAN.
YOUR ROOMS ARE THIS WAY.
WE'VE PREPARED ROOMS 401 AND 402 FOR YOU.

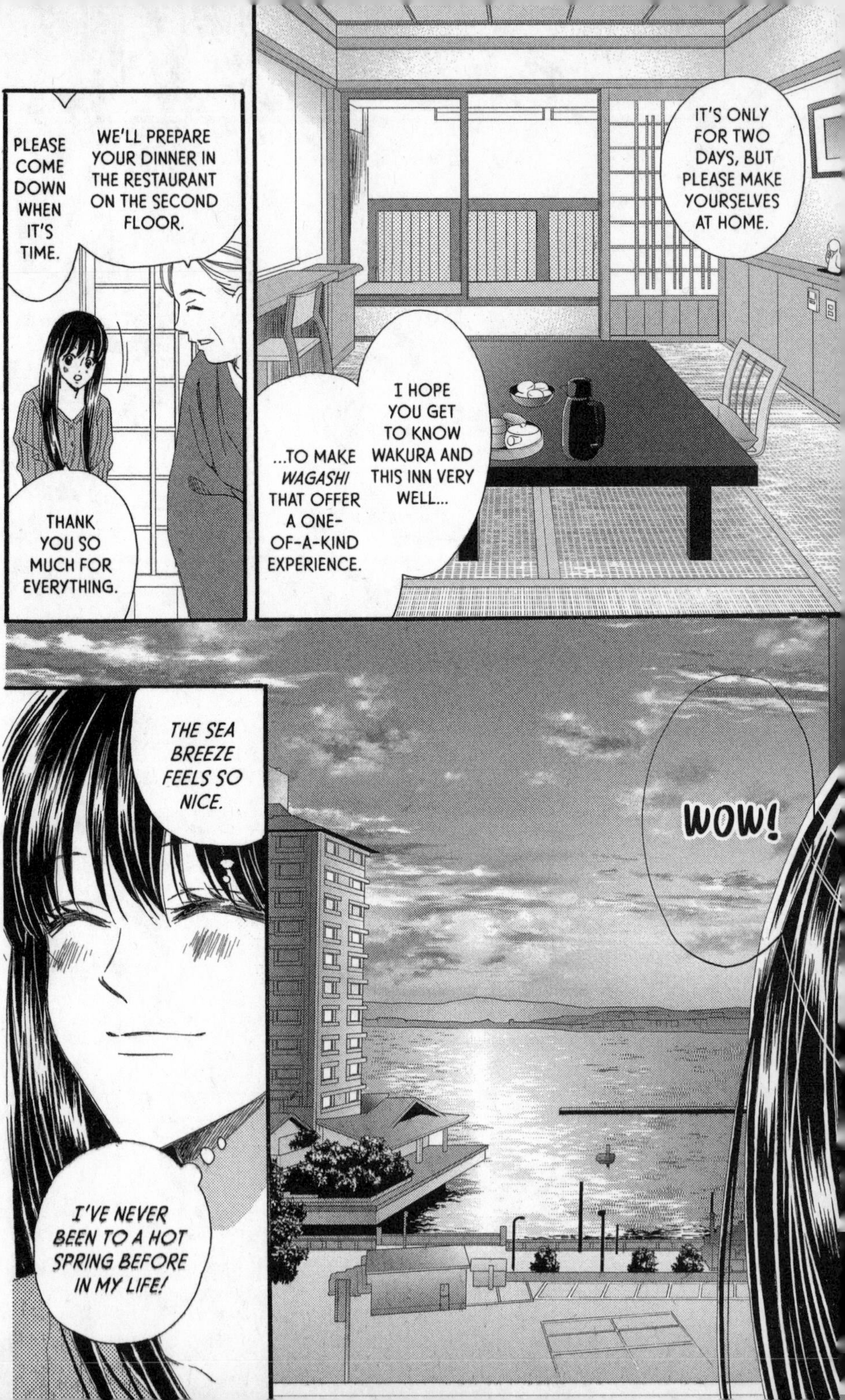
IT'S ONLY FOR TWO DAYS, BUT PLEASE MAKE YOURSELVES AT HOME.
I HOPE YOU GET TO KNOW WAKURA AND THIS INN VERY WELL...
...TO MAKE *WAGASHI* THAT OFFER A ONE-OF-A-KIND EXPERIENCE.
WE'LL PREPARE YOUR DINNER IN THE RESTAURANT ON THE SECOND FLOOR.
PLEASE COME DOWN WHEN IT'S TIME.
THANK YOU SO MUCH FOR EVERYTHING.
WOW!
THE SEA BREEZE FEELS SO NICE.
I'VE NEVER BEEN TO A HOT SPRING BEFORE IN MY LIFE!

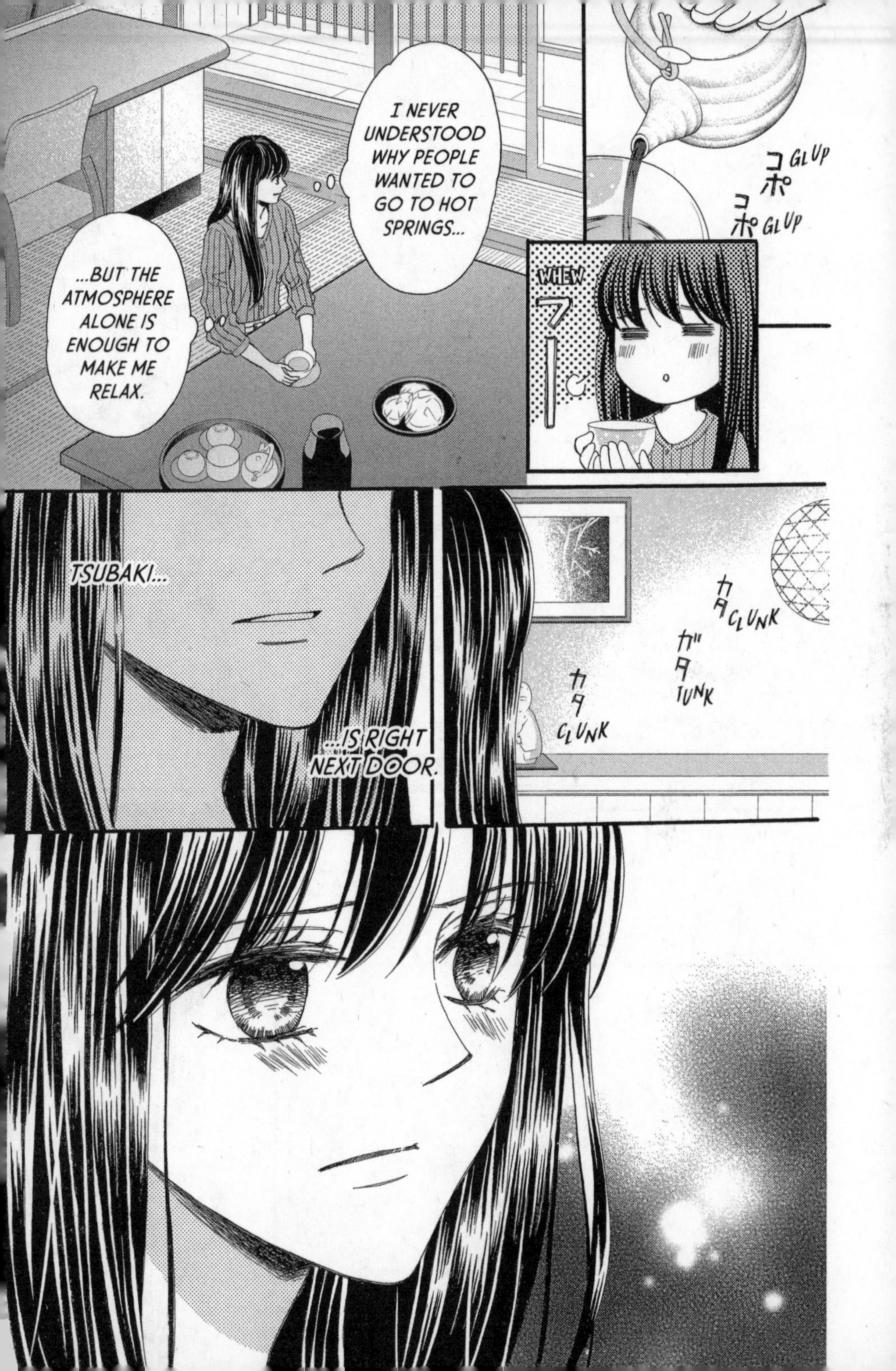
コポ GLUP
コポ GLUP
WHEW フー
I NEVER UNDERSTOOD WHY PEOPLE WANTED TO GO TO HOT SPRINGS...
...BUT THE ATMOSPHERE ALONE IS ENOUGH TO MAKE ME RELAX.
カタ CLUNK
ガタ TUNK
カタ CLUNK
TSUBAKI...
...IS RIGHT NEXT DOOR.

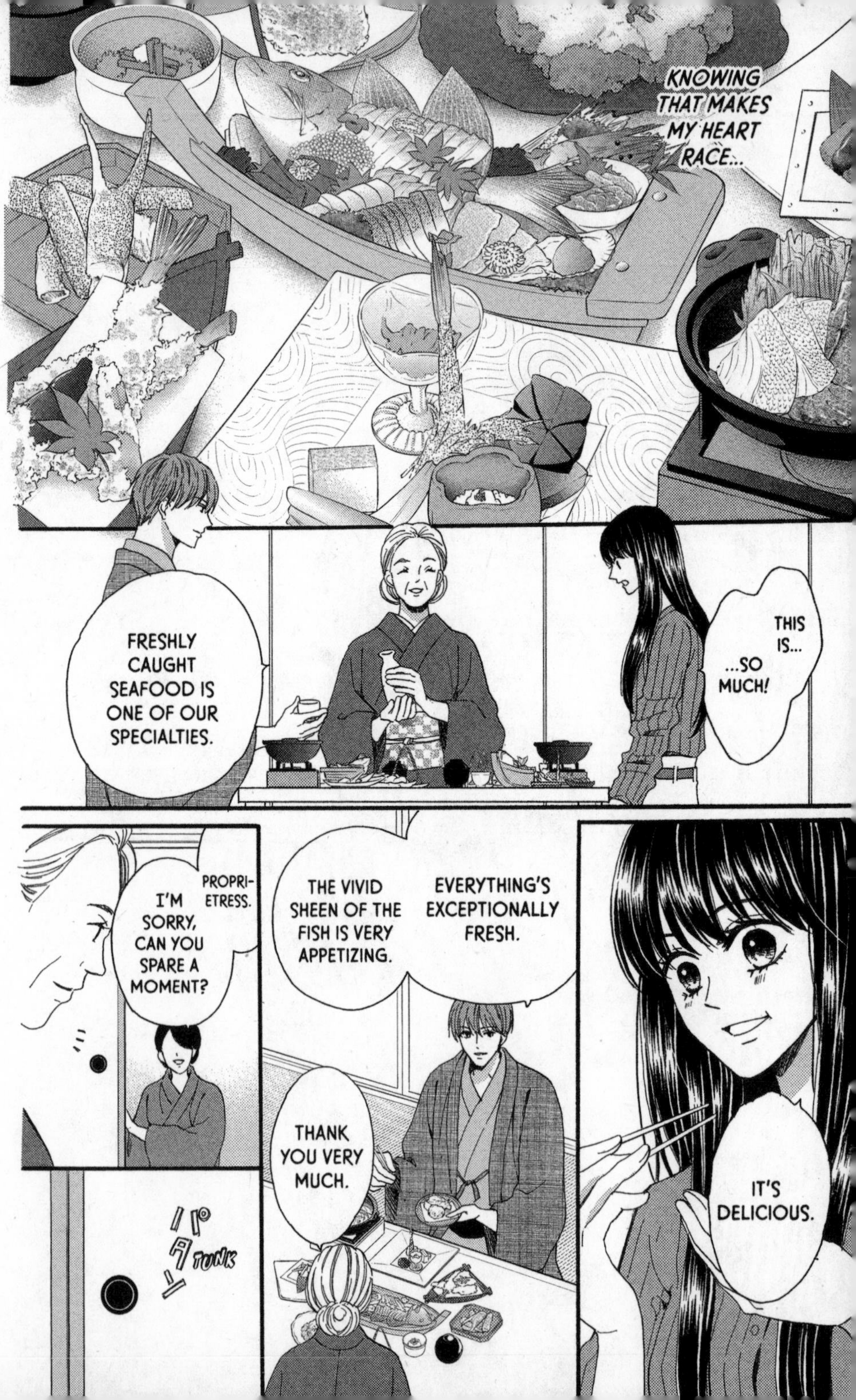
KNOWING THAT MAKES MY HEART RACE...
THIS IS... ...SO MUCH!
FRESHLY CAUGHT SEAFOOD IS ONE OF OUR SPECIALTIES.
IT'S DELICIOUS.
EVERYTHING'S EXCEPTIONALLY FRESH.
THE VIVID SHEEN OF THE FISH IS VERY APPETIZING.
THANK YOU VERY MUCH.
PROPRI-ETRESS.
I'M SORRY, CAN YOU SPARE A MOMENT?
パタン
TUNK

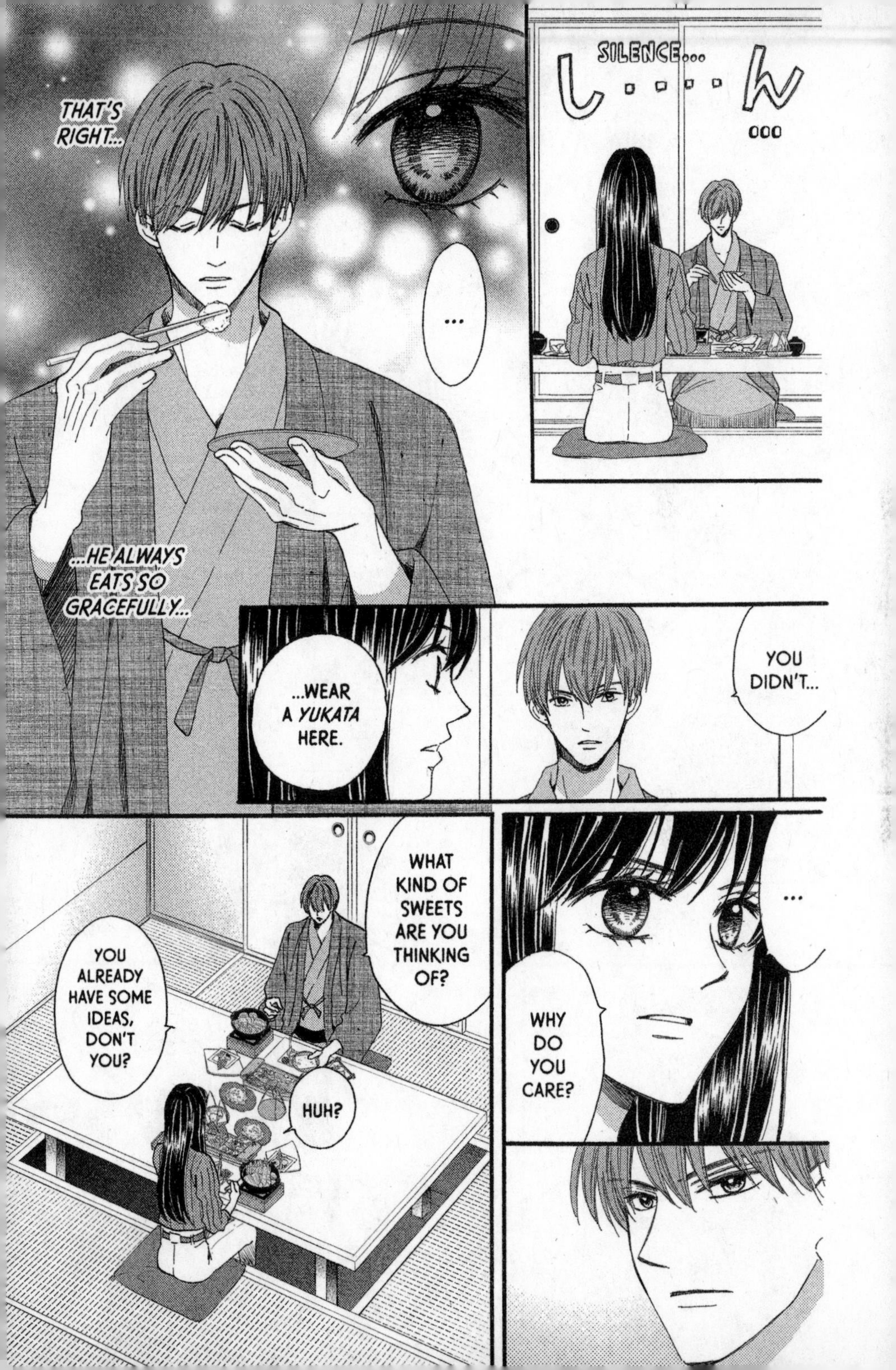
SILENCE...
し・・・・ん
ooo
THAT'S RIGHT...
...
...HE ALWAYS EATS SO GRACEFULLY...
YOU DIDN'T...
...WEAR A YUKATA HERE.
WHAT KIND OF SWEETS ARE YOU THINKING OF?
HUH?
YOU ALREADY HAVE SOME IDEAS, DON'T YOU?
...
WHY DO YOU CARE?

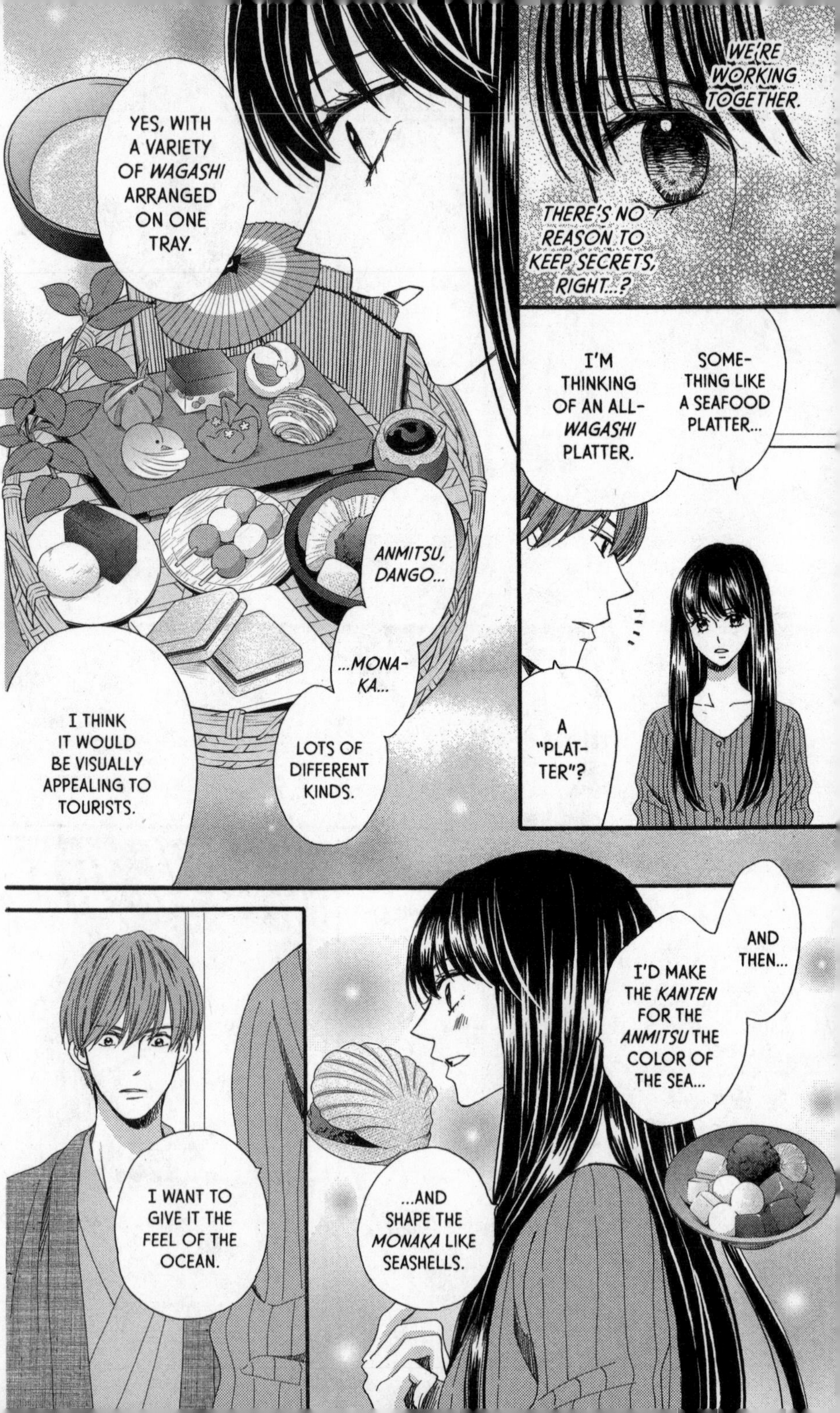
WE'RE WORKING TOGETHER.
THERE'S NO REASON TO KEEP SECRETS, RIGHT...?
SOME-THING LIKE A SEAFOOD PLATTER...
I'M THINKING OF AN ALL-*WAGASHI* PLATTER.
A "PLAT-TER"?
YES, WITH A VARIETY OF *WAGASHI* ARRANGED ON ONE TRAY.
ANMITSU, DANGO...
...*MONA-KA*...
LOTS OF DIFFERENT KINDS.
I THINK IT WOULD BE VISUALLY APPEALING TO TOURISTS.
AND THEN...
I'D MAKE THE *KANTEN* FOR THE *ANMITSU* THE COLOR OF THE SEA...
...AND SHAPE THE *MONAKA* LIKE SEASHELLS.
I WANT TO GIVE IT THE FEEL OF THE OCEAN.

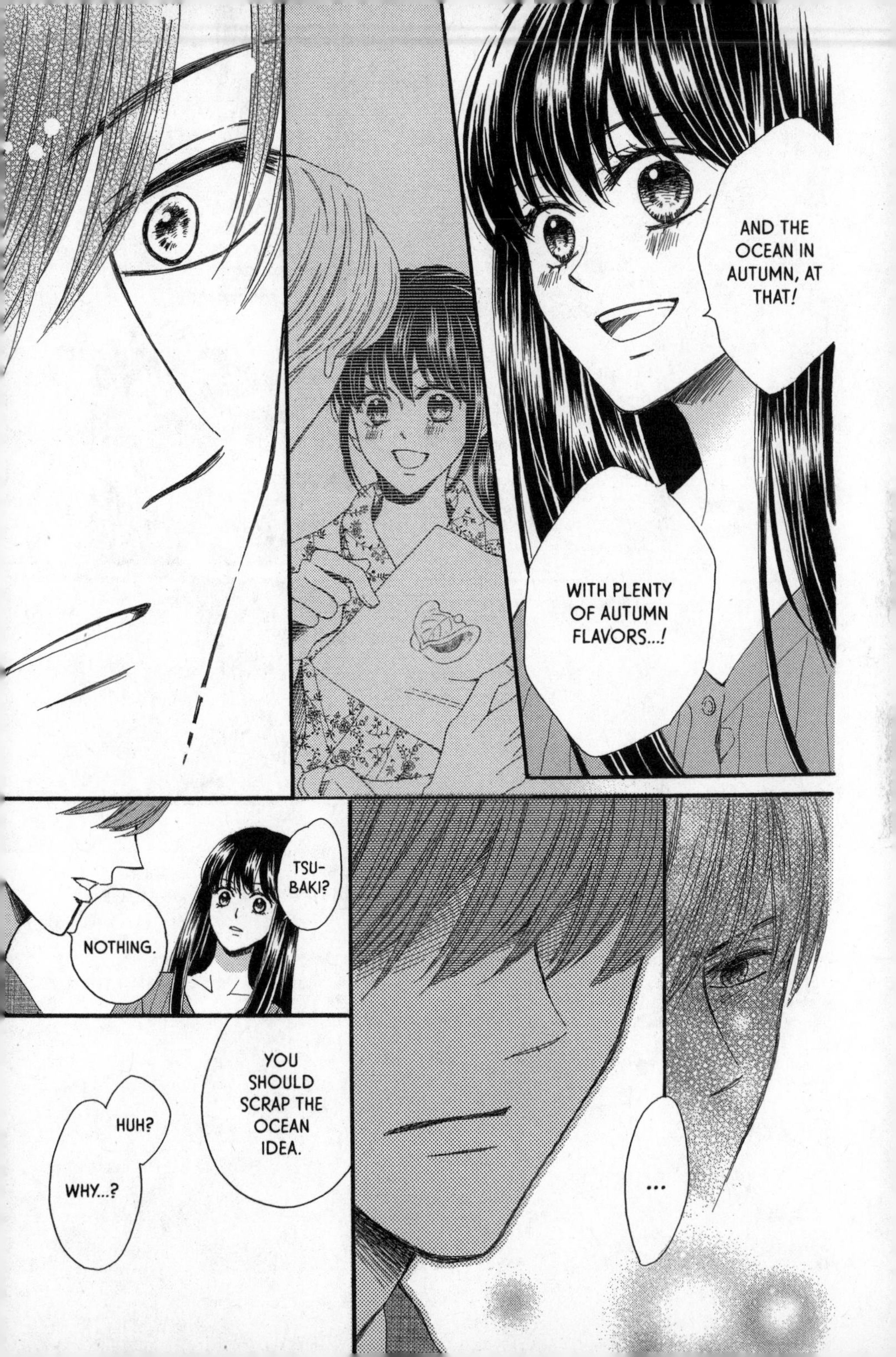
AND THE OCEAN IN AUTUMN, AT THAT!
WITH PLENTY OF AUTUMN FLAVORS...!
...
TSU-BAKI?
NOTHING.
YOU SHOULD SCRAP THE OCEAN IDEA.
HUH?
WHY...?

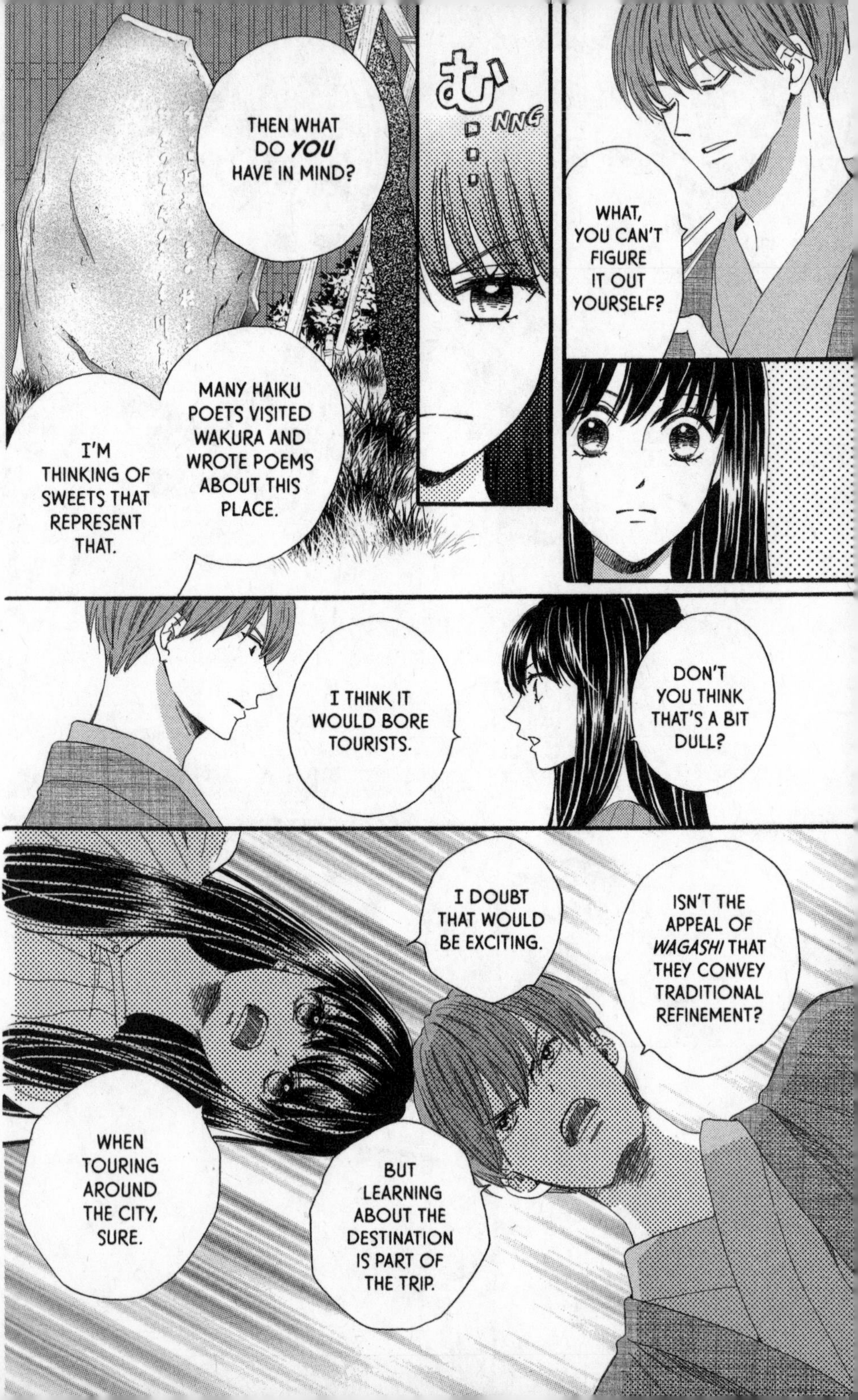

WHAT, YOU CAN'T FIGURE IT OUT YOURSELF?
む NNG
THEN WHAT DO *YOU* HAVE IN MIND?
MANY HAIKU POETS VISITED WAKURA AND WROTE POEMS ABOUT THIS PLACE.
I'M THINKING OF SWEETS THAT REPRESENT THAT.
DON'T YOU THINK THAT'S A BIT DULL?
I THINK IT WOULD BORE TOURISTS.
ISN'T THE APPEAL OF *WAGASHI* THAT THEY CONVEY TRADITIONAL REFINEMENT?
I DOUBT THAT WOULD BE EXCITING.
BUT LEARNING ABOUT THE DESTINATION IS PART OF THE TRIP.
WHEN TOURING AROUND THE CITY, SURE.

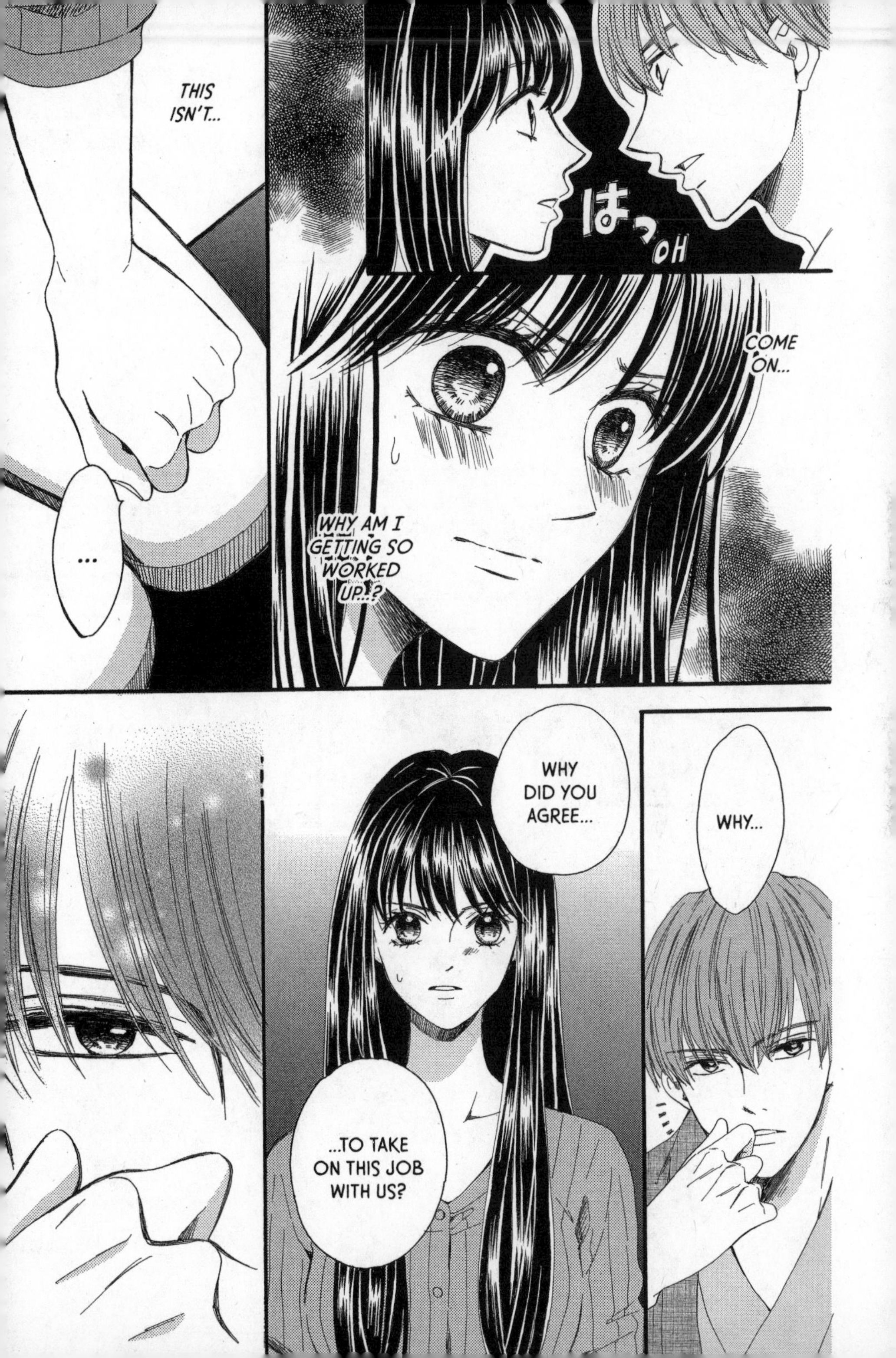
はっ OH
COME ON...
WHY AM I GETTING SO WORKED UP...?
THIS ISN'T...
...
WHY...
WHY DID YOU AGREE...
...TO TAKE ON THIS JOB WITH US?

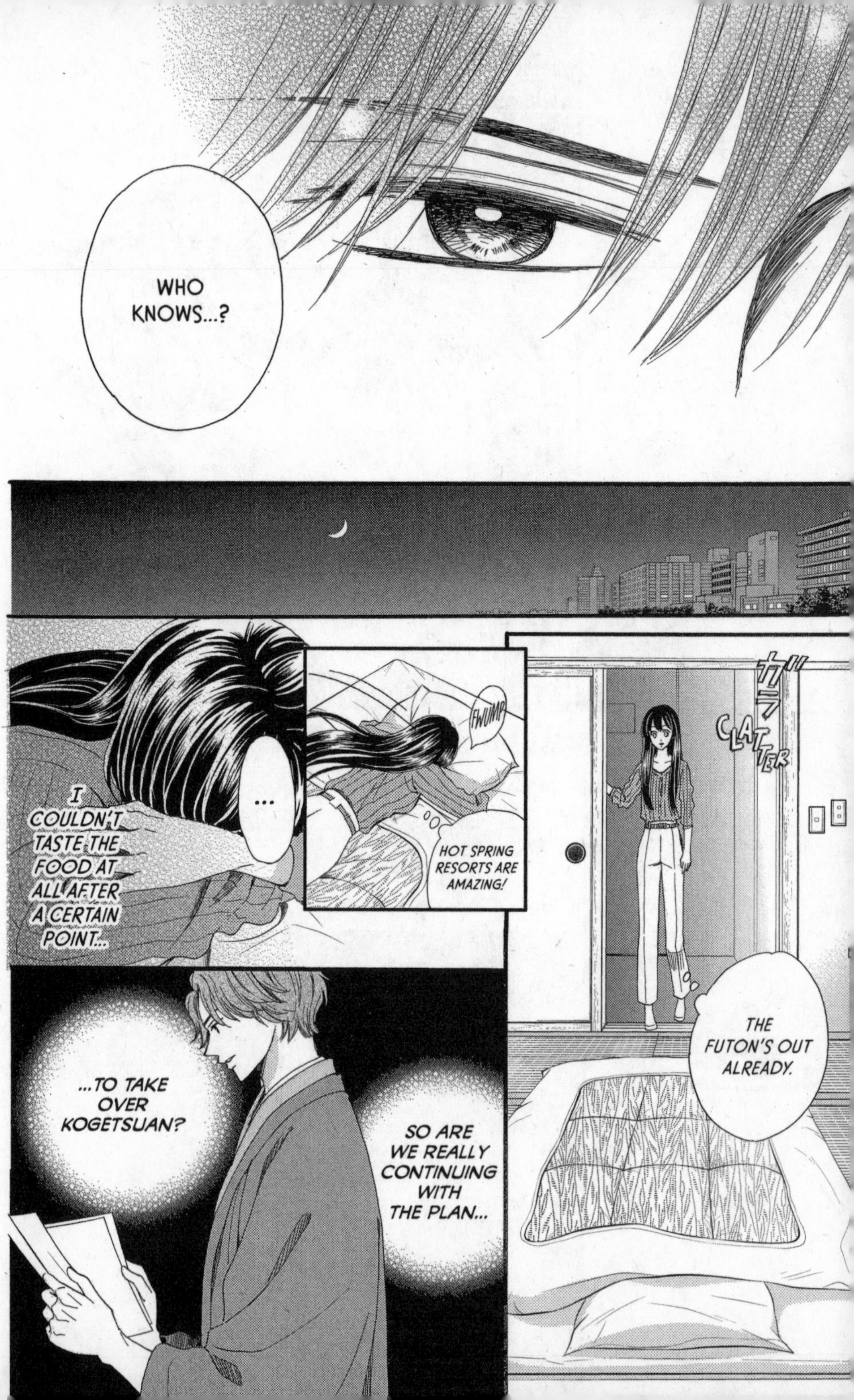
WHO KNOWS...?
ガラ
CLATTER
THE FUTON'S OUT ALREADY.
FWUMP
HOT SPRING RESORTS ARE AMAZING!
...
I COULDN'T TASTE THE FOOD AT ALL AFTER A CERTAIN POINT...
SO ARE WE REALLY CONTINUING WITH THE PLAN...
...TO TAKE OVER KOGETSUAN?

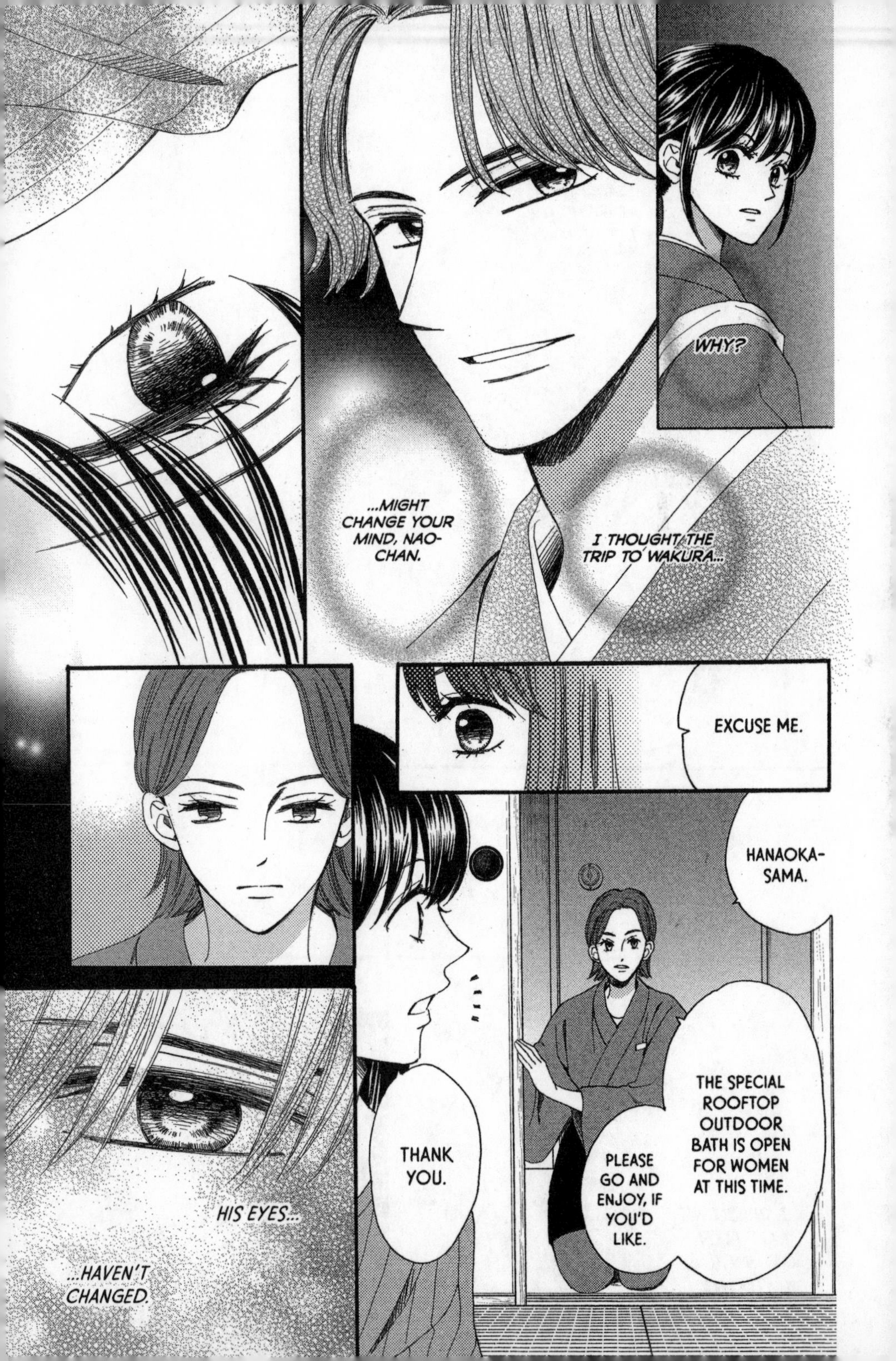
WHY?
I THOUGHT THE TRIP TO WAKURA...
...MIGHT CHANGE YOUR MIND, NAO-CHAN.
EXCUSE ME.
HANAOKA-SAMA.
THE SPECIAL ROOFTOP OUTDOOR BATH IS OPEN FOR WOMEN AT THIS TIME.
PLEASE GO AND ENJOY, IF YOU'D LIKE.
THANK YOU.
HIS EYES...
...HAVEN'T CHANGED.

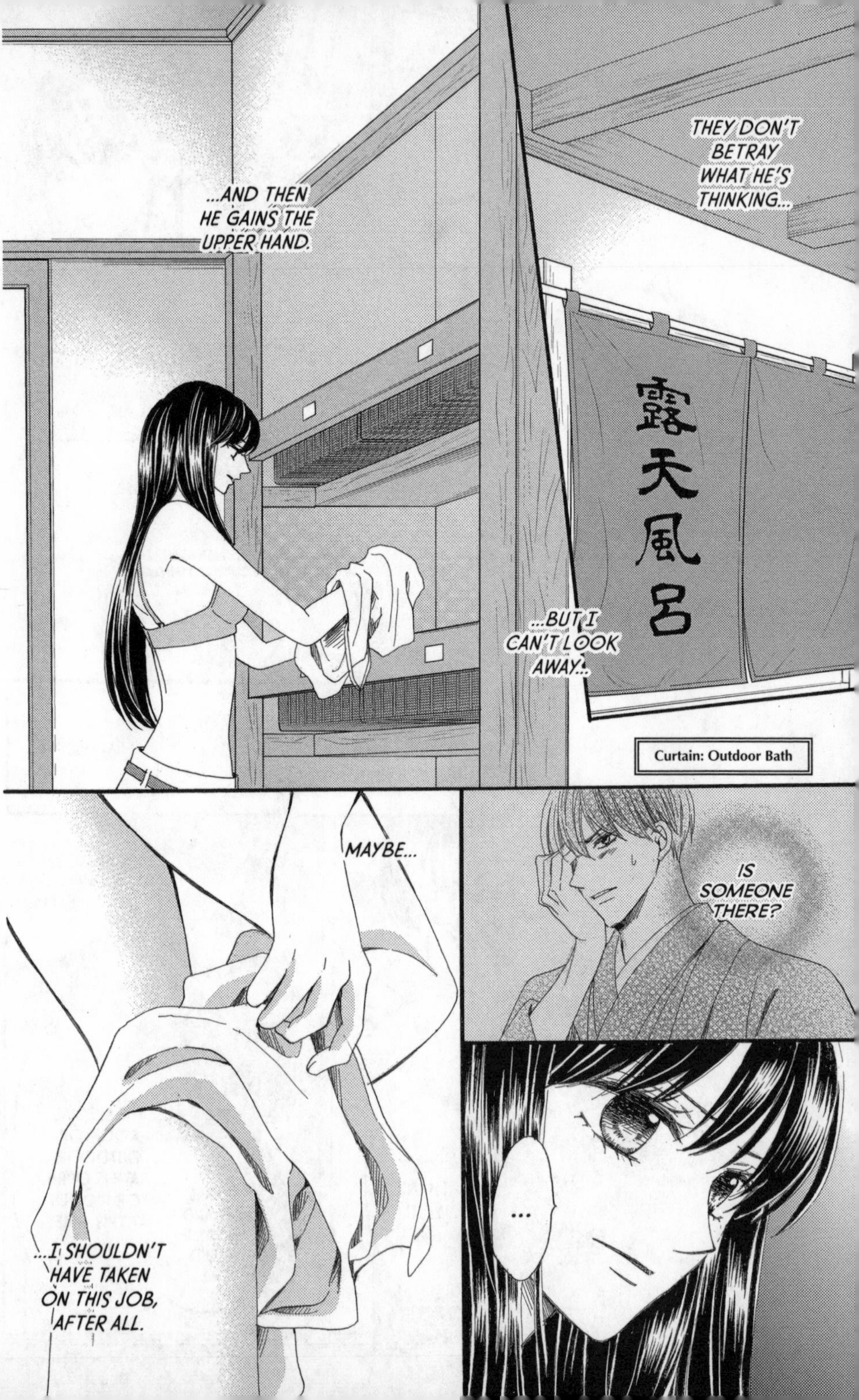
THEY DON'T BETRAY WHAT HE'S THINKING...
...AND THEN HE GAINS THE UPPER HAND.
露天風呂
...BUT I CAN'T LOOK AWAY...
Curtain: Outdoor Bath
IS SOMEONE THERE?
...
MAYBE...
...I SHOULDN'T HAVE TAKEN ON THIS JOB, AFTER ALL.

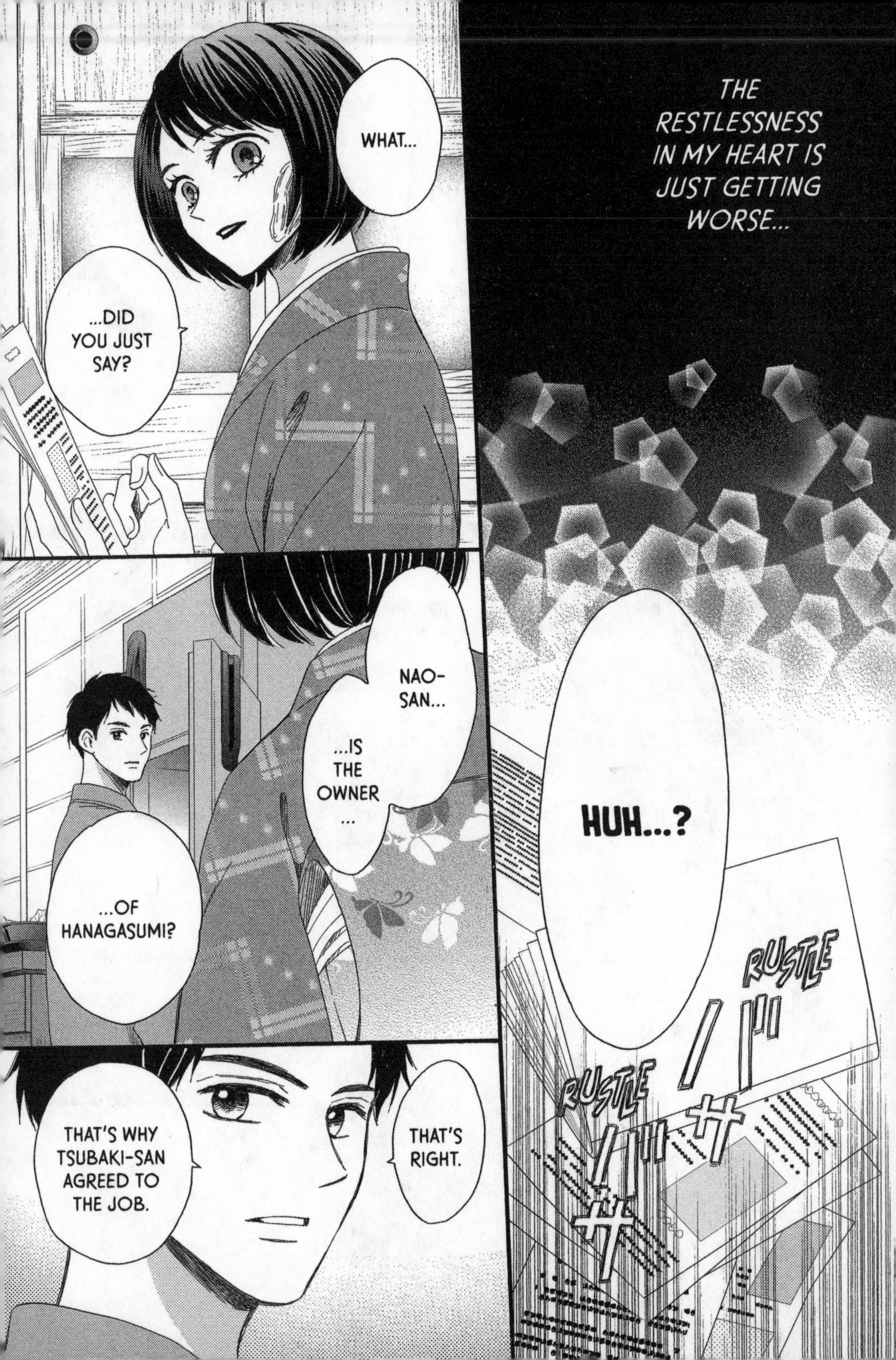
THE RESTLESSNESS IN MY HEART IS JUST GETTING WORSE...
HUH...?
RUSTLE
RUSTLE
WHAT...
...DID YOU JUST SAY?
NAO-SAN...
...IS THE OWNER ...
...OF HANAGASUMI?
THAT'S RIGHT.
THAT'S WHY TSUBAKI-SAN AGREED TO THE JOB.

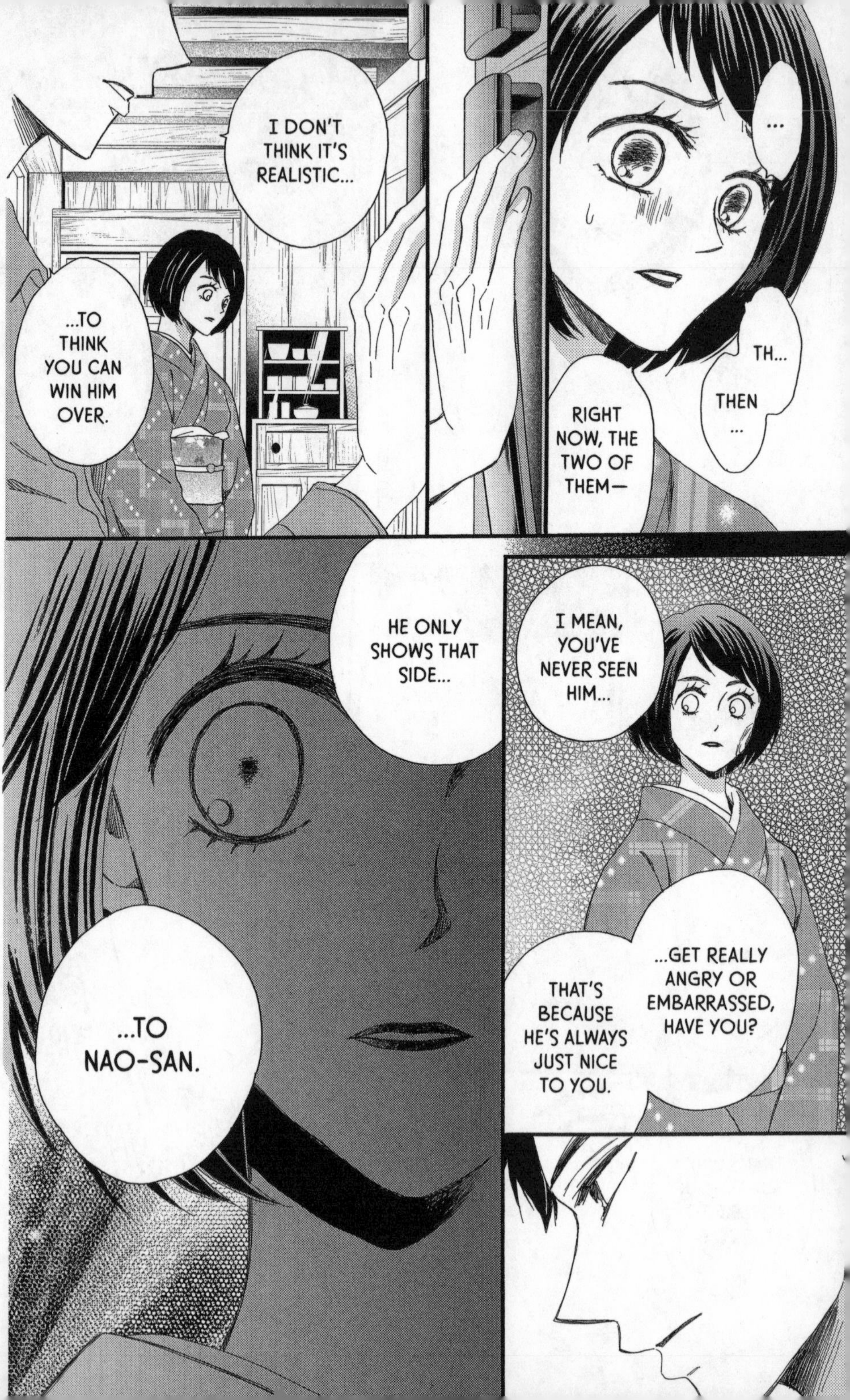
...
TH... THEN ...
RIGHT NOW, THE TWO OF THEM—
I DON'T THINK IT'S REALISTIC...
...TO THINK YOU CAN WIN HIM OVER.
I MEAN, YOU'VE NEVER SEEN HIM...
...GET REALLY ANGRY OR EMBARRASSED, HAVE YOU?
THAT'S BECAUSE HE'S ALWAYS JUST NICE TO YOU.
HE ONLY SHOWS THAT SIDE...
...TO NAO-SAN.

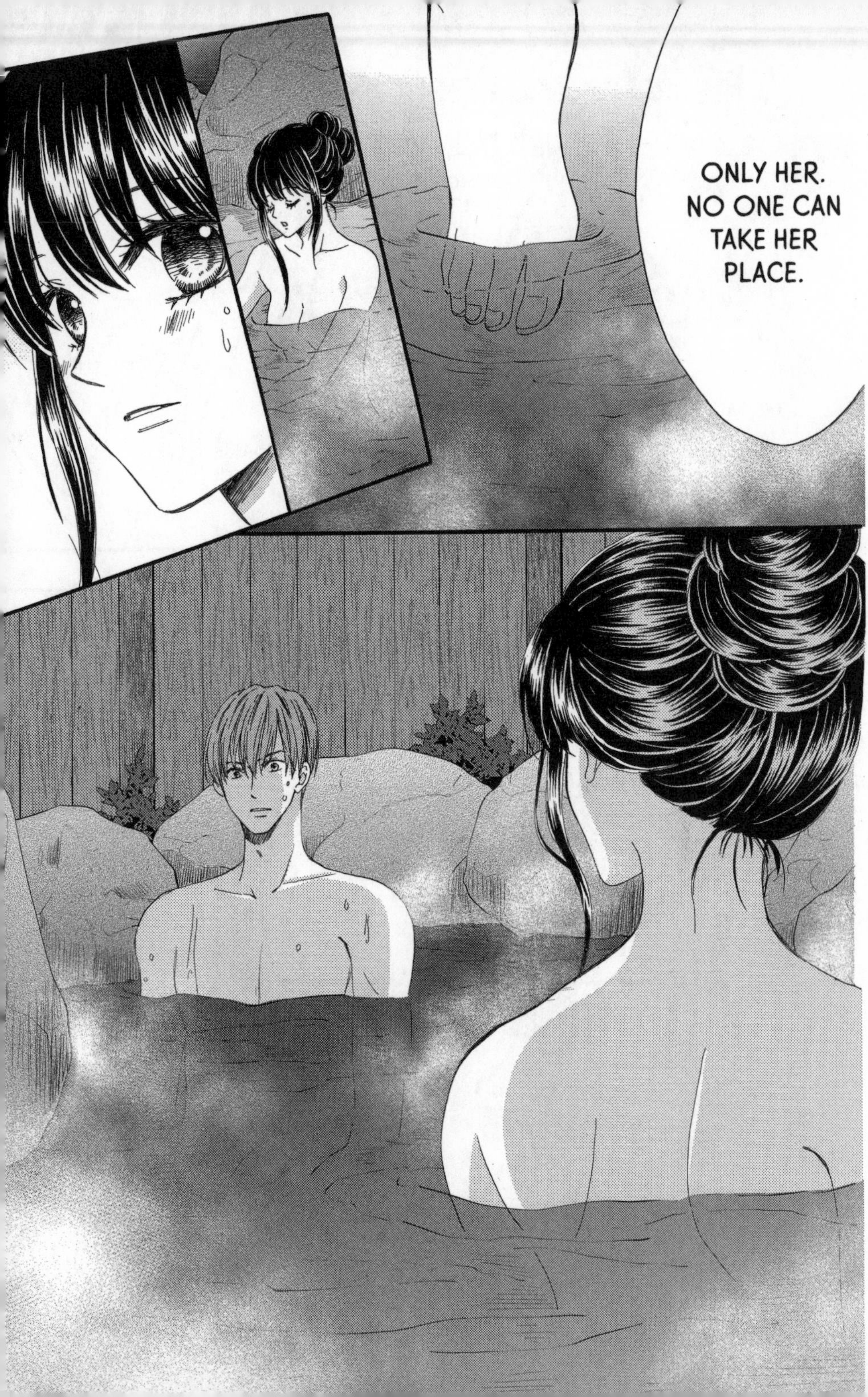
ONLY HER. NO ONE CAN TAKE HER PLACE.

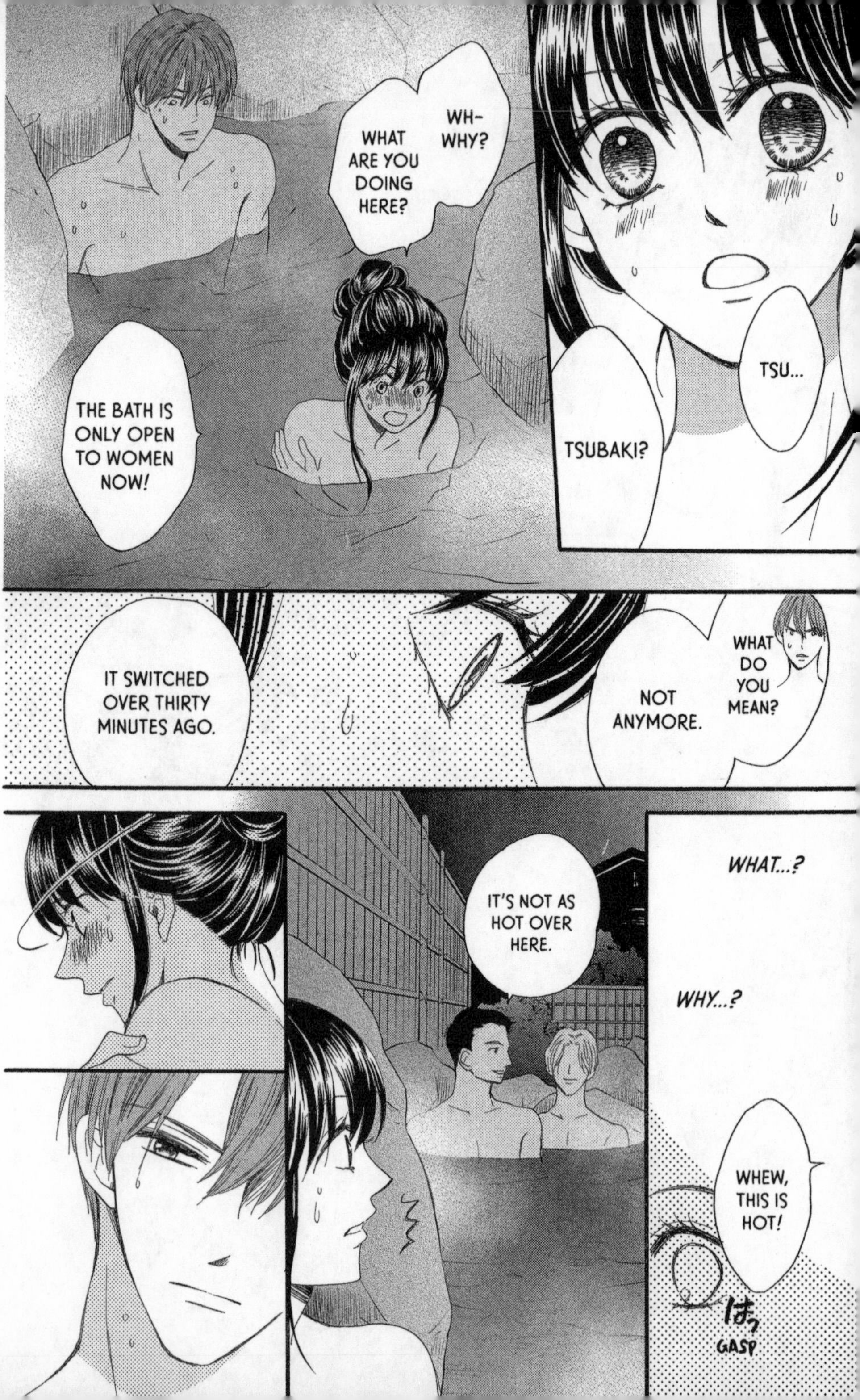
TSU...
TSUBAKI?
WH- WHY?
WHAT ARE YOU DOING HERE?
THE BATH IS ONLY OPEN TO WOMEN NOW!
WHAT DO YOU MEAN?
NOT ANYMORE.
IT SWITCHED OVER THIRTY MINUTES AGO.
WHAT...?
WHY...?
WHEW, THIS IS HOT!
はっ
GASP
IT'S NOT AS HOT OVER HERE.

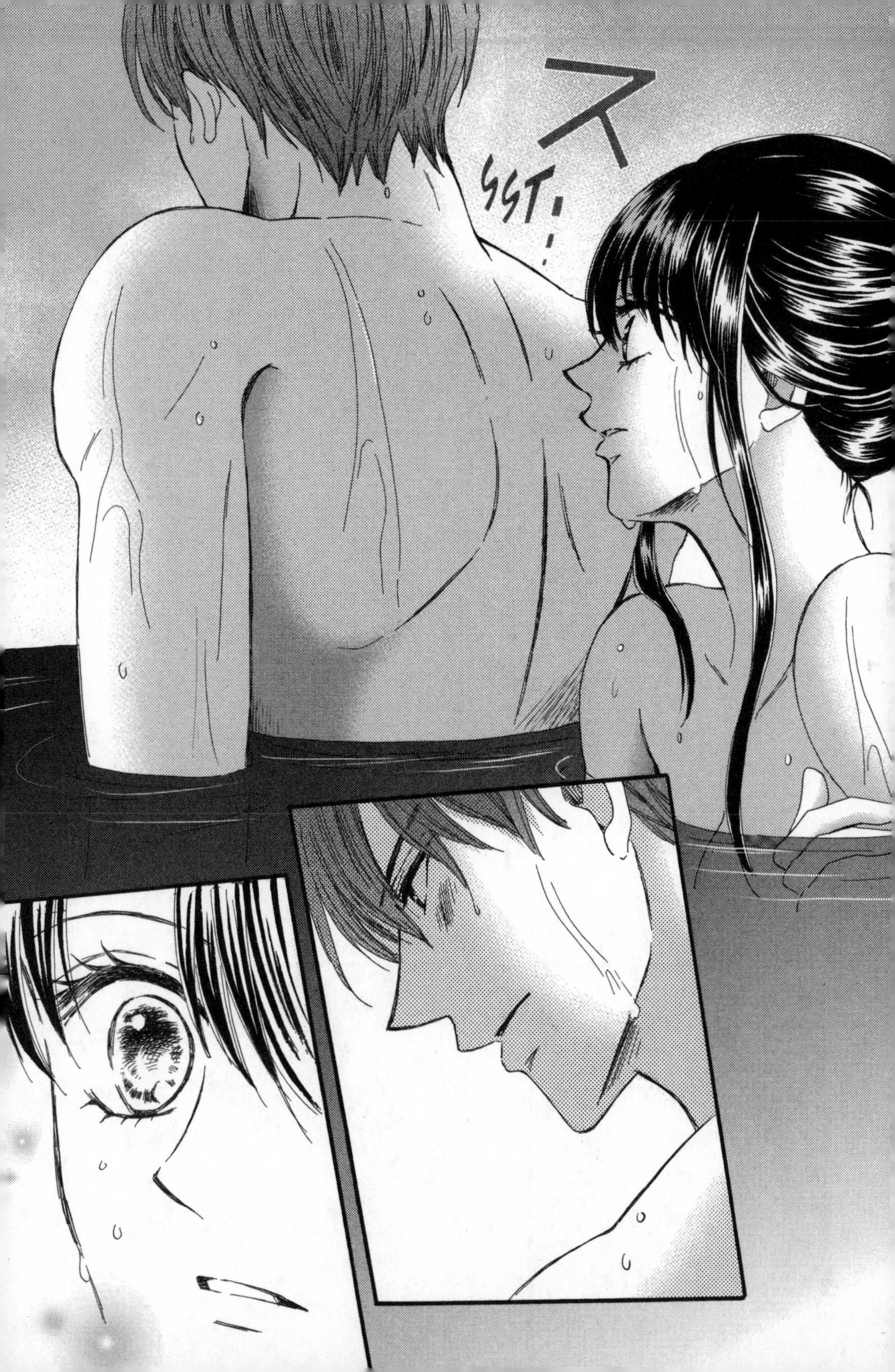
SST...

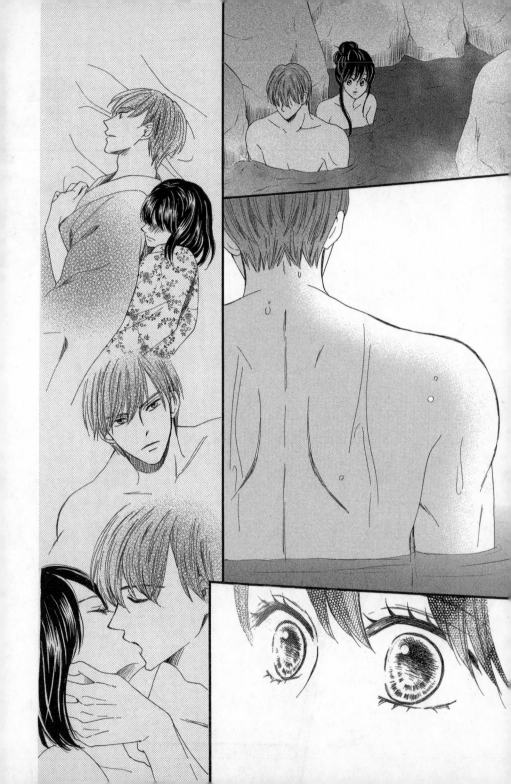

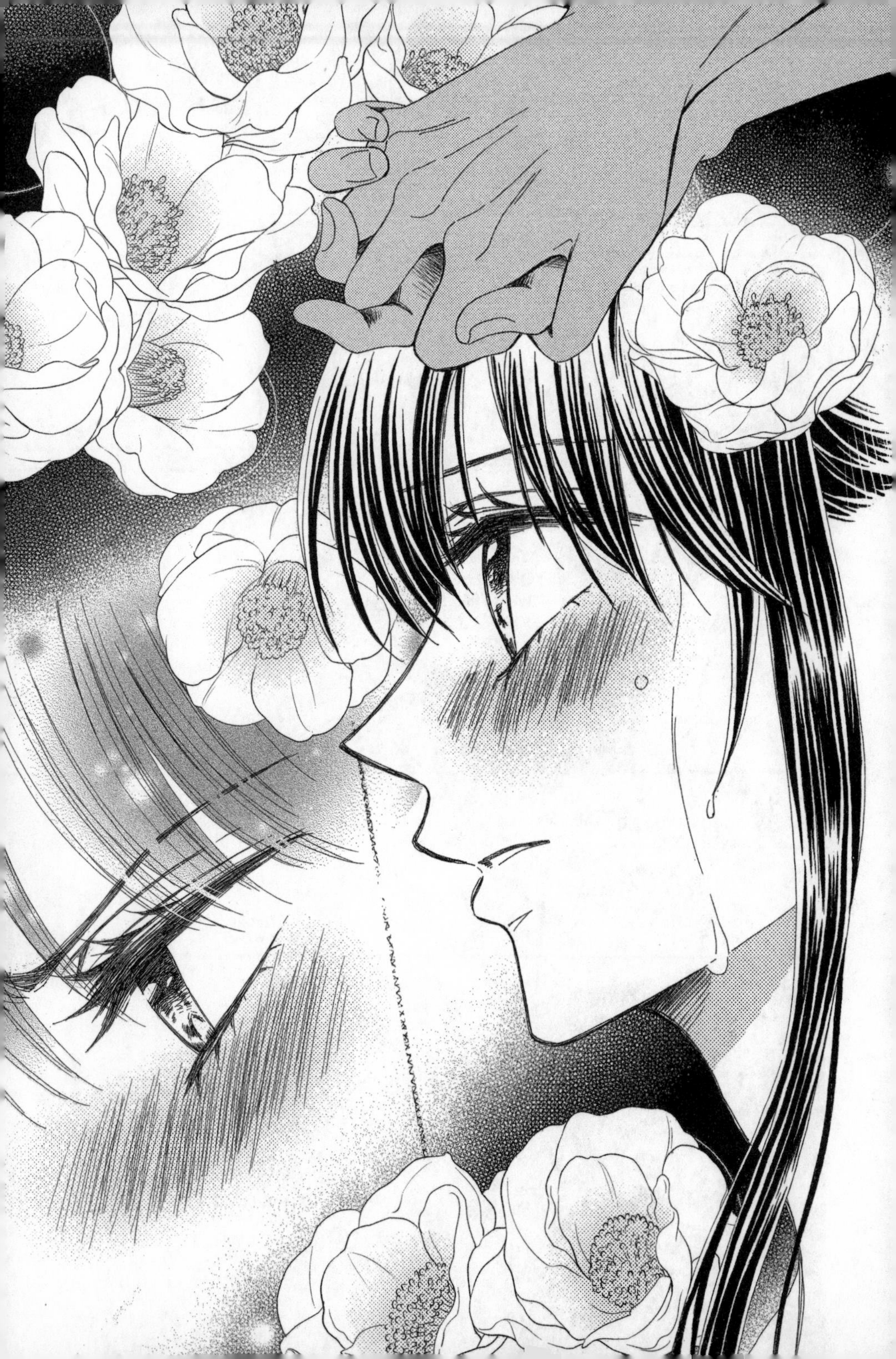

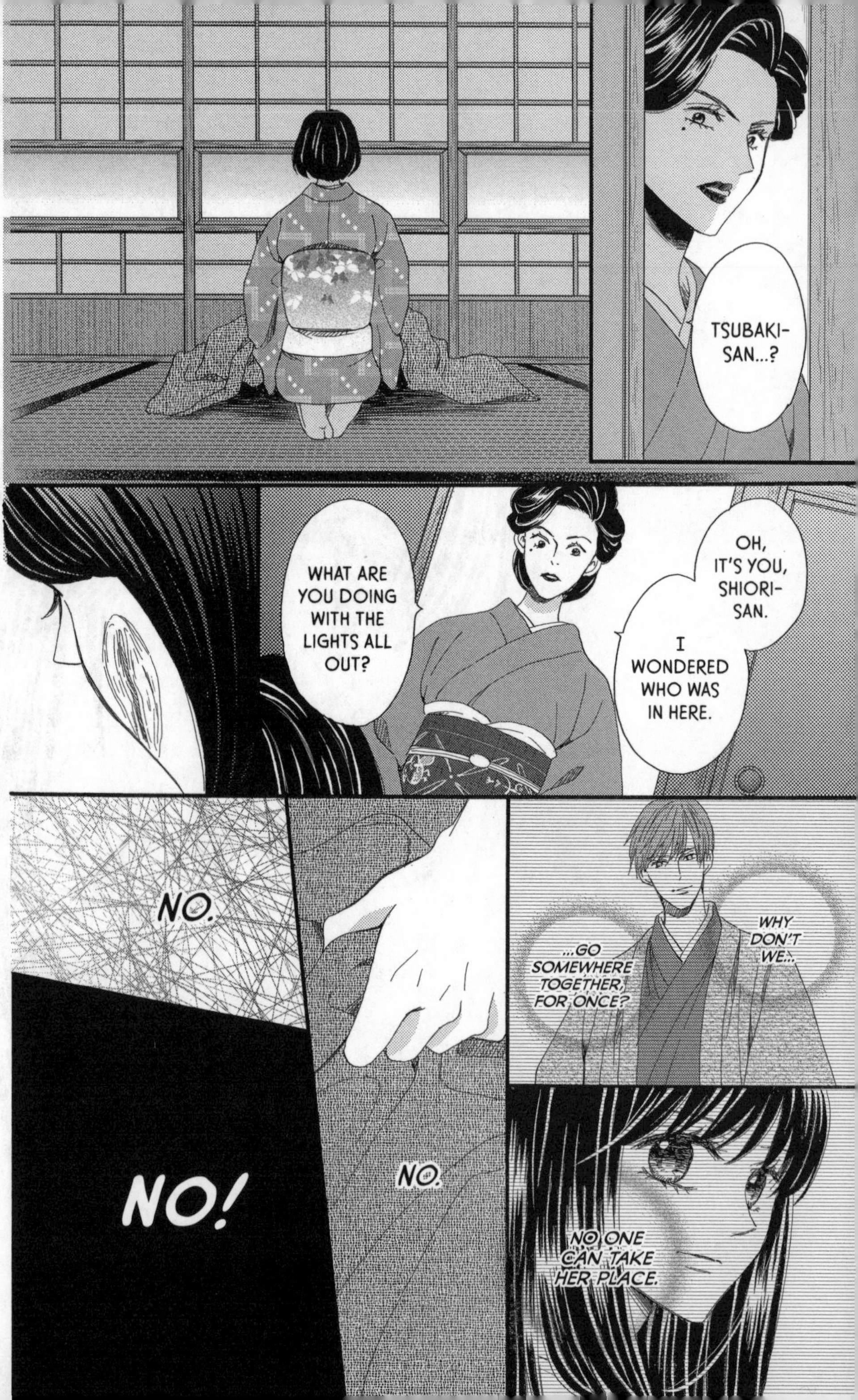
TSUBAKI-SAN...?
OH, IT'S YOU, SHIORI-SAN.
I WONDERED WHO WAS IN HERE.
WHAT ARE YOU DOING WITH THE LIGHTS ALL OUT?
WHY DON'T WE...
...GO SOMEWHERE TOGETHER, FOR ONCE?
NO ONE CAN TAKE HER PLACE.
NO.
NO.
NO!

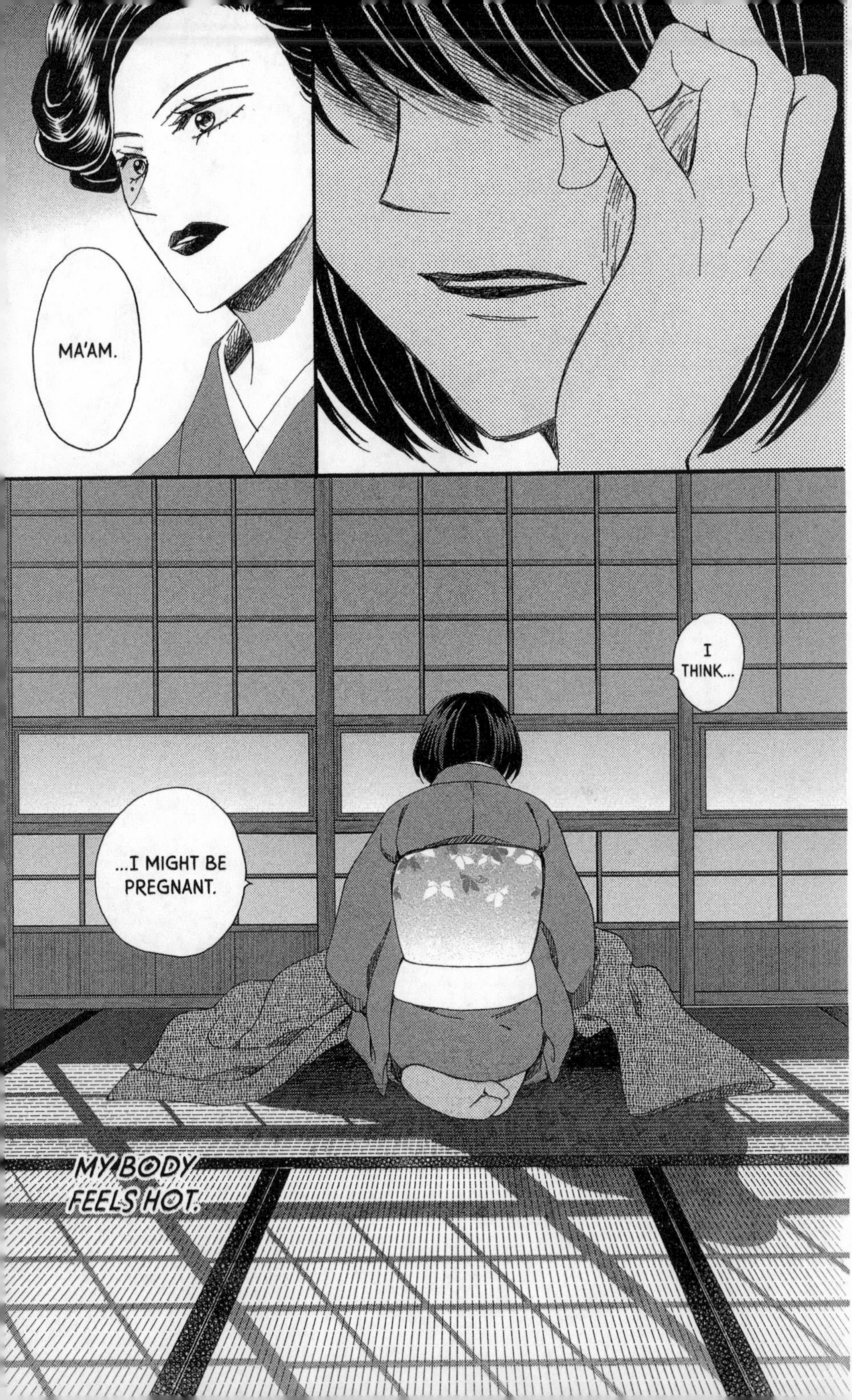
MA'AM.
I THINK...
...I MIGHT BE PREGNANT.
MY BODY FEELS HOT.

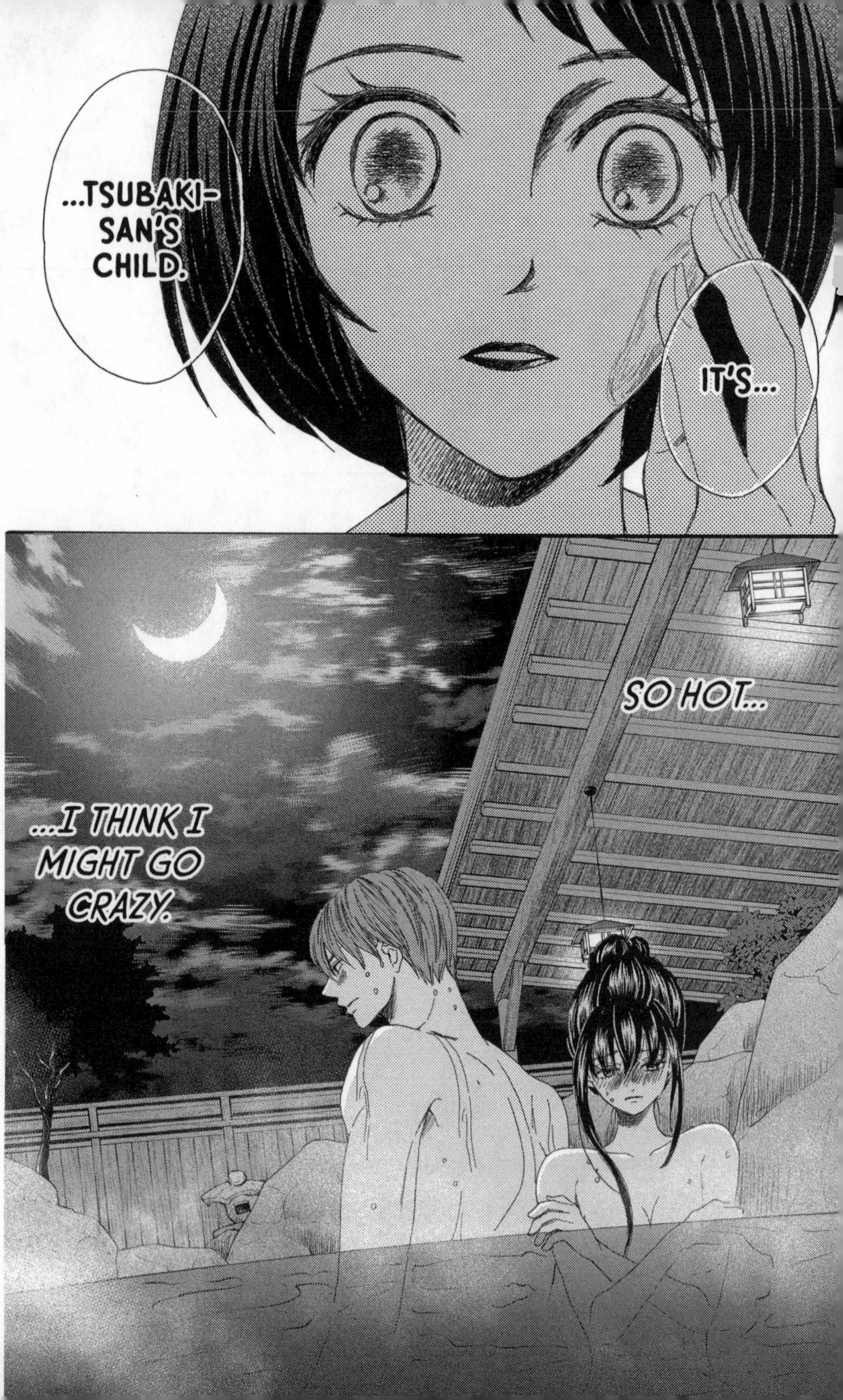
IT'S...
...TSUBAKI-SAN'S CHILD.
SO HOT...
...I THINK I MIGHT GO CRAZY.

Thank you so much,
Umesakura-sama,
Doi-sama,
Naganawa-sama,
Miyaji-sama,
Morizane-sama,

 and my editor
Chikada-sama.

Thank you very much for reading *Something's Wrong With Us*, Volume 9!

It was chaos working on the manuscripts in this volume because I was hospitalized for surgery for the first time in my life. I'm so glad I managed to get this book out! TT

We were supposed to schedule the surgery in a way that was easier, but an emergency situation led to sudden hospitalization, and the doctor told me we should operate the following day. It really threw me into a panic. I'm so grateful to my editor, the editorial department, and my assistants who dealt with the situation immediately to make sure things would be okay.

It was frustrating not being able to draw manga the way I wanted, but it's a good memory looking back on it now.

My room in the hospital was a big one with six beds, and staying there for two whole weeks (plus three days beforehand) allowed me to see many kinds of interactions between people. I now understand why there are so many hospital dramas...

In particular, there was a woman there who would tell her daughter things like, "I'm not going home after this," "I put up with it for fifty years," and "I'm going somewhere far away where no one will ever find me." Every so often I still wonder what happened to her.

On the flipside, people around me might have wondered what my deal was because I was working on my manuscripts while I was there.

Anyway, I'm all better now, so I've thrown myself back into working hard on manga!

Hope to see you again in Volume 10.

—Natsumi Ando

Next Volume Preview

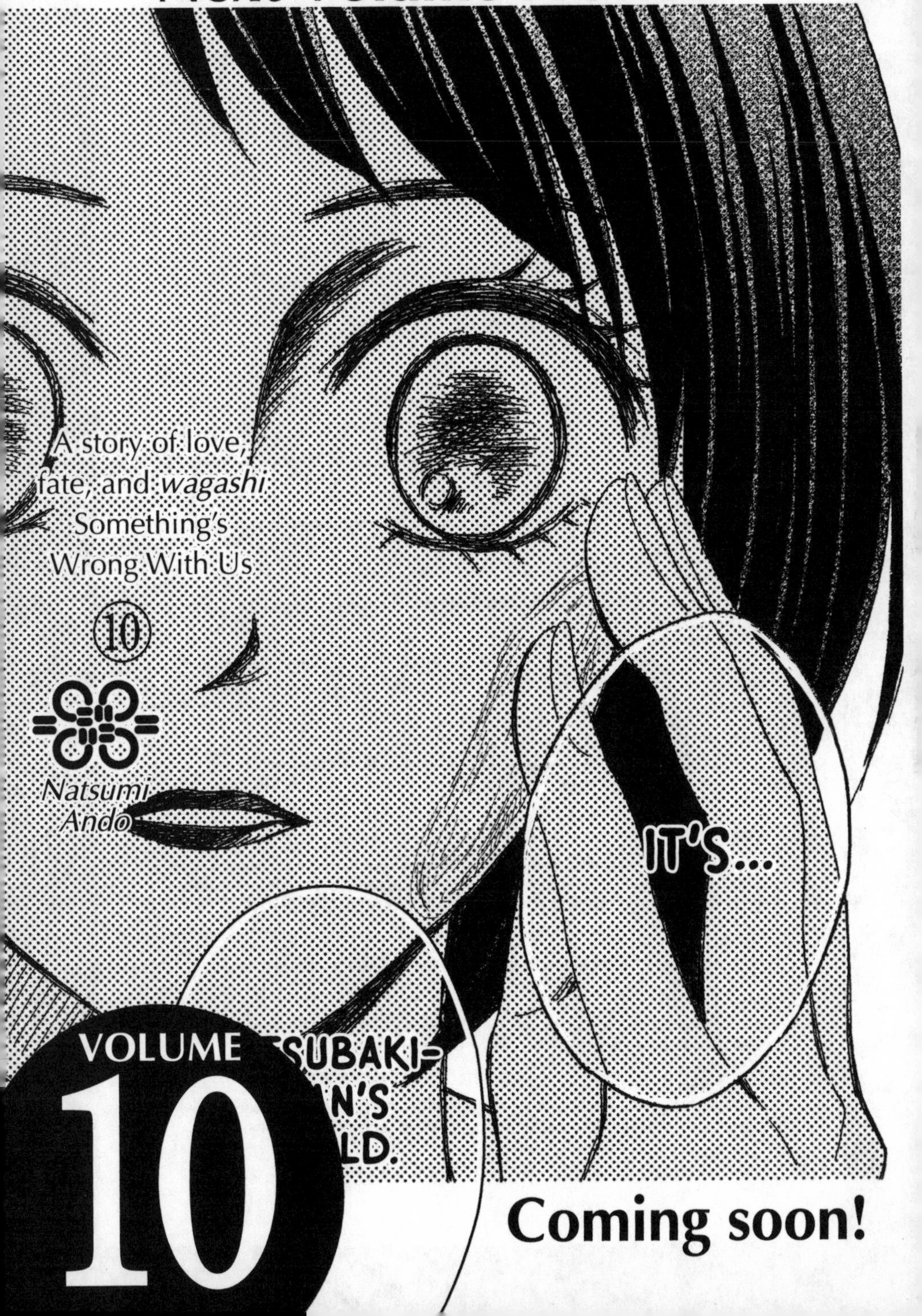

Translation Notes

wagashi, page 2
Traditional Japanese confections.

gyuhi, page 7
A softer, more delicate version of *mochi* (rice cake) made by kneading glutinous rice flour and sugar over heat. The resulting product almost melts in your mouth and stays soft for longer and at low temperatures, making it an ideal choice for cold sweets.

manju, page 9
A bite-sized bun with sweet filling, usually bean paste.

jo-namagashi, page 15
Fresh, artistic *wagashi* that are made with specific (usually seasonal) motifs.

zenzai, page 29
A sweet dessert soup made from half-crushed *azuki* beans served with grilled *mochi* in it.

yokan, page 32
A smooth, jellied sweet made of bean paste and agar.

Hanagasumi-san, page 44
Hanagasumi is not Nao's name, but when people run a business (especially in retail) they can be addressed by the store's name with the -san honorific attached.

Tsubaki-san, page 59
In very formal households like the Takatsuki family, the mother will often address her children with the "-san" honorific. "-san" is akin to "Mr., Ms., Mx." etc.

inokomochi, page 71
A rice cake filled with bean paste that is made to look like a wild boarlet. This motif only appears in November, when it is traditionally eaten on Inokonohi (the day of the boarlet) to pray for good health and many descendants.

kinako, page 71
Roasted soybean ground into a powder that has a distinctive nutty flavor.

monaka, page 79
Two crispy wafers made of rice flour with a sweet filling (usually bean paste) sandwiched in between.

daifuku, page 79
Meaning "great luck," a *daifuku* is a small ball of mochi rice cake with a sweet filling, usually bean paste. Its simplicity allows for endless variations.

robiraki, page 105
An important tea ceremony held in November to "open up the hearth," signaling the start of the winter tea ceremony season (*ro* season). While a small charcoal brazier (*furo*) is used to boil water in the warmer months to keep the heat away from guests, a sunken hearth (*ro*) is used during the winter months to keep guests warm.

higashi, page 105
Literally "dried sweets," *higashi* have very little moisture and keep for longer than *namagashi* (fresh sweets).

sencha tea, page 110
A green tea made by steeping whole green tea leaves in hot water. *Sencha* has a separate tea ceremony with its own customs and traditions, but in this case, it seems to be served after the matcha green tea (a rich tea made from powdered leaves) to close the ceremony.

yukata, page 139
A more casual version of the kimono. Yukata were originally airy, unlined robes meant to be worn after a bath. Most inns in Japan provide yukata as relaxing room wear to use on the premises.

anmitsu, page 140
A dessert of *kanten* (agar) jelly, bean paste, *gyuhi*, and various fruits drizzled with *kuromitsu* (black sugar syrup).

dango, page 140
Small *mochi* dumpling balls on a skewer.

The futon's out already, page 144
In a traditional Japanese inn, the staff set up the futon bedding while the guests are eating dinner. This way, there is more space in the room during the day.

The art-deco cyberpunk classic from the creators of *xxxHOLiC* and *Cardcaptor Sakura*!

CLAMP

CLOVER

— COLLECTOR'S EDITION —

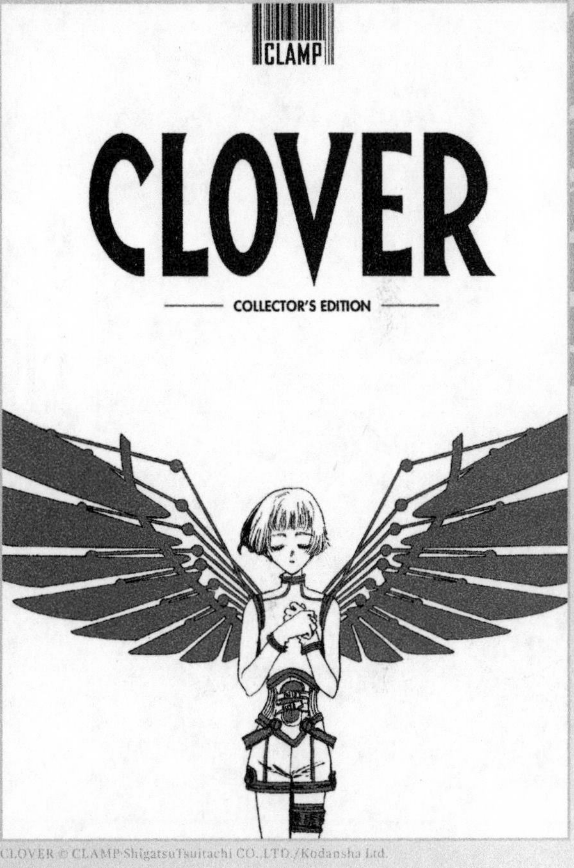

CLOVER © CLAMP·ShigatsuTsuitachi CO.,LTD./Kodansha Ltd.

Su was born into a bleak future, where the government keeps tight control over children with magical powers—codenamed "Clovers." With Su being the only "four-leaf" Clover in the world, she has been kept isolated nearly her whole life. Can ex-military agent Kazuhiko deliver her to the happiness she seeks? Experience the complete series in this hardcover edition, which also includes over twenty pages of ravishing color art!

KC
KODANSHA
COMICS

Young characters and steampunk setting, like *Howl's Moving Castle* and *Battle Angel Alita*

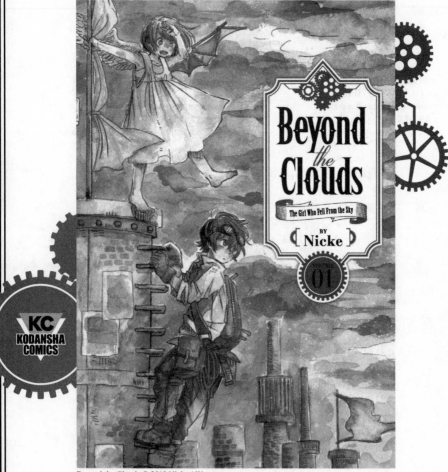

Beyond the Clouds © 2018 Nicke / Ki-oon

A boy with a talent for machines and a mysterious girl whose wings he's fixed will take you beyond the clouds! In the tradition of the high-flying, resonant adventure stories of Studio Ghibli comes a gorgeous tale about the longing of young hearts for adventure and friendship!

A SMART, NEW ROMANTIC COMEDY FOR FANS OF *SHORTCAKE CAKE* AND *TERRACE HOUSE!*

A romance manga starring high school girl Meeko, who learns to live on her own in a boarding house whose living room is home to the odd (but handsome) Matsunaga-san. She begins to adjust to her new life away from her parents, but Meeko soon learns that no matter how far away from home she is, she's still a young girl at heart –– especially when she finds herself falling for Matsunaga-san.

THE WORLD OF CLAMP!

Cardcaptor Sakura
Collector's Edition

Cardcaptor Sakura:
Clear Card

Magic Knight Rayearth
25th Anniversary Box Set

Chobits

TSUBASA Omnibus

TSUBASA WoRLD CHRoNiCLE

xxxHOLiC Omnibus

xxxHOLiC Rei

CLOVER Collector's Edition

Kodansha Comics welcomes you to explore the expansive world of CLAMP, the all-female artist collective that has produced some of the most acclaimed manga of the century. Our growing catalog includes icons like *Cardcaptor Sakura* and *Magic Knight Rayearth*, each crafted with CLAMP's one-of-a-kind style and characters!

PERFECT WORLD

Rie Aruga

A TOUCHING NEW SERIES ABOUT LOVE AND COPING WITH DISABILITY

An office party reunites Tsugumi with her high school crush Itsuki. He's realized his dream of becoming an architect, but along the way, he experienced a spinal injury that put him in a wheelchair. Now Tsugumi's rekindled feelings will butt up against prejudices she never considered — and Itsuki will have to decide if he's ready to let someone into his heart...

KC KODANSHA COMICS

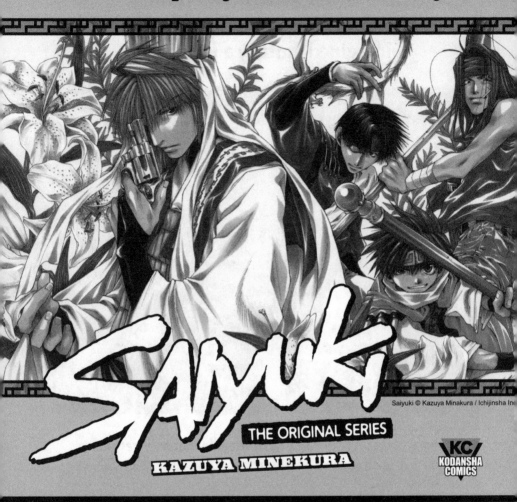

The beloved characters from *Cardcaptor Sakura* return in a brand new, reimagined fantasy adventure!

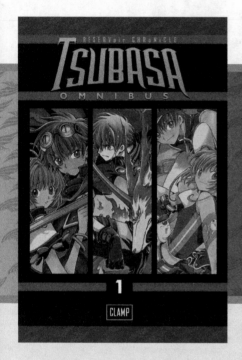

"[*Tsubasa*] takes readers on a fantastic ride that only gets more exhilarating with each successive chapter." —Anime News Network

In the Kingdom of Clow, an archaeological dig unleashes an incredible power, causing Princess Sakura to lose her memories. To save her, her childhood friend Syaoran must follow the orders of the Dimension Witch and travel alongside Kurogane, an unrivaled warrior; Fai, a powerful magician; and Mokona, a curiously strange creature, to retrieve Sakura's dispersed memories!

The adorable new odd-couple cat comedy manga from the creator of the beloved *Chi's Sweet Home*, in full color!

Sue & Tai-chan

Konami Kanata

Sue is an aging housecat who's looking forward to living out her life in peace... but her plans change when the mischievous black tomcat Tai-chan enters the picture! Hey! Sue never signed up to be a catsitter! *Sue & Tai-chan* is the latest from the reigning meow-narch of cute kitty comics, Konami Kanata.

KC
KODANSHA
COMICS

THE SWEET SCENT OF LOVE IS IN THE AIR! FOR FANS OF OFFBEAT ROMANCES LIKE *WOTAKOI*

Sweat and Soap © Kintetsu Yamada / Kodansha Ltd.

In an office romance, there's a fine line between sexy and awkward... and that line is where Asako — a woman who sweats copiously — meets Koutarou — a perfume developer who can't get enough of Asako's, er, scent. Don't miss a romcom manga like no other!

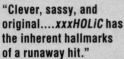

Kimihiro Watanuki is haunted by visions of ghosts and spirits. He seeks help from a mysterious woman named Yuko, who claims she can help. However, Watanuki must work for Yuko in order to pay for her aid. Soon Watanuki finds himself employed in Yuko's shop, where he sees things and meets customers that are stranger than anything he could have ever imagined.

KC
KODANSHA COMICS

A Kodansha Comics Trade Paperback Original
Something's Wrong With Us 9 copyright © 2019 Natsumi Ando
English translation copyright © 2022 Natsumi Ando

All rights reserved.

Published in the United States by Kodansha Comics, an imprint of Kodansha USA Publishing, LLC, New York.

Publication rights for this English edition arranged through Kodansha Ltd., Tokyo.

First published in Japan in 2019 by Kodansha Ltd., Tokyo as *Watashitachi wa doukashiteiru*, volume 9.

ISBN 978-1-64651-097-9

Printed in the United States of America.

www.kodansha.us

9 8 7 6 5 4 3 2 1
Translation: Sawa Matsueda Savage
Lettering: Nicole Roderick
Editing: Jordan Blanco
Kodansha Comics edition cover design by Matthew Akuginow

Publisher: Kiichiro Sugawara

Director of publishing services: Ben Applegate
Director of publishing operations: Dave Barrett
Associate director, publishing operations: Stephen Pakula
Publishing services managing editors: Madison Salters, Alanna Ruse
Production managers: Emi Lotto, Angela Zurlo
Logo and character art ©Kodansha USA Publishing, LLC